MW01518746

JIMMY GARDINER

RELENTLESS LIBERAL

1910 Foremen's march p24
Military Voters Act p.27
Tory open brain drain p33
Civil service report p79
Cabinet office - Ch.?
Conscription campaign p54 166-7
School Bd 170 -
Regina riot 182

JIMMY GARDINER
RELENTLESS LIBERAL

Norman Ward and David Smith

UNIVERSITY OF TORONTO PRESS
Toronto Buffalo London

© University of Toronto Press 1990
Toronto Buffalo London
Printed in Canada

ISBN 0-8020-2721-0

Printed on acid-free paper

Canadian Cataloguing in Publication Data

Ward, Norman, 1918–
Jimmy Gardiner : relentless Liberal

ISBN 0-8020-2721-0

1. Gardiner, James G. (James Garfield), 1883–1962.   2. Canada – Politics
and government – 20th century.   3. Liberal Party of Canada – Biography.
4. Cabinet ministers – Canada – Biography.*   5. Politicians – Canada –
Biography.   I. Smith, David E., 1936–   . II. Title.

FC3524.1.G37W37 1990   971.24'02'0924
F1072.G37W37 1990   C89-095367-8

Unless otherwise noted, the photographs are from the Saskatchewan
Archives Board.

To the Ward grandchildren and
Joshua Smith

Contents

Preface

The provenance of a book is always interesting and with this one it is somewhat unusual. Neither of us knew Jimmy Gardiner, but several years ago another volume, *A Party Politician: The Memoirs of Chubby Power,* prepared for publication by Norman Ward, attracted the attention of Jimmy's son Wilfrid, who had been reflecting on possible biographers for his father. Wilfrid had an extensive career as an MLA and provincial cabinet minister in Saskatchewan, and he and Norman Ward were brought together by a member of another lively political family, Sally Merchant, also a former MLA. It took Norman Ward only a short time to assess Jimmy Gardiner's papers and realize that they comprised an unusually rich and varied collection full of political lore; and the biography was begun. Then when the manuscript was well along, a serious illness made a co-author necessary, and fortunately David Smith, who had chosen Liberalism in Western Canada as one of his academic interests, was available and willing.

Fortunately, too, the co-authors are old friends and colleagues, and had no trouble agreeing on the book's format. Ward wrote chapters one to fourteen, inclusive, and Smith the chapters and epilogue which follow. Each author wrote freely as far as the other was concerned, and neither interfered editorially in the other's work. The whole book, that is, consists of two separate manuscripts which deal sequentially with the same subject. By sheer coincidence Ward's chapters deal mainly with Jimmy Gardiner's provincial career, and Smith's with his federal activities. The only section which necessitated any overlapping is chapter fourteen, after which the turnover from one author to the other took effect.

From the start the purpose was to see Jimmy Gardiner as he saw himself, refraining from sitting in solemn judgment on his activities, on the one hand, and making no attempt to fit him into contexts perceived by somebody else, on the other. (Like most public men, Gardiner had a capacity to arouse strong feelings about himself, and while his chief opponents, though sometimes decrying his methods, often praised him, it was Liberal associates who described him as both 'an utterly splendid leader' and 'a truly dreadful man.') Jimmy was very much his own man, and his voluminous papers make clear that he did not perceive himself to be living in a context visualized by others; it would be misleading to suggest that he did. Nor did he lose much sleep over what others thought about him. It may seem paradoxical to add that he nonetheless committed himself early to following the tenets of Liberalism, to which (as he saw them) he adhered almost slavishly; and he certainly did not invent them. But he became Liberal by choice, and the Liberalism he believed in sometimes aggravated other Liberals.

Trying to present Gardiner as he saw himself, and to understand problems as he saw them, involves also trying to sort out what he thought was important and what was not, and his accounts of events that might make sensational news in the media were often fairly laconic because he saw the developments as normal happenings in a politician's life. Once he became a Liberal MLA, for example, he assumed that his course would include rising in the ranks until he had reached the top job in the party, and at various stages in his career the press made far more of his actions than he did himself. He assumed, too, that any good politician needed an organization, and an organization always needed financial support. But he publicly said remarkably little about political money, and not much more about his organization. Critics, both academic and journalistic, have made 'the Gardiner Machine' a legend in Canada, but Jimmy Gardiner did not believe he ran a machine at all.

He believed also that his private and public lives were separate entities. The Gardiner family, from the very beginning of Jimmy's career, privately endured much that could be expoited as high drama, but he used none of it for public purposes. He was a good family man who, despite his ambitions, genuinely enjoyed being in opposition from 1929 to 1934 because of the leisure it gave him for his growing family. When he became a federal cabinet minister after Mackenzie King's return to power in 1935, one of his concerns was the effect on the family of moving from Saskatchewan, where he had a farm, to a relatively large Ontario city. But these are private matters, and to follow Jimmy's public career we have left them so. This is a political biography.

For us it has been an enjoyable if demanding enterprise, and on our way we received much help. From the start, members of the Gardiner family gave us unrestricted and exclusive access to Jimmy's papers, laying down no conditions about the biography. The staffs of the Saskatchewan Archives Board (who first put the Gardiner papers in order), the National Archives of Canada, and the archival division of the library of Queen's University were always helpful, as were Jimmy's former colleagues in interviews. The manuscript was read in whole or in part by several of our colleagues at the University of Saskatchewan, most notable John Courtney and Duff Spafford, and by three nameless readers appointed by the grant-giving forces at the Social Science Federation of Canada; always to our benefit. Our proof-reader and indexer, Geri Rowlatt, saved us hours of tedious work. The University of Toronto Press provided its reliable services, including the assignment to us of that sharp-eyed editor, Diane Mew. Financial support that made publication possible came from the University of Saskatchewan. Publication was also made possible by a grant from the Social Science Federation of Canada, using funds provided by the Social Sciences and Humanities Research Council of Canada. To all of these we offer our grateful thanks, reserving only our own responsibility for the use we made of their assistance. And for each of us, working with the other was a special adventure.

Norman Ward
David E. Smith

Gardiner in 1905, the year he arrived in the new province of Saskatchewan

The Manitoba College Senior Football Team, Intercollegiate Champions, 1909-10 (Gardiner, seated on floor, left)

Inter-Class Debating Champions, Manitoba College, 1908-9 (Gardiner, back row, right)

Inter-Class Championship Track Team, Manitoba College, 1910-11
(Gardiner, second on left)

Teacher and principal, Lemberg School, 1911 (Gardiner in doorway)

Lemberg Baseball Team, 1912 (Gardiner, front row, centre)

In the premier's office, Legislative Buildings, Regina, c. 1927

OPPOSITE
Left: Gardiner with W.R. Motherwell, campaigning in Assiniboia by-election, 1919. *Right:* Hon. J.G. Gardiner, premier, 1926–29

Hon. C.A. Dunning (third from left, front row), Canada's new minister of railways with Saskatchewan's new premier, Gardiner, and his ministers and deputy ministers, Regina, 17 March 1926
Front row: Hon. J.A. Cross, Hon. S.J. Latta, Hon. C.A. Dunning, Hon. J.G. Gardiner, Hon A.P. McNab, Hon. J.M. Uhrich, Hon. T.C. Davis, Hon. W.J. Patterson

Second row: R.F. Blacklock, J.N. Bayne, M.M. Seymour, T.M. Molloy,
A.P. Taylor, A.H. Ball, J.W. Reid, J.J. Smith, G.L. Hopkins, J.W. McLeod
Third row: A.E. Fisher, R.W. Shannon, D.P. McColl, P.G. Ward, F.H. Auld,
A.L. Geddes, M. Dingwall, W.G. Haultain, G.A. Mantle
Top row: Murdo Cameron, S.P. Grosch, F.J. Reynolds, J.M. Smith, C.A.
Mahony, W.J. McLeod, H.S. Carpenter, P.A. Harding, D.M. Woodhams

Candidates in the new seat of Melville, provincial election 1934: J.G. Gardiner,
Liberal; Elisha Forest Scharf, Conservative; Wilfrid Wass, Farmer-Labor

Family portrait, 1936: Florence, Violet, Edwin, Beth, Wilfrid and Gardiner

Arrival in Ottawa: Gardiner (standing) and Dunning (seated, both to Mackenzie King's immediate right), in a group photograph of 'government
authorities,' c. 1930s

Violet, Edwin, and Gardiner, following RCAF ceremony at Yorkton, Saskatchewan, 1941, when Gardiner pinned wings on his son (photograph from private collection)

As minister of agriculture, Gardiner addresses a dominion-provincial conference, December 1947 (NFB photograph).

Left: Gardiner visiting Britain in 1940 as minister of national war services
inspects works of the Royal Corps of Engineers. Immediately behind
him is Hume Wrong, under-secretary for external affairs.

Liberal leadership convention, Ottawa, August 1948. Gardiner congratulates Louis St Laurent on his election as leader; Mackenzie King looks on.

The Gardiner farm, Lemberg, c. 1950

Portrait of the minister, Department of Agriculture, c. 1950

Gardiner receives honorary degree from the chancellor of the University of Saskatchewan, E.M. Culliton, 1959.

Production of *HMS Pinafore* at Lemberg, late 1950s; Gardiner danced the hornpipe.

JIMMY GARDINER
RELENTLESS LIBERAL

1

The Way In

A man destined to become premier of a western province, and in due course a contender for the prime ministership of Canada, could hardly have chosen a sounder background than did James Garfield Gardiner. On both sides of his family he came from industrious Scottish stock, in whose history he became increasingly interested as he grew older. The family migrated to Canada in the mid-nineteenth century and settled at Farquhar, on the boundary that divides Huron and Perth counties in south-western Ontario, the clients of a land company that emphatically did not want idlers or remittance men taking up its territories. Jimmy was born there in 1883.

The area was alive with future politicians, and especially those to be identified with the prairies; the first legislature Gardiner sat in drew over half its members from southern Ontario. William Aberhart, who was to electrify Alberta with Social Credit at the same time that Gardiner was moving from the Saskatchewan to the national scene, was born at Seaforth, a few miles from Farquhar. Arthur Meighen was born at Anderson, and attended school in St Mary's, Perth County. Not far north-east of Farquhar was Grey County, the birthplace of John George Diefenbaker, and about the same distance directly east was Berlin, the home of William Lyon Mackenzie King. The paths of these men, and many more, were to cross and recross on western trails in an almost bewildering variety of circumstances: Aberhart to invade Saskatchewan during the provincial election of 1938, for example, in a vigorous crusade to carry the faith one step eastward, while Gardiner was concurrently trying to organize the Liberals of Alberta. Diefenbaker and King represented the same area in the House of Commons, Prince Albert.

Gardiner's Huron County background was to follow him wherever he went, and one simple chronicle can convincingly demonstrate that. Gardiner as a youth was a farm labourer in Ontario for one J.B. Gillespie, who himself later moved west. There Gillespie became a brother-in-law of W.R. Motherwell, the first commissioner and then minister of agriculture in the provincial cabinet of Saskatchewan, later twice holding the same portfolio in Ottawa under Mackenzie King. Gardiner succeeded Motherwell not only in the federal portfolio, but even took over his constituency, Melville; and there, for twenty-two years, J.B. Gillespie was president of his constituency organization.

Finally, since Gardiner spent his adult life on the prairies, whose terrain is widely (and erroneously) believed to be flat, it is worthy of note that no part of the west is flatter than the countryside of Gardiner's birthplace, which includes a waterway appropriately called Flat Creek. So even in geological terms he was born on a part of the earth about whose misty hills he was not going to be nostalgic when on the plains; and, since he kept a lifelong contact with both Huron County and Saskatchewan, he never was. How could a Huron man be homesick when, in Saskatchewan, he could play with a football team drawn from a community settled from Huron?[1]

Not all of Gardiner's early life can be seen in so sharp a focus, but little of it can be said to be shrouded in mystery. Gardiner often spoke and wrote of his past, and he wrote two books, one an autobiography but in the third person and signed by another man, the other a youthful novel he wrote while in college. The published biography, *None of It Came Easy*, by Nathaniel Benson, was ostensibly created as Gardiner's contribution to the celebration of Saskatchewan's fiftieth anniversary in 1955, and the first choice of author was the distinguished newspaper-man, B.T. Richardson. However, Richardson was overtaken by other duties, and almost at the last minute Nathaniel Benson was hired to put the book together from its subject's copious notes, which in fact constituted a first draft. Benson had only three months to rework this material, the general idea being to make it into a book designed to enlighten and inspire high school students.[2]

Gardiner's novel, *The Politician, or The Treason of Democracy*, was written in 1910–11 while he was completing a degree in history and economics at Manitoba College, and finally published in 1975. He was twenty-seven when he wrote it, his education having been delayed by his own and his family's poverty, which by that time had taken the Gardiners from Huron to Nebraska, thence to Michigan, and back home to Huron, all in search of an elusive security which Gardiner finally had to find for himself. The hero of the novel, whose life was startlingly like Gardiner's own in his experiences and activities, was also used by his creator to express – often with a sanctimoniousness likely to cause retching among anybody reaching twenty-seven in the 1980s – his own beliefs and aspirations. 'The love of the true woman endureth much,' *The Politician* records at one point; and again, 'Canada must hold fast her love of womanhood and the home.'[3]

Until writing his remarkably revealing novel, Gardiner had lived a conventional Canadian version of the log cabin-to-White House legend. (His middle name was after the twentieth president of the United States.) His mother was the daughter of a cousin of Alexander Mackenzie, the first Liberal prime minister of Canada (1873–78), and so staunch a Liberal was she that in her later years Mackenzie King added her to the list of mothers who were to be revered for the profound influence for good they exerted on their sons. When Gardiner attained the premiership of Saskatchewan in 1926, King wired congratulations to the elder Mrs Gardiner in Ontario, and to her son in Regina.[4]

The elder Mrs Gardiner was a brisk element in the lives of her children and grandchildren until her death, often communicating with her famous son in letters written in brilliantly erratic spelling.[5] His father is a more shadowy figure.[6] James C. Gardiner came to Ontario from Stirlingshire with his father Robert, and as a young man shared in his father's prosperity as he successively exploited the opportunities open to a farmer-businessman during the Crimean War and the American Civil War. His accomplishments included election as reeve of Hibbert Township and warden of Perth County, and the organization of a cheese factory and the Hibbert and Usborne Mutual Fire Insurance Company, of which he was the first president. The first James Gardiner, Robert's son, became particularly proficient as a horseman and as a ploughman (James G. Gardiner kept to the end of his days a ploughing trophy won by his father at the age of sixteen), and when a post-war economic collapse reached the Gardiners' farms in the 1880s, James C. Gardiner in 1889 took his wife, two daughters, and four sons to Lincoln, Nebraska, where he thought to use his knowledge of horses. His brother William at the same time went to Clearwater, Manitoba, a move which was to play an important part in the life of William's nephew, the young Jimmy Gardiner.

Nebraska was unfortunately in even worse shape than south-western Ontario, and the Gardiner who was destined to help cope with the dirty thirties on the Canadian prairie encountered his first drought and dust storms in the American midwest. At times the family was so poor that, as Gardiner later recalled, the only cash coming into the house was from the papers sold by Jimmy and his older brother, and the boys on occasion had to wear clothing cut from the coarse fabric used to make straw ticking. The embarrassment caused by these striped garments was to make Gardiner sensitive to children's clothes forty years later. When the family could make no headway in Nebraska it moved in 1895 to the northern tier of Michigan, where Mrs Gardiner had two sisters at Alpena. Here again hard luck followed James C. Gardiner, and his sons again had to bolster the family's income as newsboys; they performed with such zeal that they more than once ran afoul of the truant officer, which gave the budding politician opportunity to practise his skills in debating. But Alpena too became a dead end for the family. Mrs Gardiner and the children returned to Ontario, and the two older boys, at twelve and sixteen, soon became farm labourers.

Jimmy had by now attended public school in three widely separated places situated in vastly different terrains, and had known grinding poverty, drought, and depression. Like many children, he seems to have taken all that in his stride, and his memoirs include joyous chronicles of raising a shoat which a passing cowboy in Nebraska had told him he could have if he could catch it; and log-rolling on the water in Alpena, a sport about which his mother had strong negative opinions, especially after he had fallen in. Both in Lincoln and Alpena he played the usual games, and approached manhood as an adept athlete. Like his later colleagues Chubby Power and Mike Pearson, the young Gardiner's athletic prowess became connected with his political career, and he was active in baseball, hockey, and football until he entered government.

His youthful travels gave him a good deal more than muscles. In Lincoln he became aware of the multiplicity of European nationalities settling the western plains. As a newsboy in Alpena he had experiences which helped convert him to a teetotaller, chiefly because his work took him into many saloons.[7] In Alpena, too, he met the phenomenon of schools where, as he sometimes marvelled, not only did Protestants and Catholics do their learning apart from each other, but so did German Catholics and Polish Catholics and French and Irish. Partly as a result of his observations as a schoolboy in the United States, Gardiner was rarely troubled by doubts over sundry fundamental aspects of Saskatchewan's educational policies, and the clarity of his opinions helped defeat him as premier in 1929.

Jimmy was not, at twelve, in a position to take whatever ambitions he had much further. He had to work, and by the time he was seventeen had performed almost every chore on an Ontario mixed farm. He sought a different farm each year and, in his own words, 'at from $5 to $16 a month he learned to feed chickens, pigs and cattle and milk cows between five and six in the morning and six and nine o'clock in the evening after driving a team, hoeing turnips, coiling hay or stooking from seven to six with two hours for noon as was the custom.'[8] Five years of that seemed enough; when Jimmy concluded that all his siblings were planning on making their home at their father's rented farm, he decided to leave. On 14 August 1901 he joined a harvest excursion and, in response to an open invitation he had had for some time, headed for his uncle's place at Clearwater, Manitoba. It was his first major break with his family, and except as a visitor he was not to return. The trip west, as if to emphasize the finality of his departure, took four days, with the train having to be split into sections for the steeper gradients; in daily concerts on board he danced the hornpipe. His welcome at Clearwater was a warm one, for his cousin Rosetta Jane (Etta) had already been east in 1899 and a friendship had begun then which ultimately led to their marriage in 1911. But in 1901, after a summer spent mostly at the back-breaking work of stooking (at $1.50 a day), he considered himself to be at a loose end, with few prospects and a minimal education.

He tried to enlist in the Canadian contingent being readied for the Boer War, but was rejected both because of his youth and his size. He thought of trying his luck as a sailor on the Pacific, but when he broached this subject to the Clearwater Gardiners, his uncle William, no doubt abetted by Etta, offered him a job as a hired man to do chores that included driving the children the two miles to school during the winter. The school was the clincher: provided his work could be arranged so that he could attend school himself, Jimmy was prepared to remain at Clearwater indefinitely. That suited Etta.

For the next three years Gardiner gained invaluable experience in western farming to add to his Ontario background, and attended high school, where a teacher (this time the son of a former Liberal premier of Manitoba, Thomas Greenway) influenced him. Gardiner's own political views had far from jelled, but by 1904, when he completed his second-class teaching certificate, he felt he had time to enlarge his horizons. It was also time to move on: he had done enough debating in Clearwater to arouse the interests of men who thought he should be recruited into Manitoba College's team, but college took money. His teaching certificate was good in Manitoba and the Territories that were to become Saskatchewan and Alberta, and there were opportunities in the Territories, where immigrants were pouring in. He left Clearwater for Regina in the summer of 1904 on a train loaded with settlers from the United Kingdom, continental Europe, the United States, and even China.[9]

To arrive as a young man in Regina in 1904 one needed no friends to greet one: farmers hung about the station button-holing the able-bodied to press them into service as farmhands. Gardiner eluded these without difficulty and made for the Territorial Department of Education, where he met the equivalent of its deputy minister, James A. Calder, a man with whom Gardiner was to have close associations since Calder was in fact the first organizer of the institution that later became celebrated as 'the Gardiner Machine.' Neither man knew that in 1904: Gardiner was after a territorial teaching permit, which Calder issued on condition he return for further training at Regina Normal School in January of 1905. Gardiner readily agreed; staying only long enough to attend a rather rowdy public meeting held to plan the inaugural ceremonies attendant upon the creation of the new province of Saskatchewan, he left for the tiny settlement of Alpha in the south-eastern corner of the Territories. He was the hamlet's first teacher.

Teachers in the Territories could obtain posts in two ways in Gardiner's day: they could go to an agency, or they could reverse the tactics of the farmers at the railway station and follow a new batch of settlers out to their homesteads. Gardiner chose the former course and served in a sequence of hamlets and villages each of which added valuable new experiences and connections for his subsequent career. In Nebraska he had seen groups of settlers arriving from many lands, and played with their children; now he had to live with the settlers and teach their children – and not only book learning, but football, hockey, and baseball as well.

At Alpha, where he taught in the fall term of 1904, he found a community of Dunkards. At Hirsch in 1905 he served in an almost solidly Jewish settlement, and for a time taught school in the synagogue; sometimes, with the rabbi acting as translator, Gardiner served as an informal secretarial go-between in transactions involving Hirsch and outsiders. Warmley, where he taught in 1906, was predominantly an English settlement, and Vineberg (1907) had been settled from eastern Canada. West Weyburn (1909) was largely of American origin, and Lockwood (1910) included both Canadians and Americans, and a generous admixture of Austrians and Scandinavians. Lemberg, where he settled as principal from 1911 to 1914, was a larger village with a Polish name, a typical mosaic of the prairies' population. The inspectors' reports on his teaching were highly laudatory.[10]

Gardiner regarded the teaching of Canadian and British history as of particular importance to the west's cosmopolitan peoples; for while, as he noted, one could hardly hope to make the immigrant parents into 'the most loyal Canadian subjects' because they naturally looked homeward, 'we can hope however, to make of the rising generation loyal Canadian citizens, loyal British subjects.'[11] He saw British (and hence Canadian) political institutions not as the result of the thinking of idealists, or of any one generation, but pragmatically 'inspired by necessity as generation after generation has struggled on filled with a love of freedom the first germs of which were found with our Teutonic ancestors while yet they lived on the banks of the Elb [sic] and the Weser.' Gardiner's views on the teacher's role included another relevant factor: 'Outside school hours I always considered it my right while a teacher to take any stand regarding politics.'[12]

Indeed he did. Gardiner's own grand design was what lay behind his choice of schools. It included covering vast parts of the south-eastern prairie on bicycle or horseback, getting to know as many people as possible. His athletic skills were useful in giving him a quick rapport with his pupils everywhere he went, but they also meant travelling around from contest to contest, not only playing but learning the techniques of organization and management. In later years Gardiner repeatedly reminded correspondents that his first political organization had been an athletic club. The game plan also required a university degree, and at first Gardiner had law in mind, with Queen's his choice of school. As the possibilities of the expanding west were borne in on him, along with the realization that teaching afforded as sound an entry into politics on the prairies as law in the east, his mind turned to Manitoba College simply because it was nearest.

When the college offered a new course in history and economics, Gardiner set aside whatever ideas he had had about law, and registered in it. He attended Manitoba intermittently from 1906 to 1911, when he took his Bachelor of Arts and returned to Saskatchewan to accept the principalship at Lemberg. With his several years' solid experience as a teacher, and an excellent degree, the Lemberg school board had reason to feel it had a good catch. What made Lemberg particularly attractive to Gardiner was that the provincial constituency of North Qu'Appelle, which contained it, had been lost by W.R. Motherwell in 1908, and he had moved to Humboldt. So there was a potential opening for another Liberal.

The precise point at which Gardiner decided he was a Liberal cannot be determined. The Gardiner family had settled in a part of Ontario so committed to politics that, as Gardiner observed years later, 'a true return could be sent in for the poll before the day of the election came off.'[13] His mother's potent Liberal leanings were matched by the Clearwater Gardiners and his mentor there, Harvey Greenway. Gardiner himself worked as a poll clerk in Saskatchewan's first provincial election in 1905, a fragment of patronage he would hardly have had if he had been suspected of a Conservative taint. He later recorded that the Liberals' first convention in 1905 was the only one he had ever missed. Gardiner worked for the provincial Liberals again in 1908, and was a strong champion of reciprocity in 1911. Yet when accepting his first nomination in 1913 he told the convention that he was not a dyed-in-the-wool Liberal, having in federal politics voted Conservative once and Liberal once.[14] Since he was loud in his praise of Laurier and reciprocity with the United States in 1911, his lone Conservative vote must have been in 1908, the only other federal election in which he was qualified to cast a ballot.

The point is of more than passing interest, for it raises the question of how influential his training at Manitoba College was in settling his convictions as a Liberal. Winnipeg itself helped, for as the bottle-neck through which all prairie grain flowed eastward (a lot of the grain that became celebrated on world markets as Manitoba wheat came from Saskatchewan), the city was the headquarters not only of those who battened on the trade – the grain exchange, the officials of railway and elevator companies – but the farmers who organized to protest their own exploitation. In every prairie settlement early in the century the farmer bringing his wagons of grain to any elevator was largely at the mercy of those who took over its storage and transportation: people with every reason to take advantage of the farmers for their own profit were in charge of weighing, grading, keeping and moving the grain, and the growers' insecurity was worsened by the speculations of brokers on the Winnipeg Grain Exchange whose operations, though vital to the prices at which grains sold, performed no function comprehensible to the farmers who actually planted the seed. The chronicle of the farmers' attempts to organize themselves in self-defence, mainly through co-operatives, has been well told elsewhere and needs no repetition.[15] What is important here is that Gardiner was mixed up in the whole development, and not merely as an observer, almost from the start. The leading protagonists among the agriculture pressure groups were, or soon became, his acquaintances and colleagues. His experiences in Winnipeg, quite apart from the intellectual stimulation of attending college, helped convince him that publicly owned grain elevators were not the answer to the farmers' problems: they had to solve those themselves, through co-operatives.

That conclusion, one of profound importance for a man who was to be a premier of Saskatchewan and a federal minister of agriculture, was reinforced by his studies. On a fourth-year essay Gardiner wrote on 'Economic Functions of Government,' his professor of economics, A.B. Clark (a Scot), noted: 'A thoughtful and interesting treatment, from an independent standpoint. More account might be taken of the literature of the subject, and of the general limitations of State action.' The comment is revealing of Gardiner, but equally so of his tutor: what Gardiner learned from Clark, among others he read and listened to, was not merely that there were 'general limitations on State action,' but that some state actions, such as putting up protective tariffs, were positively bad. As a westerner and farm boy, of course, Gardiner hardly needed to be told that. But the systematic reading of standard economic texts (and, under Chester Martin's guidance, constitutional history) gave him a disciplined grasp of nineteenth-century liberalism he never lost.

The theoretical knowledge of economics he gained at Manitoba he enclosed in a mental capsule which, while he almost daily opened it to help expound his views on liberalism, democracy, combines, freight rates, the 'interests,' socialism, free trade and allied matters, seems rarely to have had its contents disturbed by the addition of new material. He continued to read history in a desultory manner after leaving college, and when asked in 1937 what he read, answered, 'history, economics and cowboy stories principally.'[16]

As a student Gardiner did well, supplementing his studies with a good deal of attention to the college's athletic and debating teams. His small stature might have hampered the sports career of a less determined or slower-moving man, but he regularly played positions where quickness of hand and eye – or, in soccer, of foot – could offset a slight build: he was a forward in hockey and soccer and an infielder in baseball. As a debater he was a phenomenon, speaking convincingly on either side of any resolution, and representing the college not only in contests with other Winnipeg institutions, but also against teams from North Dakota. He ended his student achievements as a speaker with the only two prizes available: he was class valedictorian in his last year, and winner of the gold medal for oratory. (He had been runner up in 1910 against Manitoba's Rhodes scholar for the year, Joseph Thorson, with whom he later served in Mackenzie King's wartime cabinet.)

In speeches and essays that are more reliable evidence of his views than his debating notes, he asserted that a lot of men are not fit for politics, because for their own purposes they were deliberately teaching the foreign-born how to manipulate the electoral system. 'Cheap politicians,' he said to a college audience, 'there is what I consider one of the greatest, if not the greatest enemy we have to fight in Western Canada.' He then developed one of the themes in his novel: 'The balot [sic] which is sacred to every lover of democracy is played with and violated in the most flagrant way, and to the lasting shame of many of our educational institutions many of those responsible are professional men.' We need, he concluded, 'political men of strong intellect, of clean moral and political character.'[17] He had already, in a third-year essay on protection, tied the cheap politicians to the main economic pressure groups: 'So closely do the interests of Politicians become associated with those of their creation – the protected interests – that it is impossible to rid the country of the responsibility of protecting these industries even to the injury of the nationally established industries of the country.' In other essays he favoured government regulation of competition in the public interest, and opposed government ownership and operation of industrial utilities; free trade, he considered, was the real answer to combines in restraint of trade, and to monopoly too, an idea he was to echo on his deathbed.[18] 'During your University debating days,' a schoolmate wrote him years later, 'I well remember you quoting the Bible to show that Joseph was the first man to get a corner on wheat.'[19]

That Gardiner should use biblical references in college debates in 1910–11 was typical both of him and of Manitoba College. He taught Sunday school throughout his days in Winnipeg, and lived in a residence whose rules, drawn up and signed by Gardiner, forbade smoking and required regular attendance at 'evening prayers and the respective places of worship on Sunday.' (The original draft included morning prayers, but that was stroked out.)[20] This piety carried over to his attitudes towards two other major matters, social welfare and the British connection.

Welfare for the maimed, the orphaned, and the invalided, the young, Gardiner approved of; when it came to the able-bodied indigent, his Scots Presbyterian upbringing took over. 'If work is at hand,' he wrote in 1911, ' ... it is punishment and not sympathy that is due the able-bodied poor.' That kind of poor was not exactly prevalent then on the Canadian prairies, but in more settled areas, Gardiner went on, 'care must be taken by government not to encourage living on the rates by adding a little of disgrace and discomfort but not enough to turn the pauper into the criminal.'[21]

A more spacious religious element entered into his beliefs on the British connection. He expressed himself fulsomely about this in his early days, for among other things it was an example he could cite in many of his debates and essays that concerned free trade. It was also mystically tied to Christianity, and that tie in turn was one reason why he was one of the earliest champions of the movement that produced the United Church of Canada in 1925. His thoughts on all this are not in a single exposition, but scattered over a series of patriotic speeches he gave to a variety of audiences:

In all ages religious belief has had considerable to do with the moulding of nationality ... to be a British citizen is to substitute for all your gods, Our Father in Heaven, for blood, sacrifices, pure worship, for learning love; for law the sermon on the Mount. To be a British citizen is to be a Christian filled with the spirit of Christ ...

If Canada is to be truely [sic] great the Church must see that our Canadian nationality is based upon the teachings of the Christian Church and that those teachings be guarded by the light and liberty of a Protestant faith ... We hope in the near future to have the United Canadian Church into which we can invite all Canadians of whatever country to worship the one true God.[22]

Readers of those heady words may be surprised to learn that Gardiner was also a stout champion of party government and its inevitable accompaniment, the caucus, as one of the most effective tools for accomplishing desirable social goals. As a man familiar with school, church, farm, and athletic organizations, he did not regard political organization as fundamentally different from any other. It might vary in structure because it was for other purposes, but basically it was simply a tool, and like any good tool, it was fashioned to serve its craftsman best. 'There is no question but that Representative Resp. Gov. is the most democratic system of gov't in the world today,' he wrote in 1911 in notes for either a debate or a strikingly combative essay. 'There is no question but that party government is a necessary part of a representative system where free discussion is allowed.'[23] In the same document he argued that the faults readily apparent in the system were not those of the system itself, but could be traced to such pressures as those which resulted in first-rate men staying out of politics for their own self-interest, or in clergymen having to avoid political controversy because to become involved was 'as much as most clergymen's appointments are worth.' The result too often was that second-rate men got elected.

It was with a missionary's zeal that Gardiner looked upon seeking a nomination for himself, and it was only sensible to seek it in an area with which he was familiar and where he was well known. The provincial constituency of North Qu'Appelle, which had been created in 1908 by a redistribution which for the first time used the lovely Qu'Appelle River as a boundary, was not an easy seat for a Liberal. Motherwell had lost it by 990 votes to 848 in 1908, and his successful opponent was to take it again in 1912 by 882 to 837; the premier of Saskatchewan, Walter Scott, had so little confidence in it as a Liberal stronghold that he did not want Motherwell to run in it again because it would not leave him free to campaign elsewhere in the province.[24] When Gardiner moved to Lemberg in 1911 (at first alone, returning to Clearwater to marry Etta at Christmas) the seat was not only occupied, but a doubtful prospect.

What was available, with Motherwell sitting elsewhere, was a possible candidature. Gardiner did not arrive in North Qu'Appelle in time to have sufficiently consolidated himself to win the nomination for the election but he did offer his services to Scott early in the year, and was sent literature from the office of the chief organizer. He worked conscientiously for the Liberal who was nominated and was so useful a campaigner that he was asked into a neighbouring constituency as a spokesman for the government at meetings convened on behalf of a redoubtable Conservative. The protocol at such meetings was for the invited spokesman to go first, followed by the candidate whose meeting it was, with subsequent rebuttals by both speakers in the same order, the final speech by the candidate being regarded as his main performance. Gardiner fastened himself onto his opponent like a leech, attending not one but a series of meetings interrupted only by a baseball tournament in which Gardiner had to play. He was so effective that after the first meeting the Conservative cut the time allocated to his opening speech from forty to twenty minutes. The Conservatives lost the election, 1,001 to 896.

That defeat made Gardiner a marked man in the district, particularly since it followed Liberal victories in the two federal seats in which he had campaigned in 1911. And the defeat of the Liberal in North

Qu'Appelle in 1912 opened the way to a candidature, for defeated candidates were regarded as expendable. The opportunity came sooner than expected; the Conservative MLA who won in 1912, J.A. McDonald, was shortly accused of having influenced the electorate in divers illegal ways, mainly bribery in the form of cash, clothing, tents, whisky, cigars, lumber, barbed wire, beer, permission to cut hay on a desirable field, and free transportation. The collection of the usual affidavits persuaded McDonald to confess mildly that while 'practically all' of the allegations contained in the petitioner's particulars 'were untrue,' he had technically breached the elections act on 'one of the minor charges' and was therefore unduly elected. A provincial court solemnly agreed, and North Qu'Appelle was open as of 16 October 1913.[25]

An executive of the North Qu'Appelle constituency association, J.B. Gillespie, wrote to the premier on 26 November to raise the question of seeking a candidate, as the Conservatives were already in the field. Scott agreed and, as was the practice in the party, emphasized the importance of local constituency autonomy in the selection of candidates, with an absolute minimum of interference from the central organization. Would not the appearance of a cabinet member at any convention, as requested by Gillespie, be seen as the hand of the hierarchy? Gillespie reassured him, and asked for either Scott himself or W.F.A. Turgeon, a member of a distinguished political family and Scott's attorney general and provincial secretary. The date was set for 23 December at Cupar; Turgeon went and spoke only after the nomination of the candidate, so that nothing ministerial could even inadvertently be mistaken as favouring one contestant over another.[26]

Gardiner's adoption was by no means a certainty, as he had two strong rivals. He was put forward by the Lemberg Liberals under the leadership of R.H. Hall, who had been a possible candidate for nomination in the constituency east of North Qu'Appelle in a previous election. Hall's motivation, Gardiner said, was that the 'young school teacher ... had done well as a campaigner for others in the elections of 1911 and 1912, and was popular not only as a teacher and in church work but also as leader among young people.'[27]

Gardiner considered both his opponents to be formidable. One, N.B. Williams, was a grand master of the Masonic Lodge, and allegedly had the party organization behind him. The other, Donald McKinnon, was Roman Catholic, and his wife came from Gardiner's own base, Lemberg. The eastern half of the seat, the Abernethy-Lemberg area, had twenty-six delegates at the convention; the Balcarres-Cupar section, to the west, had twenty-four. Turgeon came to the event having been told that Williams was a cinch to win. What he had not been told was that Hall and Gardiner had been organizing like madmen and, as Gardiner years later told his son, 'we had the convention won before we went to it.'[28]

Gardiner came third in the draw to determine the order of the candidates' fifteen-minute speeches, and his rivals acquitted themselves well. But Gardiner was not impressed; resting comfortably in the assurance that he had worked the seat well, he also knew he had done his homework for his own speech, which had been carefully planned and put through three drafts. Since it was his first major performance on his own behalf, and charted the political course he hoped to follow thereafter, it is worth sampling.[29] After the usual reference to the honour he felt in being allowed to stand, Gardiner turned to the federal campaign of 1911, when the west saw a good deal of the Honourable Robert Rogers, who had been Conservative minister of public works in Manitoba for over a decade and was in 1913 serving in Sir Robert Borden's cabinet in the same capacity; his successive appointments to the great patronage portfolios were not based on coincidence, and the Liberals called him 'Minister of Elections.'

For forty years the octopus of political corruption with its centre in Toronto has been spreading its tentacles over the whole Dominion slowly but surely sucking the life blood of Canadian Democracy. I have allowed my name to come before this convention because I believe that western Canada led by the Sask. Gov. is to strike the first effective blow at the monster of vested interests and that North Qu'Appelle is to be the field of the advance skirmish.

He then lauded the Grain Growers for their fight against 'the great c.p.r. ... in close combine with the grain dealers,' again using his college metaphor about Joseph cornering wheat, describing the Growers' association as 'one of the wonders of western organization.' He dealt with the Growers' demand for public ownership of telephones, comparing Manitoba's failure in owning elevators unfavourably (and somewhat irrelevantly) with Saskatchewan's policy of encouraging farmers, through co-operatives, to look after their own needs in elevators, hail insurance, and credit. From there he turned to Saskatchewan's interest in wider markets and lower tariffs, and spoke ill of the tariff. Lifting a passage directly from a college debate of 1910 he proceeded:

A good system of taxation must bear on all according to their ability to pay. A good system of taxation must be payable at the time when it is most easily met. From a good system the gov. gets the maximum amount of the tax collected. Under a good system of taxes a man knows exactly what his taxes amount to. Under our present system of protective tarrifs [*sic*] the consuming laboring class and the producing farming class pay the taxes while the plutocratic aristocracy of the east pocket their share of the spoils. Under our present system the homesteader pays the bulk of his taxes for years to come when he purchases his implements. Under our present system a large part of the enhanced price goes to the mfgs.[30]

The rhetorical repetition, and the homely images he used, were to become his hallmarks. So too his roundhouse swings at things Tory. He berated Borden's cabinet for its reception of the latest farmers' delegation to Ottawa, and reminded his audience that he had been a farmer himself and proposed to become one again: 'My ambition today is to be a farmer with education representing the farmer of this constituency in the legislature.'

And in conclusion: 'What the farmers of this country must have if they were going to succeed in the struggle was men in sympathy with the farmers but able to meet the interests in parliamentary debate ... I place my agricultural experience, my education, my knowledge of the province, my political experience in your hands. If you accept it I will put into the campaign all the energy I have. If you decide in favor of another I will give him all my spare time in securing the victory.'

He had chosen his role, and the convention accepted it. On the first ballot Gardiner and McKinnon tied, and the touted Williams was low man. On the second, all of the delegates of the masonic grand master swung to Gardiner.[31] From the evening of 23 December 1913, he was off and running.

For the next forty-five years.

2

Back-bencher

The province to whose affairs Gardiner committed himself in 1913 had been host to one of the greatest migrations of modern history. The area that became Saskatchewan had a population of less than one hundred thousand in 1901, almost all of it, except for some scattered settlements around Prince Albert, in the south-east corner; by 1911 settlement had spread across to the Alberta boundary, and the population had grown to 492,432. By 1916 it was 648,000 and even at that the settled area averaged only two or three persons for each square mile.[1]

The miracle of the migration lay not merely in its size (which was considerably greater than the settlement figures suggest: thousands more did not remain) but also in the variety of obstacles overcome. The settlers arrived on railroads that were still being built, and travelled locally on trails that could be quickly made impassable by rain or snow or, when dry, exceedingly unpleasant by dust; except for short spurs, the province's major centres were not linked by paved highways until the 1950s. Over those unfinished railroads and dirt trails the settlers had to bring literally everything they needed to survive, and that included traps and guns: the bounty on wolves for years after its creation was annually paid on from ten to fifteen thousand kills.

The accommodation of instant settlements had to include quick preparation of such institutions as judicial districts and schools (districts for the latter grew from 896 in 1905 to 2,932 in 1912),[2] and the statute books of Saskatchewan in its first years are a fair measure of precisely what the new province saw as its priorities. Justice and education were obvious needs; less obvious were provisions for the security of public officials, for the confinement of the insane, or the regulation of butter and cheese production.[3] The chief architect for all this building was the Liberal party.

That party did not exist as the equivalent of a provincial organization before 1905.[4] Territorial politics had been largely non-partisan, and while the parties fought on traditional lines for federal elections, they did not in territorial affairs. Partisanship for provincial affairs came much closer to reality before 1905 when F.W. Haultain, the territorial premier, appeared with increasing frequency to flirt with the idea of a local Conservative party, even presiding over its first convention in 1903. That there would be an opposing Liberal party became a virtual certainty at that point, and Sir Wilfrid Laurier ensured it by seeing to it that Walter Scott, the Liberal MP for Assiniboia West, was selected as the first premier of Saskatchewan instead of Haultain. (Scott's well-wishers included W.T. Diefenbaker, whose teen-aged son John had possibly not yet taken up sides.)[5]

For provincial purposes, both parties had to start organizing from scratch, and it quickly became apparent that the Liberals were not only more adept at it but also luckier. What territorial organization there had been for federal purposes had lain in the hands of Clifford Sifton, then Laurier's minister of the interior. In 1905 Scott selected as his colleagues in a four-man cabinet J.H. Lamont of Prince Albert, W.R. Motherwell of Abernethy in North Qu'Appelle, and James A. Calder of Regina – all four of Scots descent. The least of these as a politician was Lamont, who lasted just two years before becoming a judge. The other two, with Scott, made a remarkable team. Of Motherwell Scott wrote in 1908, 'outside of political management, Motherwell is an excellent man.' The slack was taken up by Calder, whom the premier described as 'simply an invaluable man. We have done a perfectly amazing [amount] of work in the last three years.'[6] Calder was the man who built the party.

The expanding province provided an almost ideal environment for party-building, and the party was a sensitive response to its environment. Both the governed and the governing needed a web of communications. The insatiable demands at the local level for schools, teachers, court houses, bridges, agricultural advice, railway branch lines, and so on had to be expressed to those in a position to provide them or at least facilitate their acquisition. The party, led by ambitious men genuinely desirous of providing services in return for control of the making of decisions (and the consequent exclusion of opponents who would make other and usually wrong decisions) needed supporters and informants everywhere. The mature organization that resulted from all these common needs had to be far more than an electoral device, although that was essential; it meant looking after the naturalization of immigrants as fast as they qualified, getting their names on the voters' lists once the law required it after 1908, and seeing that they actually turned out to vote.

The whole system drew its nourishment from an extraordinary network which not merely distributed but created patronage. The major impetus came from the centre, but the emphasis was always on local autonomy in all activities, ranging from the selection of the candidate for the next election down to deciding which of the two hardware stores would provide half a dozen shovels for a road crew, which of two hotels should house an itinerant school inspector, or which of two weekly newspapers should print the voters' lists. In 1907 the deputy commissioner of public works, a public servant, wrote to all Liberal MLAs for the 'names of business firms in every town and village in your district for patronage purposes in respect to livery, blacksmithing, hardware, lumber, unloading cars, etc.' It had to be done properly, for not only was the department hampered if its information was incomplete, but the member himself suffered if patronage went to the wrong person.

The people on patronage lists, it should be added, were sternly warned that their quotations had to be reasonable. A deliberate policy of abandoning the purchase of certain supplies wholesale from Winnipeg in favour of local acquisition was announced to the faithful with an emphasis on economy and quality, and a request that nobody lay in supplies in anticipation of an order from Regina.[7] How firmly the line held in any one community would depend, of course, on the integrity of the businessmen and the alertness of the candidate; it was, in effect, an honour system. The structure as a whole was confidently expected to work. One satisfied candidate spoke for them all when he told Calder: 'The bridge will help me to get the Doubtful and most of the Tories ... This road work will make more Liberals.'[8]

The machine (a term heartily disliked by all its operators, including Gardiner) was even more elaborate than the foregoing examples suggest. Within the electoral system it included not only printing the voters' lists but the appointment of returning officers, deputy returning officers, and the rental of premises for polls in some areas where the local school was unsuitable; for the single election of 1905, when the electors marked their preferences on blank paper with a red or blue pencil according to choice, it no doubt included the pencils. Friendly newspapers had to be supported. Calder, when offered some Scandinavian papers for distribution among Liberals at a price, had to reply that he had already made certain arrangements for the Swedes and Norwegians and could not afford more; but Scott had earlier taken the initiative by starting a newspaper in German, and when twenty disgruntled electors petitioned him about its unsatisfactory policies he agreed to look into it because the paper was, after all, 'supported by the party and for the party.'[9]

Patronage in staffing the civil service was of course the standard practice, and sometimes it was taken to surprising lengths. It was of great moment to the government that teachers in the provincial Normal School not be subversive of the party, while the inspectors in the field received advice such as that Calder gave one in 1912: 'I will be very glad indeed if you will give me such assistance as you can in a quiet way while on your rounds.'[10] Nor were the police overlooked: 'I think that two-thirds of the Mounted Police must be against,' Scott wrote testily in 1908, 'and it would go to show something radically wrong with the management.'[11] He had similar views about the railways: one Canadian Northern agent, he told the agent's superior in 1909, was 'a mischievous and an especially virulent enemy of ours ... I ask you to take McBain out of the Province or to relieve him from your service.'[12] Scott knew that kind of detail because Calder's organization brought it to him; and Scott himself made a practice of circularizing Liberal candidates after an election to ask for the names of outside Conservative workers who had invaded each seat, a summary of untrue opposition statements, and a description of any unfair methods, as well as material on opposition literature and unfriendly newspapers.[13] The organization did not miss much, in short; it saw to it that every country fair and every village sports day had its quota of speakers.[14]

When Jimmy Gardiner received the North Qu'Appelle nomination in 1913 he did not become merely a candidate: he became a non-commissioned officer in a versatile army. He later reminisced that as an ordinary MLA he had never had much patronage at his disposal, and in a sense he was right, for neither a candidate nor an elected member had any executive power of appointment. What a government candidate had in 1913 was a strong hand in all recommendations affecting his riding. The premier not only believed in local autonomy: in a large thinly populated area he considered it unavoidable. When he was an MP, he explained to a complainant in 1908, he had had to rely for advice on the presidents of local Liberal associations. But in the provincial constituencies, 'it is the regular practice for the Government to act only upon the advice of the Liberal candidate in the last previous election'[15] – unless he had been superseded by a later nominee. And Gardiner, in 1913, was a later nominee; whatever there was, he looked after.

Immediately after the nominating convention, of course, patronage was not uppermost in Gardiner's mind. He had been nominated to fight an election, and he wanted to get at it. Sporting a magnificent shiner earned in a hockey game, he made his debut early in 1914 before the executive council in Regina for his marching orders. He wanted the earliest possible date for calling the by-election, but the premier wanted to wait until June and he carried his colleagues with him;[16] Scott had a theory that while a candidate too long in the field might alienate too many voters and become the subject of too many unmanageable rumours, one in not long enough was unready. Gardiner arranged for a substitute teacher for January so that he could visit every part of the constituency; then he went back to teaching. After school and on weekends he campaigned.

The campaign had to have many facets, for North Qu'Appelle measured roughly twenty-five miles by fifty and contained a cosmopolitan population. It had no cities or towns, only villages; and no highways, only trails, some of which received sporadic attention from maintenance crews. The constituency's main villages were strung along a single railway which was built in 1905–6, and every one of them had a population which cut across several ethnic and religious lines. Gardiner's chosen home, Lemberg (a Polish name), according to the census had seventy-one inhabitants of British origin, thirty of German, thirty-seven of Austrian, and thirty-four of Russian. Cupar's population, by contrast, was over 10 per cent Jewish; and in Dysart the Jews comprised more than a quarter of the total. Killaly was almost wholly Austrian and Russian, the British consisting of five individuals.[17]

Hockey and, as the spring advanced, baseball, brought Gardiner in touch with one element in his district; the importance of his youthful participation in games could hardly be overemphasized, for Saskatchewan was also a young man's country politically. Gardiner was thirty-one when he took his seat in the legislature, the youngest of the MLAs whose ages are known; but at least seven of his fifty-three colleagues were also in their thirties, and fully one-third of all members had won their first election at the same age. He had contacts with the older generation through his church work and his school board; the years at Alpha, Hirsch, and all the other villages had made him feel at home with almost every conceivable nationality, a trait he never lost. But all his friends would have availed him little without organization, and to his natural gifts there he had the good fortune to add two great teachers – George Scott and James Calder. Gardiner always gave Scott, the MLA from Arm River, the credit for being his real master in political techniques, but both Gardiner and Scott worked within Calder's system, and Calder's thoroughness can be measured by instructions he sent out to alert all MLAS to a possible snap election at the federal level in 1915. His list included:

- Every single polling division and township should be examined to make certain reliable men were available.
- Every possible case of naturalization should be looked after; preferably before seeding got the farmers all out on the land.
- Ethnic leaders should be sought out in each foreign-speaking settlement.
- Any local feelings or divisions that could be exploited by the opposition should be carefully watched.

That attention to detail was applied by Scott and Gardiner in North Qu'Appelle in a campaign which, as the tempo quickened, became a miniature general election. Every minister was in it (and in the easier simultaneous by-election being held in Rosthern) and at times only one minister held the fort at Regina.[18]

The selection of issues on which to fight was of major concern, for before radio and television facilitated the creation of 'images,' what a politician said was often more important than how he said it. In the provincial election in 1912, with the great farmers' march to Ottawa of 1910 and its aftermath fresh in everybody's mind, elevators and railways, and the need for roads to supplement them, had loomed large. The federal election of 1911 had been fought on reciprocity, a subject dear to western hearts. The Conservatives' view of the issues was at first unclear, but Gardiner was never one to let other people decide what he was going to talk about. In his own account of the 1914 by-election he wrote that he was 'for Reciprocity, for government owned and operated telephones, against government owned elevators and for Co-operative farmer owned and operated elevators in competition with privately owned and operated elevators, for municipal hail insurance on a co-operative basis, for co-operative creameries and some form of government loans, and for prohibition.'[19]

Any campaign must of course be adapted to local conditions, and it is relevant that in June of 1914 prospects for the crop were excellent.

(Contemporaneously, the Banish the Bar League was planning its biggest convention to date, and on 9 June a church general assembly plumped for church union.) Since North Qu'Appelle had no daily newspapers and few weeklies, there was no general coverage of the campaign. The *Saskatoon Phoenix*, intemperately Liberal, did not consider the Qu'Appelle Valley to be within its own constituency; though it carried a weekly column by John J. McGraw on the affairs of the National Baseball League, as well as Lillian Russell's Beauty Secrets, it did not report on the North Qu'Appelle by-election until 26 June. Whatever Gardiner had done, it had worked: he took the seat from the Conservatives by 1,171 to 891, a phenomenal victory for that district; it was to be his smallest majority in a provincial election. The national Liberal organization noted the new recruit, and the *Canadian Liberal Monthly* solemnly reported in its July issue that Gardiner had carried Rosthern with a greatly increased majority, while giving all the credit for the North Qu'Appelle triumph to a man who had not run there.[20]

Gardiner took his seat in the legislature on 15 September, the first day of a special session occasioned by the outbreak of war. The building was new, having been completed in 1912, and even after its construction the assembly had had to meet for a while in the chamber designated to be the library, the library itself housed in the basement of the Land Titles Office. When the assembly was not sitting, its clerk, in a splendid economy, served as superintendent of neglected children.[21]

Nobody in Saskatchewan then was likely to be concerned about makeshift arrangements, for practically all the MLAS were accustomed to getting along without electricity, running water, passable roads or, when campaigning, comfortable beds. The luxury of the legislative building was for many a sharp break with their unsophisticated rural pasts. A sharper break for Gardiner was the cause of the September legislative session. In accordance with Scots tradition as the Gardiners understood it, one son – Jimmy, the married, settled, son – stayed home, and the rest went off to war. 'I have three brothers away to the front,' Gardiner told one wartime audience, 'and I almost shudder when I think of the possibilities of the responsibility I assume if I remain at home until this war is ended.'[22] He did remain, in due course applying for and receiving exemption when conscription came in. His brothers were less fortunate; all were killed by the war, but two of them – Bill and Robert, Jimmy's boyhood companions in Nebraska and Michigan – took many years to die.

In 1914 Gardiner fortunately had no inkling of that, and he applied himself to some of the more immediate problems of a freshman legislator, one of which was that he soon needed money to supplement his official pay. He was not the kind of man who expected to make money out of politics, and he despised those who tried: some of the most important events of his back-bench career early identified for him what kinds of elements to avoid in a governing party, and what kinds to trust.[23] But even before 1916 Gardiner had repeatedly spoken out against predatory politicians who took advantage of the trust placed in them, and they provided all the villains for his novel of 1911. Interestingly enough, one of the ways in which he tried to make money after his election was a second novel, considerably more sophisticated than the first, which chronicled the classic confrontation between ranchers and new settlers wanting the same lands.[24] The novel was left untitled and unfinished, probably because Gardiner was too busy as MLA and the Lemberg agent of the National Life Assurance Company of Canada. He also tried to sell articles to the *Grain Growers' Guide*, which did not encourage him because it had all the material it could use from the farmers' viewpoint and wanted more from the manufacturers'; and he considered briefly acquiring a press of his own when a Lemberg printer fell behind in his payments.[25] With none of these enterprises proving fruitful as a career, he made a decision which he never regretted: in 1917 he made the down payment on a farm at Lemberg. 'Pleasant View,' as he called it, was neither large nor overly productive, but it had a fine big house and supported enough mixed farming to feed and clothe the Gardiners from then on. It became Jimmy's home for the rest of his life, and he died there.

Gardiner's career as a back-bench MLA was steady rather than spectacular. He was on occasion put on the Standing Committee on Public Accounts, and served regularly on the Library Committee, which presented no reports while he was a member. More importantly, he was annually assigned to the Committee on Private Bills, which brought him in touch with a variety of elements from all over the province: municipalities, private companies, charitable organizations – anybody, in short, who needed to be incorporated, to have a charter amended, or wanted the remission of some burdensome fee. Every year the committee approved, altered, or rejected an interesting list of proposals. Although Gardiner was never elected chairman of a committee, his value as a worker is attested to by his selection as one of five members constituted as a special committee to look into charges brought by the MLA, J.E. Bradshaw, in 1916.

The Saskatchewan legislature did not record its debates in those early days, and the official *Journals of the Legislative Assembly* are so cryptic that it is impossible to tell from official sources how often or in what manner any particular member participated in the proceedings. As a back-bencher Gardiner proposed no bills and did not once vote against the government. As its supporter he asked no damaging questions, though he did put down a few which permitted the elucidation of some points more to the government's credit than anything. And since no other party had been in power, there was no opportunity to ask questions which brought out the shoddy past of the opposition. The opposition was in power in Ottawa, and that gave him scope for the moving of resolutions demanding the transfer of jurisdiction over the province's natural resources in 1917, and the repeal of the iniquitous Wartime Elections Act in 1919.[26]

In the speeches he made on these occasions, and on others both inside the legislature and out, Gardiner continued to reveal the beliefs and qualities he first showed for the record as a college student and debater. The years had broadened his interests and experiences, but his entrance into public life did not change his mind about much. In his maiden speech during the short autumn session of 1914, on the Patriotic Aids Act, he saw the war as unifying the empire because of the virtue of British institutions. He related that to the cosmopolitan character of the prairie population, similarly unified by the war, and spoke sympathetically of those of German extraction who, of all of Canada's 'great races,' would be under the greatest tensions because of the war. He reminded his colleagues that the original Lemberg, in Poland, was at that moment in the battle area, while in its Canadian namesake all the nationalities living there were already co-operating in Red Cross tag days and similar ventures.[27]

The theme Gardiner chose for his opening address was prophetic, for he used precisely the same approach over four years later when condemning the Wartime Elections Act and the Military Voters Act of 1917. Those acts in general terms extended the franchise to all adult females with male relatives in the Canadian or British armed forces, and to virtually all males in the forces whether or not they were otherwise disqualified. The legislation disfranchised conscientious objectors and those who even applied for certificates as such, including Mennonites, Doukhobours, 'and not only all naturalized British subjects born in an enemy country and naturalized after March 31, 1902, but all who even spoke an enemy language habitually and were naturalized after that date.'[28] To Gardiner and his Liberal colleagues who had worked so assiduously among the citizens of European origin, getting them naturalized precisely so that they would be able to vote, the wartime franchise adopted for federal purposes was an utter outrage. It deepened Gardiner's conviction that Tories are liable to do anything.

What particularly irked him about the wartime franchise was that it deprived British subjects of one of the basic rights they had come to Canada to enjoy; and it was all instigated by the very party which most loudly touted the values of the imperial connection. His condemnatory resolution recited the Tories' misdeeds in detail and concluded: 'Therefore, be it resolved, That this Assembly is of the opinion that the War Time Election Act and any other enactment, order or regulation, having the effect of depriving any loyal Canadian citizen of the privilege of exercising the rights of citizenship should be repealed at the earliest possible moment.' Gardiner backed up his resolution with a well-prepared speech which tied Liberalism into his argument, and concluded with a warning to those Liberals who had gone into Borden's Union government; they will, he said, 'have to answer for their actions during the time they were part of the government.'[29] The debate which followed, considering that the House roster numbered only six Conservatives in the fifty-nine seats, might have been routine, but Liberal bitterness more than made up for the thin opposition. Gardiner's resolution carried forty-four to four.

Gardiner's emphasis on things British in both his maiden speech and his major statement above was in a sense misleading as to the scope of his interests. One notable omission from his resolution concerned French Canadians and the French language, for the Wartime Elections Act, comprehensive though it was, could hardly have disfranchised French Canadians as if they were of German descent. The provincial Conservatives, to be sure, had related ideas, and had tipped their hand by going beyond their own party platform to move on 18 December 1918, that 'the English language should be the only language of instruction in the elementary schools of the Province during the regular school hours,' and Gardiner had spoken briefly but feelingly to that.[30]

Education, to both Gardiner and the party, was never confined to the formal apparatus of the school system. The party, for example, went to considerable expense to have campaign material distributed in several languages, for the proper instruction of as many voters as possible. Gardiner's strong views on prohibition gave him a special dimension not occupied by all his fellows: 'We are fighting today two enemies,' he said when seconding the address in reply to the speech from the throne in 1915 (and incidentally paraphrasing a man referred to throughout his notes as Llyod George), 'the Teutons and booze.'[31] Liquor was connected with other matters of political moment, for the growing pressure for more stringent liquor laws was part of the women's suffrage movement, while the beverages themselves were manufactured by sinister outfits usually lumped together as 'the interests'; the church, in its own way, was as involved as the political parties. Gardiner had strong views about them all: whatever else might be said of his career as a back-bencher, he could not be classified among those silent government supporters so prized by cabinet ministers who like to do most of the talking themselves.

Like many successful politicians, Gardiner set great store by the spoken word and wrote out in longhand most of his major speeches. He left thousands of pages of scripts, but even so the record is incomplete, for he also spoke frequently from notes scribbled on scraps of paper, and often departed from prepared statements anyway. (More than once he baffled reporters by handing out printed copies of a speech quite different from the one he actually made; the record was what he intended to say when he planned it, but he was always ready to adjust to his audience.) His speeches ranged over all the major issues of the day, but they are held together by a remarkable philosophical consistency, dependent in part on his religious convictions, with which he coupled pragmatic beliefs about human institutions. 'I like to think as far as possible God speaks to me as he spoke to Moses,' he told a church audience in 1914, and in the same speech he said that when he heard a preacher condemn the party system he wished he could take him into the legislative chamber and ask him 'to indicate wherein the church is any improvement on the political organization.' The church is necessary, he added, 'but with present day organization the church dare not and does not attack the industrial, social and political evils with the enthusiasm that it should.'[32] Nor was the party system perfect: in one stout defence of parties he nonetheless asked, 'Is there anyone bold enough to assert that the financial policy of either party as carried out in practice is in the interests of the whole mass of the people rather than in the interests of the few?' The theoretical answer was always at hand: 'Liberalism in the province must stand for the development of agriculture and subsidiary business even though it does at times run counter to recognized financial and mfg interests or the interests of lawyers who depend [on them].'[33]

Most of the offending interests, in one way or another, Gardiner usually managed to tie to the Tories. The Bradshaw charges of 1916, for example, did not all appear to have a connection with the trade in potable alcohols, but Gardiner was suspicious enough to allege that the distillers had hired a man to delve into the private lives of Liberal MLAs in an attempt to discredit them, while offers of campaign funds were intended to silence them; the one allegation was by implication, the second directly, identified with Bradshaw's cause. That cause, a good one, was based on information which came to J.E. Bradshaw, the Conservative member for Prince Albert City, through sources which the Liberals, who always claimed that the Bradshaw charges were part of a federal Tory plot to destroy the government in Saskatchewan, traced to Robert Rogers, the dominion minister of public works.[34]

J.E. Bradshaw held the rank of lieutenant-colonel and was active in recruiting for the armed forces, a course not necessarily calculated to make him popular in an agricultural province with heavy demands for farm labour. His first charges, though alleging, among other things, that Liberal MLAs had accepted bribes, named no individuals and were ordered withdrawn. Bradshaw's response was to broaden the scope of his charges and he shortly had the legislature in a turmoil over allegations of 'graft, incompetence, and connivance of officials' in connection with the liquor and hotel trades, the asylum at Battleford, the jail in Regina, and the Department of Telephones generally. This time he supplied names, citing Premier Scott, James Calder, W.F.A. Turgeon and A.P. McNab, all members of the cabinet, as being involved in specific wrongdoing.[35]

The legislature could hardly ignore that, and its initial reaction was to refer the charges to committees of the House, both select and standing; Gardiner was on two of them, the Committee on Public Accounts which received Bradshaw's charges about fraudulent road contracts, and a select committee examining three charges that Liberal members had exerted undue influence and received bribes over liquor licences.

The whole story of Bradshaw's multifarious allegations, and their ultimate disposition, is an incredibly complex tale not wholly relevant to Gardiner's biography. It included turbulence verging on hysteria in both legislative chamber and committee room, and a parade of witnesses who ranged from the obsequious to the truculent, one of whom was called to the bar of the House and, on proving unco-operative, committed to the custody of the sergeant-at-arms for seven days. The committees did establish one thing: there was substance to Bradshaw's charges.

Despite the conflicting evidence, the Committee on Public Accounts conceded that 'there is the gravest suspicion' that the province had been bilked on fraudulent contracts, though it did not 'deem it advisable' to try to fix the blame. The other committee on which Gardiner sat concluded that there was sufficient evidence to justify further investigation of the relationships between several MLAS and the liquor trade and, like the Committee on Public Accounts, recommended that the charges be referred to royal commissions. Since the committees consisted overwhelmingly of Liberals, and in the case of that on public accounts only Liberals participated in the deliberations, Scott's government was not in a strong tactical position to refuse their advice, and three commissions, all chaired by judges (including Haultain, the former Conservative leader) and ex-judges, were established.[36]

The commissions also found substance in many of the charges, although many also fell for lack of evidence; they exonerated seven of thirteen Liberal MLAS Bradshaw had named in his charges concerning the liquor trades, for example. Both Liberals and Conservatives thus had reason to be comforted and discomfited. Bradshaw had, however, made a tactical error in trying to implicate cabinet ministers; Scott and his colleagues may not have had the tightest control over either the public service or the party, and with patronage and low pay dominating the one and a strong tradition of local responsibility in the other, it was perhaps impossible for them to do so. What Bradshaw did reveal was that the province had several crooked businessmen and a few crooked civil servants, and four disreputable Liberal MLAS out of a contingent of forty-five.

Had Bradshaw just quietly taken his evidence to the attorney general for inquiry and action against public servants and legislators alike, it is at least possible that he might have served his own cause better. By making spectacular charges, the chief of which failed, he gave adept opponents the opportunity to argue forever that the Liberals had taken prompt action as soon as the trouble was brought to their attention, for they had swiftly purged themselves of their own offending colleagues. As Bradshaw and his forces handled their allegations, the fundamental question of how the rot had set in in the first place, in a party barely a decade old, barely got asked, let alone examined. But plainly the honour system, as applied to patronage and influence-peddling, was far from foolproof; it grossly underestimated the ways in which a successful organization headed by high-minded people will attract predators who wish to use it for looting.

As a curtain-raiser to the next provincial election, due under the provincial constitution by the summer of 1917 at the latest, the Bradshaw charges undoubtedly helped the Liberals more than the Conservatives. They were in any event overtaken in 1917 by the dramatic crisis imposed particularly on the Liberals by conscription and, for the longer haul, by the burgeoning farmers' movements with their obvious threats to the established parties. Another relevant factor was the declining health of Walter Scott, the provincial leader, and Sir Wilfrid Laurier. Scott, plagued by asthma, was persuaded to retire in October of 1916, to be succeeded by W.M. Martin, who, like Scott, was an MP who had not previously sat in the provincial assembly. Martin was chosen by the Liberal caucus, although the transfer of leadership was informally ratified by a large convention early in 1917, the first since 1905.[37] Laurier's departure in 1919 was to inject into the same stream of events the great Liberal leadership convention which chose W.L. Mackenzie King as federal leader.

It all made for a busy time for an ambitious young Liberal who needed promising distractions. For to his anxieties about his brothers overseas, Gardiner had to face in the summer of 1916 the fatal illness of his wife Etta, who had never been robust; she died in Lemberg on 10 July. Gardiner was too strong a family man to remain long without a family: on 25 December 1917 he married Violet McEwen, a Saskatchewan girl who had gone to Lemberg to teach school and play the church organ. The marriage, happy and lasting a quarter of a century, produced four children, two boys and two girls.

By the time of his second marriage Gardiner had acquired the farm at Lemberg, a symbol of his final commitment to the prairies, and survived the provincial and federal elections of 1917. The first, preceded by the change in provincial leadership and the party rally of 1917, was held on 26 June, and was an important milestone in Gardiner's career. Running in his first general election, with fifty-eight constituencies beside his own on the block, he could not rely on the whole provincial machine and had to organize the seat on his own. With an able corps of the faithful, Gardiner systematically drew up the boundaries of his polling divisions; checked off every name on the resulting voters' lists; raised campaign funds, employing a printed form designed to 'eliminate the probability of political corruption'; made his first recommendations for appointments to the new provincial police, on this occasion to help minimize the use of 'intimidation, liquor or other means ... by the Opposition'; and spoke interminably. He attended meetings on sixteen of the twenty days preceding the election, and if one deducts the three Sundays included, when he was conspicuous at church, he was in fact on the hustings every day but one.

The effort paid off: Gardiner trounced his opponent by 1,829 votes to 1,244, taking every poll but two. The party did equally well, retaining 57 per cent of the popular vote and winning fifty-one seats; the Conservatives dropped from 42 to 36 per cent of the vote, and from eight seats to seven. For the first time an independent, who later decided he was a Liberal, was elected.[38]

Gardiner's victory meant much more than that a former Tory seat had become solidly Liberal. The election turned on two issues dear to his heart: the continuing debate over separate schools, into which bitter prejudices concerning religion and language inevitably entered, for the Conservatives in 1917 were making their first major attempt to arouse the English-speaking Protestants in Saskatchewan against everybody else; and the political role of the farmers, who were themselves divided over whether their organizations should sponsor candidates or not.[39] The Liberals' stand on the school issue was unequivocal: all schools, whether separate or not, were public schools and the legislature could pass what laws it chose about language used in the buildings, whether in or after school hours.[40] As for the farmers, the Liberals' position was even simpler: they infiltrated farm organizations openly, like the honest members they were (Gardiner himself became a life member of the Saskatchewan Grain Growers' Association in 1919)[41] and used their skills not only on behalf of the farmers but on behalf of the party. It was no coincidence that while Alberta fell to the United Farmers of Alberta in 1921, and a coalition under John Bracken, in a legislature where the largest group was the United Farmers and Progressives, took over Manitoba in 1922, Saskatchewan remained Liberal until nearly the end of the 1920s. When it changed it was to a government led by Conservatives, not farm organizations.

Gardiner was by his thirty-fifth birthday beginning to appear as one of the pillars on which Liberal success rested. He was still a back-bencher, but his role after 1917 was to change markedly. A major factor in it was a fortuitous circumstance over which he had no control: James Calder, in 1917 minister of railways and highways, president of the executive council, and master of the party organization, had chosen not to succeed Scott as leader and premier. The man who did succeed, W.M. Martin, was less familiar with the provincial organization than any MLA, including Gardiner. A second relevant event was the federal election of 1917, for which Calder deserted the party to join Sir Robert Borden's Unionist government as a conscriptionist. Calder at first took the organization with him, and as a result the Unionists swept Saskatchewan's sixteen federal seats. Calder also chose, in 1921, to enter the Senate as a Conservative. This double defection (as it appeared to Laurier loyalists) left numerous legacies, the chief of which was the vacuum left in the province's Liberal machine. Conscription and its aftermath temporarily shattered the organization and was a watershed in the party's history; to Gardiner it was merely a series of events in a coherent, consistent career, for all he had to do was the sensible thing and remain loyal to the party chief.

Loyalty to his leaders was one of Gardiner's most striking characteristics, and over an issue like conscription he had not the slightest doubts. He believed, and reiterated on his deathbed, that no true Liberal could accept the coercion implicit in conscription; twenty-five years after his first brush with conscription he identified the Honourable J.L. Ralston, the leading conscriptionist in King's cabinet during the Second World War, as a non-Liberal the day he began to toy with conscription.[42] Conscription was to Gardiner like coalition, socialism, co-operatives, church union, protection, drinking, or swearing: to each there was a right and a wrong side, and a Liberal took the right. That was not to say that a Liberal might not sometimes have to tolerate the wrong side for a while, because the alternatives were even worse. When Gardiner himself was party leader, for example, he was a prohibitionist whose supporters included good two-fisted drinkers, and he knew it. But what other adults did in their private lives was their business, not his; and that too, happily, was of the essence of Liberalism.

To oppose conscription in 1917, when the alternative was to support the Unionist coalition under a Tory leader, thus came naturally to Gardiner. He, W.R. Motherwell, and four other Liberal MLAs stood by Laurier and mustered what strength they could to help the ten federal candidates who opposed Union government. The Unionists received four acclamations, were opposed only by Labour in Moose Jaw, and in one seat, Mackenzie, both candidates were supported by the government, but only one by the opposition. The Laurier Liberals in Saskatchewan, who had won 52,924 votes to the Conservatives' 34,700 in 1911, taking nine seats out of ten, won 43,491 votes to the Unionists' 81,420 in 1917; the latter forces won the civilian vote by a little better than two to one, but the soldier vote by five to one.[43]

Both the party and Gardiner's future were saved in part by the very nature of the federal election in 1917. Ruinous as it was to the Liberal organization at the time, it was equally hard on the Conservatives in the long run. The Laurier Liberals in Saskatchewan in 1917 were an odd lot, for not one of the ten federal candidates who opposed Union Government in 1917 was ever elected to a seat in either the Saskatchewan or federal houses; they were readily expendable, in short, and as one-shot wonders had no claims on the party. (The single candidate endorsed by both government and opposition did later show up in the House of Commons as a Liberal.) The Liberals could start to rebuild from a clean start, but the Conservatives were not so fortunate; of the sixteen victorious Unionists of 1917, eight did not run in 1921 (two because they were in the Senate), two (of Liberal Unionist leanings in 1917) ran successfully as Progressives in 1921, and the remaining six were defeated by Progressives. In other words, not one survived the election of 1921 as a Conservative; and the redoubtable Calder, whose skills in organization might have served the Saskatchewan Tories well, was in opposition in the Senate, with none of the perquisites that go with being a supporter of the government. Both provincially and federally, the Conservative forces in Saskatchewan were as broken as the Liberals appeared to be.

But they did not have W.R. Motherwell, the old campaigner who knew agriculture so well; or W.M. Martin, the premier; or Charles Dunning, or George Langley, or James Gardiner, the rising man. Gardiner was more active in his second full legislature than in the first, taking particularly seriously his duties as a planner of the road grid for his constituency.[44] Privately he worked up his farm, for which Violet Gardiner kept detailed day books after their marriage. As a member, Gardiner automatically attended the Liberal national leadership convention of 1919, an event which inevitably won for the party not only more publicity, but a more lasting internal stimulus, than the quiet, almost secretive, method the Conservatives shortly chose when Arthur Meighen succeeded Borden. As a junior at the Liberal rally Gardiner could hardly play a leading role, but he did back King. Later he recalled that the Saskatchewan delegation had split; the younger element was for King because he looked like a winner and had tied the future of the party to the development of social services; the more senior, led by Premier Martin, was for W.S. Fielding, and Fielding had supported conscription in 1917.[45]

Gardiner wrote to King early in 1920 to introduce himself, and to apprise him of the growing political threat of the farmers' movement.

Its only object, he told King, was to overthrow the Liberal government, and he was disheartened by its success, which he attributed less to the merits of the Grain Growers than to inactivity among the Liberals. Gardiner himself, as a Grain Grower, attended the meetings at which farmers nominated farmer-candidates for the next provincial and federal elections, but he was not satisfied that enough Liberals were similarly active.

Gardiner told King about his concerns, and concluded by offering King his services 'to assist in drawing our forces together'; and King sent a copy of his letter to Andrew Haydon, the party official who ran the committee on organization set up as a result of decisions reached at the convention of 1919. He also promised to come west as soon as possible.[46]

King's reply to Gardiner was considerably less specific than the letter he had received, and indeed is so oblique that one cannot be sure he fully grasped its message. Plainly the MLA back-bencher, ten years King's junior, was hitching his wagon to the new federal leader's star; but equally plainly he was telling King of threatening developments in the relations of the provincial and federal wings of the party. Premier Martin, anxious to placate the farmers, had taken a number of steps towards making his government more acceptable to them, and these included increasing separation between provincial and federal Liberals. Motherwell's personal dissatisfaction with Martin's course had led him to resign from the provincial cabinet in 1919, for a variety of reasons which included doubts about how Liberal Martin really was. As early as 1911 an equivocal statement Mackenzie King had made about tariff reductions had led Walter Scott, then premier, to discourage a supporter who thought a seat might be found for King in Saskatchewan,[47] and Martin shared some of Scott's scepticism about King after the latter was elected leader of the party.

The culmination of Martin's efforts came in 1920 when the premier, speaking as the party leader, divorced himself from responsibility for the organization or policies of any federal party.[48] To Gardiner, who in 1921 became a Saskatchewan member of Andrew Haydon's national Liberal committee, the whole business was disturbing in the extreme. To Gardiner a Liberal was a Liberal, and it always seemed nonsensical to him that a Liberal should behave differently at the provincial level and the federal, or support one wing of the party but not the other. Yet paradoxically, provincial Liberals in the early twenties, in order to ward off the farmers' movements (which would enter the political arena as the Progressive party), were acting almost as if the federal Liberals under King were the enemy; while after the elections of 1921 the federal Liberals, in power with Progressive support, began to woo the same Progressives in ways that unsettled loyal Liberals in Saskatchewan.

Gardiner tried to stimulate both provincial and federal organizations, but was too late federally. He had already irritated some of his colleagues in the Grain Growers by working as a straight Liberal when Motherwell unsuccessfully ran in a federal by-election in 1919, and he appeared, especially after he had spoken out at a Grain Growers' convention, to be a better Liberal than a Grain Grower. The Liberals did not even nominate candidates in five seats for the federal election of 6 December 1921, and in the nine seats in which there were three-way contests among Conservatives, Liberals, and Progressives they carried only one, that of Motherwell. They had done much better provincially in June when, although their vote slipped from 57 to 52 per cent, they still took forty-five of sixty-three seats; the Conservatives won two, the Progressives six, and the other ten went to people loosely called Independents, who were variously backed in mixed degree by Conservatives and Progressives. The provincial election was a curious one; despite the competition among the three groups, there were only five three-way battles but thirty-five two-way fights, two-thirds of which featured Liberals versus Independents. Equally unusual was the fact that sixteen Liberals received acclamations.

One of them was Gardiner, whose rout of the enemy in North Qu'Appelle was now absolute. The acclamation was itself a measure of his growing power, for the sixteen seats which the opposition left unopposed in 1921 went generally to leading Liberals. It was Gardiner's last election as a back-bencher, and he was mildly disappointed that it was not even a fight.

3

The Ascent Continues

The federal and Saskatchewan elections of 1921 pointed up for Gardiner one of his favourite themes. If one meets a threat to the Liberal party as an unashamed Liberal, one can win, as the provincial party did; but if one waffles, or compromises, or fails to field a full company of candidates, one gets trounced, as did the provincial parties in the other two prairie provinces, and the federal party in Saskatchewan. That federal wing, as Gardiner observed, found that it was hard to organize in 1921 where no straight Liberal had run in 1917, and let five of the sixteen seats go by default.[1] Only W.R. Motherwell won for the Liberals, in Regina.[2] Progressives took the other fifteen constituencies.

The lone Liberal success had unforeseen consequences for Gardiner. Motherwell's well-known lack of political capacities rendered him an unlikely liaison between the Saskatchewan Liberals and Ottawa, and that was the vacuum Gardiner stepped into, just as he ultimately took over the organization after Calder. He was unexpectedly aided by the way Mackenzie King managed his parliamentary forces: 'Caucus here,' Motherwell told Gardiner after King's first victory as prime minister, 'means that the Cabinet goes there to listen, rather than impose their views on Caucus, and that the private Members do the talking. Under such circumstances, it leaves not a single soul from the Prairies to talk up in caucus a low tariff, or the implementing of the Liberal Platform.'[3] Gardiner was not a man to leave the prairies without a voice, and he had already offered King some gratuitous advice about acting to extend the franchise to foreign-born women before the Progressives proposed it and claimed the credit.[4]

Events at the provincial level also helped move Gardiner up. Where at Ottawa the Progressives, with sixty-four seats or sixty seats (depending on how one counted), kept King in office, in Regina they held only six seats in their own name, along with the sympathies of the ten Independents returned in 1921. Their influence was waning, but they were still strong enough to play a role in changing the premier of Saskatchewan. W.M. Martin had leaned over backwards not to offend the farmers' various political movements, and had done so again in the provincial election of 1921. In the federal election of the same year, however, he quixotically emerged as a stout federal Liberal and opponent of the Progressives. Whatever his motives, his volte-face made it impossible for him to continue as the leader of a party in whose province all but one federal seat was held by a Progressive. He was succeeded by Charles Dunning, an old Grain Growers' supporter, on 5 April 1922.[5]

Gardiner, though not then in the cabinet, was already sufficiently conspicuous to be talked of as a possible provincial leader, but his partisanship too had to be reckoned with; had the farmers been better organized they might even have kept him out of Dunning's ministry. 'Mr. Gardiner is spoken of,' J.B. Musselman, a leading official of the Saskatchewan Grain Growers wrote of Dunning's potential colleagues on 3 April, 'but Mr. Gardiner is decidedly unpopular with the Grain Growers generally.'[6] But Gardiner was himself a member of the Grain Growers, a farmer, a veteran MLA with a blameless record, and a particularly deft hand at organization. He had also been a consistent Liberal, loyal to the national leader and the party. According to Gardiner's own account, the backing and filling of the Saskatchewan government under Martin, particularly in its relations with Mackenzie King, had been so unsatisfactory that the caucus insisted on the strengthening of the provincial cabinet with old-fashioned party-liners, and as a result both he and Dr J.M. Uhrich became ministers.[7] Uhrich was to remain in Liberal cabinets until the CCF victory of 1944, and he ended his days as lieutenant-governor. Gardiner, following a different route, entered Dunning's cabinet as minister of highways, the communications department with which the party organization was associated.

It was an important assignment for the fledgling minister, for it placed him in a position to be of special service to the national leader, who in due course accepted the offer of a Saskatchewan constituency (Prince Albert), and occupied it from 1926 to 1945. Equally important, the appointment helped him manage his relationships with Motherwell, King's minister of agriculture after the election of 1921, and Dunning, the provincial premier from 1922. For it was close to impossible for an ambitious Saskatchewan politician to be both a Motherwell man and a

Dunning man, and it was important to Gardiner that the two were two thousand miles apart. Motherwell needed a Saskatchewan agent to handle both his and the federal party's interests, and Gardiner was ideally suited to the task. Dunning, on the other hand, was a suspect figure. He had not stood firmly with Laurier in 1917, nor had he taken an unequivocal Liberal line in the by-election in Assiniboia in 1919; had he been clearly partisan, indeed, he would almost certainly not have attained the premiership in 1922.

Gardiner and Dunning always corresponded with a cool politeness, but Gardiner could never free his mind of the suspicion that Dunning was not a Liberal at all, but an opportunist who saw a more secure future for himself in the Liberal party than in any other. In his last days Gardiner spoke freely of Dunning, recalling darkly that he had spoken against George Scott, Gardiner's political mentor, alleging that he would probably have considered running for the Conservative leadership had he failed to obtain the Liberal.[8] Dunning, for his part, treated Gardiner with unfailing courtesy, and when Gardiner's own premiership was temporarily ended in 1929, typically sent a solicitous offer of help for Gardiner's unemployed staff.[9]

Gardiner was not a man to let his personal feelings hamper his political courses, and in 1922 the Department of Highways was ideal for his purposes. His work kept him out of Regina a good deal. The department, by its nature, was not often involved in controversial policy; the province's basic road grid had been laid down (with the assistance of Gardiner and other MLAs) in 1918, and for the calculable future all any minister had to do was see that construction was carried forward. Since the provincial system of rural municipal organization had been built before both the emergence of the automobile as a popular form of transportation and the rapid growth of the major towns, a continuing adaptation of departmental administration to local conditions was necessary. Gardiner's main piece of legislation as minister of highways was a reorganization act which, significantly, centralized more power in the hands of the minister and the department.

When Gardiner took office, the law recognized only main highways and other roads, and permitted grants to municipalities for local maintenance. The department's annual report for 1923 noted that 'it was still evident ... that in many cases the grant was not being used for the purposes intended by the Legislature,' and some municipalities used it so ineffectively that they forfeited it.[10] Gardiner's legislation of 1923 abolished the grants and required the minister to classify roads into provincial highways which received federal assistance, main market roads, colonization roads, and local roads.[11] The province would accept full responsibility for main highways, and a shared responsibility for market roads; but local roads were not provincial roads, and the municipalities would have to look after them.[12]

The department under Gardiner's direction enjoyed four years of unbroken expansion. It built highways both by contract (523 separate arrangements in his last year, 1925–26) and directly by departmental crews (478 stretches in the same year). It operated over forty river ferries between spring run-off and autumn freeze-up. Its correspondence division sent out 43,601 communications in 1921–22, and 53,506 in 1925–26, and the main highway system was extended by between 285 and 484.1 miles annually. Highways expenditures were broken down by constituencies, so that every MLA could decide whether he was getting his fair share, and Gardiner, who lightened provincial spending in areas where federal subsidies were heaviest, had more difficulty convincing Liberals about the fairness of their shares than he ever did opponents, especially when the lowest bidder on work was an outsider. By Gardiner's last year in Highways, Saskatchewan had more miles of road per capita than almost anywhere else in the world.

Gardiner had little difficulty with the legislature. He was not hounded by searching questions, nor did he have trouble getting his programs approved; and the same was true of the other jobs assigned him. The most important of these was the Bureau of Labour and Industries (Labour did not become a portfolio in its own right until the advent of the CCF in 1944), as head of which he sat on the Lignite Utilization Board with representatives from Manitoba to assess the future development of the provinces' soft coal deposits, a venture which also gave him contact with the federal Department of the Interior.[13] His labour duties, by a coincidence, gave him one more interest to share with Mackenzie King. Premier Dunning, as conservative about labour as any leading member of the Grain Growers could be expected to be, thought that King's predecessors had gone too far in being agreeable about the standards sought by the International Labour Office attached to the League of Nations, and even complained about the costs of the Dominion-Provincial conference King convened in 1922 to talk about them, among other things.[14] Gardiner shared some of Dunning's caution, and observed in 1925, when the provincial cabinet was having its regular meetings with the Trades and Labour Congress (one of several interest groups which the cabinet met by custom, usually annually) that 'most of those whom [the eight-hour day] would affect do not want it.'[15]

His duties did not give Gardiner a spectacular career as a minister, and if he had done nothing else in public life he would now be forgotten. He was unquestionably a good minister, a conscientious performer showing the same capacities he had earlier revealed in playing and organizing baseball and hockey; but, as in those sports, he was at best a small-time semi-pro as a minister. But he was also a politician, and while the legislature probably contained half a dozen men who could have run the Department of Highways as well as Gardiner, he was the only one who was also in charge of the organization. The unique relationship that this gave him with the prime minister, the premier, and Motherwell, the federal minister of agriculture, requires further examination.

Motherwell's colleagues did not all regard him as a king among politicians. Nonetheless, it was Motherwell who on Gardiner's accession to office sent him a touching homily on how he should comport himself in his new dignity. Gardiner, in 1922, so unaccustomed to dictating to a secretary that he used to wait until after office hours to type important letters himself,[16] had been a minister barely two weeks when Motherwell addressed him in fatherly tones. He should move from the farm to Regina, Gardiner was told – a step he had already decided on. 'It is not wise to make many changes in the first six months. Glide into your work easily, keeping your eyes and ears open for prospective changes later on.'

Gardiner was also advised to convene meetings of his heads of branches: 'They like this and it won't do you any harm, so long as you keep from undue familiarity which, of course, must be avoided.' Social life was of course necessary: 'In deference to public sentiment, even though you do not feel very much like it ... a little more expense in clothes and trimmings generally, but that is the price we have to pay for serving the public.'[17]

Gardiner's deployment of the party organization in the early twenties had clear aims. The federal Liberals had to be rehabilitated in the west. Equally clearly the Progressives had to be destroyed. The Conservatives offered a far smaller threat; and anyway, Gardiner had 'no hesitation' in saying he would rather vote and work for Conservatives than Progressives.[18] That attitude stemmed in part from his dislike of third parties, but also from his disapproval of farmers isolating themselves in their

own political movements. Dunning had said, when assuming the premiership, that he hoped the Grain Growers (to which, after all, many
Liberals belonged) would remain neutral in provincial politics,[19] and it
was one point on which he and Gardiner could agree. The trick was,
considering the Progressives' near sweep of the province's federal seats
in 1921, to persuade them to do it.

Gardiner was well aware that the Progressives' electoral success at one
level would encourage them to move on to another, and the Liberals'
large majority at Regina gave him a breathing spell he was less sure he
had in the federal arena. So far as he could see in 1922, it was worth
working on the Grain Growers from within, and as a farmer he had
every right to do so; the Conservatives were at it too. That party, after
wandering almost headlessly for several years, began to show signs of
revival early in Gardiner's ministerial career, and in 1924 chose as leader
a man of undoubted ability, J.T.M. Anderson, a school inspector of long
standing whose interests in 'new Canadians,' among whom he had done
a great deal of work, had moved him to write a book on their education.
The Conservative resuscitation had Progressive connections: a year
before Anderson was chosen, when an employee of the highways department thoughtfully sent Gardiner a copy of a Progressive circular run
off in a business college attended by his daughter, Gardiner was able to
identify most of the recipients as former Conservatives, now presumably
Progressives; he distributed the list to Liberal workers.[20]

It was one thing for Liberals to use their influence as members of the
Grain Growers to try to keep the organization neutral in Saskatchewan
politics, and they did. Gardiner himself, thanks to smooth work at the
constituency level by R.H. Hall, was appointed a delegate to the Grain
Growers' convention of 1923 in Saskatoon,[21] and there he opposed the
Grain Growers' involvement in politics.[22] But it was something else to
get involved with the farmers' political organ, the Progressive party. Its
federal wing, as the force keeping King in office in Ottawa, was in a
position to expect some sort of co-operation from Liberals at the local
level in Saskatchewan, such as trading off federal seats against provincial.
The strong tradition of constituency autonomy in the Liberal party, and
the looseness of the Progressive organization, made it difficult for any
centralized authority to have a policy on such a matter; and in any event,
Gardiner's idea of co-operation was that the highest form of it consisted
of Progressives throwing their weight behind Liberals. That kind of
conviction led him to urge R.H. Hall to attend a Progressive constituency

convention and object to a federal party intruding on provincial affairs; and five Gardiner men did actually attend a Progressive constituency convention called to choose delegates to a provincial meeting of the party.[23] In due course Gardiner received a list of all those who attended the provincial convention.[24]

Gardiner could operate in that manner through his own constituency organization; but there were fifty-five other constituencies over which he had nothing like as much direct influence. In some areas, some kind of collaboration might be needed with the Progressives – a party which was based on a Grain Growers' Association 'out to get control of every Government in Canada.'[25] There is no evidence that the provincial and federal elections of 1921 changed Gardiner's mind about that, but they did alter the circumstances within which he had to work. When he acquired responsibilities for the Liberal party organization in 1922, in a spirit which his own records suggest was faint, he at least considered closer ties between the two parties. In November of 1922 Gardiner told a colleague that sundry plans to amalgamate Liberals and Progressives were proceeding slowly, but there was no indication in the correspondence of what he was doing to expedite them. A Liberal meeting preceding a by-election in October 1923, in Milestone, was opened up to become a joint meeting with the Progressives; but both parties fielded candidates, and the Liberal won.[26] Three years later, after the provincial election of 1925 but before the federal, Gardiner was reporting gloomily: 'We have been very much disappointed, so far as any of the constituencies where an attempt has been made to get Liberals and Progressives working together, is concerned.'[27]

It is not easy to believe that so skilled an organizer could have been unable to bring the two parties closer if his heart had been in it. The Progressives were faltering badly as early as 1923,[28] and in need of any help they could get. Mackenzie King, uttering in 1926 a view he had held since 1921, wrote to Gardiner: 'Knowing ... what the nature of the Conservative campaign against us is certain to be, I feel it most important that we should keep Liberals and Progressives firing at a common enemy and not be thrown into the position where as a Party we will be fired at from the one side by Conservatives and from the other by Progressives.'

Gardiner's response to that was a wire: 'Think it important no statement be made concerning Progressive Liberal co-operation until you come West.' He reported in the same message that he and Robert Forke (a federal Progressive leader) were speaking at a joint Liberal-

Progressive convention in Qu'Appelle.[29] And that was exactly Gardiner's view of co-operation – Forke was moving towards King, whose cabinet he soon joined.

The truth is that Gardiner by at least early 1925 was convinced that the crisis was passing. Barely a year earlier he had told his chief that it was hard in the west to counter the arguments of those opposed to King's government,[30] but his optimism in 1925 was solidly based. It came from a growing conviction that the strategy with which to beat the Progressives had been found: it was not to collaborate with them, but to disarm them. That had been Motherwell's idea from the start. The way to stop the Progressive steamroller, he had written on 5 January 1922, was to give 'such legislative reforms from Parliament Hill here that will leave our reasonable farmers very little, if anything, to agitate about.'[31] That was not hard to agree with; but how did one go about it in a Parliament where the governing party was supported by sixty-five members from Quebec, twenty-one from Ontario, but only three from the prairie provinces?

One small glimmer of hope lay in the representative system which, as a result of the census of 1921, gave eleven additional members to the prairies. That gave the west another grievance, for the holding of an election in 1921, before the census was completed, meant that the prairies were deprived until 1925 of the representation they were enti-tled to, and for the second time, since the sixteen additional seats going to the prairies after 1911 had not had effect until 1917. The catching-up process in the 1920s was to hurt the Progressives, for as a movement which scorned the low practices of the two old-line parties, they did not have the machinery to adapt readily to the reorganization required by a sudden jump in parliamentary representation.

That was not true of the Liberals. Saskatchewan's rise from sixteen to twenty-one federal seats was greeted cheerfully by the governing party, not least because its leaders drew the new map. They were in no position to inflict a shameless gerrymander on the electorate, for the parliamen-tary committee on redistribution set up in 1922 was for the first time broken down into provincial subcommittees,[32] and Motherwell, as the lone Saskatchewan Liberal, had no party colleagues on his; but the map was drawn in accordance with well-established traditions. Motherwell wrote to Gardiner on 30 September 1922, offering him census data to use in making a rough draft of a map, and passing on suggestions from Prince Albert and Last Mountain, the latter of which coincidentally 'would reduce Saltcoats [constituency] to about the right size and increase our chances of winning there.' (The constituency was altered and under a new name, Melville, carried by Motherwell and Gardiner consecutively until 1958.) Gardiner produced a map drawn by Dunning and himself, based on an equalization of populations, and asked to be consulted about any further changes. In due course Motherwell took its first version to the subcommittee and Gardiner then sought the help of the party's national organization to work on the redistributed seats.[33] In the federal election of 1925 the Liberals took fifteen of the province's twenty-one seats, the Progressives the other six; the Liberals raised their victories to sixteen in 1926.

The decline of the Progressives in the early twenties owed less to redistribution and its accompanying reorganization than to other factors. The farmers appeared increasingly divided over the form their political activities should take, and distracted as well over arguments for and against a co-operative wheat pool to offset the private elevator companies, and a federal wheat board to market the grain.[34] By the spring of 1925 the Saskatchewan Grain Growers' Association was, in Gardiner's opinion, less powerful than the relatively junior Farmers' Union, a delegate from which he wanted courted in Ottawa; at the same time, characteristically, he wanted a particular policy announcement made before a widely touted farmers' delegation reached the capital, because the group was not solidly Liberal and there was no sense in sharing credit with the outsiders through an announcement made after their visit.[35]

That kind of tactic, adapted to varying circumstances, was one Gardiner used repeatedly in undercutting the Progressives. As a farmer his interests were in most areas very like theirs. He may have scorned their espousal of proportional representation, fixed election dates, and other parliamentary tinkerings; but when it came to the tariff, freight rates, bank credit, the Hudson Bay Railway, and similar matters that made western interests different from eastern, he was with them all the way. That was one reason why he saw no need for the farmers to take political action outside the Liberal party; it was also a reason for trying to push King in directions in which his central Canadian supporters were loathe to move, simply because they did not grasp western needs.

Two separate examples dear to westerners, the Crow's Nest Pass railway rates and the protective tariff, can be used to exemplify Gardiner's lobbying of King and the federal cabinet. The Crow's Nest Pass Act of 1897, by which the Canadian Pacific Railway guaranteed low rates on eastbound grain and grain products and westbound commodities of stated types, was suspended by order-in-council in 1918, and again by statute in 1919; when the suspension expired in 1922 it was again extended in a manner which forced the government to make a major decision in 1924. As Gardiner saw it, the federal government then had to make a choice: either to seek a further extension of the suspension – that is, perpetuate high freight rates both ways for products of fundamental importance to the west – or let the suspension end, thus returning to the lower levels set in 1897 and vexing eastern interests, especially those of the CPR.

In Gardiner's eyes the government chose to end the suspension and the railway meticulously applied the terms of the statute of 1897; that meant, for example, that Regina and Calgary benefited from the reversion to the old rates but Saskatoon and Edmonton did not, because they had not been on a CPR line in 1897. Thus, at a time when the Progressives appeared to be on the run, they had been handed a major political issue and a new lease on life. Gardiner importuned King to do something promptly, and King responded reassuringly that he was 'in entire accord' with Gardiner's views, but unfortunately 'thus far here there has been considerable difficulty in securing unanimity of opinion on the part of members of the Government.'[36] Gardiner, by now an old hand at dealing with obtuse easterners, patiently waited. He was agreeably surprised when in the same month he heard from King that the Crow's Nest Pass rates, 'though belated to a degree which I personally greatly deplore,' were safely reinstated. Gardiner's reply, in the light of the rates' subsequent history, contained a striking passage, in which Gardiner observed that the rates 'are so far out of date ... that it would be idle to think that the Crowsnest Agreement could be re-established and retained in its present form for any considerable length of time.'[37] To Gardiner the west's victory over the Crow's Nest rates, whether or not they lasted forever, was a symbol of the Liberals' rejuvenation, and Motherwell told him his 'cracking good letter' on the Crow's Nest rates had 'helped us wonderfully.'[38]

Gardiner was not so successful in his attempts to bend the tariff towards the west, and that was all the more frustrating in that all he sought was implementation of the party's own platform adopted in 1919. The tariff plank, presented by his colleague George Langley, then minister of municipal affairs in the Saskatchewan cabinet, said 'That ... wheat, wheat flour and all products of wheat, the principal articles of food, farm implements and machinery, farm tractors, mining, flour and sawmill machinery and repair parts thereof, rough and dressed lumber, gasoline, illuminating, lubricating and fuel oils, etc., nets, net twines and fishermen equipments, and fertilizers, should be free from customs duties as well as the raw material entering into the same.'[39]

Western Liberals were generally satisfied with the plank, and were disconcerted when W.S. Fielding, King's minister of finance, from the start presented to Parliament budgets that appeared to ignore it. And they were outraged when he finally repudiated the platform. Questioned by Arthur Meighen in 1922 about his position on the Liberals' tariff plank, Fielding blandly told the Commons: 'I have never voted for the tariff items of the Liberal platform and never concealed the fact that I did not approve of the platform in that respect.'[40]

Gardiner was so exercised over these exchanges that he told Motherwell that if Fielding remained in Finance he would have to oppose the government in the west in the next election. He had opposed Fielding for the leadership in 1919 because he suspected his views, he said, and here he was in the key portfolio actually trying to undo the platform. Some of the other ministers were little better; for instance, Motherwell pointed out that Fielding seemed to think that the last resolution on the tariff offered by the Liberals when in opposition was the party's platform, despite the convention's decision.[41] One more difference between the west and the east, it seemed, was that western politicians set more store by the party's declared policy.

Gardiner continued to grumble about Fielding's budgets, and in 1923 finally took on Fielding himself, urging that at least some progress, however slight, be made towards the 1919 platform, particularly in regard to increasing the preference on British goods and cutting the tariff on items necessary to the west. Fielding replied in an agreeable enough tone, but pointed out that he could not alter the British preference until Canada had signed a trade treaty with France. Since British preference was specifically mentioned in the 1919 plank on the tariff, and treaties with France were not, Gardiner did not think Fielding had provided a particularly good reason for inaction. After enduring another disappointing federal budget in May, over which he brooded a good deal, he decided to abandon general pressure and go in for specifics. So he wrote to King in December of 1923. Fielding was then seriously ill, and Gardiner expressed conventional regrets, adding that he nursed 'a desire to have the Grand Old Man of the Liberal Party bring down a budget which would remove the impression created by his remarks of the last two sessions' on the tariff plank.

He went on to urge on King three minimum steps required to rehabilitate the party in the west: 'In the first place, a carefully selected list of farm implements should be placed on the free list. Small reductions on a long list of articles will not get results. Secondly, the Government should build the Hudson's Bay Railway to the Bay ... Thirdly, some step should be taken to restore public confidence in our banks.'[42]

King's reply to this was little more than an acknowledgment, ending with a pious expression of hope 'that in the main we may find it possible to work along the lines you have indicated.'[43] This stung Gardiner to bolder action, and with a third federal budget in the offing he sought to anticipate it by having the Saskatchewan legislature pass a resolution endorsing the party's 1919 tariff plank. Oddly enough, his own motion watered down the plank: instead of using the 1919 statement in toto, he rewrote its main section to free only 'a carefully selected list of the implements and machinery of production, and building materials.' Two of the six Progressives in the legislature moved an amendment which substituted most of the wording of the original plank, which the Liberals could hardly refuse. The final motion, as amended, was the platform plank of 1919 almost word for word, and it passed without division.[44] Gardiner took it personally to Ottawa; he timed his visit so that he got there before a delegation from the Canadian Council of Agriculture presented a brief to the cabinet on the same topics.

This time something gave. The intransigent Fielding, possibly softened by his illness, was unable to give his own budget speech for 1924, but his substitute, J.A. Robb, was able to announce some changes which gladdened the hearts of westerners. They were not all that Gardiner wanted, but a step in the right direction, and he accepted then cheerfully, as did Motherwell. They congratulated King 'on the spirit of Liberalism displayed in the Budget.'[45] King's reply was a curious one. Having resisted the party's 1919 resolution on the tariff for three years, he seemed to feel that a nod in its direction ended his responsibilities; he advised Gardiner 'that it only requires the leadership of our Western friends to keep Liberalism at the head of the procession from now on.'[46]

Gardiner had been striving to provide that very leadership since he took office, and had begun to feel he was fighting a losing battle. The Crow's Nest rates and the tariff were probably his main targets in the early twenties, but he fought on every front. A continuance of the wartime Wheat Board, about whose peacetime existence there were legalistic doubts;[47] the granting to the prairie provinces of jurisdiction over their natural resources, which Gardiner urged in a major legislative address, provided a substantial federal subsidy went with them because of what had already been alienated by federal authorities;[48] the completion of the Hudson Bay Railway, about which the assembly regularly passed resolutions; the granting of the full franchise to alien-born women, which Parliament agreed to in 1922;[49] prohibition; legislation on church union – all these by turns preoccupied him, and he sought all solutions through the party, that mighty agency whose own interests were identical with the community's.

He believed that he had been on the losing side nationally in 1917 and it was to happen to him provincially in 1929, again on a matter of principle. The party might be criticized for its tolerance of human frailties, but to Gardiner it was the highest practical expression of human organization for good. Gardiner's opponents, who sometimes saw his devotion to the party as a kind of weakness, would have been surprised to know that when he compared the party with the church it was usually to the latter's disadvantage.

He was a staunch churchman, a pioneer in church union, and a delegate to the great union convention of 1925, and his interest in schools in due course led him to serve as his own minister of education; but nothing in the church or the educational system consumed his energies like the Liberal party. In the early twenties, busily reorganizing the party's structure, he was so successful that in 1926 Dunning told J.W. Dafoe that the organization was no longer the party's agent, but its master.[50] The observation would have puzzled Gardiner, who regarded all sections of the party as parts of the same enterprise, and it always surprised him if, for example, when he worked for the Liberal cause against Progressives in Manitoba, he was regarded as an interfering outsider.

To be a full-time minister also in charge of organization meant that Gardiner needed help. On assuming formal command of the machinery in 1922 Gardiner had chosen as his chief lieutenant J.J. Stevenson, destined to end his days as a senator. Stevenson in 1922 was forty-nine years old, by trade a lumber merchant and farmer. Stevenson set about at once to erect a new structure, partly because the Liberals were then in poorer shape than at any time since 1905. The national convention of 1919, with its promise of new directions in the platform, and its choice of King over the suspect Fielding, had given the westerners new hope; but promises and hope were mere words without organization. Besides, Gardiner believed – and the conviction grew on him with experience – that continued reorganization was a creative activity in itself: every election of a constituency executive should see the old guard, needed for continuity and knowledge, complemented by new blood, needed to provide the future's old guard.

Dunning appears to have given Gardiner a free hand in the organization, for there is nothing in their correspondence in the way of instruction or even suggestion; people who wrote to Dunning on organizational matters were referred to Gardiner. There is nothing either to indicate that Dunning anticipated the full use that Gardiner would make of his powers, making himself indispensable not only to the provincial party but to the national leader. The first he accomplished by the thorough-going revamping of the party's structure. Stevenson, who lived in the northern settled part of the province and brought to the party a needed counterweight for its heavily southern leadership, wasted little time getting to work. Gardiner drafted a call which went out over Stevenson's signature to 'nearly all Liberal members.' It announced the need for a thorough reorganization, and the opening of a central office in Regina with Stevenson in charge. He planned to have a minister speak in every constituency during the summer of 1923, and appealed to the members to arrange 'representative meetings' at which at least one carload from each polling division would attend to hear the minister outline the government's policy and record.[51] That call was dated 15 May 1923, but Stevenson had been at work long before that. By November of 1922 he had taken over handling the local post office patronage for Motherwell; even that early, only Gardiner and Stevenson had access to the information needed for the job.[52]

The mature organization was a nice mixture of centralized direction and local autonomy. Gardiner was a strong believer in small local conventions (which he frequently called primaries) in which representation was based on two delegates (plus two alternates) from each poll, regardless of the number of Liberals in the poll, because the fixed number avoided all sorts of trouble that arose when one started to decide how many electors were Liberal and how many were not. The chosen delegates had a clearer status and function when there were only two of them.[53]

The centralization of the organization was clearly in the hands of Gardiner, for as minister of highways he had not only status and responsibility, but command of the staff of highways inspectors who were the core of the party's paid workers. Throughout his years in Highways, Gardiner had an ambivalent attitude towards the partisan civil servants; for while there can be no doubt that they were partisan, writing detailed reports on political affairs and helping with organizational work, Gardiner attempted to keep official Highways business separate from the political. On occasion he not only defended the ability of his assistants, but even tried to convince people that they were non-partisan. In the legislature on 17 December 1925 he took up charges of partisanship among his staff, pointing out that the accusers never produced any evidence, and that under his regime highway inspection costs had dropped from $132,000 to $87,000, and the staff from twenty-seven to thirteen.[54] The public accounts bore him out.

Yet his files as minister of highways abound with political letters, and his correspondents clearly assumed that the public service was, or should be, partisan. Several times he was asked to send a worker to help organize: the worker was almost always a man on Stevenson's staff, or a road inspector. Stevenson himself had a black list of federal civil servants of the wrong kind in Saskatchewan. Gardiner, quoting Stevenson, told Motherwell in 1924: 'So long as the Civil Service continues in personnel as it is at present it will be impossible for us to get anywhere, as these people are offsetting every move that is made to tend to place the Liberal party in better standing in different communities.'[55] It was presumably some of these who, as policemen zealously collecting federal excise revenues from those making home-brew, led the teetotal Gardiner in 1925 to plead with Jacques Bureau, the minister in charge of customs and excise, to call them off: 'These searches and prosecutions over the province are creating a great deal of trouble and turmoil in the midst of our election.'[56] Gardiner, on another tack, urged on Motherwell in 1925 the desirability of extending the parliamentary session in Ottawa as long as possible in order to keep the Progressive MPs in the east, so as to avoid unseemly Liberal-Progressive confrontations in the provincial campaign, in the interests of preserving Progressive support for King's government.[57]

It was all a complex network of relationships, some overt, some subtle. The organization had many critics, for as well as its partisan opponents it always had to cope with those who considered organization in politics, unlike that in churches, social clubs, athletics, government departments, and companies, to be a bad thing per se. Partisan the organization unquestionably was, but it had one solid virtue Liberals always prized: it worked. It worked behind the scenes, keeping Gardiner and Stevenson in close touch with politics everywhere in Saskatchewan. Openly it delivered fifty of the province's sixty-three provincial seats in 1925, and fifteen and sixteen of twenty-one MPs in that year and 1926. It delivered a seat for the prime minister when he needed it in 1926, actually returning him three times in seven months. It won recognition in a second Saskatchewan cabinet post in Ottawa, removing Dunning to join Motherwell. Inevitably it created its own opposition, and the Conservatives bestirred themselves under the most formidable provincial opponent Gardiner was ever to face, J.T.M. Anderson. And his work led Gardiner himself to another long upward step, into the provincial premiership.

4

Reaching the First Summit

Jimmy Gardiner, reminiscing in his last days, recalled an assessment of Mackenzie King by Laurier: while King might get elected to Parliament once, no constituency would return him twice. Down to 1926 his judgment of the electorate was almost completely vindicated, and by the twenties King was well on the way to becoming one of the most travelled members in parliamentary history,[1] with several federal seats behind him.

Neither Laurier nor King could have been aware of the electoral skills of James Gardiner and his Saskatchewan guerillas, since down to the 1920s they had hardly started to operate. Gardiner's handling of the organization for both the provincial and federal elections of 1925 had impressed King, and he had praised Gardiner with a fulsomeness which was to become misleading. 'I know how much is owing to your splendid organization of the campaign,' King said in a handwritten postscript to a letter congratulating Gardiner on the return of the Dunning government; and of the federal campaign, which affected him more immediately, he wired: 'Cannot express to you too sincerely my admiration and gratitude.' Shortly after he wrote: 'If the day has been saved to Liberalism in Canada it is becoming increasingly apparent that it is Saskatchewan that has saved it.'[2]

The saviour was probably more struck by another passage in the same letter: 'I am looking forward, as you know, to seeing you enter the larger sphere of politics and to your cooperation in the work of organization of adjoining Provinces ...' That was a sentence to encourage a less ambitious man than Gardiner, and he made immediate plans to visit Ottawa, leaving the west on Christmas night of 1925. By that time the federal election was over, Saskatchewan had returned to the Liberal fold, and

King was seatless. Gardiner went east with the notion that so indispensable a man as himself might be in a position to strike for a federal portfolio.

Satisfied with his conversations in the east, he returned home to arrange for the resignation from Prince Albert of Charles McDonald, a freshman Liberal MP whose defeated opponent was a J.G. Diefenbaker. McDonald deserves a special footnote in history; in the House he did not speak once, and when in 1935 he was appointed to the Senate he died before being sworn in, the only Canadian to be a member of both houses of the same parliament without uttering a word in either.

King was soon again unable to express too sincerely his gratitude to Gardiner and the Prince Albert Liberals, and Gardiner threw himself into a brisk campaign, hoping at first for an acclamation. Polling day was set for 15 February, which made nomination day 1 February; Gardiner had an organizer in the seat before 18 January, on which day he wired Senator Andrew Haydon, the Liberal money man, to 'put us in position rush campaign.' On 19 January Gardiner advised Haydon that the Progressives were not going to oppose King, and that an acclamation was likely unless eastern Conservatives put up a hopeless candidate, a step they decided not to take on 25 January. Then at the last minute they changed their minds and put up as an independent an attractive young war veteran, D.L. Burgess. 'The campaign,' Gardiner recalled years later,

was run from the City of Toronto. Toronto Telegrams were shipped in by the ton and a Mr. Heeney from Windsor, then a member of the House, and Mr. J.J. Maloney, afterwards organizer of the Ku-Klux-Klan against the government of Saskatchewan, were sent to the constituency with the newly launched Stevens' charges with regard to the Customs Department.

I took charge of the organization in the constituency at the time, and still recall ... [that] I stated to you that the first battle to save liberalism in Western Canada from a certain group in Canada would take place in the constituency of Prince Albert within the next two weeks, and that it would be followed up in Saskatchewan whether I was leader or someone else, and that I intended to finish the first battle before paying any attention to the leadership of the Province of Saskatchewan.[3]

That 'certain group' was to reappear, but in February of 1926 its influence was slight; King outpolled Burgess by over three to one. He thanked Gardiner, at a loss to express his appreciation for what was 'no doubt ... one of the most significant [victories] in the history of Liberalism in Canada.'[4]

Gardiner no doubt agreed. After his great electoral successes on two levels in Saskatchewan in 1925, and after finding a seat for the national leader, he had high hopes of going on to Ottawa. King's letter of 3 December 1925 had referred, after all, to 'the larger sphere of politics,' and Gardiner had not unnaturally taken his chief's words to refer to two separate endeavours: federal politics; and Alberta and Manitoba, where the Liberals were floundering, and where as a federal minister he could legitimately participate.

A few days earlier Gardiner had in fact told Andrew Haydon that he could handle organization on the prairies *only* if he were a federal minister, an important point since Dunning appeared to feel he could handle the job from Saskatchewan.[5] Gardiner's hopes were kept alive well into 1926. King wired Dunning on 25 January, asking him to show the telegram to Gardiner, referring to the 'absolute necessity of ensuring strengthening of Government ... by inclusion of yourself and Gardiner and one or two others as Ministers before the House reassembles.'[6] That seemed clear enough to Gardiner, but in less than two weeks the 'absolute necessity' had melted in a February thaw. Saskatchewan's revitalized federal Liberal wing clearly deserved more representation in the cabinet, particularly since Motherwell continued to be unsatisfactory as a liaison with the Saskatchewan party. But Gardiner was a Motherwell man, less anxious than even Motherwell to placate the Progressives. King, still needing Progressive support in the House of Commons, would hardly have strengthened his hand by taking into his ministry the combative Gardiner. At the same time Motherwell, although then sixty-five, was not yet ready for retirement; adding both Gardiner and Dunning to the federal cabinet would have given Saskatchewan three former local ministers at Ottawa, an all but indefensible number. King's logic is apparent: he had to take in one more Saskatchewan minister, and that meant Dunning first, not Gardiner. Dunning was the premier, and a moderate where the Progressives were concerned.[7]

The news again reached Gardiner through Dunning. 'I find that during my absence,' King told the latter on 6 February, 'Cabinet representation from Saskatchewan has been much discussed among Saskatchewan Members and that they are practically unanimous that at present time it would be unwise for both you and Gardiner to come even if as they understand Gardiner were to be substituted for Mr. Motherwell. I believe this latter arrangement can be worked out satisfactorily once this session is over.'[8]

Gardiner was not pleased over his place on the priority list, especially since the crucial telegram reached Dunning when Gardiner was absent from Regina working on King's behalf. He wrote stiffly to King on polling day in Prince Albert:

I have been shown the telegram which you sent to Mr. Dunning during the time I was in the north. Since obtaining the information which it contained, the only statement which I can make here is that I intend to remain in Saskatchewan. The political situation here does not permit of my being able to judge as to what will take place following such an announcement, but I presume that the immediate developments will make it impossible for me to give you any assurances whatsoever with regard to the future.[9]

Gardiner had made clear to Dunning more than once that he could not manage the party on the prairies except as a federal minister, which he saw as a positive reason for going east; but he also saw himself in danger of being trapped in the premiership of Saskatchewan. 'Everything which has taken place to date,' he told King, 'has been to the end that should I be compelled to take charge here, I might be compelled to remain indefinitely.'[10] He was at the same time expressing himself more strongly to his old companion, Motherwell, to whom on 3 February he had snorted about the Progressives: 'If our organization defeating all but four places them in a position to select cabinet I never want to be in it or assist in its return.' He returned to the same theme on King's polling day. 'If it is a disadvantage to a provincial Liberal organization to go out and assist in winning a Federal election, then the only thing remaining for a Liberal provincial organization to do is to keep out of Federal politics in future.'[11]

Gardiner might thrash around, but by mid-February of 1926 it was too late to change the prime minister's choice. King had a scouting report from Andrew Haydon dated 23 November 1925, in which Haydon had told him that Gardiner 'would like to go to Ottawa, but prefers Saskatchewan and yet if he were in the Federal field bossing the organization of the three provinces he would be happy ... [He] will want to be Premier if he stays.'[12] Gardiner's own concerns about being compelled to become premier did not worry King, who wrote to Gardiner on 22 February: 'The events over the weekend here have convinced me that any course other than the one step at a time would have been hazardous at Ottawa whatever its consequences in other ways might have been with you.'[13]

Gardiner did not find time to write again until 5 March, by which time he had been premier for a week, and was the recipient of a congratulatory telegram from King, a copy of a similar missive to Gardiner's mother, and a letter covering both.[14]

It was Dunning's view that it was the Liberal organization, not a good mother, that put Gardiner in power in 1926. Dunning's choice would have been Charles M. Hamilton, who had been minister of agriculture under both Martin and Dunning, and Gardiner's immediate predecessor as minister of highways in 1921–22, after which he became minister of municipal affairs until Gardiner became premier; under Gardiner he was to continue in Agriculture until the party's defeat in 1929. Also in the running were Samuel Latta, a veteran of three portfolios, the most important being Education from 1921 on, first elected in 1912; and Archibald McNab, who had held only two portfolios but dated his career as a member from 1908.

Gardiner, though the junior minister in this formidable quartet, was still the one with the party organization. Latta had been minister of highways from 1917 to 1921 and the organization, as already noted, usually went with that department. But Latta's years were those immediately following the conscription crisis of 1917, when James Calder, the creator of the machine, had defected to the Unionists and taken most of it with him. Had either Latta or Hamilton, who succeeded him, been charged with rebuilding the organization while in Highways, and been even moderately successful, the organization would almost certainly not have been assigned by Dunning to Gardiner in 1922; Gardiner was not really Dunning's kind of politician, whereas Latta and Hamilton were. In any event, by 1926 it was too late: Dunning did not know, J.W. Dafoe reported in due course, 'whether Gardiner had induced the organization' to choose him as leader, 'or whether the organization had decided to have its own man on the job'; but it had happened.[15]

That explanation overlooks two important facts: the organization Gardiner managed existed mainly outside the Liberal caucus in the legislature, and did not claim to dominate the caucus; and Gardiner was the unanimous choice of the caucus as leader. Dunning, on being asked by the lieutenant-governor for advice on his successor, had requested time to consult his legislative supporters. The consultation took the form of a caucus at which four names were put in nomination on the understanding that, in accordance with party practice, only one name would be selected for nomination to a subsequent convention. Gardiner was that one, and the convention unanimously endorsed him. He was sworn in as premier, president of the executive council, and minister of railways on 26 February 1926; he also continued as minister of highways until 10 November.

Gardiner considered the premiership second best, but characteristically he at once set about making the most of it. The unknown future held on the federal side the results of the customs house scandal and ensuing constitutional crisis of 1926, followed by another general election; none of these would hurt Gardiner. Closer to home there was his first cabinet, and the re-ordering of party matters that inevitably followed a change in leadership. The first of these was relatively simple:·· he kept on his erstwhile rivals for the leadership, and there were two other holdovers, J.A. Cross, who had been attorney general under Dunning and continued in the post, and J.M. Uhrich, the other partisan taken into the cabinet with Gardiner in 1922. Gardiner brought in two contemporaries destined, like himself, for distinction: T.C. Davis, who could have become premier after Gardiner but chose instead the bench and then diplomacy;[16] and W.J. Patterson, who did succeed Gardiner. In November 1927 Gardiner added another sturdy partisan, George Spence, who later became administrator of the Prairie Farm Rehabilitation Act.

The eight-man cabinet lost two members in its three and a half years in office; Cross resigned to sit as an ordinary MLA and McNab accepted a post in the public service. Cross and McNab, perhaps because of their short tenure, were the only men to hold single portfolios in the ministry. All the rest had two or more, frequently simultaneously, while Gardiner went into five; and individual portfolios were juggled among as many as three ministers. That was in sharp contrast to Dunning's cabinet, which had been all but static from 1922 to 1926, but not those of Dunning's predecessors. Gardiner's shifts differed from his predecessors' in one important respect: they were seen by some as part of a genteel purge. The *Western Producer* predicted editorially, and accurately, on 21 October 1926 that McNab and Cross, as Dunning men, were to be moved on.

Dunning himself saw Gardiner's moves as a purge. 'One gathers after talking with Dunning,' Grant Dexter reported from the press gallery to J.W. Dafoe in December, 'that the retirement of McNabb [*sic*] was a personal affront. He intimated also that Cross had been marked for the block and also Hamilton.'[17] Since Gardiner had always had his doubts about Dunning (and in the same letter Dexter reported that King was now having them too), he could not have surprised many seasoned political observers by dropping Dunning men. Dunning's cabinet was one designed to reconcile Liberal-Progressive differences and he himself, Dexter reported, was a 'sort of half Progressive – doesn't see anything wrong with a Progressive.' Gardiner's first cabinet was solidly Liberal, with Gardiner defining Liberalism.

Whatever its internal problems, the cabinet's first months were placid enough. Formed within eight months of a provincial election which gave the Liberals a huge majority, it was free of all the usual tensions created by the prospect of imminent changes in legislative personnel. At first it appeared that the cabinet's task was to be largely one of housekeeping, building on the rapid expansion of the province, whose peak was not yet seen to be passing. The province's irregular disturbances over the language of instruction to be used in the schools, which invariably raised religious issues, seemed to have died down after a minor flare-up during the provincial election of 1925.[18] The wheat economy had, it is true, faltered after the end of the First World War. Wheat prices had soared to an average of $2.51 per bushel for No. 1 Northern in 1920, and then dropped to $1.08 in 1923, and both the yield per acre and the number of acres sown to wheat had also fluctuated, though less violently. But by the time Gardiner became premier the worst seemed over, and he took office on a rising tide of optimism.

Saskatchewan in the 1920s was Canada's third most populous province. Migration out of the prairies was high, but so was the growth in new settlement. The 1931 census showed 921,785 persons for Saskatchewan, an increase of 830,506 since 1901, and of 164,278 since 1921. New land in the 1920s was still being broken, particularly across the northern and south-western edges of the arable areas. Roads, railway branch lines, electrification, and other amenities were all being extended as fast as human ingenuity and limited resources would allow. Railway mileage, for example, which was 2,225 in 1907, was 6,415 by 1921, and 7,259 by 1926. The number of registered motor vehicles, which had stood at 22 in 1906, was 61,184 in 1921, and 128,426 in 1929, and telephones were multiplying at similar rates. Enrolment in the public schools, which stood at 25,200 when the province was created in 1905, was 227,300 by 1929.[19]

This phenomenal growth was accompanied by an inevitable lag in conveniences that received a lower priority than the requirements of settlement, communications, and trade. Saskatchewan farms by the end of the decade were above the national average in their equipment of automobiles, radios, and telephones. But of all the farms in Canada in 1931, 11.7 per cent had running water in the kitchen, while in Saskatchewan the figure was 1.4 per cent; 4.9 per cent of the total had running water in the bathroom, but in Saskatchewan only 1.2 per cent; 10.1 per cent of the total had electric light or gas, but in Saskatchewan only 2.9 per cent.[20] It was an economy that put enormous burdens on farm women, and one of Gardiner's interests as leader was to stimulate the organization of both women and youth in the Liberal party.

That same economy, viewed with the west's recurring optimism, involved a colossal job of administration, but all with an assured end in view. A future of negative population growth, of crushing debt and depression, and of years of drought, was in nobody's mind. When Gardiner expressed to King his reluctance to take charge in Saskatchewan, he spoke the literal truth: no great challenge was involved in taking charge of an enterprise with an unlimited future.

When he had his first cabinet shuffle on 10 November 1926, Gardiner brought in no new men. The most significant change was his own assumption of the provincial treasury whose incumbent, W.J. Patterson, took over the Department of Highways from Gardiner, but not the accompanying party organization. Gardiner made only one budget speech as his own minister of finance, on 15 February 1927, and it was an almost routine accounting for, and defence of, the government's raising and spending of the taxpayer's money. The amounts today seem absurdly small: for 1925–26 a total revenue of $11,404,332, derived in the main from three sources: federal subsidies, provincial taxation, and provincial licences and fees. By far the largest expenditure was for education (36 per cent of the total), followed by highways, public health, and law enforcement, the last a lively task in a province where bootlegging provided the principal cash crop for numerous citizens.

Gardiner's lone budget speech was revealing of his own priorities. 'We have been prophesying better conditions,' he said, 'confident that they would come, because at all times we have been persuaded that the productiveness of our soil and the thrift of our people could be relied upon.' He then went on to explain in conventional terms why an expanding economy needed to borrow ('I am sure that no other province owes more to the influence of credit than does Saskatchewan'), and cited the advantages of borrowing for public institutions, and to back individual farmers through the Farm Loan Board, and farmers' co-operatives.

He reviewed the Liberals' record in public health, highway construction, public works, and the operation of the provincial police, saving until the last the general topic of education at all levels, on which he spent the most time. He foresaw for education a possible innovation: instead of unconditional provincial grants to local school boards, 'the Government should rearrange the school grants ... in such a way as to bring relief to weak districts; to give encouragement to school districts to improve the standard of their schools rather than merely to supplement the local taxes.' The primary purpose of that was not educational, but administrative: the Department of Education was to be given adequate funds to do its work, 'more particularly in supervision, without making the department appear to be the spend-thrift department of the Government.'[21]

If the provincial front was quiet in Gardiner's first year as premier, the federal was not. King's shaky majority in Ottawa would have had its hands full if its sole task had been placating the Progressives over such varied topics as the tariff, freight rates, and the Hudson Bay Railway, while not alienating central Canadian support; although ultimately the party was to benefit from the aftermath, it hardly needed the celebrated customs house scandal of 1926. The Saskatchewan wing under Gardiner was to benefit even sooner, chiefly because the scandal gave him another exhilarating campaign into which he could throw his forces.

The scandal itself has been well chronicled, and needs only summary here.[22] The federal election of 1925 had returned to the Commons 101 Liberals, 116 Conservatives, 24 Progressives, and 4 others, and King's government, though consistently carrying divisions with varying majorities, was nonetheless in constant danger. A parliamentary committee reported on 16 June 1926, that the Department of Customs and Excise 'has been slowly degenerating in efficiency and that the process was greatly accelerated in the last few years. Apparently the Hon. Jacques Bureau, then Minister of Customs, failed to appreciate and properly discharge the responsibilities of his office.' H.H. Stevens, a leading Conservative MP, then moved to instruct the committee to stiffen its criticisms of the government, and his motion was followed by a subamendment offered by J.S. Woodsworth, then a Labour representative, which would have had the contrary effect.

The Woodsworth motion, supported by the Liberals in the Commons, was defeated, but the prime minister did not take the vote as one of want of confidence. A second amendment, again more critical of the government, was ruled out of order by the Speaker but his ruling, supported by the government and challenged by the opposition, was overthrown. A motion to adjourn the proceedings to give King more time for bargaining with the Progressives, supported by the government, was also defeated. After considering various possibilities, including the position of the government even if it succeeded in defeating the Stevens motion, King decided to duck the issue and ask for a dissolution of Parliament. The governor general, to King's surprise, declined his advice and King resigned, abandoning office without any of the conventional consideration governing the take-over by his successor.

The governor general asked the Conservative leader, Arthur Meighen, to form a government and he, hampered by an ancient statute that required newly appointed ministers (as recipients of offices of emolument under the crown) to vacate their seats and seek re-election while holding office, had recourse to an acting ministry of ministers without portfolio, each of whom, without additional remuneration, administered two or more portfolios. King and his lieutenants gave the Meighen cabinet its head for a day or so, then attacked its constitutionality in a debate which produced from the Liberals a two-pronged motion making mutually exclusive points:

1. That the said hon. gentlemen have no right to sit in this House, and should have vacated their seats therein, if they legally hold office as administrators of the various departments assigned to them by orders in council.
2. That if they did not hold such offices legally they have no right to control the business of government in this House and to ask for supply for the departments of which they state they are acting ministers.

That curious resolution, which might have been rejected by a less fatigued House, or perhaps by a House with Meighen in it (for his seat was vacated when he accepted the prime ministership) passed, thus defeating the government. Meighen then obtained the dissolution King had asked for, and the 1926 election campaign was on.

Gardiner, viewing all these events from his western plateau, almost certainly did not know that in the excitement following the refusal of his advice for a dissolution King had three times urged on the governor general that he seek British advice 'as to what you should do in the event of the Prime Minister asking for dissolution.' Since King made much of imperial interference in the ensuing election campaign, without hinting that he himself had suggested it, it is at least possible that Gardiner might have queried some of King's tactics. It is more likely, however, that he would have loyally followed King in any event, on the comprehensive grounds that he was not a constitutional authority, and that Liberal advice on constitutional matters, even at its worst, was still preferable to Tory.[23]

It would have been out of character for Gardiner not to accept the Liberal mythology about 1926, and on all the other major issues of the campaign he supported King, naturally putting his own interpretation on them wherever co-operation with Progressives was concerned. Among the issues, those which loomed largest in Saskatchewan were the old standards. The federal constitutional crisis was not, by its very nature, likely to have wide appeal in Saskatchewan in 1926. Saskatchewan was not Quebec where, as Chubby Power had noted, 'the fact that a leader of a political party had not only talked back to a representative of the imperial government but had defied him and was actually campaigning against the power and strength of the imperial government was sufficient to carry all before it.'[24] Saskatchewan, shortly to erupt in a wild display of pro-British – or, more specifically, pro-WASP – sentiments, in 1926 gave sixteen of its twenty-one seats to the Liberals for other reasons, the chief of which was Gardiner. So far as the constitutional issue was concerned, his government's main contribution appears to have been the initial wording of the motion which brought down the Meighen government, which, according to T.C. Davis, was drafted in Regina in the office of the attorney general.[25]

The significance of the 1926 federal campaign to Gardiner as premier and party organizer was that it was his first test in the dual capacity. He had won his spurs in the provincial and federal elections of 1925 as a junior, and it was important to him that he improve on previous performances. The campaign he conducted in Saskatchewan was routine enough: the Liberals versus the field, with particular attention to those who looked most threatening, whether Progressive or Conservative. But a new dimension was created with Gardiner's responsibilities outside the province, and particularly in Manitoba, where his duties seem to have been so loosely spelled out that he may have merely assumed them, as one Liberal helping others. In Saskatchewan, by contrast, there was no doubt about his role; he fought the 1926 federal campaign there as he fought all his own campaigns. Voters' lists were checked out poll by poll, so that before election day Liberal workers had a clear idea – in some districts almost to a voter – how the citizens were likely to vote. Gardiner worked for King in Prince Albert and Motherwell in Melville, and both of them obtained substantially more votes than in

1925. He persuaded Dunning to spend several days in Saskatchewan, 'in order to defeat a feeling which was circulating to the effect that he was loosing [sic] ground here.'[26] Dunning won narrowly in his first contested federal seat, Regina, and elsewhere the Liberal triumph was all but total. The Liberal vote, 46,447 in 1921, had been 82,810 in 1925; it rose to 125,849 in 1926, while in the same period both Progressive and Conservative totals showed gratifying declines. Of the sixteen straight Liberal victories on polling day in 1926, eleven were two-way fights, and in nine of those the vanquished was a Conservative. The Progressives were runners-up in only five seats, three of them three-way fights: Liberals came second in three of the four Progressive victories, and failed in the fourth because they did not contest it. The remaining seat was won by a Liberal Progressive, formerly a straight Progressive. When all the votes were counted the Conservatives had again been shut out of Saskatchewan, the Progressives all but routed.

There remained the usual post-election routine, the chief task being the arranging of by-elections for King, Motherwell, and Dunning, all of them made necessary by the law which had facilitated Meighen's undoing. All three were returned by acclamation on 2 November. With the successful management of one provincial and two federal general elections within a scant sixteen months, and all the requisite ministerial by-elections looked after, Gardiner could contemplate with satisfaction a Liberal party safely in power in both Regina and Ottawa. But if he thought he could relax for a while, he was underestimating Manitoba.

Gardiner's initial assumption was that Liberalism in Manitoba was not to be considered different from Liberalism elsewhere. He was involved in Manitoba even before the campaign of 1926, for it was his understanding not merely that Liberalism was Liberalism, but that his responsibilities for the party on the prairies were related to his remaining behind when Dunning went to Ottawa. He saw himself as more than the premier of Saskatchewan; he was the leader of western Liberals. His experiences in Manitoba were shortly to show him that a party leader without a local power base cannot expect the kind of results he could seek confidently when at home in Saskatchewan.

Gardiner took his broader responsibilities seriously, and as early as mid-March of 1926, when he had been premier for barely two weeks, he wrote to several correspondents about a recent speech he had made to a United Farmers' meeting in Portage La Prairie, and told them that what was needed to get Progressives to fight under the Liberal banner was 'the proper kind of organization.'[27]

That view was going to meet with resistance from some influential Manitobans. J.W. Dafoe, both privately and in the *Manitoba Free Press*, had for months been promoting 'the idea that a coalition is necessary' between Liberals and Progressives in the House of Commons,[28] and at the end of the year told his chief, Sir Clifford Sifton that he (Dafoe) 'should not be in the least surprised if King and Gardiner, between them, should succeed in consolidating the Western Progressives into virtually an opposition party within the next five years, in which case much of the work which we have done here in the last year would be destroyed.'[29]

Gardiner's view of the same matters, which affected his entire reaction to Manitoba politics, is worth quoting at length. He was credibly informed early in 1926, before the fall of King's government, that Brownlee's United Farmers' government in Alberta and John Bracken's coalition government in Manitoba were to be returned with Liberal agreement, or at least little opposition. Gardiner, who equated both his neighbouring premiers with the Progressives, was quick to seize on any rumour which suggested Liberal support of either. One of the villains of his youthful novel of 1910, *The Politician*, was the Honourable Charles Clifford, who could not have been anybody but Sir Clifford Sifton. One of the main protagonists of the book, speaking of Charles Clifford as the acknowledged 'leader of the party in the West,' said that 'he has shown himself a man without strength of character and unworthy of the strong support he has been given.' Gardiner wrote to Motherwell in April of 1926, in much the same vein, and added:

It is my opinion that the Free Press has never lost us a single vote in the province of Saskatchewan since 1917 because of its unfriendly attitude to the Liberal party, and I am fairly certain that its friendliness to the Government will not return a single additional Liberal from the city of Winnipeg, and it is very doubtful if it will have very much influence in the rural sections of the province of Manitoba. Dafoe and his staff of editorial writers in Winnipeg are too much concerned about questions of which farmers and other ordinary people in Manitoba care little, to bother writing editorials which are going to influence public opinion very much ... We do not need the support of Sifton and his Free Press to win in Western Canada, whatever his influence may be in Eastern Canada, and it is my opinion that it will militate against our winning in the West rather than otherwise, particularly when his support is obtained by friendliness to the Progressives which places him – because of his relationships with a few men in Winnipeg who are supposed to have been friends of the farmers – in a position to hold the balance of power at Ottawa.[30]

These battle lines, with Gardiner seeking the defeat of Progressives in Manitoba as assiduously as in Saskatchewan and leading Manitoba Liberals regarding Progressive support as indispensable, lasted as long as Gardiner played a role in Manitoba. King shared Gardiner's opinion of non-Liberals, but at the federal level he needed Progressive support wherever he could get it and, as he later reminded Gardiner, 'in Manitoba the Progressives have been recruited from the Liberals and are for the most part Liberal at heart.'[31] That was true, and Gardiner knew it intellectually, although privately he considered Bracken 'traditionally a Tory.'[32] But in Saskatchewan he saw the Progressives, dominated by former and continuing Conservatives, as a major threat to the Liberals – a threat that would grow if Progressives, under whatever name, continued to hold Alberta and Manitoba provincially. Although he frequently acknowledged King's need for Progressive support, he never really accepted it; nor could he take seriously alleged distinctions between Liberals in different areas. He was thus for many years a thorn in the flesh of many Manitoba Liberals at federal and provincial levels, and did not cease to grumble about those self-seeking Winnipeg leaders who put expediency ahead of Liberal principles. In the federal election of 1926 Manitoba returned seven Liberal-Progressives, four Progressives, four Liberals, and two Labour. Gardiner did not think much of that performance.

If Gardiner's role in Manitoba had been confined to the federal election of 1926 he would not have found himself subsequently so unpopular in both federal and Manitoba circles. King himself had invited Gardiner's intervention in Manitoba in 1926, and specifically enjoined on him the desirability of paying attention to Arthur Meighen's constituency, Portage La Prairie, which King thought correctly could be won 'with a determined effort.'[33] When early in 1927 the Manitoba provincial Liberals decided to keep their party's identity separate from Premier Bracken's cabinet, and chose former judge H.A. Robson as their leader, Gardiner praised Robson to King, adding that he knew of nothing 'which will advance liberalism so much in the west as the return of a goodly number of supporters of Judge Robson' in the provincial election then under way in Manitoba.[34] Robson welcomed Gardiner's support warmly, and the latter supplied him with campaign materials. In response he received another invitation; 'We understand each other,' Robson wrote to Gardiner in April of 1927, 'and know the situation so please don't hesitate to do or suggest anything you see fit and *don't wait for us* ... A man in every seat and "no arrangements" is the only way to approach the matter.'[35]

The Manitoba Liberal leader thus started off as a man who suited Gardiner, who hardly needed to be asked to work for the cause. As the Manitoba provincial campaign of 1927 progressed (polling day was 28 June) the party's optimism – and Gardiner's – grew, and if nothing else came of the campaign, Gardiner expected at least 'a real Liberal organization ... when the election is completed.'[36] When John Bracken tried to make something of the presence of outsiders in his province during the campaign, Gardiner was able to point out that Bracken himself was billed as the chief speaker at a Progressive meeting in Saskatchewan.[37] Gardiner seems to have thought that constituted a stand-off, but the electors of Manitoba were unconvinced: on 26 June the candidates labelled 'Government' won twenty-nine seats, one more than in 1922; the Conservatives rose from six to fifteen; and the Liberals remained at seven.

Gardiner remained unconvinced that there was anything less than a solid Liberal party in Manitoba. He counselled Robson in a post-election letter: 'There is only one way to eliminate the Progressives, and that is by defeating them. Wherever there is a Progressive element of any considerable strength it has not been found possible to negotiate with them.'[38] Gardiner stayed high on Robson's list of advisers until the end of the year, when he was invited to Manitoba to address a meeting: 'No doubt you saw,' Robson told him, 'that they have advertised you as another Sir Wilfrid Laurier.'[39] Nonetheless, it was Gardiner who declared war on the party's federal wing. On 17 January 1928 he wrote to King to complain of the lack of consultation with western Liberals about a mooted federal appointment for T.C. Norris, a former premier of Manitoba, and laid the blame mainly on Dunning – an attribution which caused the prime minister 'pain as well as surprise.' Gardiner enlarged his complaint to take in more prairie Liberal MPs, asserting in part: 'Every time I go to Winnipeg I get more proof of the fact that Regina influence with Manitoba Liberals is being undermined from Ottawa ... We are definitely convinced here that in self defense we must see that both these governments (Alberta and Manitoba) are defeated.'[40]

King's reply, delayed over six weeks because the prime minister had hoped to see Gardiner to discuss the whole issue in person, began by reminding Gardiner that the Progressives were allies, not enemies, and especially in Manitoba, where the Liberals' federal needs were matched provincially. King expressed dismay at the hostility being aroused against the Progressives, and startled Gardiner with a new view of the Manitoba leader: 'Judge Robson, when he was in Ottawa, was quite outspoken in his view that in this particular a mistake had been made, and that any hope of the Tory Party being held in check in the Province of Manitoba lay in a working together of Liberals and Progressives alike in provincial and federal fields.'[41]

Manitoba, Gardiner must have thought ruefully, truly is different from Saskatchewan. King's letter gave him the first indication that he had lost Robson as an ally. Correspondence between the two came to an abrupt end, and Gardiner's file entitled 'Manitoba Politics' petered out.

Early in 1929 the premier of Manitoba, whom Robson had characterized in October of 1927 as stupid, proposed an alliance between his government forces and the Liberals, and a flurry of excitement developed over whether Gardiner might intervene. Perhaps to forestall Gardiner, J.W. Dafoe wrote a forthright letter to King denouncing as 'the most hopeless nonsense' any talk of the Manitoba Liberals taking advantage of the current position in the province to assume power. 'You will be told,' Dafoe advised the prime minister, '– perhaps from Saskatchewan; the Liberals from there have been mischievous and uniformed advisors of the Manitoba Liberals – that this is the time for the Manitoba Libs to go it alone and they are wrong as on previous occasions.'[42] But for Gardiner, at least temporarily, the Manitoba adventure was over.

That in Saskatchewan was not. Gardiner's Manitoba experience shed a revealing light on his chosen role as a leader of Liberals in the west: on the one hand it throws into relief his concurrent actions as premier of his own province, and on the other it anticipates his later intervention after 1935 in Alberta. In Alberta, as in Manitoba, he was to be invited in, and then accused of interfering in local matters not only without being adequately informed, but in a manner inimical to the interests of the local party. In the short run the record suggests Gardiner may have been wrong in the advice he gave in both neighbouring provinces. In the long run he was dead right: he feared that Liberal deals with other groups or failure to fight consistently as Liberals would endanger the party's life in Alberta and Manitoba, and in neither province, for the rest of his career, did a straight Liberal party flourish.

And even in Saskatchewan, in the late twenties, the Liberal party was headed for trouble.

5

The Uses of Power

The stability of Saskatchewan in Gardiner's first year as premier is attested to by a single statistic: he assumed power on 26 February 1926 but saw no cause to have the legislature summoned until 18 January 1927. Of his three predecessors, only Scott had let as much as six months elapse before meeting the assembly, and he had the excuse that until the first provincial election in mid-December of 1905 there was no assembly to meet. Both Martin and Dunning, appointed premier in 1916 and 1922 respectively, took office with a legislature already in existence; but both met the legislature in a little more than three months.

The delay in Gardiner's case was attributable partly to the Liberals' majority, which presented so solid a front to the small bag of Progressives, Conservatives, and Independents in opposition and disarray that there was little incentive for them to clamour for a session. There was no pressing need for legislation, for the province's economic revival in the mid-twenties occurred within a basic framework of extant laws. Forces already at work were to lead the Gardiner government to seek enactments about electrical energy, but they had not surfaced in his first year in office. When they did, the government's policy was as much a reaction to politics as it was an outgrowth from convictions about state ownership of public utilities.

To Gardiner, that was to be as it should be. His retention of the party organization while premier may have been unprecedented, but he saw it as essential to carrying out the principles of Liberalism. It was also essential to his own sense of responsibility for what he did in the party's interest. If, as he believed, the Liberal party was the most effective instrument for good (and he did not disagree with a correspondent who once suggested to him that the difference between practical Christianity and practical Liberalism was infinitesimal, with any edge there was belonging to the latter)[1] it would have been unwise for him in 1926 to delegate management of the party organization to even so reliable a minister as T.C. Davis, his minister of municipal affairs, let alone a former rival for the leadership or a Dunning man. When Dunning was in Regina and Motherwell in Ottawa, Gardiner enjoyed an almost ideal position for an ambitious man, running the Saskatchewan organization for one and acting as the federal-provincial liaison for the other, while coincidentally becoming extremely useful to the prime minister. With both Dunning and Motherwell in Ottawa, the former apparently in the ascendant as the latter aged, simple caution obliged Gardiner to keep full command of the Saskatchewan forces. Quite other reasons would soon appear.

Gardiner told friends that the duties of the premiership kept him from reading 'a great many of the books I would like to,' and said wistfully that, before becoming premier, 'my greatest pleasure and personal benefit was derived from meeting and associating with the leading clergymen and ministers.'[2] His office was not short of reading material (in 1926 it was receiving nineteen daily and one hundred and twenty-eight weekly newspapers, each labelled for its political complexion)[3] nor did he lack the company of more raffish citizens than the clergy were likely to be. A strict teetotaller and prohibitionist himself, Gardiner was too realistic to expect either the public in general or the Liberals in particular to follow him slavishly where alcohol was concerned. 'It is dangerous,' he had said of the temperance movement early in his career, 'to attack any established custom or practice as a government until public sentiment is behind the movement.' A little later he charged that the liquor interests had hired a man to delve into the records of Liberal MLAS with the purpose of discrediting them.[4] And just as he was a teetotalling leader who could not afford to drive away tippling supporters, he was also an upright man who knew that the party sheltered men willing to be more careless about the uses of political power. He knew because a group of them once offered him a deal, and when he turned them down, although they continued to claim to be Liberals, it earned him their lifelong enmity.

The feeling was mutual. To Gardiner it was unthinkable that one should use elective office to line one's own pockets, and his conviction led him on occasion to put too much trust in loyal Liberals. The group who had approached him early in his career with offers of generous financial support in return for guarantees of government business had clearly underestimated him. Gardiner had known the group (an enterprising lot whose leaders he frequently named) as opponents of the Wheat Pool and of his own leadership because he was a Pool supporter; he had good reason to believe that some of them had diverted to their own use funds meant for the Liberal party.[5] Some of them were what were later called influence peddlers and, as Gardiner often remarked, every premier has to cope with them. A political organization, he said, is always surrounded by possible evils, and those in charge must always be on guard against them.

The persistence of Gardiner's unwanted 'ring' matched his own. Its members not only opposed him on Pool legislation, but later fought for private distribution of electricity as against the public utility Gardiner wanted. Having failed to prevent his succession to the leadership, they sought to undo his government in subsequent by-elections and the general election of 1929. They sought to acquire control of a Regina daily newspaper (an episode in which Gardiner thwarted them deftly) to provide a strong anti-government voice in the capital, and a few years later, when Gardiner was temporarily managing Liberal affairs in Alberta, he found them up to the same tricks in Calgary. Their fell hand was to be seen, nearly twenty years after Gardiner had left Saskatchewan for the national scene, still trying to influence the provincial Liberal succession. It was then that Gardiner told a confidant that they had tried to frame him as they had J.E. Brownlee, the premier of Alberta driven from office by scandal in 1934. They were everywhere, in short, and their predations were still dominating Gardiner's thoughts when he lay dying.[6]

The significance of 'them' to Gardiner was obviously considerable. The gang was small, the same names recurring in his references to it. He lumped them all in with the better-known powers of darkness: the Toronto and Montreal financial interests; the Tories; the Winnipeg Grain Exchange; and all those prepared to form coalitions for whatever purpose. His experiences led to two inseparable courses. His government dealt directly with suppliers, eschewing third parties of any kind (the resulting practices, virtuous in intent, readily leading to favouritism in areas outside the leader's purview). And he continued to retain control of the party's organization. The institution that became celebrated as the 'Gardiner Machine' was to him the opposite: it was a device to ward off machines.

Gardiner's opponents considered his organization, which he once described as 'perfect,' at worst corrupt and 'vicious,'[7] at best a vehicle for maintaining power through winning elections and the judicious use of patronage. Gardiner himself did not think patronage had much to do with elections,[8] and the party lost the only provincial contest into which he led it as premier. Nonetheless, his government was careful to fend off attempts to regulate the letting of contracts, or to limit the use of the appointing power in manning the civil service. The Conservative leader, J.T.M. Anderson, in one typical resolution, moved 'That all contracts of $500 or over for the construction of public works and for the purchase of public supplies and Government printing should be awarded only after fair public tender therefor.' The Liberals' response, also representative, was to amend Anderson's motion to read, 'where practicable tenders should be called ...'[9]

The practices employed in letting contracts varied greatly, and owed much both to tradition and to Gardiner's belief that public monies should not be used for private gain. Thus tenders might be called for public works, including roads, and the minister responsible then had little difficulty proving that the lowest tender had been accepted. Rarely did anybody try to follow through an individual contract to discover if, in accordance with Canadian experience, the initial price of a contract was later augmented by provisions passed by the legislature in supplementary estimates; when somebody did, the answer was often yes. The government also followed tradition in purchasing printing from friendly newspapers; a question in the legislature, asked after Gardiner had gone into opposition, revealed that the *Regina Leader* had received $2,486,384 in printing contracts during the Liberal regimes from 1905, not a cent of which had been subject to tender.[10]

The only full-length study of the Saskatchewan Liberal party has set forth, with documentation, how both the civil service and the purchasing of services and supplies for its use were riddled with political considerations. Gardiner countenanced such practices because, with a good public policy like the Liberals', the end justified the means; but 'he strongly disapproved of using public office for private gain.'[11] An earlier writer, Escott Reid, has described the organization as having two parts, 'one formal and ineffective, the other informal and effective ... The formal organization constituted a democratic façade which hid from the common gaze the naked autocracy of effective party management.'[12]

There is no evidence that Gardiner ever read Reid's assessment of his machine, and if he had he would have been astonished. While the party's workers in each constituency unquestionably consisted of more than the elected members of the local executive, Gardiner always regarded the individual constituency organizations as of great importance to the party's total operation, and constantly advised and cajoled their members to keep active in the interests of Liberalism. His interest covered the most minute details, such as the usefulness or otherwise of having clergymen on local executives. In March of 1926, long before his own organization became notorious, he wrote: 'The only machine that is worth while is one which is to be found right out in the local polls, which is the most serviceable, the hardest to get at by those who are trying to work against us, and the kind which we have throughout the province of Saskatchewan.'[13] Gardiner wrote too many letters in that vein to permit a reader to conclude that he himself considered the party's formal organization a façade.

He had, too, a rationale for political elements in the public service: 'Our opponents are inclined to contend that the outside service spend too much time trying to keep the government right with the public and argue that this constitutes political interference. I may say quite candidly that no government can be stronger than its civil service and that every government expects that the civil service will spend its time in putting over the policies.' If the government was one led by a dedicated, doctrinaire Liberal, manning the public service with like-minded supporters was common sense, and the line separating the public interest from the party's inevitably became so indistinct that for some purposes it disappeared. This is not to defend Gardiner's widespread use of patronage, and his condoning of it in others, but merely to present how he saw it himself.

The legend of the Gardiner provincial machine has nonetheless been writ large, and not only by its critics. By coincidence it was the first party organization to be described systematically,[14] and the legend is such that it is not easy fifty years later to put Gardiner's organization in perspective. It is therefore important that major segments of it were examined in detail in inquiries initiated by his opponents after 1929. The reports included three special audits, one general and two specifically of the Department of Telephones and the Farm Loan Board; an investigation of the administration of old age pensions; an examination of the civil service; and a royal commission which studied charges laid by J.F. Bryant on the basis of statutory declarations made by a few members of the provincial police. Not all those reports have survived, and the findings of those that have vary from none of significance to clear evidence of maladministration of justice in particular cases. None of the findings could be considered striking in a time when civil services generally had not yet been overtaken by the merit system. None of them turned up anything that could be called corruption in high places, and Gardiner was able to tabulate most of the searchings into his immediate past on a sheet he entitled, 'Cost of Proving Liberals were Honest in Administration.'[15]

Of most general interest was the Public Service Inquiry Commission, created almost as soon as J.T.M. Anderson became premier in 1929. It was chaired by M.J. Coldwell, on the threshold of his distinguished career as member and federal leader of the Co-operative Commonwealth Federation, and included a Conservative cabinet minister, J.F. Bryant, and a second layman. The commission was given broad powers 'to inquire into and make recommendations in regard to the conduct of the Public Service' of Saskatchewan, and it had its origin in a long-standing pledge of Anderson's for civil service reform. Anderson had served for years as a professional educator in the Department of Education, all of them under Liberal administrations. That fact Gardiner frequently alluded to as living proof that the Liberal public service was not based solely, or even largely, on patronage, while Anderson was as often able to retort that he favoured the reform of the civil service because he had been in it and knew what he was talking about.

Gardiner had not unnaturally been sensitive to Anderson's repeated calls for reform of the civil service, and in the legislature's last session before the election of 1929 went out of his way to put on record the opinions of one Fred Telford, a peripatetic expert from the Bureau of Public Administration of Washington, D.C. Saskatchewan's control of the civil service, Telford found,

is being exercised with considerable discretion ... You pay less attention to the formal selection of employees than is common in some of the British Dominions and in the United States, but at the same time you are taking steps to assure the employment of the right kind of persons. I was particularly interested in the work being done to fix the hours of work, to regulate salary adjustments, to control the size of the civil establishment, and to provide for such working conditions that the employees can do their work effectively ... I was much interested, too, in the retirement system which has been installed ... I was astonished to note the low cost at which this administrative control over personnel problems and work is being done.[16]

That was a handy letter to quote at Anderson but Mr Telford, while hailed by Gardiner as 'perhaps the greatest authority on Civil Service organization on this Continent,' had spent only one day in Regina. The Coldwell commission spent five and a half months studying practices elsewhere, holding hearings throughout Saskatchewan, taking the first long cool look ever directed at the province's administration.

Its report was highly critical in places, but it did not damn the Liberals' regime as many confidently expected. Indeed, it was of such limited political use that, apart from being tabled in the legislature, it was never published. The report began by setting administration in a historical context, noting that the transition from patronage or spoils to merit systems was a characteristic of governments throughout the world, and suggesting that the time had come for Saskatchewan to catch up. It almost excused the Liberals historically, pointing out that in the rapid settlement of the province 'the Service was itself a growth, rather than a planned and organized development.'[17] It went on to describe the benefits to be derived from an impartial, decently paid, and properly organized public service on the British model. It then documented the state of affairs in Saskatchewan, when seen against what had been proven possible abroad. The Saskatchewan evidence was collected at first hand, mainly from meetings with public servants of all ranks (who appeared on their own initiative) and the commission also called in the president of the Saskatchewan Government Services Association.

The commission's findings are not all relevant here, but the most important among them, as far as Gardiner was concerned, were these:

1. The Civil Service commissioner, whose office was established in 1913, had statutory authority of such limited nature that he could recommend for appointment only clerks and stenographers, and even so 'there were cases in which he felt bound to make appointments ... on the recommendation of the Ministers ...' All other appointments 'were made on the Minister's say so.'
2. 'No system of open competitive examinations for entry to the service, or of examination for promotions has been set up.' There was similarly no system of classification within the service.
3. 'We are of the opinion that the salaries paid in certain branches of the service are unjustly low and not in the public interest.'
4. 'The heads of Commissions and Boards are men possessed of high professional qualifications and administrative experience.'
5. 'In the case of certain inspectors on the "outside staff" of a department, the

minister makes the appointment, it being considered advisable "to have a local man who knows the district and the public there." '

6. 'Unquestionably a system of individual selection has many merits, and may in very many cases not be abused. It is the system adopted in the commercial world, and was the logical system when the provincial public service was small. It will readily be admitted, however, that it is open to great abuse.'

7. The lack of any system for transfers and promotions was a source of dissatisfaction in the service.

8. 'If ... the public servant desires that security which we believe essential to the welfare of the service, and holds his position by appointment from an impartial Commission, then he must remain strictly impartial in his actions ... Enough emerged ... to suggest to our minds that, in certain parts of the service at least, undesirable practices had taken place.'[18]

It was hardly a report to make Gardiner feel disgraced. He could not deny what the Coldwell commission said about the lack of proper systems for entry, promotion, transfer, classification, and so on, nor would he have cared to; the system of personal selection he had inherited was, he believed to the end of his days, just better. Although he and his ministers were of course responsible, the report linked no minister to the 'undesirable practices' on the political side, nor did it suggest that the practices came about on orders from above. A similar commission in any other province, in short, would probably have produced a similar report, and there were several precedents outside Saskatchewan to suggest that reports elsewhere might have been far more damaging.

Paradoxically, during the same period that Coldwell and his colleagues were working to free the public service of partisan influences, Gardiner had been trying to free the Liberal party of the public service. He had been growing increasingly sceptical of the value of having party workers on the public payroll, as compared with those who were either paid by the party or worked voluntarily for love of the cause. In Saskatchewan's early history the financing of party affairs through salaried public workers was always tempting, not just because they were paid but because, in days of poor communication and transportation, civil servants were among those who could get around the province most easily. It was no coincidence that the organization went with Highways, and until he became premier, Gardiner not only accepted what he had inherited but improved on it, adding additional inspectors such as those who examined hotels, none of whom apparently even bothered to file departmental reports for the work they were ostensibly paid for.[19] Barely into his first premiership, however, he was beginning to have serious doubts about party workers who were paid by the state, and the clearest short expression he gave to his views is in a letter written some years later when he was trying to revitalize the Liberal party of Alberta. A correspondent there had sent him a detailed plan to use the prairie census of 1936 to count political inclinations among the electorate, and Gardiner discouraged him, concluding: 'The most effective political worker is one who has no employment with the Government, and works for the cause because he believes in it.'[20]

In Saskatchewan in the late twenties, Gardiner was shifting hardened veterans out of their oldest haunt, the inspectorial forces in Highways. In his first full year in the department, 1922–23, the public accounts showed that the inspectors numbered sixteen who received payments, mainly for expenses, out of the legislative votes for revenue, and twenty-two, many of them the same men, who were also paid out of the capital account, and in that vote most of them were salaried. The best known among them (Jim Cameron, whose specialty was picking candidates, Archie McCallum, a trouble-shooter and fixer, and Billy McKay, whose forte was making trouble for opponents)[21] were moved almost at once from the revenue to the capital vote. Their combined expense accounts for 1924–25 and 1925–26 consumed approximately 70 per cent of the total payments allotted. At the same time, the number of inspectors paid out of capital dropped, in one year, from twenty-two in 1922–23 to nine, and it stayed there, or below, until Gardiner left office in 1929. In 1926–27 the expenses of the three specialists dropped to a little over 40 per cent of the total, and by the next year the accounts showed only one of them still on full pay, Cameron and McCallum having drawn much smaller amounts, as did McKay also in 1928–29. Public accounts over half a century old are tricky to interpret, as they perhaps were when they were new; but the figures do support Gardiner's contention that he was shifting the organization, and his explanation is clear. Writing in 1936 to one of his successors in Highways, Gardiner said forcefully:

I think it would be an absolute mistake to place the organizers in Saskatchewan on Government pay, either in Saskatchewan or at Ottawa. If the Liberal Party cannot finance these two men they had better close up shop. We have had one demonstration of the fact that the people of Saskatchewan will not stand for a party organization paid with Government funds. Our main difficulty at that time was that we did not make the change early enough.[22]

The removal of the Liberal organization from the public service was not the only matter about which it was impossible to convince some people in the late twenties. In the other major inquiry into the Liberal government initiated by Anderson, a royal commission was appointed to investigate certain spectacular allegations made by J.F. Bryant. The charges were serious, involving among other things political interference in police activities and the administration of justice, and were initially made by policemen. Their investigation was to the Liberals peculiarly vindictive, for some of the charges went back beyond 1922, some concerned persons no longer active, and the Saskatchewan Provincial Police was actually abolished in 1928. Nonetheless, three judges were commissioned to conduct an inquiry with the aid of two counsel, one of them named John Diefenbaker.

The report of the royal commission, published in 1931, is a curious document, but one revealing of life in small southern towns in Saskatchewan in the twenties. The stars included policemen, doctors, and Chinese restaurant owners, not to mention Jim Cameron and Archie McCallum, the prominent organizers. The charges were conscientiously taken up seriatim by the commission, and either confirmed or set aside one by one.

Again, not all of the judges' findings are relevant to Gardiner's career. One case, indeed, turned out to be no more than peevish complaints from a zealous policeman who had a regrettable blot on his own record for which he had been dismissed from the RCMP; the judges' report on his most serious charges not only cleared but reflected some credit on T.C. Davis, the last Liberal attorney general in charge of the provincial police. But Davis's predecessor, J.A. Cross, was found to have acted improperly in the unexplained dismissal of a constable considered by his superiors to be a good man.[23]

Other typical findings on the Bryant charges implicated Jim Cameron in an attempt to get an inspector to work for the Liberals; found that several policemen were known to be active Liberal workers; and established that some police refrained, on instructions, from enforcing laws that might have hurt Liberal chances 'in a great many instances.' The single episode in the report involving Gardiner personally went back to his days as a private member, and concerned his alleged interference in the remittance of a fine in a narcotics prosecution of a druggist at Lemberg. The judges found that Gardiner 'had been instrumental in having the charge laid' in the first place, and that whatever he did 'was for the purpose of remedying what he believed to be an injustice.'[24] The Gardiner government did not fare as well: the report on the Bryant charges painted 'an unmistakable picture of politically tainted justice in the province during the Dunning and Gardiner administrations.'[25]

The report nonetheless offered so little ammunition to the Anderson government that not much was made of it. It was tabled in the legislature on 27 February 1931, and T.C. Davis shortly took the opportunity to point out that there was no evidence that either he or his predecessor had, as attorney general, directed an inquiry into the Ku Klux Klan of which the report had been critical. When Premier Anderson said that the government would not prevent any MLA from initiating a discussion of the findings, Gardiner took the stand that propriety required that somebody connected with the government should move for the report's adoption, and a debate could then be held.[26] The *Journals* of the legislature reveal no such motion.

Gardiner's challenge to the government would not have been issued if he had not felt he had a good case. In one prosecution arising from the charges, involving the administration of the Weyburn Hospital, the Anderson government had in effect lost.[27] From the start of his premiership Gardiner was not only aware of problems with the police but concerned about them, and tried to clean the force up in a series of steps which led to its abolition. One of the ministers he inherited from Dunning was J.A. Cross, who served both premiers as attorney general. According to evidence given to the commission on the Bryant charges, Cross's predecessors had given the provincial police commissioner 'a free hand in the administration of the Provincial Police Force, while holding him personally responsible for maintaining its efficiency.' Cross, who had been a colonel in the army, had apparently followed that policy under Dunning; but under Gardiner he had become an activist, reducing his commissioner to what the latter himself called 'a cog in the wheel.' The judges in the Bryant charges thought Cross, while 'actuated by excellent motives,' was mistaken, because it brought the police into an area 'too likely to encourage designing persons to try and affect it on political grounds, while it laid the Government too easily open to the imputation that the police were subject to political control.'[28]

But Cross's activism could not have been solely responsible for causing political interference with the police. Judging from the records of such toilers as McCallum and Cameron, it is likely that Liberal organizers would have been trying to use the police no matter who was premier or attorney general. Like the highway inspectors themselves, the police had good reason to travel all over at public expense but, unlike the inspectors, they were endowed with some genuine power. As Gardiner observed, an over-zealous or unpopular policeman could cause his political superiors only trouble, and it is inconceivable that either he or Cross's successor, T.C. Davis (a Liberal of whom even Mr Diefenbaker speaks well),[29] would have willingly countenanced what the commission on the Bryant charges revealed.

The provincial police were a problem on another front: the laws they enforced included some not held in great affection by large segments of the public, such as the Liquor Act. So astute a politician as Gardiner was unlikely to overlook that, and he early concluded that Saskatchewan was over-policed. Two years before becoming premier he had told Motherwell that he thought Saskatchewan had three or four times the number of constables it needed (145 as against 45 in Manitoba), adding that in the light of that opinion he objected strongly to reductions in RCMP detachments friendly to the Liberals while unfriendly ones were left at full strength.[30] A few months after becoming premier, Gardiner told the federal minister of justice that 'the policing of this province is rapidly developing into a condition which is likely to bring the whole matter into the field of political controversy.' He proposed several alternatives that could either have seen the province take over the duties of the Royal Canadian Mounted Police, which was briefly Gardiner's first preference, or the Mounties take over the duties of the provincial police, which was Lapointe's. Gardiner, convinced that two separate police forces, both under Liberal governments, could lose the party more seats than any other single factor, did not oppose Lapointe's choice, and late in 1927 asked his own attorney general to negotiate the transfer of all provincial policing to the RCMP. To this Cross objected strongly, and Gardiner offered him the education portfolio; Cross decided instead to retire, and T.C. Davis became attorney general, his first task to 'clean out the Saskatchewan Provincial Police';[31] the provincial police act was repealed at the next session of the legislature. About fifty of those rendered unemployed by the legislation joined the RCMP.

The record is clear that the force, originally created to enforce prohibition at a time when the First World War was cutting heavily into the manpower needed to staff the RCMP, was subjected to a variety of political influences at several levels. It was Gardiner's deathbed recollection that the first members of it were all selected by Liberals, and their unofficial duties included attending and reporting on opponents' meetings.[32] The royal commission proved conclusively that Liberal organizers, as well as policemen, misused the force. It should be emphasized that the Bryant charges affected a small number of people, and that the historical record of the whole force was not discredited, nor was it discreditable.[33] Nevertheless, the inescapable result of the investigation was that Gardiner's opponents had little trouble attributing the charges, properly inflated with the passage of time, to the 'Gardiner machine,' so that one of the Bryant counsel, John Diefenbaker, can remember the commission's report as one which 'documents the whole sordid story of the early Gardiner machine.'[34] The report had actually a narrow focus on certain specific allegations, and Gardiner's own papers make clear that from the first year of his premiership he was trying actively to do something about the police, and in 1927–28 did so.

That fact, like his efforts to shift party organizers off the public payroll, did not prevent the Liberal organization from becoming a major issue in the election of 1929. Those parts of the reports of the Coldwell commission and the inquiry into the Bryant charges which could have been turned to the Liberals' advantage were of course not available since both investigations, like the various other audits and surveys into the Liberals' management initiated by J.T.M. Anderson's government, were *ex post* phenomena. All the surviving reports together did not substantiate the picture, widely used during the campaign, of a predatory political party whose every move was dictated by an unscrupulous leader. Anderson, ironically enough, complained frequently in the twenties that he, as a party head and leader of the opposition, could not be held responsible for the excesses of some of his supporters, particularly those favourable to the Ku Klux Klan. That did not prevent equally zealous Liberals from spreading the unfounded rumour that he and others, including John Diefenbaker, were actually members of the Klan. Similarly, when Anderson supporters attacked Gardiner's administration, it availed the Liberals little to quote Anderson's own words about the largest element in it, the civil service. Speaking in the legislature on 27 January 1928, Anderson said: 'With regard to the Civil Service, I would like to pay tribute to the work of most of the members of the service which is, in the highest degree, efficient. The political activities of some of them I do not blame them for. It is not their fault, but the fault of the system that permits it.'[35]

The last part of Anderson's statement, not the first, became an election issue, and it was a typical campaign distortion. Gardiner's supporters, for their part, showed no backwardness in following suit, and since both sides between them tried to exploit issues that covered broadly every topic about which electors can be aroused, the 1929 campaign was the most ferocious in the west's history. As is often the way, it was fought first in miniature, in a by-election in 1928.

6

The Loss of Power

Gardiner would have approved of Winston Churchill's dictum, 'No part of the education of a politician is more indispensable than the fighting of elections'; and Churchill, interestingly enough, was one of the authorities Gardiner consulted after the Saskatchewan general election of 1929, because he happened to be in Regina.[1] But an election is only a means to an end, and every successful politician has his hands full as soon as it is over. Gardiner's short-lived premiership from 1926 to 1929 required a good deal of attention to party organization, but as premier he had to cope primarily with issues that bore little relation to that.

Almost all of them were inherited, and it was his peculiar fate that in the late twenties the most important of them came to a boil at the same time. He had himself, before he became premier, made a major speech on Saskatchewan's proposed acquisition of its natural resources, and as premier played the leading role in the negotiations that led the federal government to relinquish them.[2] Crown lands involved settlement policies; the federal government had kept them in the first place to facilitate filling them up. That inevitably involved a railway and an immigration policy, which freed the province from many responsibilities in the same areas as long as it did not have its natural resources. Natural resources were also the basis of electrical energy, and the province's growing needs for power had been reflected in Dunning's promise of a royal commission on electricity during the campaign of 1925, with whose report Gardiner had to deal.

Immigration and settlement included educational policies, and well before Gardiner's time that had raised controversial questions about the languages in which children were to be instructed,[3] and the admission or otherwise of religious observances and symbols into the schools.

Some settlers came from backgrounds where a more liberal view of the manufacture and sale of alcohol was taken than in Saskatchewan, and they joined native Canadians in using the lands they had acquired as the sites for illicit stills; many in the southern parts of the province found running beer and liquor into the United States a profitable occupation which, if carried out with judicious care, was not necessarily illegal in Saskatchewan. The domestic bootlegging, as Gardiner frankly conceded, was almost impossible to control from any centralized office such as the attorney general's office; given the scattered nature of the population, only local people could keep it down.

One citizen who fell out with the liquor laws was to cause Gardiner, a prohibitionist, a great deal of difficulty. A federal Royal Commission on Customs and Excise, at work in the late twenties, recommended that legal action be taken against one Harry Bronfman on two sets of charges; but federal and provincial legal officials held that there was insufficient evidence on which to prosecute. Gardiner was accused of protecting bootleggers such as Bronfman in return for campaign funds, and the opposition and its press made a considerable fuss over it. When the Conservatives attained power they prosecuted Bronfman, and he was acquitted.[4]

Gardiner, as a farmer, teacher, family man, and teetotaller, had personal interests in all these and related matters, but it was his professional interests as a politician that were to get him into trouble over them. Paradoxically, it was his own familiarity with the issues that led him to underestimate not only the first rumbles of the gathering storm, but also his chief opponent, J.T.M. Anderson. Each of the major issues had its own history and Gardiner knew it in detail, but he was unprepared to accept the possibility that an electorate to whom he explained everything rationally and repeatedly (so much so that he had to rest on occasion when his voice gave out) could be persuaded to vote against him in large numbers over non-issues. The hottest dispute of the twenties in Saskatchewan, over the use of religious symbols in the public schools, was often dismissed by Gardiner as not a true political matter at all; and when it turned out to be, Gardiner confessed that he was disconcerted by the ease with which the electorate could be stampeded.[5]

Religion, although the most conspicuous topic, was not alone in providing a focal point around which anti-Liberal and anti-Gardiner forces could rally. Gardiner's government aroused powerful private interests when it opted for public control of electricity through a provincial power commission, perhaps its most important single decision.[6] Education acquired new institutions under Gardiner: after the failure of a four-province conference, Saskatchewan began a school for the deaf and blind, and special schooling arrangements for immigrant adults were made. On the welfare front the Liberals introduced old age pensions in 1928 and extended legislation for relief and debt adjustment in the following session. Elsewhere the government opened up several dozen new school districts each year, tried to keep abreast of the burgeoning prairie municipalities with frequent legislative additions and amendments, and continued building roads, on the premise that the province at the time needed many long highways of a secondary nature rather than a few shorter stretches of gravel or pavement. For that, they were later to be accused of having neglected the roads, a charge which Gardiner numbered among those he considered ridiculous.

The forces that were to defeat the government in 1929 first came together in a by-election in 1928 in Arm River, a large rural seat with no major towns, occupying almost the exact geographical centre of the settled part of the province. It was good fighting ground for Liberals and Conservatives, but had gone solidly Liberal in every election since its creation in 1908. The 1928 contest was the twelfth by-election since 1925, and all but one of them had been won by the government. And Arm River was unique in two counts: Gardiner did not have to hold the by-election, but deliberately chose to do so in what in Quebec is called 'faire un maitre' – 'to bring about a test of whether his authority was still supreme.'[7] And the Ku Klux Klan, its sympathizers, and fellow-travellers were an important factor.

The Klan in Saskatchewan has now been well chronicled. Gardiner, with his usual thoroughness, collected all the information on the Klan he could get, and actually sent a detective to Ontario, Michigan, and Indiana to gather data, including transcripts of court cases where Klan leaders who later showed up in Saskatchewan had been tried. He had copies of letters between Klansmen, as well as dozens of typed pages listing the names of Klan members, and clippings from a variety of journals and newspapers. By 1928 he was, in short, as well informed about the Klan as any outsider could be – and that was undoubtedly better than the rank and file of the outfit itself.[8]

Precisely when Gardiner first sighted the Klan as a threat is not clear. His initial view was that the Klan was merely a front for his opponents, and not in itself a threat; the fact that J.J. Maloney, who had worked for the Tories in Prince Albert in 1926, supported it gave him the confirmation he needed for that. In February of 1928 he declined to attend a meeting sponsored by the Klan, but a few days later the Klan publicly supported him on a minor action concerning the province's Official Guardian.[9] Gardiner began his general files on the Klan in May of 1927, and in July he told a meeting in Regina, without naming the Klan, that he thought the purpose of the organizers was to collect as much money as possible and then disappear with it, as they had done elsewhere.[10] A month later he was taking the Klan a little more seriously, but he nonetheless wrote coolly to the prime minister:

At the same time that this new organization made its appearance there developed a great deal of activity in all localities where an Orange lodge is located. From each of these localities has come information to the effect that all the leading Orange Conservatives are spreading propaganda to the effect that the Catholic Church is controlling the activities of both the Federal and Provincial Governments. Large bills are now appearing at different places in the Province advertising Dr. Edwards as the speaker under the heading 'Shall Saskatchewan Be Free?' I do not know that this propaganda will do us any harm politically either from the Federal or Provincial point of view, as it seems to be rallying to its cause those who have been very rabid against us and at the same time the bitterness with which they attack the Roman Catholic Church will, in all probability, compel a great many to vote Liberal who would not do so otherwise.[11]

Gardiner at the time considered the Klan to be a simple, straightforward racket whose sole function, whatever its political implications, was to line the pockets of its organizers. Its rationale, as described by one of its own leaders, Pat Emmons, was to send into some unsuspecting community an organizer who would quietly find out what, at its baldest, the inhabitants could be aroused to hate. Since there was a general shortage of blacks in the west, no productive work could be based on them. But there was a generous supply of several kinds of ethnic and religious groups, many of them clustered in identifiable enclaves. In Moose Jaw the Klan, which always claimed to be 'a good clean Christian organization,' had considerable success in churning up the citizenry about prostitution in the city's downtown area. The wise organizer, that is, selected an issue that was locally exploitable, and it hardly mattered what it was so long as it worked. The Klan's anti-Catholic and anti-Jewish pitch, Emmons assured an interviewer for the *Canadian Jewish Review*, had nothing to do with the Klan's real functions; it was for 'the boobs.'[12]

What really mattered was collecting money (with which, in Saskatchewan, at least three Klan leaders subsequently absconded), and the Klan made its money by selling memberships in an association whose rituals and regalia owed much to freemasonry. The ritual depended on documents which were copyrighted, to protect innocent Klan organizers from losing their livelihood to unscrupulous plagiarists. The fee for joining was generally thirteen dollars, of which the organizer kept eight, sending the balance to head office. But there were also expensive regalia, gowns and hoods, and, for the chosen, advanced degrees which cost more than the initiation fee. The Klan's Saskatchewan creed was a grab-bag: 'The Klan believes in Protestantism, racial purity, Gentile economic freedom, just laws and liberty, separation of Church and state, pure patriotism, restrictive and selective immigration, freedom of speech and press, law and order, higher moral standards, freedom from mob violence, and one public school.'

'Methodists and Baptists have such a horror' of Roman Catholics, Gardiner observed in 1928, and that provided one pillar of the Klan's support. The Klan's methods, of exploiting feelings about almost any people set apart by language, religion, custom or dress, had an appeal: 'We had a good run and lots of fun' for the money, a member cheerfully testified, and the fun included such practices as calling teaching nuns 'she-cats,' terrorizing people belonging to selected groups, and spreading malicious rumours about people who opposed or criticized the Klan.[13]

A typical Klan pamphlet which Gardiner used frequently in letters and speeches contained these words:

One more point about the present attitude of the old stock Canadian. He has revived and increased his long-standing distrust of the Roman Catholic Church. It is for this that the British and Native Canadians with the Klan as their Leader are most often denounced as intolerant and prejudiced. This is not because we oppose the Catholics more than we do the alien but because our enemies recognize that patriotism and race loyalty cannot safely be denounced, while our own tradition of religious freedom gives them an opening here ... the real indictment against the Roman Catholic Church is that it is fundamentally and irredeemably in its leadership, in politics, in thought, and largely in membership, actually and actively alien, un-Canadian and if anti-Canadian it is this and nothing else that has revived hostility to Catholicism.[14]

Gardiner was to receive many letters of thanks from appreciative

French Canadians and other Catholics during the Klan's operations, for from the start he never faltered in opposing it. He was at first astonished and then appalled at what Klansmen did in the name of religion. As a liberal with a doctrinaire faith in the worth of each individual, he found it genuinely difficult to comprehend individuals who employed hatred against other individuals as if it were a normal and useful part of human relationships. As a politician he early noted the affinity between some ideas of the Klan, the Orange Lodge, and the Conservatives, whose leader was himself a well-known Orangeman and Mason.

By a coincidence, a friend of his youth had told him to watch out for one J.S. Lord, a Conservative member of the New Brunswick legislature who, travelling west as an organizer for a Bible students' league, was also organizing for the Klan. Gardiner kept an eye on him but, because Lord was a Conservative, 'refrained from meeting him at all.'[15] When he first attacked the Klan in the legislature in 1927–28, he knew what he was talking about. When challenged to repeat his speech outside the House, he did so not once but often.

Gardiner's reason for attacking the Klan was simply stated. He told his own constituents in May of 1928: 'I consider it the duty of the first minister of this province to, so far as possible, protect its citizens against the attacks of all scoundrels both from within or without Saskatchewan ... to protect our institutions of Government from the attacks of dangerous individuals, not after the harm has been done, but the moment they begin their evil work ... [and] to issue a warning to even those who are anxious to give away their money to a group of time serving grafters.'[16]

The Klan could hardly ignore words like those from the premier of Saskatchewan, particularly when he seemed to be uttering them somewhere every two or three days. Early in June of 1928 J.H. Hawkins, a Klan leader, issued a challenge to Gardiner to debate the Klan's role. Gardiner was reluctant to accord the Klan that much importance, but agreed to meet Hawkins at a Konclave at Balcarres. The Balcarres group had a mind of its own and refused to let Gardiner attend its meeting, and the venue was changed to Gardiner's own village of Lemberg, fifteen miles to the southeast. There, on 29 June, the citizens of Gardiner's constituency filled the skating rink to hear two unquestionably able orators entertain them.

Hawkins was an attractive man, and he looked enough like J.T.M. Anderson to be mistaken for him. On his own admission, he was versatile (a member of the bar in two states and an optometrist) and his chief point on that Lemberg night was to dissociate himself from the Klan in the United States. The Klan in Canada was entirely separate, and a purer better association at that, which had purged itself of every objectionable feature that stood in the way of equal rights for all men. Hawkins concluded by saying that the Saskatchewan Klan was not political, but if it were it would be Liberal because eight of its ten governors were Liberal.[17]

Gardiner, whose files showed that the only difference between the Klans in the United States and Canada was where the money went, would have none of that. In a well-documented speech he set forth precisely how he saw the Klan, which was as it was.

Gardiner, having damned the Klan with the aid of law cases and its own documents, felt he had pushed the Klan so that it could only run downhill from then on. But he continued to underestimate the Klan's political force. He was aided in that by what he considered statistical proof. One typical supporter of Klan ideas, though identifying himself as chaplain of another organization, once told him: 'We the officers and members of the National Association of Canada view with alarm the influences exerted by Quebec over the seperate [sic] school question in Alberta and Saskatchewan, and we understand that you Sir have given your consent to the Federal Government to sell 2 millions of acres for the purpose of continuing seperate [sic] schools.' Gardiner replied in effect that neither the chaplain's assumptions nor understanding rested on a grain of truth, and added gratuitously that he was surprised that so un-Christian a body should have a chaplain at all. It was, he wrote, 'the narrowest, most unBritish and most sectarian organization, barring one, which I know of anywhere in Canada.'[18]

The one, of course, was the Klan, and by January of 1929 Gardiner was beginning to suspect that the truth, as an answer to the Klan and those who accepted its support, was not going to be enough. In electoral matters those who accepted Klan support were the Liberals' opponents, especially the Conservatives and what he always considered their natural harness-mate, the Orange Lodge, of which he saw the Klan as a lunatic but equally natural fringe. The common target of the triumvirate in the late twenties was the province's school system and what went on therein. Gardiner's view was that they were almost wholly preoccupied with what did *not* go on therein.

The alleged crisis in the educational system surfaced most clearly in the by-election in Arm River in October 1928, although it had appeared elsewhere, and continued to be a major element in the general election of 6 June 1929. By then other issues had come into sharper focus, partly because the Klan, running short of fresh issues and organizers, was past its prime. In Arm River in 1928 the Klan, contrary to Gardiner's expectations after the great debate, was still active, but even so, schools, religion, and ethnicity were not the only issues. The immigration of 'aliens' was a related and aggravating topic to many, and it did Gardiner little good, either before or after the by-election, to reiterate census results which showed 'we have 820,000 people in the Province of Saskatchewan, and 624,000 of them were actually born within the British Empire; and of that 624,000 some 361,000 were actually born in the Province of Saskatchewan. Again, 161,000 of them were born in other Provinces of Canada.'[19]

His point was that the Tories' continual attempts to portray a Saskatchewan in danger of being overrun by foreign hordes rendered undesirable because they variously wore sheepskin coats, spoke broken English, and ate garlic, made no sense. But Anderson was a specialist in the teaching of new Canadians, and his credibility was greater than that of mere statistics. He could, moreover, conjure up statements of Charles Dunning in support of his general position: 'We want no cesspools in this country,' he quoted in the legislature from a speech Dunning had made in 1923. 'We want to see people of sound healthy bodies, active and intelligent and industrious brought into the country; people who can be absorbed into an enlightened citizenship. We want to see people who will not change our institutions but maintain and foster them.'[20] Gardiner would never have uttered the first sentence quoted, but he did stoutly maintain that Canadian immigration policy actually produced the kind of settler desired. He could support his stand only with uninteresting facts.

Immigration, in any event, was not seen by the Liberals to be even of particular provincial interest as long as the federal government retained control of the prairies' natural resources, and they in turn provided fruitful political arguments. The story of the dominion's original retention of Manitoba's resources in 1870 and Alberta's and Saskatchewan's in 1905, and their subsequent return in 1930, is another of those chronicles that is interesting in itself, but provided only a series of incidents in Gardiner's life. From the start Gardiner believed that jurisdiction over Saskatchewan's resources belonged in Regina and, almost without exception, so did every other provincial politician and party. Federal politicians from Sir Robert Borden on also favoured it, but Borden as prime minister was lukewarm to making deals of profit to provinces governed by non-Conservative parties, and the provinces concerned were all determined that any deal over resources would have to be profitable. All three prairie provinces had been receiving grants in lieu of the revenues they might have obtained from the resources, and all three believed that to obtain the resources and lose the grants would be to exchange a reliable asset for an unknown liability. In the meantime, the federal government was busily trading the resources off for its own purposes. In the legislature in 1925 Gardiner had sounded a recurring theme in Saskatchewan politics, one on which he never changed his mind:

To sum up, what is the price we have paid for our public domain to be a part of a Canada united from coast to coast? We have given:

To Railway companies	15,177,063 acres
To Hudson's Bay Company	3,183,600 acres
To Colonisation through homesteads	27,616,000 acres
To Colonisation through pre-emptions	7,663,300 acres
TOTAL	53,640,063 acres

If we were to receive settlement for these lands on the same basis as Prince Edward Island received consideration in 1873, we would be entitled to $2,482,000 per annum in perpetuity in addition to the return of those lands and resources not yet alienated.[21]

That quotation posed many of the questions that Canada's politicians took two decades to answer and none of them involved the lands' original owners, the Indians. Why were British Columbia and Prince Edward Island treated differently than Manitoba where their resources were concerned, when all three became part of Confederation in the 1870's? Why were Alberta and Saskatchewan treated like Manitoba? If the Maritimes received special compensation from Ottawa in the 1920s on the grounds of need, as recommended by two royal commissions, what did that imply for the prairie provinces, none of which was affluent either? Did the prairies' resources belong to the provinces as a matter of constitutional right? With the lands alienated at differing rates in all three prairie provinces, and sometimes for differing purposes, what formula would treat all three fairly if the lands were transferred? The whole problem in due course produced a considerable literature, both journalistic and academic.

Some of the best of it was written by Chester Martin, Gardiner's professor of history at Manitoba, and that helped give Gardiner a well-stocked armoury with which to approach Ottawa. He was aided, sometimes more than he wanted, by one Bram Thompson, a Regina lawyer who had made a hobby of British and Canadian land law, and thrust his views on Gardiner and the public at the slightest provocation.[22] Gardiner, according to Thompson, was the first premier of Saskatchewan to accept the view that the lands and resources belonged by right to the provinces, and press on Ottawa that all unalienated lands in Saskatchewan should be handed over to the province, with adequate and continuous compensation for those already alienated.[23] King was at first reluctant to admit that the provinces could have both lands and subsidies, but by 1927, when at the dominion-provincial conference of that year Gardiner presented his case forcefully, King was ready to yield, and all that remained was to work out the details. It was, Thompson noted, 'truly a victory for Premier Gardiner.'[24]

Paradoxically, it was to do Gardiner little good. The working out of the details, in King's deliberate fashion, required due consideration of how best to manipulate the return of the lands in the interests of Liberal-Progressive co-operation in Manitoba, and even after Manitoba's lands were returned to the province a royal commission had to be appointed to devise a formula for compensation, which was to treat Manitoba as if it had had its resources since 1870.[25] A lesser commission might have found the task impossible, but its chairman was a Saskatchewan man, W.F.A. Turgeon, and an acceptable formula was forthcoming. Gardiner meanwhile was bargaining hard for Saskatchewan, urging that Saskatchewan's compensation should extend its boundaries northward to the Arctic Ocean, thus giving the province a salt-water port. He did not get that, nor did he get the resources. At a conference in Ottawa in February 1929, when negotiations were well advanced, Gardiner formally declined for Saskatchewan the terms offered Alberta,[26] and no settlement had been reached when he went out of office in September.

Gardiner was able later to taunt J.T.M. Anderson for having accepted Saskatchewan's resources on terms that he had refused, but during the Arm River by-election of 1928 Gardiner was himself taunted for having not yet, despite his frequent public utterances, obtained them. He was also tested in Arm River on a related issue – his power policy – which, like the natural resources issue, had a long and complicated history into which Gardiner stepped relatively late. The issue, though critical, could be stated relatively briefly: should power in Saskatchewan be developed by private interests or public enterprise, or a combination of both which gave public guarantees to private undertakings; and if by public enterprise, should control rest locally with municipal governments, or be centralized under the province? Should the province be served by a few large generating stations, or dozens of small local plants? And should the power come from hydro development or steam plants using coal?[27]

Gardiner's papers, usually a sensitive reflection of his views, do not reveal any long-standing convictions about electrical energy. But they do suggest that he looked on its manufacture and distribution as falling into the same category as the marketing of grain or the building of a telephone system: if it appeared that the best way to solve the major problems was through a co-operative encouraged by the government, or by direct government take-over, the Liberal approach was to decide which way to move and then do it. He had inherited from Dunning a royal commission on power, and that put a constraint on his speeches until after the commission reported.

Gardiner's administration may have nudged the commission along the route it wished it to take[28] – an intervention by no means unknown in Canada, and perhaps perceived in 1928 to be particularly advisable by a premier who had not selected the commissioners. In any event, the commission's recommendations contained nothing to frighten a prairie Liberal. The core of its report, published in July 1928, urged public as against private ownership, with province-wide coverage under one central administration as the ultimate goal, starting with the acquisition of facilities of the three largest cities.[29] It meant a gradual approach to a large goal, and that was Gardiner's own approach. He embraced the commission's recommendations publicly, and was shortly pointing out that they embodied the traditional Liberal and co-operative principles that had already been so strikingly applied to telephones, hail insurance, creameries, and grain elevators. Nonetheless he kept his options open. In announcing the negotiations with Saskatoon for acquisition of the plant there, he said: 'We are prepared to go a long way to retain public ownership but are not insistent that such ownership of necessity should be vested in the Provincial Government. It would appear, however, that the nature of this utility is such that even under public ownership it can give the maximum of service under central control.'[30] In due course the legislature enacted the statutes required to set up the relevant department and the Saskatchewan Power Commission.

That commitment to public enterprise in electricity was to give the Liberals a powerful argument against the socialist Co-operative Commonwealth Federation (CCF), soon to be born, for it allowed the Liberals to point to one more area where what the socialists appeared to favour had already been done by Liberals. In the short run it had an impact in the Arm River by-election, for it set well-financed private interests against Gardiner, and he had no difficulty in identifying them once more with his old enemies of the 'ring.'

It is not easy sixty years later to picture a by-election in a placid rural constituency fought over such issues as religion in the schools, languages of instruction, natural resources, and power policy, but it happened. And Gardiner, having deliberately opened the seat, equally deliberately provoked all its opponents by opening his campaign on 3 October with a swinging speech which touched on virtually everything his opponents had complained about. Never a temperate speaker on the hustings, Gardiner courteously invited J.T.M. Anderson up to the platform, let him speak first and then, so far as the partisan audience was concerned, demolished everything Anderson had said.

'Tory Attacks Melt as Premier Clarifies Government Policies,' the *Regina Leader* said in a sub-headline over the report of Gardiner's speech on 4 October, and it was one of the least accurate reports the newspaper could have carried. Gardiner himself, at the end of the campaign, said it was the 'most bitterly fought by-election' he could remember, as well as 'one of the most important victories' the party has won, a triumph over the combined forces of the Tories, the Klan, the power interests and the 'ring.'[31]

The list of casualties was accurate, but the result was no triumph: in a phenomenal turnout of the electorate (91 per cent as against 52 per cent at the general election of 1925) the Liberals, in a seat that had been theirs for twenty-three years, won by 2,764 votes to 2,705.[32] Since in the other by-election where the Klan had participated, the much less safe seat of Maple Creek in 1927, the Liberals had routed a lone Progressive 1,476 to 502, Gardiner knew that he now had on his hands a fight of some magnitude.

Apart from the vigour of Anderson's campaign in Arm River, Gardiner was impressed by the amount of money the Conservatives seemed to be attracting. The usual source of Conservative money, according to his information, was in central Canada, but now they were raising money locally. Anderson himself had said that the party had $362 when he assumed the leadership, and as recently as 1926 he had partially relinquished his leadership to go into business, continuing only as House leader; he was persuaded to resume full leadership early in 1928. By December of that year Gardiner was telling the national office that the Conservatives were unusually active, in better hands than they had been since the war. He expressed a hope for plenty of three-way fights in the next general election, but unfortunately the Progressives and Independents were, unlike Anderson's forces, in decline. Still, he was optimistic; even after Arm River he was underestimating the forces lining up against him. He found it difficult to take seriously his opponents' nonsensical assertions about Catholic dominance of the Liberals and their government, about insidious ethnic and religious elements undermining the school system, and alien forces threatening Saskatchewan's clean British way of life.[33] He continued to counter these and similar charges in perhaps the only way he knew, with facts: the Liberals' only real weapon, he often said (and the party's official pamphlets supported it), was their record. He had used the weapon at Arm River, and the seat had been held. A few weeks before Arm River he had reassured the Saskatchewan conference of the United Church with more facts, failing to observe that it was surely unusual that a conference of Protestant clergy should need reassuring at all.[34]

In December 1928 Anderson moved an omnibus amendment to the address in reply to the speech from the throne. It included an ambiguous expression of regret over the government's failure 'to introduce remedial legislation for the purpose of clearing up troublesome and difficult situations in regard to the administration of our public schools.'

On 20 January 1929 Dr Anderson moved to amend the school act: '(1) No emblem of any religious denomination, order, sect, society or association, shall be displayed in or on any public school in the province, nor shall any person teach or be permitted to teach in any public school in the province while wearing the garb of any such religious denomination, order, sect, society or association.' The amendment would have deprived any offending district of provincial grants; and in the light of the premier's utterances, Anderson thought, 'this Bill should meet with the approval of every member of the House.'[35]

If Anderson thought that, Gardiner replied, he was remarkably ignorant of school policy in Saskatchewan and the other provinces. Gardiner went through the practices of all the provinces concerning religious symbols and garb in the public schools, and he was followed by his attorney general, T.C. Davis, who reviewed their legislation. The extent of their research, indeed, revealed how genuinely concerned they were about the headway the opposition was making.

Saskatchewan's public school system differed from that of most of the other provinces that had separate schools in that the publicly financed schools could be either public or separate, and the separate could be either Catholic or Protestant. In all cases the local school boards had clearly understood rights and duties. The system, in essence, guaranteed educational rights to defined minorities under defined circumstances, and was based on an important right written into the constitution of the province when it was created. Gardiner's argument was that Anderson's bill, though deceptively simple, involved a fundamental violation of the principles underlying an educational structure that worked.

The bill, Gardiner asserted, presumed the existence of some kind of problem of which, so far as his department knew, not a single example existed at the moment. He conceded that there had been a few related incidents in the immediate past, but all these together added up to a minuscule concern, and the notion of any planned or real take-over of Saskatchewan institutions by any sect was absurd. He used a sample of the statistics he was to offer increasingly as the general election approached. Of the seven cabinet ministers, six were Protestant. Of sixty-three MLAs, fifty-seven were Protestant. Not one of the top executives in the Department of Education was a Catholic – indeed, there were only two Catholics in the department's service. In the service generally Catholics held 12.8 per cent of the positions, as compared with 20 per cent of the population at large.

Of 8,114 teachers in Saskatchewan, 64 were sisters teaching in the public system, 23 more in Catholic schools founded under a statute of 1875, and 66 in the separate schools. Of 4,822 school districts, 43 employed nuns. And of those 4,822 districts, 31 were separate, 8 of those Protestant. Virtually all the relevant figures showed Saskatchewan to have lower proportions of teaching nuns and Catholic school districts than almost any other province. The problem at which Anderson's bill was aimed was negligible; and when an occasional flare-up did occur, over a crucifix in a classroom, or something equally earth-shaking, the sensible solution, Gardiner argued, was to leave it to the local school board. It was a good speech and, followed by Davis's legal analysis, an overwhelming one. If logical arguments and facts won elections, Gardiner should have been home free. But even he may have been beginning to feel unsure. His speech ended:

I would say that, as the Prime Minister of this Province, I would leave public life in disgrace and dishonour if I were to betray the principles which underly the lasting settlement which has been established in this Province resting on the good feeling that exists as between the peoples of different nationality and race ... though we were to face political defeat in accomplishing it, [I] believe we are doing the proper thing in defending the principles I am proclaiming tonight.[36]

If Gardiner had spoken so loftily only in public his speech might have been dismissed as rhetoric, but his private record on the combined Conservative–Orange Lodge–Klan pressure on the school system is unflawed. Not once did he offer a compromise that might have swung support from their side to his.

On all the other issues of 1929 he was naturally willing to try to win support wherever he could, but most of the other issues were either related to the school question or were difficult to exploit. He was trying to move the party's workers off the public payroll, but that was difficult to explain without admitting that they were on it in the first place. The transfer of natural resources, though proceeding well, was not completed. It was difficult to counter Anderson's pleas for a policy of encouraging immigration from Britain when, because of the natural resources, the province had not yet developed an immigration policy. The government's power policy was set, but by 1929 had only begun to be applied, and could thus be open to attack from almost any angle, even to a general charge that it did not exist. On the school issues Gardiner was convinced he was right, but fighting Anderson and his supporters on them was one of the most baffling experiences he had yet had.

How, in any sensible community, could a series of utterly non-existent 'problems' over language, crucifixes, and nuns' habits in the public schools have so many thousands of electors excited, so that even the usually taciturn Saskatchewan School Trustees Association was passing resolutions? Anderson had admitted that he had no objections to members of religious orders teaching in the public schools provided they did so in mufti.[37] If the objection was to religious influences in the schools, what could it matter what the teachers wore?

As for the threats from Quebec and French Canadians, the federal government had a policy for repatriating French Canadians, most of them moving back to Quebec from the New England states. In the hands of the Conservatives, and especially the Orange Lodge and the Klan, that migration became another gibbering mob threatening the foundations of civilization in the west and, added to the dangerous immigrants from Europe, created a veritable tidal wave certain to overcome the decent if left unchecked. The facts again were simple: French Canadians were scattered widely in Saskatchewan, comprising in all about 8 per cent of the population. Their language, as the *Saskatchewan Liberal Handbook for 1929* spelled out accurately, 'may be used in the First Grade during the first year, but no longer and nowhere else.' Otherwise, English was the sole language of instruction.[38]

If Gardiner was puzzled by the furore over schools and language, he had at least more concrete problems to deal with. Anderson, his confidence growing as supporters flocked to his banner, and fortified by the results in Arm River, was able to embarrass Gardiner on another front where he was vulnerable, and where vague unsupported charges were also productive. The Liberal organization was put under increasing scrutiny in 1928–29, and Anderson was able to manoeuvre Gardiner into a position where it appeared that he was refusing to let Jim Cameron, the veteran organizer, appear before the legislature's Committee on Public Accounts.

Howard McConnell, the Conservative victor in a by-election in Saskatoon in 1927, moved in the legislature for an examination by the committee of the expense accounts of the big three Liberal organizers, Cameron, McCallum, and McKay, when in the Department of Highways. On 15 January 1929, the committee asked for and received them, thoughtfully adding to the documents requested J.T.M. Anderson's accounts as an education inspector in 1920 and 1921. Cameron appeared in the committee room, and McConnell was given every opportunity to examine him. By a series of delaying tactics, McConnell was able to postpone his examination, and in the event, Cameron never gave his testimony on whatever it was McConnell sought. It was not difficult thereafter for Conservative speakers to claim that McConnell had been thwarted by an arrogant Liberal majority.[39] The Conservatives' suggestion of a cover-up attracted wide attention, particularly when a second of the organizers, Billy McKay, was sensationally brought into the news a few weeks later. Late in May George Bell, one of the leaders of the 'ring' Gardiner so cordially despised, released a confession of McKay's about his culpability in a newspaper football pool swindle. Under a black headline in inch-high type saying 'Liberal Attacks Gardinerism,' the subheads ran: 'Says Premier Deliberately Uses Crooks: Lifelong Liberal Says Only Hope for Party is Defeat of Present Machine-Ridden Government.'[40] Those headlines, over a detailed story and a photograph of McKay's confession, appeared in the *Regina Star* (Bell's own mouthpiece acquired after he had been eased out of the *Regina Leader*) on 30 May 1929, a week before the general election.

McKay's confession was dated 29 December 1921, and Gardiner not only knew all about it but had dealt with it fully and frequently before. Just before the Arm River by-election J.F. Bryant, the Tories' expert charge-maker, had used the story and provoked Gardiner into a lengthy prepared statement which dealt with McKay's past. His main points were that McKay, whatever his past, was a capable official who had done nothing to warrant dismissal. If Bell had a case, he should lay charges. Gardiner maintained his position whenever the McKay case came up.[41] But Anderson and his allies had proved themselves past masters in concocting charges that were either too vague to cope with or brought up too late to do anything about.

Gardiner knew by nomination day that all the non-Liberal political forces in Saskatchewan were arrayed against him. He knew that his stands on the school issues and the Klan's fulminations on aliens had won for the Liberals new support; but all the Catholics and European-born together were a minority of the electorate. He had tried to broaden the base of his support through the recent enfranchisement of women, urging their election to local executives, and proposing a redrawing of rural poll boundaries so that house-bound farmers' wives would find it easier to vote.[42]

His chief opponent, however, was a quick learner, and one of the lessons of Arm River was that in a two-way fight the Liberals were vulnerable. Since Anderson left no political papers except the few in others' files, evidence of collaboration among the anti-Liberal forces is hard to find. But it is highly suggestive that although in 1929 seats were contested by Liberals, Conservatives, Progressives, Independents, and a forerunner of the CCF which called itself Economic Group, there were multi-party contests in only thirteen constituencies. In the other forty-seven, Liberals faced only Conservatives in twenty-six, only Progressives in six, and only Independents in fifteen; five of the fifteen Independents ran as Conservatives next time around. Equally revealing are the candidatures. Although they were hoping desperately to form a government, the Conservatives in 1929 ran only thirty-eight candidates for the province's sixty-three seats, and thus alone could have afforded only six losses if they were to have a bare majority. There were sixteen Progressives and twenty-two Independent candidates. The Liberals ran a full slate, one candidate having a Liberal-Labour tag.

Unlike in the Arm River by-election, in a general election Liberal forces had to be deployed throughout the entire province, except for the two huge northern seats where the voting was deferred. Inevitably it weakened them, and Gardiner tried to take up some of the slack by having himself and his ministers booked into meetings all over. As early as April his voice was troubling him and he tried to limit himself, especially in poor weather, to one speech a day.[43] He was also interested in political broadcasting through linked radio stations, and passed on a suggestion to that effect to the organization.[44] As a good churchman he knew that the United Church held its annual conference in late spring, and chose the election date after determining the date of the conference; five hundred absent clerics from his own church might well cause a few seats to go the wrong way.[45]

To the last Gardiner remained doggedly optimistic, refusing to believe that the solid citizens of Saskatchewan would vote for candidates espousing lunatic issues, whether with the support of demagogues such as J.J. Maloney or more urbane persuaders like J.T.M. Anderson. Three days before the vote he wired Mackenzie King, 'Campaign progressing well.'[46]

On election night Gardiner sat quietly listening to the results. He knew early that he was in serious difficulty: the urban polls, reporting first, saw the Tories sweep all six seats in Regina, Saskatoon, and Moose Jaw, four of them gains over 1925. Yorkton and Swift Current also fell, one another Conservative gain, the other going to a former Progressive running as an Independent. In the north T.C. Davis held Prince Albert, but with a sharply reduced majority. It was soon clear that the Liberals had been all but wiped out in the cities, and the rural seats continued the collapse.

Gardiner himself had little trouble in North Qu'Appelle, his majority actually increasing marginally. He won in a three-way fight, over a Conservative and a Progressive, and in the other three-way fights the Liberals, as he had anticipated, did well, taking eight out of thirteen. But everywhere else his colleagues were struggling, and when the counting was over the score (excluding the two northern seats) was Liberals twenty-six, Conservatives twenty-four, Progressives five, Independents six. The Liberals were the largest group in the House, and final tallies were to show them to be by far the most popular single party: 46 per cent of the popular vote as against 36 per cent for the Conservatives, 7 per cent for the Progressives, and 9 per cent for the Independents. Even if they won both northern elections later in the summer the Liberals would still hold only twenty-eight of sixty-three seats.

What to do? On the night of 6 June Gardiner telephoned the news to Mackenzie King's office and went to bed.[47] He may have lost a battle; but he had kept the faith.

7

An Uneasy Succession

As Gardiner sat in his office on 7 June the calmness with which he had notified King's office of his defeat began to be overtaken by a number of nagging queries about exactly what had happened. He had lost; but to whom, and on what issues? The non-sectarian schools on which Anderson had harped so much were not mentioned in the Conservatives' platform; that document cited only 'thorough revision of the educational system of the province,' assigning it equal weight with 'furtherance of scientific research' and 'eradication of bovine tuberculosis.' Freeing the schools from sectarian influence was a specific clause in the Progressives' platform, as it was in the regular resolutions emanating from the Klonvokations of the Klan.[1]

If the school issue tied all three opposing groups together, as he believed it did, where did that leave the Independents, who were not so visibly organized? If the Liberals won the two deferred elections in the north they would then, with the support of any one of the other groups, have a majority in the assembly, whereas all three would have to coalesce against the Liberals to form a government. On the other hand, two Conservative victories in the north would mean that they, too, would need only the support of one other group to form a government. If there was some kind of anti-Liberal coalition, how was it that both Conservatives and Progressives had opposed Liberal candidates in eight constituencies? Could a coalition based on nothing more than a common opposition to the Liberals really survive in a post-election government that combined high-tariff Tories with low-tariff Progressives? Besides, were not the Progressives unequivocally on record against coalition, at least as far as elections were concerned? Their annual meeting of 1928, which drew up their platform, explicitly opposed 'any arrangements or negotiations with either the Liberal or Conservative political parties.'[2]

The resolution did not seem to have influenced most of the Progressives' local constituency organizations, and enough was said during the campaign about the distinctive policies of the non-Liberal groups to encourage Gardiner to believe for a few days after 6 June that all was not lost. He was further encouraged to delay a decision about his position by the slowness of the vote-counting in a few seats. It was not until the afternoon of 8 June that the final tally was in: Liberals twenty-six, Conservatives twenty-five, Progressives five and Independents five.[3]

During the counting of ballots Gardiner toyed with the idea of sounding out the possibilities of Progressive and Independent support but, according to J.W. Dafoe, he talked to the wrong people – party executives who could not speak for the elected members. Gardiner was reportedly ready to offer the small opposition groups two cabinet posts and the Speakership,[4] and confirmed the negotiations in a wire to King on 8 June and later in correspondence involving M.J. Coldwell. Earlier that day King had advised Gardiner to call the two deferred elections at the earliest possible date and then summon the legislature to force the various opposition groups to come out in the open. Gardiner replied: 'If no understanding reached with Progressives hope to follow your suggestion.'[5] But Gardiner heard on 11 June that all three opposition groups were going to meet to proclaim their union for certain purposes and wired King that under the circumstances all he could do was resign. On the same day the groups met to elect Anderson (who resigned as leader of the Conservatives) to head a single group acting in concert, and to call for Gardiner's immediate resignation. On 13 June King told Gardiner, 'have come to feel that to tender resignation would be proper course for you to pursue.'[6]

It was one thing to resign in cold blood, as it were, and another to resign after forcing the opposition to defeat him. The latter course might be unavoidable, but the former was foreign to Gardiner's character. To abandon the field without any kind of commitment from his opponents was poor strategy: they had been elected on separate and in some ways conflicting platforms, opposing each other in several seats, and that could be used as a reason for deciding that they should take office only after some unequivocal further action. For several days, Gardiner considered exhaustively all the options open to him, and concluded that he should have the legislature summoned. He reached the decision after a caucus of Liberal members and candidates held on 15 June, following which he announced that the cabinet held 'that responsible self-government calls for a decision by the Legislature itself, not by informal group caucuses held behind "closed doors." ' He promised that in the meantime his government would make no appointments beyond those demanded by the public interest.[7]

King agreed. Although he had earlier felt that the summons could await the deferred elections, he now urged Gardiner to make the necessary announcement before the Progressives and Independents announced their intentions. But those groups forestalled King's advice by their meeting on 11 June. So on 17 June King advised Gardiner not to wait for the deferred elections: 'Your position should be that you are endeavouring to save public in long run by holding on till exact decision can be definitely and constitutionally ascertained.'[8]

The two Liberal leaders were complicating their own course through a misconception of the constitution. King, when faced with a situation somewhat analogous to Gardiner's after the federal election of 1925, had solemnly announced that he had three alternatives: to ask the governor general for an immediate dissolution of Parliament; to ask His Excellency 'to call upon the leader of the largest political group to form a Government'; and to have Parliament summoned at the earliest practicable date.[9] There is no evidence that Gardiner considered trying again by asking for a second dissolution; and, unlike King in 1925, he was himself the leader of the 'largest political group' following the election. But he did believe that he had the right to pick his own successor, and here again he faced a dilemma; it was one thing to assert that right, but it was quite another if it involved advising the lieutenant-governor to offer the reins of government to J.T.M. Anderson, a notorious Tory and creator of non-existent issues in whom, to put it mildly, he had no confidence.

He therefore dawdled. The Progressives were divided about what kind of support they should give Anderson. On 20 June an informal meeting of the Progressive Association produced a statement which held that their five MLAs should vote for any motion of non-confidence in the Liberal administration, but not enter the cabinet or attend either a Liberal or Conservative caucus.[10] On the same day T.C. Davis sent Gardiner a thoughtful memorandum which, after postulating that the public would catch on to the fact that the Liberals had been defeated on fictitious issues based on utter falsehood, went on to argue that it was better for the Liberals to be defeated by a coalition than a single party, since the coalition would of necessity be weak and destroy itself.

For the same reason the Liberals should not consider entering a coalition. Davis wanted the opposition to be put in a position where it could not advise a dissolution before proposing a legislative program. An immediate dissolution, Davis thought, might wipe the Liberals out; therefore, assuming that in the near future they were going to be defeated, the Liberals should agree to an adjournment of the legislature after it had been called, to permit the new administration every facility to get itself organized and prepare legislation.[11]

This was advice more to Gardiner's way of thinking. The general election of 6 June was, at month-end, incomplete in two ways: there were the two empty northern seats, and recounts were pending in two other seats. The recounts followed a schedule laid down by statute and the courts, but the government could choose the northern dates. It set the election for Ile à La Crosse for 16 July, Cumberland for 12 August. The date for Cumberland meant that, by the time the official writ was returned, summer would be nearly over and the legislature could not be called before early September.

Gardiner was assisted in his tactics by his opponents. The Progressives were on record repeatedly in favour of the principle that a government should be able to resign not when it chose to on any issue, but only on a clear vote of want of confidence. The combined opposition groups in 1929 followed up their meeting of 11 June with a petition to the lieutenant-governor which recited the events of that day, the fact that Gardiner had not heeded their call to resign, and went on to remind His Honour that   .

the said Government is carrying on as if it had not been defeated ... to call a special session of the Legislature in order to have your petitioners repeat in the Legislature what they have already stated over their signatures is entirely unnecessary and at the same time is an expensive procedure, because if the said session of the Legislature is called it is the intention of your petitioners to express at the earliest possible moment, by a vote in the House, their lack of confidence in the Liberal Administration.

The petitioners concluded by praying that 'Your Honour dismiss your present advisers at the earliest possible moment and call upon Mr. J.T.M. Anderson to form a new Government.'[12]

That singular document could hardly have been better drafted by Gardiner himself. The legislature, and no other body, was the proper and constitutional place to settle the fate of a government, and Gardiner had every right to face it. It would be unconstitutional for a representative of the crown to dismiss a ministry on the advice of the opposition, and Gardiner could, and did, make such a request sound unconstitutional. The petition, with the deferred elections, gave Gardiner several weeks to prepare the hoops he hoped Anderson and his allies would in due course jump through. And in all this, it must be remembered, he convinced himself he was not simply clinging to power: he was trying to preserve a system he profoundly believed in, and which his opponents did not understand.

The summer gave him time to size up the new recruits on the other side, many of whom he did not know. Those he did know included some impressively able men. Anderson's record as a public servant was beyond dispute; M.A. MacPherson was a brilliant Regina lawyer; two other lawyers, the turbulent J.F. Bryant and Howard McConnell, were perhaps less distinguished professionally, but disconcertingly adept on the hustings. And in those four was obviously the core of a formidable cabinet. The five Independents included three known Conservatives who had run as Independents for such local reasons as the avoidance of a three-way fight that might have elected a Liberal; and two former Liberals, one on his way out of the Progressives, the other a man who compromised on an Independent nomination after declining a Conservative. The five Progressives, variously Liberal and Conservative in previous incarnations, were veteran members of their group. One Independent was reportedly a communist, and perhaps for that reason a man about whom it was difficult to learn much. Whatever their pasts, Gardiner thought that most of these members would support Anderson's government even though, in the case of the Progressives, they could have exacted more concessions from a Liberal administration.[13]

That opinion was unchanged after the Liberals had won the two northern seats and Gardiner had the legislature summoned on the first day possible, 4 September. With the smaller opposition groups in mind, an inordinate amount of attention was given to what the speech from the throne should contain, Liberal opinion ranging from those who favoured a long set of offerings to those who wanted a single alternative – throw us out or support us. Part of the preparation for the session was an independent audit of the province's books, done for the government by the firm of Price Waterhouse. Gardiner had no fear of an independent audit because he was sure any genuine investigation would give the Liberals a clean sheet. But during the campaign the Conservatives had raised such a clamour about corruption and the need for reform in the civil service that Gardiner wished to be ready for them when the legislature met. Price Waterhouse was chosen partly for its reputation, and partly because it had no offices in Saskatchewan.[14]

The report of the auditors was presented to W.J. Patterson, the provincial treasurer, on 29 August and its tone was pleasing to Gardiner: 'We are pleased to state that we found the books and records of the Treasurer's Department in good order, and that all the officials and employees with whom we came in contact afforded us all the facilities for the conduct of our work.' That was the conclusion of the report, and the preceding paragraphs were in a similar vein. The auditors were mildly critical of the practice of presenting the accounts on a cash rather than a revenue basis, suggested that closer attention should be paid to accounts receivable, and indicated that they had not had time to carry out as complete a survey as they would have liked. But they conducted an exhaustive examination of the major accounts, and found nothing significantly wrong.

An audit can, of course, find proper central books which mask practices which might make the blood run cold among the government's outposts. But Gardiner was not lacking confidence, and he incorporated references to the report in the first drafts of the speech from the throne for the September session. What is equally interesting is that the Conservatives tried to prevent the tabling of the report, and did not follow up the completion of the audit. Instead they pounced on specific branches of the government which the Price Waterhouse report listed as among those which the auditors had not had time to look into in detail.[15]

The speech from the throne which Gardiner worked on during the summer of 1929 was no ordinary document. Unlike most speeches, it could not present an ordinary program of legislation for the ensuing year. It hardly seemed appropriate to laud the government's record. By late July (Gardiner's own copy of the opposition's petition of 3 July has on it in his handwriting, 'Reached the Governor 28th day of July')[16] Gardiner knew he was drafting a speech for a government soon to depart. His particular intention was to draft a statement which would force the Progressives and Independents to declare publicly which of the two older parties they chose to support. He still nursed a dim hope that the Progressives and some of the Independents might, as low tariff men (and despite his earlier attempts to undo the Progressives) prefer the Liberals. It was a vain hope, but he and T.C. Davis spent many happy hours preparing for the session. The record does not show how often Davis's booming laugh, or Gardiner's more subdued chuckling, hung over the plans to back Anderson into one corner over the election of the Speaker, and the two smaller groups into another over the speech. But it is impossible to believe that the two leading Liberals did not enjoy their work that hot dry summer.

The early drafts of the speech contained a detailed account of the political events of 6 June and after, and pointed references to areas which had already been hit by drought. Gardiner was unsure of how much he should say about problems with which his administration would almost certainly not have to deal, and sent a draft of the speech to Mackenzie King. King was critical of it and, while stressing that all final decisions must be made by Gardiner, more or less rejected it. 'The impression conveyed by the Speech, as drafted,' he wrote Gardiner on 21 August, 'is that it is in the nature of an argument and is, in part, special pleading.' He told Gardiner that he need not justify having the legislature summoned, or explain political events since the election. King also queried the references to the drought and the need for the legislature to vote money for relief, because that would commit the Liberals in advance to supporting votes for money which would probably be spent by the Anderson government. The absence of any reference to relief, King suggested, might well mean that Anderson would have to start his regime by asking for money for it, and the Liberals would then be free to hammer home what an unpromising beginning Anderson had made.[17]

It was all shrewd advice and Gardiner accepted it. The result was a speech, one page long in typescript, which – whatever else could be said about it – was unusual. The real substance came in two sentences:

In the circumstances, my advisers are of the opinion that the earliest possible opportunity should be given to Independent and Progressive members to declare, in accordance with known constitutional practice, to which of the two historic parties they are prepared to give their support. Pending a decision in the matter of political support, my advisers are of the opinion that it is not desirable to submit a programme of legislation for the consideration of the members.[18]

What 'known constitutional practice' Gardiner had in mind is not clear: there was no constitutional reason why the Liberals themselves could not support the Conservatives, or vice versa. But the intent was clear: the speech posed a problem to the Independents and Progressives in Gardiner's own terms, and suggested to the Conservatives that once they attained power their first priority should be 'a programme of legislation' rather than a quick dissolution.

Before the speech could be read a Speaker had to be chosen, and here again was an opportunity to score a point. The Saskatchewan custom for electing a Speaker required two members of the cabinet to offer one name from the government side, which the legislature, led by large majorities down to 1929, routinely approved. In 1929 it was a virtual certainty that the opposition, temporarily a majority itself, would not tolerate that. What Gardiner sought was a tactic which could not produce a defeat of the government over the choice of Speaker, and therefore leave him free to get his speech from the throne on record. T.C. Davis's deputy wrote a learned memorandum on the legal procedures of electing a Speaker, and on 23 August Davis wrote another to Gardiner, advising him that 'there being no organized House until the Speaker is elected; therefore, there can be no defeat in the House without the Speaker in the chair.' Just in case the possibilities of that struck anybody on the opposition side, Davis pointed out further that Anderson's cohorts might 'consistently defeat any of our nominations and thus prevent the House from functioning at all.' He suggested the advisability of having ready the names of a Tory, a Progressive, and an Independent who could be nominated in turn if their first Liberal nomination was rejected.[19]

The only possible result of an opposition tactic like that would be an unwanted dissolution, Davis thought; neither he nor Gardiner considered the responsibilities of a government which stayed in office while unable to get a Speaker elected. Gardiner, his files now swollen with precedents and quotations, sought to minimize the chances of the undesirable dissolution. The device he hit upon was to have a Liberal MLA nominated as Speaker by two back-benchers 'to emphasize the fact that politics should in no way enter into the matter of constituting the House.' That ingenuous assertion, establishing a bizarre precedent in itself, left the Liberals free to claim that the vote on the Speakership 'cannot be accepted by the Government as in any way affecting the present position of the Government, either in relation to the House or in relation to the Crown.'[20] That was drafted partly to remind the Progressives and others opposed to partyism in general that they were on record in favour of the principle that a government could be defeated only on a specific vote of want of confidence. It was also notice to those who had already announced that they hoped to defeat the Liberals over the election of the Speaker.

In the event, the members assembled in Regina on 4 September for a session which was, from first to last, peculiar. But in every way except one it went exactly as Gardiner, with Davis's help, had planned it. Two Liberal innocents moved and seconded the nomination for the Speakership of John Parker, the member for Touchwood since 1917. Anderson and E.S. Whatley, a Progressive, moved and seconded that of J.F. Bryant, the member-elect for Lumsden. Parker's nomination was defeated thirty-five to twenty-eight, and Bryant's was accepted.

Bryant took the chair, the lieutenant-governor read the speech from the throne, and Gardiner and Davis moved that the speech 'be taken into consideration now.' Anderson moved in amendment that 'it is expedient that His Honour's Ministers should possess the confidence of a majority in this Assembly and such confidence is not reposed in the present Ministers of the Crown.'²¹ Anderson barely spoke to his amendment for, with the trust that came from having attended at least two caucuses of the opposition groups which agreed unanimously to knock the government over, he did not want to delay the vote. Davis and Gardiner made an equally perfunctory attempt to have Anderson's amendment ruled out of order on the ground that it negatived the main motion, but Bryant ruled against them and Gardiner agreed that it did not really matter anyway. The great debate was on.

Except that there was no debate. The only thing that Gardiner had not anticipated was that the opposition would put up no arguments but, apart from occasional interjections, sit solidly while he and his ablest lieutenants made long speeches on which they had been working for weeks. With the House full and the galleries packed, Gardiner, Davis, and Patterson sought in vain to open up a broad discussion of the campaign and the government's true record, ironically aided by the obvious inexperience of the Speaker, the only member they were able to provoke into saying much. Once the opposition's candidate had been installed in the Chair and the government made plain that that was not an expression of lack of confidence in anybody, T.C. Davis laid down the Liberals' first barrage, ostensibly speaking to Anderson's amendment. Davis then addressed himself to the Independents, asserting with what he described as irrefutable argument 'that a man, at one and the same time,' cannot 'be an Independent and also a [sic] Opposition candidate.' Davis reminded the Progressives of the irreconcilable differences between themselves and the Conservatives. Anderson shortly tried to have Davis called to order, and the Speaker, somewhat to the Liberals' surprise, defended the broad latitude he was allowing Davis: 'This is a British Parliament,' he ruled. 'We are not in Russia.'

Within a few minutes the relevance of Davis's remarks was again being discussed but Anderson 'waived his point' and Davis was permitted to proceed even though the Speaker himself felt he was out of order. His speech led remorselessly to the Liberals' main point: 'The question for the Progressives to decide, therefore, is whether or not they are going to assume the responsibility of putting a Tory Government in power.' Since the Progressives had already made up their minds to support Anderson, and said so, Davis was hardly standing on the firmest of ground. But the whole speech was part of a strategy: the Liberals could, Davis argued, recommend Anderson as premier after the Progressives had made public that they had abandoned their opposition to the party system and allied themselves with a party government. It was to the Liberals a good speech, which included much useful material for the future and visibly heightened the opposition groups' impatience to get at the business of government; and it was based throughout on the false premise that Gardiner had the right to recommend his successor to the lieutenant-governor.

No opposition member showing a disposition to speak, Davis was followed on 5 September by the provincial treasurer, W.J. Patterson, whose chief ambition that afternoon was to read parts of the Price Waterhouse audit of the province's books, which he had shrewdly tabled before anybody knew what he was about. When he began to speak to it, he was challenged by Howard McConnell because the session had been called for a single purpose, to decide who was to govern, and the report had not been tabled properly anyway. The Speaker confessed that he thought the audit had been tabled, and permitted Patterson to proceed. Patterson did so, offering a fair assessment of the audit. The opposition refrained from challenging him on substantive matters, Anderson contenting himself in the main by reminding Patterson that as recently as last session the legislature had voted down a proposal for an independent audit, and asking where the authority for this one had come from, and the cost. Patterson countered with two accurate statements: he was, after all, provincial treasurer in charge of such matters; and the cost was $16,104.

By the time Gardiner rose there was not much new that he could add to the government's case. He had a well-prepared speech which went further than Davis had in explaining and defending the party system as such, and he challenged the two smaller groups to stand up and say on the floor of the legislature on which side of the chamber they were prepared to sit after a change of government. When he sat down to await a reply, there was only silence. The truth was that everybody knew the answer, and the legislature was getting a trifle jaded. Gardiner, although he was in his usual combative form, was barely interrupted throughout his presentation. The last substantive words he spoke in the legislature during his first premiership were simple: 'We are prepared, Mr. Speaker, as a Government, to hand over our trust to any other Government. We shall do so prepared to fight our way back to the Treasury Benches on the Liberal principles we have stood for, we hope for another twenty-four years in the Province of Saskatchewan.'

Gardiner was followed by Whatley of the Progressives, who uttered eight sentences: the government had clearly lost the electorate's confidence, he said, and 'we have no alternative under the existing party system but to support a new government.' A.C. Stewart, for the Independents, said the same things as Whatley but took four times as long because he stopped en route to taunt the government for having wasted over twelve hours in needless debate, for not having prosecuted Harry Bronfman, and for having at last seen the 'thralldom' of Saskatchewan to the Gardiner machine ended.[22]

The rest was almost anti-climactic. No Conservative spoke further and Anderson's amendment passed by thirty-four votes to twenty-seven. For the first time in Saskatchewan's history, late on 5 September 1929, a government had lost the confidence of the legislature, and a non-Liberal government, its shape not yet certain, was due to take office. For routine purposes it was agreed that Gardiner should continue as House leader for the completion of a few non-controversial bills, the least controversial a money bill to indemnify the members for attending the session. The opposition poured out into the corridors cheering and laughing, and Gardiner went to the caucus room to meet with his members. The next morning he tendered his resignation, advising the lieutenant-governor to summon Anderson. Anderson was sworn in on 9 September.[23]

The change-over itself took several days, while the newspapers busied themselves with finding out what Gardiner's unemployed former ministers were going to do for a living, and which of Anderson's would have to move to Regina. The Liberal MLAs had touched Gardiner after his defeat by giving him a purse of gold and an illuminated address signed by all of them which concluded: 'Our faith in your leadership remains unshaken and you may be assured of our continued and unswerving loyalty in opposition as in power.'[24] The address helped commit him to carrying on as leader, which had its own implications for his personal life, since he would be unable to revert to the relatively uncomplicated world of an ordinary MLA. There was no suggestion at the time from any part of the Saskatchewan party that he should step down, although J.W. Dafoe doubted if he could continue: Gardiner, he told Harry Sifton, 'is a political anachronism – a survival of a stage of political development which we have definitely passed in the West.'[25] Dafoe's letter would have aroused Gardiner: his commitment to fight the Progressives everywhere, which Dafoe so deplored, was part of his commitment to Liberalism, and to be called an anachronism for adhering to enduring principles would have struck him as sheer nonsense.

Besides, what had his government done wrong? The independent audit by Price Waterhouse had revealed nothing seriously amiss. Gardiner's correspondence shows him as serenely confident that further investigations, even under his opponents' auspices, would reveal little more than the usual silt from a smooth stream that has been flowing for years. And on the whole he was right. The Coldwell commission on the public service was to find evidence of some political interference, but not enough to support allegations of wrongdoing; and in any event, Gardiner considered the Liberals' selective system was superior to so-called merit systems. The royal commission on the Bryant charges did find unmistakable evidence of improper activity in the provincial police in specific instances in limited areas, but Gardiner himself had taken the initiative in disbanding the force.

Those two inquiries bore more closely on parts of the party organization than did two other major audits which it is convenient to describe here, as they were of sections of the administration which Anderson took over in 1929. The Anderson ministers did not, although they talked about it, follow up the kind of general scrutiny began for the Liberals by Price Waterhouse. They did, however, follow up two branches which that company had listed as among those it had not had time to examine in detail, the Farm Loan Board and the Department of Telephones. These two audits, in a word, backfired.

The Farm Loan Board, by its very nature, attracted a clientele unable to borrow money elsewhere, and under the best of circumstances was difficult to run on what are usually called businesslike lines. It had enough critics that the Conservatives had promised to investigate it if elected, and in due course they appointed one Walter Weston, CA, to audit the board's books.

Weston went to work at once with two associates, both of whom aroused the Liberals' suspicions from the start because they were, respectively, an outspoken critic of the Farm Loan Board and a defeated

Conservative candidate in the 1921 general election. Their report, tabled on 11 February 1930, was on the surface a damning indictment of the board. Howard McConnell, who spoke to it, went out of his way to emphasize that the personal integrity of the three board members who had administered its affairs was never in question, but their supervision, in Weston's words, meant that the 'Board has been hopelessly mismanaged.'[26]

The Weston report made the expected sort of allegations, and the Liberals were unimpressed. The report admitted that the board had made many good loans, but in too many instances loans were granted on inadequate inspections, sometimes even against an inspector's recommendations or, Weston suspected, on no inspection at all. In one section Weston had found that, 'While there is no documentary evidence that the Government interfered with the management and operations of the Board, there is evidence that outside influences did improperly affect the Board's policy.' While he was provincial treasurer, W.J. Patterson, like his predecessors, had repeatedly emphasized that the government did not interfere with the Farm Loan Board, and he took a dim view of the gratuitous implication that there had been interference which could not be documented. Besides, Weston emphasized that while shoddy practices in the board prevailed, 'I have not asked the Board why it did all these things and therefore have received no explanations.'[27] It was a singular statement for so devastating a report to make, and the government agreed to refer the report to the legislature's Standing Committee on Public Accounts.

The committee was all the Liberals needed. Gardiner and his followers were successful in having the members of the board called as witnesses. Their evidence, supplemented by a longer look at Weston's statistics, resulted in a bland document of little use to the new government. It repudiated, in effect, the Weston report.[28]

The other audit of the Liberals' administration pursued by the new government had an equally eccentric history. The audit of the books of the Department of Telephones was initiated by the Anderson government soon after taking office, and a reputable accounting firm, O.J. Godfrey and Company, presented its report on 21 December 1929. The Liberals had difficulty obtaining a copy, and were surprised to find that there was a second audit report on the telephone operations, dated 5 February 1930, by G.B. Munnoch and Company, identified by the minister in charge, again Howard McConnell, as 'efficiency experts.' The opposition received the two reports just two days before the minister made a speech based on them, and it was obvious to the Liberals that McConnell preferred the report by Munnoch. A scrutiny of the two reports explained why: it was apparent to the slowest mind on the Speaker's left that the government had commissioned the Godfrey firm hoping to receive another Weston report, and when Godfrey's audit found little that was wrong in the Department of Telephones, it was audited by the more sympathetic Munnoch.

The government of course denied that, although it never did produce a convincing reason for having two consecutive investigations of the telephone operations. The first audit was quite acceptable to the Liberal opposition: Godfrey, W.J. Patterson said, although known to be 'not on my side of politics,' had nonetheless 'prepared this report with a serious consideration of what the duties of an auditor are ... He was anxious to retain the reputation he properly holds in this province as a competent auditor.' Patterson readily agreed that, as provincial treasurer, he had found the department difficult to administer. Despite many conferences between officials of the Treasury and the Department of Telephones, it had been hard to reconcile the views of the Treasury men with their orientation toward bookkeeping, and those of the telephone engineers whose interests in technical matters made them impatient with statistical post-mortems. The difference between the Godfrey and Munnoch reports Patterson summarized in a short paragraph intended to point to the analogy between the Weston report on the Farm Loan Board, and the comments of the Committee on Public Accounts on the Weston report, which he knew was to be presented shortly: 'He [Godfrey] says in another place: "We find the numerical differences between the actual stock [in the stores] and the Head Office records to be so slight as not to be worthy of mention"; but if Munnoch found a discrepancy of one glass insulator, he would write a couple of pages about it in his report!'

And so it was: the technical details of the two telephone audits are not relevant to their political significance. What strikes one about the investigations is how odd it was that the two parties had four reports from which to choose. Patterson even tried to have the Godfrey and Munnoch reports sent to yet a third tribunal, but failed.[29]

None of the reports, and to them can be added the Coldwell commission and the royal commission on the Bryant charges discussed earlier, substantiated the extravagant allegations about the corruption of the Gardiner machine or the inefficiency of the government it supported. One conclusion that does stand out is that in a technical – or perhaps 'business-like' – sense, the administration of Saskatchewan under the

Liberals was old-fashioned. The party's twenty-four unbroken years in power had required it to take responsibility for the creation of roads, bridges, schools, court houses, telephones, and a host of other works and services at an almost explosive rate, when what mattered was getting something done, not accounting tidily for it afterwards. On a larger and more horrendous scale, Canada has faced the same problem, vastly different in degree but not in kind, in two world wars. Gardiner inherited most of the matters for which he was responsible and, like his predecessors, did not attach a high priority to what he would have considered mere bookkeeping. Dunning, after all, was widely touted for his efficiency, and in due course went into private business; and everything that the Anderson government investigated and audited had been taken over by Gardiner from Dunning.

Anderson of course inherited the same institutions from Gardiner, and an interesting footnote on what he had time to do with one of them has been written. An independent young scholar, George Britnell, in 1934 wrote a master's thesis on 'Public Ownership of Telephones in the Prairie Provinces' and said in it of Saskatchewan's accounts that they 'were more hopelessly confused and inadequate than those of Manitoba or Alberta have ever been.' The changes made as a result of the audits were baffling to Britnell, but he could get no explanations from Regina.[30] At the same time, Britnell noted wonderingly that despite the enormous increase in services there had been no increase in rates in Saskatchewan from 1908 to 1929. And that, not sloppy accounting, was the sort of thing that mattered to Gardiner.

To Anderson too, as it turned out. It has been necessary to establish, somewhat at the expense of historical chronology, that Anderson did not, despite the excited allegations of the campaign, take over a hopelessly corrupt or inefficient administration. In the problems he too faced, the priority had to be given to solutions. The summer of 1929, for Anderson, had been filled with victory picnics and parades, and the session which defeated Gardiner was hailed as a triumph. But when Anderson jubilantly took office on 9 September 1929, the drought had already begun; and the New York stock market crashed on 29 October.

8

A First Taste of Opposition

'I am today,' Gardiner wrote to Mackenzie King on 9 September 1929, 'awaiting the arrival of Dr. Anderson who is to take over the Government this afternoon.' He expressed satisfaction with developments since the election, and thought even the votes in the legislature, the one part of the proceedings the party had not controlled, 'will benefit the Liberal Party to a greater extent in the future than any other Party.'[1]

The Liberals' final fling before Anderson took over was of course to sink into insignificance in the face of the onslaughts awaiting the prairies. Gardiner could not have known that, but his boundless confidence would probably have led him to regard the 'Dirty Thirties' as the natural outcome of being without Liberal governments in Saskatchewan and, soon, in Ottawa. His MLAs went home in good spirits, Gardiner told King, and he felt his position as leader had been confirmed. He planned to retain direction of the party's organization, with George Spence supervising its general control, and Mary McCallum Sutherland, an able worker on whom Gardiner placed much reliance, managing the women's side. Gardiner's initial reaction to his occupancy of the office of the leader of the opposition was thus very much 'business as usual.' Another government had assumed power, but nobody in his right mind could conceive of that as anything more than a period to be waited out.

Gardiner was, indeed, to find being stripped of power while still at the centre of things a pleasant experience, and he more than once described his opposition years as among the happiest in his life.[2] That was partly for domestic reasons: three of the four Gardiner children had arrived by 1929 – John Edwin in 1919, Florence Ellen in 1921, James Wilfrid in 1924; a fourth, Violet Elizabeth, was to be born in 1932. For a young family whose father had just been liberated from the never-ending demands of cabinet life, the period in opposition provided the green years. The whole family could even leave Regina to return to the farm at Lemberg, which it did in 1932.

Oddly enough, there is virtually nothing about his opposition years in his notes for *None of It Came Easy*. The omission suggests that twenty years after they ended, the sessions in opposition did not loom large in his mind. But in 1955, when the book was published, Gardiner was still deeply enmeshed in the daily give-and-take of politics, and there is in the book almost nothing about that either. He was just as enmeshed while in opposition, for the loss of power cost Liberals the use of many facilities, and therefore necessitated intensified efforts if the party was to remain a fighting machine. The efforts had to be concentrated in two main areas: internal affairs, and the Liberal response and reaction to the activities of others.

Some of the politics of opposition began the day Anderson formed his cabinet. As well as being the first non-Liberal executive in the province's history, it was also the first to include representatives of more than one party. To play down its party bases it chose to be called a Co-operative Government. It contained the first ministers without portfolio in Saskatchewan, one Conservative and one Progressive. The ministers with portfolio included Carl Stewart, who had been chosen not by Anderson but by the Independents. Six of the ten members (the largest cabinet so far) were from urban centres, and not one was a full-time farmer. On paper they were an impressive lot, the two doctors and four lawyers among them (Anderson had an LL B) sharing thirteen earned degrees. Several had extensive experience in municipal councils. Gardiner, who observed the appointments with a sceptical interest, was obliged to make a major decision: should the Liberals contest the ministerial by-elections made necessary by the acceptance of offices of emolument?

Since there were to be eight by-elections (the two ministers without portfolio were exempted) a decision to contest would be costly for the opposition, but it would also give a stimulus to reorganizing the party. A few Liberal victories, furthermore, might restore Gardiner's majority. On the other hand, seven of the eight ministers had won handily in June, most of them by record-breaking majorities, and the one who appeared vulnerable, J.A. Merkley of Moose Jaw (a two-member seat), had nonetheless relegated a straight Liberal opponent to fourth position. It was not a promising outlook and Gardiner, who promptly summoned a group of leading supporters for a discussion of party tactics, found little enthusiasm among them for a series of scattered fights.

Besides, the federal Liberals, anxious to aggravate as few Progressives as possible before the federal election expected in 1930, were also opposed to contesting the by-elections.[3]

All the ministers were returned by acclamation, and attention then turned to further by-elections arising under the Controverted Elections Act. In Saskatchewan then, as elsewhere in Canada, political parties commonly collected (and sometimes even planted) evidence against each other as a form of insurance for their own seats. The usual practice, when both sides had good cases, was to circumvent the law by negotiating saw-offs, and that was followed in 1929. Gardiner's attitude towards the saw-offs paralleled his view on the by-elections – he felt all should be contested, or none.[4]

No by-elections were held because of the Controverted Elections Act, although an eccentric one occurred in Estevan when the MLA elected in 1929, a Liberal, resigned. In the by-election in December 1930, one McLeod, after winning on the first count, lost on an official recount to a Conservative, McKnight, but petitioned the legislature on the grounds that ballots that would have confirmed his victory had been tampered with before the recount. Gardiner, who had campaigned vigorously in Estevan, with his hand strengthened by a judicial investigation which supported the claim that ballots had been tampered with, persuaded Anderson that the seat was rightly McLeod's. Following a precedent set in 1907, the legislature ordered the certificate for Estevan amended to return McLeod.

Gardiner enjoyed the whole episode and Mackenzie King, by then in opposition himself, saw in it the hand of Providence. 'There is usually some by-election,' King wrote, 'which more than anything else spells out the ultimate doom of an Administration and I believe such will prove to be the case with the seat you have just won.' At the moment King wrote those words the recount had established that the Conservative, not the Liberal, had been victorious. Ironically enough, McLeod was himself later unseated because, the Liberals alleged, McLeod's opponents had connived at getting unqualified electors to vote in the original by-election to guarantee a court case over the seat. Despite frequent urgings from Gardiner and Davis, among others, no one was prosecuted for setting up a controverted election, and Estevan remained vacant from late in 1932 until the general election of 1934.[5] Estevan truly provided a major event, for it both strengthened Anderson and his supporters in their co-operation, and convinced Gardiner that he was right in refusing to have anything to do with it.

Not that he needed much convincing. The by-election took place fifteen months after Anderson took office, and while it was the first significant test between the two sides, Gardiner had chosen his role in any confrontation long before that. The dust had barely settled in Saskatchewan when he was surprised to receive from the party's national office, through Andrew Haydon, an offer of $500 to be spent on a long holiday. Haydon did not say that the federal Liberals wanted Gardiner out of the way while they drummed up support among the Progressives, but it was natural under the circumstances for Gardiner to suspect that. If the purpose of the holiday, he wrote, was to keep him from meeting some 'so-called Liberals and quite a number of self-seeking progressives,' the money could be 'better used to assist some real Liberal back to office.' On the other hand, he added, he had been serving the party to his own financial disadvantage for nearly thirty years; if the purpose of the offer was to show some appreciation of his work, and put him in the most 'reasonable state of mind to confront either Tories whom I admire, or fair weather Grits whom I tolerate, or Progressives whose real desires have already been demonstrated,' he might go. And he did; on his return he wrote to thank King.[6]

That letter, Gardiner's first long report on local politics since September, was written in longhand on plain paper, from Gardiner's Regina home. Those seemingly trifling facts are revealing about the amenities that Gardiner lost along with the election of 1929. The office facilities available to the opposition were hardly adequate and the party's headquarters had to be shifted from the legislative building. That meant a new expense for a party that was concurrently being deprived of a lot of services, but Gardiner considered it unavoidable: he had no confidence in any legislative staff provided by Anderson's forces. The party's mobility was sharply cut, for party workers in opposition could no longer hitch rides on cars from Agriculture or trucks from Highways, or, in the guise of inspectors, drive the vehicles themselves. That increased the value of the free passes on railways provided to MLAs, but since they were the only people who could move about as before, the party's whole orientation towards the electorate was changed. Some supporters were slow to grasp that. In the old days, Gardiner wrote in 1930, 'most of the arrangements for activities started from Regina ... We are now forced into the opposite position where the very lack of funds to move our people around makes it necessary that any activity must start with the local people.'[7]

The loss of power in 1929, indeed, revealed more clearly than any event until that time the nature of the Liberals' organization. Charges about the corruption of the machine blew about like tumbleweeds during the 1929 campaign and its aftermath, but little had been proved. Nonetheless, while it was plain that the celebrated Gardiner machine never was the devilish horde that legend made of it, and Anderson's investigations confirmed that, it was equally clear that it was not wholly manned by a heavenly host.

Setting aside the probability that at least some public servants in Saskatchewan in the 1930s, in defence of their own jobs, might have been willing to tell Anderson and his ministers anything they wanted to hear, one firm indicator of the number of Liberal activists in the public service can be found in the toll of those dismissed after 9 September 1929. Anderson told the legislature on 10 February 1930, when being taunted by Gardiner over the turnover of civil servants since he took office 'that many had been investigated for political activity, but for compassionate reasons it was decided not to molest them ... [We] have proceeded most cautiously ... and that is why only six percent of the civil servants of this province have been replaced since the 9th of September.' Anderson himself gave the size of the service at 1,700 when he became premier, which meant that he was conceding the replacement of 102 persons. Earlier he had conceded 88 dismissals.[8]

Anderson's figures were presumably accurate, but they were based on a technical definition of civil servant. Of all public servants, including those not covered by the feeble Civil Service Act, a return tabled in the House by the premier on 25 March revealed that a total of 476 had been let go from twenty-one departments and agencies. A week later, in response to an Order requesting the names of employees engaged since 9 September, Anderson tabled a list of 588. Clearly, reform of the civil service was not going to come before the Anderson government had reformed it in its own special way.[9]

In the mean time, the Liberal newspapers were having a field day listing the names and offices of the departed, many of whom began to jam into Gardiner's office seeking help. Gardiner could do nothing for most of them, although the former legislative librarian, W.F. Kerr, shortly became a party organizer. Gardiner was not particularly censorious of the Co-operative Government's course, for he believed in patronage and would have done the same himself. And later he did, when he was returned to power in 1934. What he objected to was Anderson's pious claim to be a civil service reformer.

Anderson was naturally under colossal pressures from supporters to reward the faithful who had gone so long without recognition; and he was also inexperienced. Gardiner, sitting directly across from Anderson in the assembly, must often have wondered what manner of man he was, and how his premiership would affect Saskatchewan and the Liberal party. The two men had known each other since undergraduate days, although Anderson was not one of his fellow alumni of whom Gardiner spoke in fond recollection. As an MLA and then a minister Gardiner had known Anderson as a conscientious public servant almost obsessed with certain beliefs about education, which he had pressed on the government first in official reports and then in an admirably lucid book, *The Education of the New-Canadian*, published in 1918. In one sense the book is unusual, for Anderson was a civil servant when he wrote; it is, at least by implication, a strong condemnation of major aspects of the government's education policies.

It is also a strange book to read in the 1980s, when concerted efforts are being made to preserve Canada's bicultural beginnings and multicultural history. Anderson's view was the exact opposite: diversity must be stamped out, and the public school system was the tool to use. 'There must be one medium of communication from coast to coast,' he wrote firmly, 'and that the English language.' Elsewhere he spoke warmly of the need to have immigrants earn their part in 'the greatest Empire on earth,' and was critical of their ability to qualify for the franchise simply by staying around for a few years. While he spoke of the older immigrants' large-heartedness and hospitality, he also wrote of 'the retarding influences of certain members of the clergy and a few nationalistic agitators,' of the 'barbarous pronunciation' given to simple English words, and of the 'seemingly crude human material which may be moulded into enlightened Canadian citizenship.' What was needed for that was not just ordinary teachers, but those prepared 'for missionary work in these foreign settlements.'[10] Anderson usually spoke in the most optimistic tones of the offspring of the seemingly crude human material he found in some settlements, but it is not hard to find in his book the roots of the messianic zeal with which he went after religious symbols and garb in the schools a decade later.

With one of Anderson's premises Gardiner could agree, for as long ago as his principalship at Lemberg he had told an audience of parents that the older immigrants could hardly be moulded into 'the most loyal Canadian subjects' because of their affection for their homelands. Gardiner had a far keener appreciation than Anderson of the position of French Canadians in Confederation, and believed that sound political institutions generally, and not merely the schools, were the instruments required for producing solid citizens. He had lived with the 'New-Canadians' as a fellow citizen. He thought in the early twenties that Anderson's position as director of education among New Canadians, which had developed from his book, was a disposable frill,[11] and its abolition may have been a factor in moving Anderson into politics.

Anderson's expertise as an educator and civil servant were to do him little immediate good as premier. It was as if, after spending several decades in preparation for taking over the management of the public service generally, and the schools in particular, he found on assuming office that those two topics were almost irrelevant to what he had to cope with. The euphoria of 1929 hardly had time to wear off before it was swept away by grim and worsening realities for which Anderson had become politically responsible. Saskatchewan's plight would have been serious enough had it been caused only by the collapse of the agricultural market; but the deepening drought added a grinding element that nobody could do much about. The province's northern areas were relatively untouched by the drought, but the crops they did produce could hardly be given away. The southern areas could not produce crops large enough even to feed the cattle. What was sometimes even worse, farm animals could not be watered. Better off than most, Gardiner was able to keep between forty and fifty head at Lemberg, but he too ran out of proper feed in more than one winter.[12]

Gardiner was better off than most, too, in having his legislative indemnity ($2,000), his salary as leader of the opposition ($3,000, one-third of the premier's salary), his farm, and little public responsibility for anything. If this were a biography of Anderson and his government, it would be necessary to recount in greater detail precisely what they had to cope with, and thus show the full picture of what Gardiner missed. The chronicle, which has been well told, can be outlined in part in cold statistics. The farm price of wheat fell from $1.03 per bushel in 1929 to 35 cents by 1932. The value of all products sold off Saskatchewan farms was $273.6 million in 1928, $179.7 million in 1929, and $66.2 million in 1931. The index numbers of prices received by prairie farmers for No. 1 Northern wheat was over 150 in both 1929 and 1930, but down to 60 in 1932, and 52 in 1933, while at the same time the index for what farmers paid on a list of necessities fell less drastically, from 94 in 1929 to 42 at its lowest in 1933. The government's revenues from staple sources plummeted (motor licence fees, for example, were $2 million in 1929–30, and half that in 1931–32), and its deficit, $518,000 in the former year, was $5,820,000 in the latter. The costs of direct relief rose from minuscule beginnings to average nearly $5 million in the years 1931–32 to 1934–35, and the total figures for all relief, including agricultural aid in feed and fodder, seed, and freight subsidies, averaged nearly three times that for direct relief.[13] The total for relief fell not far short of the province's budgetary expenditures on everything else.

The statistics are impressive enough, but what they hide in human terms is worse. As if drought and almost non-existent markets were not bad enough, the farmers were beset by stem rust and grasshoppers. Single young men without farms were encouraged into work camps run along military lines. Governments had to decide whether to move food and water for people and animals into some areas, or move the people and animals out. They also had to decide how to relieve people of heavy tax arrears without destroying the municipalities and school boards that needed the money, and how to adjust farm debts contracted with banks and other lenders when crops, prices, and markets were all incomparably better. The government of Saskatchewan, which took office so confidently in 1929, was two years later reduced to promising that 'no one would be allowed to starve.'[14]

It was an extraordinary statement for any Canadian leader to have to make, and in what led up to it, and what followed, it must be recorded that Gardiner offered remarkably little help. It was not because he was uninformed about what was happening, or without compassion for the suffering and deprivation he saw all around him. His own farm, supported in part by his income as a legislator, was nonetheless in the area designated as the worst by the Saskatchewan Relief Commission. But he believed in the parliamentary and party systems as a matter of principle, and had no confidence in the Tories' ability to do anything right even on their own, let alone under a coalition. Clearly that government needed opposition, and if he had to choose between helping Anderson weather a temporary crisis to which Conservative policies had contributed, if they had not created it, and seeing that the parliamentary and party systems survived, he had to choose the latter. It was plainly the Liberals' duty, Gardiner wrote late in 1932, to save the country from the Tories and radicals on either side, who had a lot in common besides their constant desire to restrict somebody's freedom. A year later, lumping Tories in with war scares and narrow nationalism involving tariffs, he saw them as always hand in hand with 'reactionary minds suggesting control of every individual act'; and Liberalism the only hope for the future.[15]

To see Liberal politics in the early thirties in proper context, it is necessary to examine Gardiner's activities after he went into opposition. His immediate preoccupation with by-elections included paying attention to the party organization, for the kind of activity needed, with the Liberals in opposition, would depend initially on the decisions made about the by-elections. There was hardly time, during the plans for the short session of September 1929 and the post-session decisions, for systematic consideration of the reasons for the party's defeat in June, but they too would help shape the organization for opposition and the next general election.

The notes Gardiner provided Nathaniel Benson in 1955 for *None of It Came Easy* show that a quarter of a century after the event he had narrowed down the cause for defeat to the school issue which the Conservatives had been trying to exploit since 1905. In 1929, 'with the help of some visiting itinerant Klansmen preaching religious bigotry and educational intolerance of minorities,' the Tories gave the issue one 'final effort,' and it was temporarily successful.[16] In his considerable post-election correspondence several other factors were also large in his mind. Thus when the celebrated Father Athol Murray wrote him a touching letter of thanks for his vigorous defence of minorities, and particularly Roman Catholics, Gardiner cited the Klan, which the Liberals had forced into the open. To another correspondent he wrote that he had felt the Liberals' time was beginning to run out when he became premier, the implication being that almost any issue might have been used to turn them out.[17]

Analysing the results for W.R. Motherwell, Gardiner related his loss on the school issue to the party's strength in Quebec as well as Saskatchewan, and the long term of office in each province. The Liberals' strong organization, though 'a perfectly proper one,' was much misunderstood as if 'it controlled, rather than persuaded, the votes of the people.' Five days later he told his old friend the Reverend C. Endicott that the long period in office and the Klan could not have defeated him: 'that which did us the greatest harm ... was the insidious campaign carried on by the Bell interests through the Regina Star and Standard.' While it was pleasant to have a clear conscience, Gardiner added, it was 'nevertheless disconcerting to know that the people of the province can be stampeded.' The personal attacks on himself, Gardiner told another correspondent, were made 'because of the fact that I had stood in the way of some interests in Saskatchewan securing financial benefit at the expense of the people.' And to that subject Gardiner often attached the unscrupulous Tory tactics of sowing distrust, then remaining silent, then whipping up feelings about it in the few days before the actual vote. On occasion he lumped all the reasons together to claim that his government had fallen before the forces of high protection in many forms.[18]

All these reasons had little to do with the Liberals' policies as a government, but Gardiner was well aware that they too had not all been wholly acceptable. The great fuss over the school issue he had considered deliberately manufactured. His convictions on that point were confirmed towards the last days of the Anderson regime, when the beleaguered premier, in response to one more Liberal motion in the legislature, had to table a sessional paper which revealed that while in September of 1929 there were seventeen Roman Catholic properties being used for public school teaching, in December of 1933 there were twenty; and whereas the public schools employed eighty-four nuns when Anderson took office, they employed ninety-three at the end of 1933 (all of them presumably in mufti).[19]

On other fronts Gardiner considered his party more vulnerable. In general, he told an editor, many sound voters thought the government needed a stronger opposition, and miscalculated. More specifically, he explained that his party's stand on electrical power had upset numbers of businessmen, including his old foe George Bell, who had worked against him both in Arm River in 1928, and in 1929. A related policy concerned the grain trade, for which Gardiner had supported the Wheat Pool as against the Winnipeg Grain Exchange and private interests. 'This,' he wrote, 'had more to do with the defeat of the government in the last election than most people realize.'[20]

Not one of Gardiner's varied assessments of 1929 showed anything resembling contrition. 'The only man who knows what party means,' he had written early in his ministerial career, 'is the man who is prepared to stand by a set of principles in the hour of defeat as well as the hour of victory.'[21] He was ready to do that in 1929, and ready too to explore with interest the problems of standing by a set of principles in the unprecedented experience of opposition. But merely asserting principles was not likely to be enough, nor would simple opposition to the Co-operative Government. Liberalism needed a party whose leaders believed in it; and a party required organization. How does one do that without the amenities of power? If one reason for defeat was the organization's strength, however misunderstood by the electorate, how did one safely weaken it? Was the loss of the governmental facilities a sufficient weakening, or of the right kind? Faced with questions like that, Gardiner came to the same conclusion that John Barrymore offered when asked how he got around the stage so well as a crippled Shakespearean king: 'I merely turn one foot inward and walk the best I can.' So Gardiner in 1929: Liberalism had not been changed by a defeat, but it had been crippled. Gardiner decided to walk the best he could.

How thoroughly Gardiner adapted the post-election reorganization of the party to his assessment of the reasons for its defeat it is not now possible to say. He felt that the party had not been diligent enough in wooing the young, and attributed that in part to the history of the province. No organization of Young Liberals had been necessary in the early days, because then everybody was young, and all elected bodies had a full complement of young men.[22] In the same way, though for a different reason, the party had been slow to organize its female supporters, because for over a decade after 1905 women had been excluded from the franchise. He was not satisfied that the party had made proper use of radio.

In all these areas work had begun before 1929, for Gardiner was not the kind of politician to overlook either new electors or ways of reaching them. When he appointed George Spence and Mary Sutherland as organizers in September 1929 he was simultaneously looking for somebody to work with the young. By 1933, by which time he had perceived that wooing the young was one of the most promising ways of undercutting the new left-wing movement led by M.J. Coldwell, he was telling supporters that in his own constituency he had a Young Liberal Club in every town and village and he had 'never seen anything go better.' To those who were sceptical of the youths' value he explained how they could study, improve upon, and spread Liberal doctrine.[23]

The organization of women was in progress before 1929. Because women found it more difficult than men to get away from the farm, the coming of the franchise had necessitated a considerable reorganization of rural polling divisions. That in turn required consideration of whether in rural areas women should have their own organization, as in the towns, or be urged to join the same committees as men. Mary Sutherland, appointed to take charge of such matters in 1929, was nearly as assertive in her Liberalism as her revered chief, whose attitude to women in the party, she told him in 1932, was 'very nearly perfect.' One of her activities was the organization of radio clubs, where the women would forgather around a loudspeaker, listen to a political address, collect a dollar or two in funds if possible, and report the speech in the neighbourhood thereafter. The Liberals' use of radio clubs was soon to become so sophisticated that Gardiner came to believe that the party should have a professional expert to manage political broadcasts. A Liberal Broadcasting Club, operated by a group of young people, was formed in Regina to sponsor broadcasts every week during the winter months, raising funds through social functions and levies on elected members.[24]

Funds were needed, of course, and the difficulty of raising them plagued Gardiner's forces after 1929. Gardiner and his political friends repeatedly commiserated with each other about the almost total absence of money, and he told many correspondents, 'our main difficulty is the standing difficulty of an opposition, namely that of getting funds.'[25] There was no money for travel or to rent halls and, apart from any space a friendly newspaper might offer, none for advertising. In 1933 the party had trouble financing the printing and distribution of its platform.[26]

But it was not quite destitute. Its twenty-eight MLAs were all drawing annual indemnities of $2,000, and most of them could be relied on to donate time and an occasional dollar to the party. All were expected to pay $10 annually into the radio fund. They wrung every drop of free publicity they could get from the legislature's sessions. They all had a few friends who could be counted on to help and, spurred on by Gardiner, the party never did slump into the slough of despond that opposition parties in Saskatchewan's two neighbouring provinces did. In August 1932 the organization launched a new venture, the *Saskatchewan Liberal*, a newspaper not always published on schedule. In its first issue Gardiner referred optimistically to the breaking of the drought, which was not readily apparent to everybody. Although the average cash returns for each acre of wheat sowed were indeed generally better that summer than in 1931, this fact Gardiner could not have known at the time. By May 1933 the paper had twenty-five hundred subscribers and Gardiner was aiming to quadruple that, using a competition among the Young Liberal clubs to peddle it. The contest put the journal 'beyond our quota,' and the five top salesmen received a free trip to a national convention in Ottawa.[27]

The *Saskatchewan Liberal* was one of the party's more conspicuous internal enterprises in opposition, a way of 'showing activity.' Equally conspicuous were some of the outcroppings of the party's general organization. Parts of that organization were hardly ever discussed by him in public except defensively, and in his notes for *None of It Came Easy*, political organization is one topic about which he says nothing. That was not because he thought there was anything wrong with it, but it was simply an instrument, a means to an end. Behind the scenes, from 1929 to 1934, the Saskatchewan Liberal party worked as it had always worked, except that it found the work a lot harder.

As in 1926, Gardiner looked to every constituency executive to reorganize itself, which always to him meant not only electing the usual president, vice-president, and so on, but getting rid of the complacent and bringing in new blood. After 1929, in addition to the work of George Spence (who was also an MLA) and Mary Sutherland, Gardiner expected every district to be worked in by either an MLA or a federal MP. He himself did nearly all the writing of publicity for the first three years, and although as the tide began to run against the government more help came to the Liberals, he continued to rely heavily on the elected members. He was constantly urging them to be out and about at all gatherings where they would not be intruders. (He donated a curling trophy for the championship of North Qu'Appelle, 'to promote intercourse.') By 1933, when the tide had clearly turned, the party's treasury was still so low that Gardiner had to miss a national conference in Ottawa because its timing precluded him from taking advantage of special Christmas railway fares. Yet as early as October 1932 the Liberals had thirty candidates in the field for the next election, which meant that local executives had been able to finance thirty conventions. Not all of them immediately became as active as Gardiner hoped, and a year later he wrote of some of them, 'I have tried to stir them up but there seems to be no way.'[28]

To these varied attempts to keep the party moving, in 1930 Gardiner tried to add a political spectacular – a leadership convention. The time was ripe; for with the depression, politics in Saskatchewan, never weak, had regained some of the values as free entertainment it had been losing to the automobile and the movie house. There is no evidence that Gardiner was thinking of relinquishing the leadership, and in any case he could hardly afford to give up his salary as leader of the opposition: between providing for a growing family and helping support the party, he was chronically short of cash at the time, and in 1933 was obliged to borrow on his insurance.[29] What was worse, he could no longer keep up with all the charitable contributions expected of a politician. The Liberal provincial executive at first refused him a provincial convention in 1930 but shortly changed its decision. A convention was scheduled for 15–16 June 1931, at Moose Jaw, at which Gardiner was re-elected leader unanimously. That was all but a foregone conclusion, but the convention served its real purpose: Gardiner was on extended speaking tours in the weeks preceding it, and received excellent press coverage.

The same convention produced a platform of more than passing interest, to which it added footnotes in subsequent annual meetings up to 1934. The finished platform reflected the Liberals' paper response to the rising CCF, and included references to a publicly owned central bank to issue all currency, 'crop or weather insurance,' a minimum wage and unemployment insurance, and the desirability of returning to the attack on combines and cartels which had been slackened to encourage production during the war. As usual, it also covered a broad spectrum that included external affairs.[30]

Gardiner wrote a formal statement on the platform of 1931, which he described as 'explained by James Gardiner, Leader of the Party,' and it is notable for its concentration on the more conventional issues of agriculture, natural resources, secondary industries, debt, taxation, and interest rates, and its omission even of hints of the newer topics such as the central bank and labour legislation. He repeated the platform's condemnation of the governments then in power in Canada and Saskatchewan, and added to it some ideas not found in any of the party's resolutions. The most interesting of these first referred to 'the cost of having no government but a group of inefficient members of the legislature responsible for the existence of this present so called administration.' Gardiner rewrote that to substitute, 'the cost of having a coalition or cooperative government with none of the restrictions and discipline which a well organized party places upon its leaders.'[31] The revised version permitted Gardiner to assail the Anderson government with a different set of weapons to those he could use on R.B. Bennett and the federal Conservatives, who did constitute an organized party. With both he concentrated on principles and policies, eschewing personal attacks on the two leaders, a tactic of which he was generally critical.[32]

The Liberals' internal activity naturally involved federal matters. The national leader sat for Prince Albert, and as long as he was prime minister the seat had to be looked after, particularly since King himself had no time to do so. That remained true when he became leader of the opposition in 1930. Just as well, perhaps, since it may be doubted whether King knew how to nurse any constituency, let alone a free-wheeling one on the northern fringes of settlement in Saskatchewan. Gardiner, as the provincial leader, found himself concerned with the federal authorities in a variety of affairs for which he considered himself a Saskatchewan or western representative. Thus in March 1930 he took up the interests of the Saskatchewan coal industry, in light of the tariff on machinery and the pressures for subsidies coming from Albertan and British Columbian producers. In 1933 he lobbied to keep open the Canadian National Railway shops at Melville. He made at least one trip east to try to negotiate between western debtors and eastern financial institutions. He helped a debater argue against the amalgamation of the legislatures of the three prairie provinces into one. When in 1933 King raised the possibility of 'a certain gentleman' becoming the Liberal candidate in the vacant federal constituency of Mackenzie, Gardiner demurred that 'it would not be advisable for him to leave the provincial field.'[33]

Another matter concerned arranging for the national leader to come west at the right time, to the right place, with the right companions, for a trip of the right duration, after which he would write letters of thanks to the right people. Gardiner made himself less conspicuous when King was in the province, and would not make a major public speech while he was around.[34] He did, however, when King was in Saskatchewan in 1933 for a tour of Prince Albert and adjoining seats, perform as starting pitcher in a picnic baseball game in which he also hit a home run. King hit only a three bagger.[35]

Tours with picnics and similar activities may seem trivial, but they received an immense amount of attention. Gardiner believed profoundly that good political practice required a meticulous attention to detail; and on a broader landscape, good practice required Gardiner to play a new federal role after the Conservatives took office in Ottawa in 1930. Even before that, of course, he had campaigned with his usual vigour; his organization, managed for the national election by Jack Stevenson, a well-known businessman whose son later married the Gardiners' older daughter, had been the federal fighting wing. In the legislature Gardiner made a speech on federal affairs which he himself entitled 'Address delivered by the Leader of the Opposition in the Saskatchewan Legislature during the Federal Election of 1930' – prematurely, for the legislature rose in April while the House of Commons sat on until 20 May. But everybody knew the Commons' legal life was ending, and Gardiner was ready for its demise with an all-purpose broadside which tied the tariff to the Tories, and both to hard times. The powers of darkness had never been on the side of the Liberals, and the Liberals alone were entitled to credit for what had been done with such western benefits as the Hudson Bay Railway, the Crow's Nest freight rates, and the St Lawrence Waterway.[36]

The campaign for the federal vote on 28 July, Gardiner expected, would in Saskatchewan parallel that of 1929, and the religious controversy aroused then, he said, had as its real long-term purpose the defeat of the federal Liberals. But he also expected other issues, and his legislative speech was a fairly accurate indicator of what happened. Education and religious symbols were not federal issues, and the furore over them in 1929 had been overtaken by July of 1930 by more pressing economic problems; the religious issue was not the kind that could be kept at a high emotional pitch for long, anyway. Gardiner entered the 1930 campaign believing (so he told King) that 'the compromises of the past while essential to our remaining in power for the time being were fatal to the building of a strong Liberalism which would weather the storm of misrepresentation indulged in during the last campaign.'[37] He wrote those words with specific reference to the federal Liberals, whose cautious steps towards free trade had never really satisfied him.

He adhered to his anti-tariff line in the campaign. While, like any good politician, he varied his attack so that by the end everything that was relevant -- and numerous things that were not – had been used by both the Liberals and their opponents, the 1930 election was fought on hard issues. The Conservatives were in better shape financially than Gardiner could remember, and even before the Commons rose on 20 May Gardiner had warned King to expect a real fight in the west.[38] Gardiner was right, and after a campaign in which he was as usual all over the place, the Liberals won eleven seats of the province's twenty-one (a drop of five from 1926), while the Conservatives went from none to eight, and the Progressives from five to two. Except for Quebec, the Liberals' Saskatchewan showing was the strongest in Canada, both in the popular vote and seats won.

Gardiner saw eye to eye on nothing of political significance with the new prime minister, R.B. Bennett. Gardiner disliked Bennett, and on his deathbed was still expressing the conviction that Bennett had financed the Ku Klux Klan in Saskatchewan – a belief to which Gardiner's own records give no support. But apart from that, Gardiner was a doctrinaire believer in free trade, and Bennett was the opposite. No single example could better illustrate their differences than a juxtaposition of Bennett's and Gardiner's views on British preference and free trade within the empire. Bennett's biographer, Ernest Watkins, has written an admirably clear account of Bennett's trade policies which includes these words: 'He had already rejected from mind the concept of "Empire Free Trade" ... Canadian industry was not strong enough to withstand the full impact of unchecked competition from the United Kingdom. But an association of nations which imposed a common tariff barrier against all imports from outside ... would be one that should be able to flourish even in times of deepening dislocations in world trade.'[39]

The Saskatchewan Liberal party was not exactly enchanted by the protection of Canadian industries for whose products western farmers had as a result to pay higher prices, and its 1931 platform said, among other things: 'We pledge our party to: (a) a further extension of the principle of British preference until all the necessities of agriculture are placed upon the free list so that goods which can be supplied more cheaply from within the Empire will be procurable at prices which will lessen the cost of production in agriculture.'

To such statements Gardiner subscribed wholeheartedly; Bennett's trade policy, whatever he might call it, was to Gardiner protectionism, and that was related not merely to bad times but increasingly, in Europe, to preparation for war.[40]

The hostility engendered by trade differences was doubled when it impinged upon electoral matters. The climactic year was 1933, when a federal redistribution occurred and a crucial by-election took place. In the redistribution the Saskatchewan Liberals were little more than helpless bystanders, but Gardiner had to do his best to keep fully informed because a provincial redistribution had been effected in 1932 and the double shifting of constituency boundaries created havoc in his well-organized party.

With the constituencies of the party's national leader and another former minister in his care, the federal redistribution made Gardiner about as nervous as he ever got, and he was not calmed by the development of the whole enterprise into the rowdiest boundary-drawing in Canadian history. It began in the House of Commons in November 1932 and, after committee hearings which saw 'maps torn up, threats and invitations to mortal combat,' and a subsequent impasse, the boundaries gravitated upwards in 1933 to 'older heads of this house,' and final bargains were struck on the floor of the Commons between R.B. Bennett and King. The Saskatchewan map, because it contained the constituency of an almost morbidly sensitive leader, gave both major parties particular trouble, but there was not much Gardiner, back home on the farm, could do about it.[41]

He wrote to King on 3 April 1933 to say that he did not know what was going on, but had heard that the southern part of Prince Albert was to be lopped off, an operation which, he believed, the Liberal MP on the redistribution committee (Fred Totzke) should resign over rather than accept. King worried about whether Totzke could be relied on to protect his leader or whether he should seek a nomination in a new seat into which a large part of his old one seemed to be going, and chafed especially because the other former minister, Motherwell, appeared at the end to be escaping almost unscathed. For his part, Gardiner received the proposed Saskatchewan map on 12 April and at once objected to some of the proposals because they ignored natural boundaries.

As has so often happened with both Conservative and Liberal maps of Saskatchewan, factors other than mere boundaries were to be decisive in the next general election. But neither King or Gardiner could be sure of that in the spring of 1933. King could protest, and did. But picking up the pieces of the dislocated organization fell to Gardiner, and the work progressed so well that as early as 26 July, on his western trip, King wrote in Saskatchewan of his new riding, 'Clearly they are beginning well on the detailed organization of the polls, and the word comes that voluntary help is easily enlisted. I was much enheartened by what I saw.'[42]

Gardiner may have been a bystander at the federal redistribution, but he was a prime mover in the federal by-election held on 23 October in Mackenzie, a constituency on the provincial border to the east of Saskatoon. The name has since 1933 been associated with a huge seat running from the southern third of the province up to the Northwest Territories, but the election in that year was held on boundaries drawn in 1924, when Mackenzie was a compact oblong. It had been won handily in 1930 by a Progressive, but he had faced two opponents who both ran as Liberals and split the vote. When the seat fell vacant, King at once saw a Liberal victory in the by-election 'as likely to have more significance than anything else which may happen between now and the time of a general election,' since a CCF win 'would set the West ... on fire with c.c.f. enthusiasm,' while a Tory success would hurt the Liberals everywhere. He put Gardiner in charge, not so much by direction as indirection. 'I know ... that it does not require so much as a suggestion to have you do in the circumstances whatever at the moment will best serve the larger cause.'[43]

Gardiner, who never needed to be urged into a political fight, responded in kind. 'It looks as though there will be four candidates,' he told King early in April, 'in which case we should win without a doubt.'

And he was right.[44] The ensuing contest was one of those by-elections into which all the parties, not being otherwise occupied, threw their full forces. King made a point of visiting the seat, noting gloomily of the Liberal candidate (J.A. McMillan) that he was 'not very prepossessing – very self-opinionated and fussy – a Scotchman from Nova Scotia,' but nonetheless hospitable, and King spoke on his behalf both from McMillan's front steps and at a formal meeting.

Throwing his cohorts into the battle with his usual enthusiasm, Gardiner took to flying to save time,[45] and he enjoyed the experience immensely. The details of the effort no longer have much relevance, but the results foreshadowed the next years of the province's political history: Liberal 5,926, CCF 4,312, Conservative 1,541, United Front (Communist) 713.

Gardiner saw Mackenzie as he saw all elections: organization and conviction were the twin pillars on which he based his attitude towards his role in opposition. It did not matter in which order one named them, since either was useless without the other.

9

A Government in Depression

Anderson's first speech from the throne, read by the lieutenant-governor on 6 February 1930, was a brave document.[1] It did not attempt to minimize the seriousness of unemployment and poor crops, but opened with references to them. It then proceeded through other major topics, most of which Anderson touched on in debate. In speaking to the address in reply, Anderson devoted more time to education than any other subject. Gardiner interrupted him frequently; he had been Anderson's immediate predecessor in the education department and was inclined to chafe under Anderson's comments on the political influences he claimed to have found in it. Anderson's summation of his first major address as premier concluded with a barb aimed at Gardiner, pointing out that he himself and Howard McConnell for four years 'sat as members for the City of Saskatoon and not on one single occasion were we asked to accompany a delegation to the Government.' I want opposition members, he said, 'to feel free to come to this Government and I will assure them they will not be penalized the way we were while we were on the opposition benches.'[2] Gardiner, who believed that merely being a Tory penalized a man, said nothing.

Since Anderson left no personal papers apart from letters saved in others' correspondence, it is not possible to assess how difficult and frustrating, and ultimately destructive, he found the cares of office. But despite drought and depression, his government was a productive one which, through heroic effort, did accomplish something. Its inquiries into the alleged sins of the Liberal administration may have been largely abortive, and its educational reforms aimed at problems which Gardiner regarded as non-existent. But it did much more than that. It successfully completed the acquisition of the province's natural resources. The

Anderson government, while finding rocketing debt and dwindling reserves a deterrent to highways and public works programs, strove valiantly at least to maintain standards for health, welfare, and education, and even managed a few innovations: a Cancer Commission; a School for the Deaf; a Public Service Commission. The Saskatchewan Relief Commission, set up in 1932, did work. Although ceaselessly denounced by Gardiner as a body of political workers, the commission in 1933–34 alone assisted families totalling 213,367 persons, moved 632 carloads of settlers' effects in relocation efforts, and transported 953 carloads of animals to better grazing.[3] Anderson's government was one that in happier circumstances might well have left an enviable record.

The environment it had to work in, and the record it produced, made great days for an opposition party. Anderson displayed considerable skill in keeping his own supporters in the legislature loyal to him under trying pressures, and the only major assault on his leadership came from a group of 'True Blue Conservatives' opposed to the coalition behind the Co-operative Government. In 1932 the provincial president denounced Anderson's policies at the party's annual convention and was repudiated. In 1933 he returned to the attack and Anderson, after resigning as leader, was re-elected in a convincing show of strength.[4] At no time, either in the legislature or out, does Anderson's pre-eminence as leader of his party and head of the Co-operative Government seem to have been in jeopardy; and that was an impressive vote of confidence.

The Liberals did not join in it. It was Gardiner's view that Anderson's reaffirmation as leader of the Conservatives was proof that the Co-operative Government was a Tory administration in disguise, and as such to be pilloried. Anderson had barely been in office a month before Gardiner told an audience at Shaunavon that 'the new Government has violated every pledge ... made to the electorate.'[5] That statement, made before the Anderson administration had even met the legislature, was typical of one side of the Liberals' implacable hostility to it. For the period 1929–34 one could document dozens of speeches at meetings all over the province at which Gardiner and his colleagues spoke ill of the government. Yet in the total collection there is nothing more revealing than the single statement quoted above. An opposition's function in a parliamentary system was to oppose, and Gardiner's Liberals were as loyal to him in that purpose as Anderson's supporters were to him.

Inside the legislature, both the rules and custom aided the Liberals' cause. Anderson innocently assisted them in several ways. Both before the legislature met in 1930 and in his first major speech in it, he insisted that 'one of the conditions upon which co-operation was decided upon was that no appeal would be made to the people of this province except where the government has been defeated on a straight vote of "want of confidence." '[6] That gave the opposition two potential tactics: they were free to belabour the government with no danger of precipitating an unwanted election as long as they moved no direct confidence vote; and they could confine their motions of confidence either to topics on which they knew they could not topple the government, or to topics on which they would like to defeat the government, and at the very least force Anderson's supporters on the record on issues selected by the Liberals. Then in the autumn of 1931 Anderson announced that no general election would occur before the end of the legislature's regular life. There is no evidence that Gardiner, convinced that his party could govern better than the Anderson forces, would not have welcomed an election any day, but Anderson's announcement left him free to demand an election at any time over any issue he chose; and he did.[7] Handled well, a challenge to the government could make an opposition look good.

Legislative procedure also gave the Liberals ample scope to harry the government. The annual debates on the address in reply to the speech from the throne and the provincial treasurer's budget speech, about two weeks later, were by custom free-wheeling discussions during which any opposition member could bring up almost anything he had on his mind. Since the throne speech always had to mention relief and unemployment, and the budget cite rising debt and sometimes new taxes, both debates were made to order for an aggressive opposition. An experienced debater, Gardiner knew that every bill introduced by the government gave the opposition a selection of routes for criticism. If the Liberals approved a proposal, they were always free to argue that the government was pursuing a desirable goal the wrong way. If they disapproved, they could oppose it both in principle and in detail as fiercely or as casually as sound tactics suggested. Often, as with the return of the natural resources, electrical power, or debt adjustment, they could demonstrate that a worthwhile policy had begun under a Liberal government, while Anderson's attempts to carry it further could be variously said to constitute too little too late, or the weakening of a desirable established practice, or what the Liberals had been doing all along anyway. Occasionally, as with education and the creation of a civil service commission to implement a merit system, they could argue that the reform brought in by Anderson was to solve a problem manufactured for electioneering purposes and, in the case of the public service, brought in after the patronage system had been allowed to replace several hundred Liberal appointees with Conservatives. Gardiner also noted that one of the Government's major creations, the Saskatchewan Relief Commission, was set up outside the Public Service Act.

The Liberals were often able to bolster their charges with facts elicited from the government in the House. Unlike a premier with a majority drawn from his own party, Anderson was not in a position to refuse to answer some damaging questions, or give evasive answers to others, since his own supporters (over whom he made no overt attempt to wield the usual legislative whip) included members as curious as the Liberals over what his cabinet was up to. Apart from schools and the public service, the Liberals established that at least some highway contracts were let without tender after 9 September 1929, and that nearly 40 per cent of the firms that had received highway contracts in 1930 had never had a contract with the department before. Another return showed that while a higher proportion of printing was purchased by tender by the King's Printer in each year from 1930–31 to 1933–34 than in 1929–30, the non-tendered total always substantially exceeded the tendered.[8]

The Liberals' use of questions and motions for returns was in truth phenomenal. One hundred and sixteen questions were asked in the House in Gardiner's last year as premier, an election year, and four hundred and twenty-four in 1931, the peak year for questions in Anderson's regime. Returns ordered totalled nine in 1929, and seventy-eight in 1931, and recorded formal divisions rose from five in 1929 to a peak of twenty-eight in 1932.[9] In 1930 especially, Anderson's own supporters added to the statistics, for they were full of queries about Gardiner's management of the government; but as the legislature's life ran on, the Liberals took over. Their task was facilitated by mere numbers, for after 1929 they constituted the largest opposition the legislature had ever seen. They also knew exactly what information to seek, and contrived to present a portrait of Anderson's supporters which looked as if he was backed by an organization remarkably like the despised Gardiner machine, only less efficient. By comparison, the ebullient T.C. Davis observed to Gardiner, 'the Patronage System is in full swing. I am going to demand all letters from Diefenbaker here re appointments,' (a motion he did not in the event present) adding that the Liberal machine had been but 'a toy engine' compared with the Co-operative. (Of Diefenbaker, his opponent in 1929, Davis later wrote that 'his proper place would be as a third-rate vaudeville performer in a four-a-day vaudeville house.')[10]

The legislative committees, always a lively part of the Saskatchewan assembly, provided yet another forum for the Liberals. The committees were in one way less useful than the legislature, for their deliberations were more narrowly focused and not always as fully reported. But they were smaller than the whole House and, in a period when the cabinet's majority was neither large nor drawn entirely from one party, easier for the opposition, with all its experienced members, to manipulate. The Liberals' most important committee victory was the repudiation of the Weston report on the Farm Loan Board by the Committee on Public Accounts, of which Gardiner was a member. There were some signal defeats; but even then the opposition could usually get on the record a division over some issue in which victory for the government was not an unequivocal benefit. (One Gardiner motion was defeated by the passage of an amendment from the government side that was almost absurdly irrelevant, and when the Liberals returned to power in 1934 they expunged it from the assembly's journal.)[11] Even when the government agreed with the opposition, Gardiner was able to find issues to embarrass Anderson because they obliged him as a Saskatchewan premier to oppose the federal Conservatives. Thus motions in favour of British preference in trade, presented by the Liberals and opposed to the expressed views of R.B. Bennett, passed the legislature by majorities as large as sixty-one to one and fifty-seven to none.[12] After 1929, in short, Gardiner offered a prototype for any leader of the opposition.

Anderson can hardly have been surprised by Gardiner's manoeuvrings over possible coalitions that might have lightened the burdens of the Co-operative Government. The first suggestion of coalition, and the only one Gardiner took seriously, would indeed have kept those burdens at zero, for in the early weeks following the election of 1929 he did have to consider the certainty that whoever was to be premier would have to be supported by a coalition. Even when all three groups opposing the Liberals had proclaimed their union, there remained one major imponderable: one of the ablest among them, M.J. Coldwell, was not in the legislature, and it was Gardiner's understanding that Coldwell was utterly opposed to a coalition of his group with any other.

The behind-the-scenes activities which developed over discussions with Coldwell, and in due course with Anderson, took on a comic opera atmosphere familiar to anybody who has watched human beings trying

̦otiate a settlement on matters over which they are deeply divided. One side has to take the initiative and that, to minimize early concessions or signs of weakness, has to be done as obliquely as possible. The other side, assessing the approach with a different set of assumptions and expectations, hears it assigning its own meaning to key words. The two separate with divergent interpretations of what has transpired. Subsequently, their memories having refined the interpretations further, they are publicly accusing each other of misrepresentation and worse, the initiator stoutly denying that any offer, concession, or promise was made, the other insisting that he was tendered a specific benefit which he refused. Both sides are right throughout. That is precisely what happened in the Liberals' approaches to Coldwell.

Part of the misunderstanding arose because Gardiner forgot one important fact. Writing to a trusted associate, Tom Wood, Gardiner asserted: 'The fact is that no offer was ever made to Mr. Coldwell direct or indirect to enter a Liberal Government.'[13] Coldwell nevertheless told a meeting, reported in the *Regina Leader Post* on 6 January 1933, that in 1929 an emissary of Gardiner's, whom he identified as a man of unquestionable integrity, had offered him the office of minister of education. Gardiner replied that he did not doubt Coldwell's word, but that he had no recollection of either the emissary or the offer. The emissary, who turned out to be P.M. Anderson, a well-known Liberal lawyer, confirmed to Gardiner that he had, in the heat of immediate post-election affairs, gone from Gardiner to Coldwell as an envoy, but that he had merely canvassed possibilities with Coldwell, and made no specific offer.[14]

The whole episode might have remained hidden had not the formation of the Farmer-Labour party and later the CCF changed the picture in the legislature. (The Farmer-Labour party, which grew out of a unanimous resolution in favour of direct political action passed by the United Farmers of Canada, Saskatchewan Section, in February 1930, became the provincial arm of the CCF, formed in 1932.) Both parties were viewed with suspicion by Gardiner, because they seemed to be extensions under fresh names of the old Progressive factions. This led him to underestimate both the needs the parties sought to meet and the quality of their leaders. If socialism was desirable in the province, he told an avid young left-wing supporter early in 1933, 'it is well to remember ... that the Liberal Party is the only socialistic party in Saskatchewan.' Its record included co-operative elevators and creameries, farm loans, hail insurance, a government telephone system, municipal health and hospital units, free tuberculosis treatment, maternity grants, old age pensions, mother's allowances, control of tuberculosis in cattle. 'Its policies called for unemployment insurance, extensions of state medicine, debt adjustment, and centralized state issue of currency.'[15]

A year later he reminded the same correspondent that the ideal of the Liberal party 'is the greatest good to the greatest number ... If individuals like Mr. Coldwell pretending reform strike off to satisfy personal ambitions it only weakens the force of reform.'[16] He had a similar opinion of other early left-wing politicians: Salem Bland, the crusading theologian, and J.S. Woodsworth, of whose work with the foreign-born J.T.M. Anderson had spoken highly in his book,[17] had, Gardiner said, 'a record which will not bear investigation. Irwin [William Irvine, who sat in the Commons for the UFA] and Coldwell are just followers of these two clerics who have had altogether too much of their own way.' He wondered why 'no one reminds Woodsworth of the fact that he has never done a days [sic] work since he ceased to make use of the training the church gave him free of charge.'[18]

That singular view of Woodsworth's accomplishments carried over to Gardiner's appraisal of the Regina Manifesto, which he dismissed as 'the most ridiculous piece of political literature put out by any party.'[19] Nonetheless, its authors and their supporters were public men, and had to be dealt with. Thus, when the Farmer-Labour group was created, and attracted the loyalty of many former Progressives (two of whom took the new party's name in the legislature in 1933 but continued to support Anderson), it occurred to Gardiner that the time was ripe to see Coldwell again. Gardiner always distinguished clearly between the Farmer-Labour party, which he saw as purely provincial, and the CCF, which sought national status. The role of the former seemed inconsistent with continued support of the Anderson government. He noted with interest its vigour in organizing, which early made him see it as the possible party to beat in the next election. By 1933, however, he advised a trusty colleague that 'I feel that the Conservative party because of their funds are likely to be our real opposition after all.'[20] Yet eighteen months earlier he had seen Coldwell to discuss the potentialities latent in a legislative defeat of the Co-operative Government.

Once again Coldwell and Gardiner had widely differing versions of what transpired. Coldwell's view was that he had again been offered a cabinet post, Gardiner's was that he had seen Coldwell in his capacity as spokesman for a group whose role might conceivably involve defeating

Anderson and then helping form a new administration without a general election. Gardiner was always clear that he had not offered Coldwell a portfolio. If a defeat for Anderson were followed by the formation of a Liberal-Farmer-Labour cabinet, Gardiner said, he would not select the individual(s) who represented Coldwell's group nor, if the Farmer-Labour group named Coldwell, would he have any part in finding him a seat. Coldwell (who claimed to be courted also by Conservatives and, like Gardiner, thought by late 1932 that an election should be held), received extensive newspaper coverage of his wooing by the Liberals, and when Gardiner countered it went out of his way to emphasize of Gardiner, 'I have disagreed with him in the past but I have respected him as I usually respect honourable opponents.' But now, Coldwell added, he wondered if a man with such a poor memory could be trusted to recall his promises.

Gardiner, for his part, also expressed a low opinion of Coldwell's recollections, but cheerfully admitted that he had always tried to make a convert of him. The whole controversy became so absurd that finally in February 1933 the two got together. Afterwards Gardiner drafted a statement which included an admission that he had forgotten sending P.M. Anderson to see Coldwell in 1929: 'I could not recall this gentleman being authorized by me to see him upon this particular mission but if the gentleman stated it to be so there could be no doubt about it. I saw the gentleman in question and after talking to him could remember the incident and shall now set down the particulars.' Coldwell suggested that everybody now shut up about it; thus ended the Gardiner-Coldwell non-coalition.[21]

The same could not be said of the action on the Gardiner-Anderson front. Where Coldwell was not even a member of the legislature, Anderson was premier and negotiations between him and Gardiner thus took a different form. As head of a government supported by at least some Progressives, Anderson would almost certainly know of the Gardiner-Coldwell connection of 1929, and he could hardly have missed its subsequent exposé in the press. By that time the *Saskatchewan Liberal* had begun to appear, and in its first issue Gardiner had written: 'It is a time when the best brains and best thought of all forward looking groups should be brought together in a spirit of cooperation and helpfulness, under the highest ideals of Patriotism, yes, and of Religion, that we might triumph over trials and tribulations.'[23] But if Anderson thought Gardiner might be amenable to some sort of coalition under the right circumstances, he did not read his *Saskatchewan Liberal* carefully enough.

Gardiner did not include Conservatives in 'all forward looking groups,' and his message was not addressed to Tories.

Nevertheless, Anderson early brought up the subject of coalition, and all the initiatives came from him. His first steps towards it came with the proposal, made publicly on 23 July 1931, that all political partisanship be set aside for twelve months until 'this period of human suffering is over.'[23] That optimism was gone by the time the year was up, and in the late summer of 1932 Anderson's minister of highways, A.C. Stewart, approached two former Liberal ministers, Gardiner and T.C. Davis, and Charles McIntosh, the member for Kinistino, with a series of unusual offers, none of which he had the authority to make. Dr J.M. Uhrich, who had been minister of health from 1922 to 1929, sent his chief an undated note in 1932 which said that on or about 1 September he had called on McIntosh and 'he informed me that some time previous he met the Hon. Carl Stewart [who] asked him to enter the Saskatchewan Government as a Minister ... Mr. McIntosh said that he was considering the matter.' Early in September Gardiner was waited upon by Stewart at the farm, and Gardiner at once reported a startling suggestion to King: 'Mr. Stewart ... offered me the Presidency of the University with the suggestion that if I would accept it they were prepared to take three of my ex-ministers into the government.'

W.J. Patterson, the MLA who was to succeed Gardiner as premier in 1935, was at the farm when Stewart called, and heard of the offer, which included other curious options. Stewart and Gardiner conspiratorially sat outside in a car while the offer was heard, after which Gardiner and Patterson drove the nine miles west to W.R. Motherwell's farm, where the party's president and secretary had gathered for a conference. The entire Liberal top brass thus knew of the offer, and the one absent member, T.C. Davis, was shortly informed in his own way through yet another offer. Gardiner soon heard from Prince Albert that the indefatigable Stewart had also spoken to Davis. He swore Davis to such secrecy that the latter felt reluctant even to tell Gardiner about it, although he had told Stewart he could do nothing without the sanction of his leader and the party. Stewart, expressing indignation over all the broken confidences, denied stoutly that he had made any offers to anybody, but three eyewitnesses, writing independently from widely separated points, all recorded that he did.[24] Later, Anderson heard of Stewart's odyssey with considerable surprise.[25]

By that time Anderson himself had begun serious attempts to get some Liberals, with or without Gardiner, into a coalition. Even while

Stewart was on his rounds, Anderson had in Winnipeg made a statement remarkably similar to Gardiner's message in the *Saskatchewan Liberal*. Not long after, he appeared to believe that neither Coldwell nor Gardiner would ever join him, but he did invite Liberal MLAS to do so.[26] Nonetheless, on 7 November 1932 he sent Gardiner a note asking for 'a confidential talk.'[27]

Gardiner replied from the farm on 11 November in fairly stiff terms, telling Anderson of Stewart's offer of the university presidency (which was, incidentally, not vacant, but filled by a man who greatly admired Gardiner), of other approaches to himself and others about some rearranging of the government, and declined to have any talk in confidence. Anderson wrote again on 19 November, this time expressing his desire to see Gardiner about the possibility of the government and opposition 'uniting in the interests of our province.' The two met the next day, Anderson pressing for coalition and Gardiner proposing what he called 'the Baldwin-MacDonald arrangement at the end of the first Labor Government in Great Britain.' By that he meant that the Liberals would be co-operative about relief and debt adjustment, since there were no serious differences between their respective parties on either the problems or the solutions; and that being the case, the two sides could co-operate without coalition. To ensure co-operation, Gardiner proposed that a committee chosen from the Liberals would sit with some of Anderson's ministers 'to settle upon legislation and votes immediately necessary to deal with the present situation,' after which, following the British precedent, an election would be necessary at the end of the session in which the two parties had collaborated. Anderson was to take that proposal to his caucus and come back to Gardiner with a definite proposal, either of coalition or a committee such as Gardiner proposed.[28]

Whether Anderson met his caucus at once is not clear, but he made the meeting at least temporarily irrelevant by going to Winnipeg to make a speech to a Conservative gathering which was apparently intended to make his position public. His proposal for coalition, he said, 'had been turned down by the Liberals who had countered with an offer of a truce for the winter on condition an election were held next summer. These terms the Premier refused and negotiations were broken.' He added that there 'will be no election until July or August, 1934.'[29] Gardiner understandably took the reports to mean that negotiations were now over, and made a formal statement to the press on 19 December summarizing events as he understood them.

Gardiner's press statement ended with a sharp personal reference: 'If Dr. Anderson is properly reported from Winnipeg he has proved that his political opponents cannot afford to treat him with the courtesy which his position would otherwise command.'[30] Anderson was sufficiently exercised by the statement that he responded the day it appeared. He reminded Gardiner that he had been speaking to a Conservative club, at which he was 'sure there was no press representative.' The newspaper story, whatever its source, 'was exceedingly distorted.' Anderson's response was obviously meant to be conciliatory, but he could not resist reminding Gardiner that their understanding included undertakings by Gardiner that (a) he would get in touch with the premier after returning from a meeting in the east, and (b) he would refrain from holding public meetings apart from one already scheduled. Gardiner had done neither.[31]

Gardiner's reply, seven times as long as Anderson's letter, dealt seriatim with every point the premier had raised, and several he had not. The exchange between the two warriors became one more of those 'you said – I did not' passages which revealed nothing more clearly than that two honest men were in disagreement and neither intended to back down. Anderson at least tried to keep his letters short but the leader of the opposition, with less to preoccupy him, mercilessly recorded every detail. Anderson emphasized that he did not seek coalition to get legislation through, but on principle 'because I think it is in the best interests of this Province that it should be consummated.'[32]

Gardiner declined to offer any new initiatives. 'I would hesitate,' he said, 'to express views which might be interpreted as inviting myself and collagues [sic] into a government ... You are in a position, as Premier, to make definite proposals regarding coalition.' That last statement was in accord with Gardiner's view of responsible government: a responsible minister accepted responsibility, and there was no way a leader of the opposition could take steps to alter the personnel of a cabinet. 'State clearly to us,' he urged Anderson on 29 December 1932, 'the matters which a coalition is to be formed to deal with, the nature of the coalition to deal with them, and the support which such a proposal can obtain from your side of the House, and I will immediately be prepared to place the proposal before the Liberal party and transmit to you their answer.'[33]

Anderson thought it unreasonable of Gardiner to refuse to divulge his own and the party's views on coalition, but agreed that the next step was a proposal from himself as head of the government. In a letter of

12 January 1933, which explicitly denied that any minister or anybody else had been authorized by himself or the cabinet to make offers of cabinet posts to Liberals, he requested of Gardiner: 'Will you kindly place before your Council my request that I be advised as to the attitude of the Liberal members of the Legislature on the matter of coalition ... I should like the Council to feel at liberty if they so wish, to have one or more of its members meet me with a view to discussing the situation.'[34] Anderson concluded with a parting shot: the statement that Gardiner had been offered the presidency of the university was 'ridiculous on the surface,' and he refused to discuss it. Gardiner agreed it was ridiculous, but true nonetheless.

The premier's offer was promptly transmitted to members of the Liberal executive, and duly considered by the party's council at a meeting in Regina in January 1933. The Liberals' answer, not surprisingly, was rejection. Their reply on 25 January 1933, recited six 'whereas' clauses which variously claimed that the premier had in fact made no offer and had insisted he could carry on without coalition, that the two parties 'are so fundamentally opposed one to the other as to make compromise impossible,' that the legislature's life was soon to end and it was advisable to seek a fresh mandate, and that the Liberal MLAs 'have always been and are now willing to co-operate with the Government in all necessary measures for the welfare and good government of the Province.' Anderson may have had his doubts about that, but he could have had none about the resolution's operative clause: 'Therefore be it resolved that this Council is of the opinion that coalition is not in the best interests of the Province.' Anderson acknowledged receipt of the resolution, observing that it 'will obviate the necessity of placing before you a concrete proposal setting forth the conditions of any coalition, a course which I should have followed had your council expressed a willingness to consider coalition in the interests of our Province.'[35]

The coalition negotiations, such as they were, were over. It was natural that Gardiner and his colleagues were accused of putting party ahead of province, as was M.J. Coldwell. But Gardiner was being loyal to some of his most cherished beliefs. It was true that he saw no purpose in 1933 in boarding a ship that was so obviously foundering, although he saw a certain consistency in that too: Tories in trouble, he often averred, always turn to coalition. But coalition between two forces so opposite as the Liberals and Conservatives, he was convinced, could never work: 'Coalitions always become spending machines because they cannot agree on anything other than spending themselves into popularity.'[36]

If negotiations over coalition were over, neither Gardiner nor Anderson was quite through with related manoeuvres. Gardiner put down on the order paper a resolution calling for a committee of five MLAs, three to be chosen from the cabinet by the government and two from the opposition by the Liberals, to confer on having legislation introduced 'upon Debt Adjustment, Tax Consolidation and other matters arising out of the depression, which will meet with the unanimous approval of the members.' Anderson and his caucus objected to it, for while they appreciated the proffered co-operation they thought the committee was too small to be fair to all the groups on the government's side. On 8 February the premier suggested instead a committee of fifteen (five members each from the Conservatives, the Liberals, and the remaining parties), of which three would be ministers. The Liberals countered the next day with a conditional acceptance of Anderson's suggestion, but reiterated that Gardiner's committee of five was the better way 'whereby the news of one caucus can be transmitted to the other until a common conclusion is reached.' The ignoring of the Independents and Progressives was deliberate, for by 1933 the Liberals were insisting that the Co-operative Government was a straight Tory government aligned with Bennett and protectionism, and as a united opposition they were not prepared to take the initiative in any official recognition of the lesser parties supporting Anderson.[37]

Gardiner's resolution, seconded by T.C. Davis, reached the debate stage on 13 February, and Anderson at once moved an amendment for the formal select special committee of fifteen he had already proposed to Gardiner. His amendment would have had the committee confer on 'Debt Adjustment, Tax Consolidation, Relief, Unemployment and other matters arising out of the depression, with a view to examining legislation introduced by the Government and suggesting amendments thereto, if such are thought necessary.' The Liberals at once objected that Anderson's amendment was a whole new motion, and therefore out of order. The Speaker sustained the objection and the government substituted a second amendment which, without altering the substance of the one ruled out of order, reduced the membership to ten, four each from the Conservatives and Liberals and two from the rest. That too was objected to and the debate was adjourned without a division. The protagonists then had a meeting, as a result of which both Gardiner's resolution and the second amendment were withdrawn and Gardiner, seconded by Anderson, moved:

That, in view of the abnormal conditions existing in the Province, a Committee be named, four to be chosen from the Conservative group, four from the Liberal

Opposition and three from the other groups in the House, which will confer from time to time upon legislation relating to Debt Adjustment, Tax Consolidation, and other matters arising out of the depression, with a view to securing, if possible, unanimous approval of any such legislation.

The resolution passed unanimously, and the efforts it had called forth exhausted the combatants. The committee, if it ever met, left no trace even of the names of its members.[38]

But Anderson had not exhausted his attempts to get at least some Liberals on his side. Consistent in the course he had followed since becoming premier, he kept issuing public invitations to MLAS not supporting the government to do so, and in 1933 his activities culminated in an offer of a cabinet post to Charles McIntosh, who had been dithering over his position to such an extent that by December it was Gardiner's opinion that it hardly mattered what he did.[39] That was partly because McIntosh, who had on occasion voted independently of the Liberals, had been the only opposition MLA to respond openly in late 1932 to a blanket invitation from Anderson to support the government. The other Liberals, in response to a questionnaire sent out from party headquarters, had stayed solidly loyal, but McIntosh had written a letter to the press which, while not revealing his own intentions, pleaded with the two party leaders to bury their differences in the common interest.[40]

Finally, at the opening of the legislative session in 1933, McIntosh crossed the floor to support the government, and on 23 April, well after the end of the session, he became Anderson's minister of natural resources, a portfolio held until then by the premier. A by-election to confirm him in his office of emolument was still necessary, for while the ancient practice of having new cabinet members seek re-election *en masse* had been abolished in 1930, anybody joining the executive more than six months after a general election still had to seek confirmation. In any event, the circumstances in which McIntosh became a minister made it politically desirable to test the electorate's opinion of coalition, which Anderson was anxious to do. The Kinistino by-election of 22 May 1933, like that in Arm River in 1928, became one of those epochal contests that foretell the future.

The seat, which lay in rolling parkland south-east of Prince Albert, had been considerably altered by a provincial redistribution in 1932, but the new boundaries did not take effect until the next general election. The Liberals sought somewhat half-heartedly to make the redistribution itself an issue when they asserted, not without justification, that the redistribution had been a gerrymander. They themselves, paradoxically, despite their reputation as operators of a party machine, had never been widely accused of gerrymandering: that was not because of any special virtue but because their majorities in most legislatures had been so large that a flagrant redrawing of boundaries would have affected Liberals.

What particularly irked the opposition in 1933 was that Anderson proposed as an economy measure to cut the membership of the legislature from sixty-three to fifty-five and, although that involved changing many boundaries, refused to accept a motion of Gardiner's to refer the map to a committee. The Conservatives were not themselves in a position to force a map to their own advantage without considering their other supporters, but all the groups on the government side were concerned less about Liberal seats. Of ten constituencies that bordered on Alberta, for example, five went Liberal in 1929. When redistribution in 1933 cut the total to eight, the seats least touched were those held by three Conservatives and a Progressive. The two Liberal seats of Maple Creek and Happyland, divided horizontally since 1916 into a north and south riding along a parallel of latitude, were divided vertically in 1933 by a north-south line. Seven seats on the American border were reduced to six, and the two least affected were the corner seats, both held by Conservatives. The two northern seats of Ile à la Crosse and Cumberland, both Liberal, were thrown into one huge riding covering the northern half of the province. Almost wherever one looks at the before-and-after maps, the reduction in the legislature's size appeared to be at the expense of Liberals: of seventeen seats sufficiently altered to justify abandoning their old names, fourteen had elected Liberals in 1929. Anderson himself indirectly confirmed the intent of the redistribution: in the Winnipeg speech already cited, he said: 'They fought our measures every inch of the way so for good measure we put through a redistribution bill.'[41]

It was a good issue for the hustings, and given other times would have been useful; as it was, its main accomplishment was to set a precedent for another redistribution, this time under Liberal auspices, in 1938. What was uppermost in all activists' minds in 1933 in Kinistino was coalition, both in principle and as embodied in McIntosh's own record as a defector. McIntosh himself underlined his position by insisting that he was still a Liberal and running as such. He was opposed only by another Liberal, J.R.G. Taylor, who had taken the seat in 1917 and 1921, so that the electors, who had given the party large majorities since the election of 1912, could only refrain from voting if they did not want to vote Liberal. They chose to vote, and in the largest turnout to date McIntosh, who had taken the seat by 3,193 to 2,361 in 1929, lost by 4,186 to 2,163 in 1933.[42]

It was a stunning vindication of Gardiner's refusal to accept coalition which, with his usual confidence, he had anticipated. He told Mackenzie King three weeks before polling day that he had 'reports from all parts of the constituency this morning which will indicate that we can win the seat.' The one aspect of the campaign which rather surprised Gardiner was that his extensive campaigning in Kinistino, a farming area, had led him at first to expect strong support for McIntosh from those who sympathized with the Farmer-Labour party. Instead, the 'radicals' voted Liberal:

At Liberty Hall, which has been recognized as one of the more Communistic communities in the province for many years, the vote was 87 to 18 in our favour. Mr. Motherwell will be able to tell you that when he spoke there in '21 they raised the red flag and sung [sic] the Red Flag and refused to sing God Save the King. They invited me to a meeting on the second last night of my campaign ... and sang God Save the King more heartily than any other audience.[43]

To Gardiner the Kinistino triumph was a signal to start at once completing the provincial nominating conventions for the next election and a powerful stimulus to start work for the forthcoming federal by-election in Mackenzie, which embraced a good deal of the provincial seat. To McIntosh it was the end of the road. To Anderson, Kinistino was the end of any stray remaining hopes he might have had for coalition. He continued to talk of it; as late as March 1934 he told a radio audience somewhat wistfully that he would have preferred a cessation of party welfare, but made clear that with a man like Gardiner, who would not even support the wartime coalition of 1917, that was impossible.[44]

Kinistino, late in May, was for Anderson's government the disastrous prelude to one more disastrous summer of heat, drought, and grasshoppers, and after that, one last disheartening session of the legislature. That March an agricultural paper had reported that the payment of interest due on Saskatchewan's farm debt alone would require 'about four-fifths of all wheat available for sale from the 1933 crop.' The wheat crop in the summer of Kinistino was the smallest since 1920, but it still provided 74 per cent of the revenue derived from farm products.[45] Four years of living with facts such as those were enough to break any government, and Anderson's handsome face was beginning to show unmistakable signs of strain.

Gardiner, by contrast, after Kinistino began to think as if his period in opposition was already over. Should W.R. Motherwell, who had more than once been spoken of as nursing the federal seat of Melville until Gardiner was ready for it, be brought back into the provincial cabinet? Or should he, at seventy-three, be persuaded to retire altogether? If Gardiner went to Ottawa in King's new cabinet, who should succeed him in Saskatchewan? Thoughts like that were in Gardiner's mind during the bleak winter of 1933–34, and they were not the preoccupations of a man dismayed by years of drought and grasshoppers, or depression and opposition.

10

Triumph

Gardiner was so sure of victory in the forthcoming provincial election that in December 1933 he told a friend that the children did not want to move back to Regina 'next year.' In the same letter he denounced the platform of the CCF as unadulterated nonsense, observing that 'if we have many more experiments in this western country under the name of farmer governments we will all have to move out.' He had not yet received any literature on Social Credit, but with his usual eye for possible opponents he had asked William Aberhart to send him some; when Aberhart obliged (charging twenty cents for the pamphlets), Gardiner concluded that the sound parts of Social Credit were already in the Liberal platform, and he approved in general terms the reliance on private enterprise for production, on governmental issue of currency, and a proposal for unemployment insurance.[1]

The kindly view of Social Credit that Gardiner took at first was not to survive long, as rumours of anti-Liberal alliances among socialists and Social Crediters began to reach him. Some early CCF supporters did toy with Social Credit theories, but there was also some understandable confusion over the names which identified the movements, not to mention the prominence of a man named Douglas in each. As long as it was untested at the polls, Social Credit had an air of anti-capitalist respectability that did not immediately alienate supporters of the CCF, some of whom in Alberta helped encourage the importation of Major Douglas. The socialist leaders in Saskatchewan, like Gardiner himself (who refused public debates with M.J. Coldwell and T.C. Douglas in 1933 partly because he did not want to appear to champion capitalism against socialism) naturally wooed voters wherever they could be found. The anti-Semitism with which Social Credit was later associated had not yet surfaced and Gardiner, as honorary vice president of the Hebrew Liberal Association, was more inclined to attribute the stirring up of anti-Semitism to the CCF. Coldwell, unwisely in Gardiner's view, had taken several organizers with Jewish names into the Kinistino by-election, and thus unnecessarily aroused among the conservative electorate feelings that had not been apparent before.[2] Soon Gardiner felt bound to take into account the Deutsche Bund, whose activities were not wholly repugnant to Liberals of German extraction.[3]

In 1933–34 that ominous development was still a few years away on the prairies. As 1934 began, Gardiner knew he had at least one more legislative session as leader of the opposition, for Anderson kept insisting that no election would be held before the constitution required it. That meant that the 1934 session would be the first to be held under the certainty that it would be followed by an election, for the only previous legislature to run well into the final year of its legal life, that of 1912–17, might have been extended had wartime conditions justified it.

The 1934 session, if the Liberal platform of 1931 meant what it said, was also likely to be the last held under the one-man one-vote system: the party's policy said simply, 'the Liberal Party is in favor of the single transferable ballot,'[4] by which it presumably meant a ballot on which the elector, instead of voting with a single x, ranked the candidates by voting 1-2-3, and so on. There is no evidence in Gardiner's papers that he or anybody else had worked out what full proportional representation would mean: had it applied in 1929 they would have won the same number of seats that they did. Early in 1933 Gardiner suggested pushing for the transferable ballot, but the reason he gave was not related to voting, but the tactical one of preventing M.J. Coldwell's supporters from seizing the initiative 'in proposing advanced measures to the house.'[5]

Gardiner was not ordinarily inclined to tinker with established institutions, and it may be doubted if he or the Liberals fully grasped what they were pledged to. When on 17 March 1932 two Progressive members moved 'that the single transferable ballot should be used in Provincial Elections in all constituencies where more than two candidates have been nominated,' both Gardiner and Anderson supporters joined in defeating it by thirty-six to twelve. On 9 March 1933 the same Progressives repeated their motion, adding 'that in plural member constituencies proportional representation be made applicable.' That time Gardiner and his party, together with Independents and Progressives and two Conservatives, supported the proposal and it passed. Nothing came of the motion, but it is of some historical interest: it could have helped only those who opposed it, and hurt only its chief supporters. The Liberals, who may have thought they were simply favouring preferential voting, took no action when they returned to power.

The regular session of 1934, summoned to meet on 15 February, was preceded by a meeting of an ebullient Liberal caucus scenting victory. Anderson's last speech from the throne, though showing the scars of his five-year struggle against practically everything, was a measured document which, while citing familiar facts about drought, relief, unemployment, tax arrears, and debt adjustment, still included some bright assurances and some major new policies. The public health programs had been maintained. The shipping season through the Hudson Bay route had been nearly doubled, and Lloyds of London, after direct negotiations, had reduced marine insurance rates by a third. Four thousand settlers had been assisted into the north, and the unsuitable lands they had abandoned were to be studied for uses other than farming; a forestry commission was to be established to examine the possibilities of reforesting the waste lands. The speech also announced plans to study the conservation of run-off water through the use of dams and natural basins where feasible. The Prairie Farm Rehabilitation Act, with which Gardiner's name was to become inextricably associated, was, ironically, conceived by his ablest provincial opponent.[6]

Although Gardiner and Anderson collaborated on a vote of thanks to those outside Saskatchewan for assistance sent to alleviate the results of drought and depression, and they were on the same side in several divisions, their togetherness was limited to issues settled by overwhelming majorities. Their only partisan significance, where there was any, turned on a negative consideration: useful steps to enhance the public weal could be criticized, but not opposed by any party aware that the next election was only weeks away. The Liberals lost two votes of want of confidence in the government, the first a general one, the second a more specific condemnation of the government's failure to accept the lower tender in sundry purchases, and otherwise throwing money away.[7]

The single issue which most roused Gardiner during the session was one not even hinted at in the speech from the throne. Early in March Anderson proposed, in two simple bills, to abolish the position of minister of education (which he himself held), and put all school administration under a commission of three. He likened his proposals to the system in Nova Scotia, which had no single minister of education but assigned

the entire cabinet a role on educational matters, with a provincial superintendent of education, appointed by the lieutenant-governor-in-council but removable only by the legislature.

It is possible that Anderson expected the Liberals to support his bills,
for their platform said: 'Resolved, that the Department of Education
should be so administered as to remove the discussion of school matters
entirely from partizan political controversy.' That sounds unequivocal
enough, and it *was* unequivocal if one understood what it meant: 'partizan political controversy' was what Anderson and his supporters had
stirred up in 1928–29, while non-partisan educational administration
was what the Liberals claimed to have provided from 1905 to 1929.

One of the historical reasons for the system in Nova Scotia, as Gardiner
well knew, was that the province encompassed in a small territory large
proportions of opinionated Protestants and Roman Catholics, and a
single minister of education would have had to come from one group
or the other. The same conditions did not exist in Saskatchewan, but
Gardiner was still prepared to consider the adaptation to Saskatchewan
of the structures used successfully in the Maritime province. But the
essence of Nova Scotia's scheme was that it retained control of perhaps
the most important single provincial function in the hands of responsible
ministers, where Anderson's proposals would have destroyed that. 'The
people must have control,' Gardiner averred, 'and they must have direct
control through a system which places responsibility on the government.' Gardiner and his forces used every available device to block or
delay the passage of the bills but Anderson, his mixed majority holding
together with striking singleness of purpose, got them through, conceding only that the Education Commission's members would not be
appointed before the election.[8]

The divisions over education showed that Gardiner and Anderson
were as far apart on major policies as they had been in 1929. A member
of the press gallery noted that the assembly had so far had a good-
natured session, thanks in part to Anderson's conciliatory role as an
elder statesman who strongly favoured a coalition free of partisan influences.[9] He could hardly have said the same of Gardiner, who remained
as combative as ever. For his purposes the election campaign of 1934
began in earnest the day the legislature met, and he used every opportunity to expound his and the Liberals' views on items of his own selection.
At times his choice was such that his observations seemed like an obbli-
gato to the offerings from the government side. Gardiner based his

attack on the speech from the throne on school finances, the Estevan by-election of 1930, expenditures in Highways, and the mounting provincial debt. He returned to Highways in his address on the budget, adding a gratuitous warning to civil servants who may be appointed to permanent positions under legislation before the House that the Liberals would not recognize them. A government whose life was ending, Gardiner said, had no right to make permanent appointments, a constitutional doctrine all the more novel in that it was propounded over two months before an election had even been called.[10]

The legislative session of 1934, in short, may have been unique on several counts, but it found Gardiner at the same old stand, vigorously pushing for the things he believed in. He was not alone: T.C. Davis took a particular interest in patronage matters in Prince Albert, and the employment of his opponent of 1929, J.G. Diefenbaker, as counsel for the royal commission on the Bryant charges, gave an added incentive to inquire into the costs of the investigation. When the government Department of Telephones placed insurance on its buildings in Prince Albert, Davis was pleased to be told that the agent who obtained the largest cut of the pie was an E.J. Diefenbaker.[11] The agent of the attorney general in the constituency was replaced by one S.J.A. Branion, who was to be Davis's Conservative opponent in 1934. King's Counsels blossomed among Tory lawyers, and since all the appointments had to be gazetted, it was not even necessary to ask questions about them to speculate about who was in the government's favour, or who was being courted as a potential future candidate. Throughout the life of the legislature, which ended its final sitting on 7 April 1934, with the traditional throwing of books and papers, the Liberals pieced together an astonishing amount of information about the activities of the Anderson administration, and none of it convinced Gardiner that it was in any serious way a 'reform' government.

The legislature was formally dissolved on 25 May; but since everybody knew that once the House had risen without prolonging its own life thus making an election in June a certainty, the campaigning had already begun. Both Anderson and Gardiner started formally the first week in May, the premier confidently claiming that 'There is no doubt whatever but what the Government will be returned with a substantial majority.' The cabinet set 19 June as polling day, a decision announced casually by Anderson in the middle of May during a short stop at Chaplin, a village one hundred miles west of Regina. By that time the Liberals had a full slate of candidates at work; the Farmer-Labor party, running as the Saskatchewan wing of the CCF, was one short; the Conservatives three.[12]

The large representation of socialist candidates was an ominous portent for the Conservatives. Their predecessors in 1929 had been especially anti-Liberal, but they had also been co-operative with Anderson. Partly for that reason, neither in 1929 nor after did the Conservatives seem to appreciate the value of a province-wide set of constituency organizations. The Farmer-Labor men may have thought they had little in common with Gardiner, but they too believed in organization, and Gardiner publicly acknowledged their skill at it. Besides, where the socialists were showing strength it was at the expense of the Co-operative Government. Gardiner was being told from all quarters that the Liberal party was in excellent shape, the Conservatives the opposite, while in between was the new third party. The election of 1934 was clearly going to be different from that of 1929.

Just how different not even Gardiner could have guessed. It was easy to discount Anderson's claim of a certain majority, or that of a spokesman for Farmer-Labor, Frank Eliason, who late in May averred that thirty-five seats were safe for the CCF.[13] Gardiner himself, opening his personal tour on 16 May in Prince Albert, drew large crowds of a sort likely to make a man optimistic; but he was too seasoned a campaigner to be misled far in that direction. He had attracted huge audiences in 1929 and lost, and in 1934 Anderson and Coldwell, the latter handicapped because as a school principal he could get out of Regina only on weekends, were being well received too. Both Liberal and Conservative front-benchers covered the province, in the usual attempt to have at least one future, former, or current minister speak at each major urban point, and as many rural stops as possible in between.

It was an exhausting schedule, but it was obvious that Gardiner, Davis, and the other Liberal heavy artillery greatly enjoyed it. Coldwell, too, was in his element, and more than one Liberal was surprised to find that the socialist leader, although pursuing lofty aims, was on the hustings a real scrapper. Among the cabinet a similar energy was displayed by J.F. Bryant and by Carl Stewart who, having already run as a Progressive and an Independent, in 1934 made his debut as a Conservative. On Anderson the evidence is less clear: he often seemed tired by his responsibilities, as well as by continuing denunciations from an erstwhile Conservative party president, Dr D.S. Johnstone of Regina, who in 1934 threw his support to Gardiner on the grounds that the Liberals would at least be a responsible government.[14]

The choice of a small waystation instead of a major centre, or a radio network, to announce the election date was one indication of Anderson's attitude. Another was opening his campaign on the handling of relief, which he may have chosen because, as he said at the time, the Liberals had opposed 'virtually all measures ... [for] alleviating human suffering and bettering conditions generally.' Certainly the Liberals had opposed, but generally where human welfare was concerned they had challenged the means rather than the ends. Gardiner professed surprise over the choice of relief as an issue, for everybody agreed about the need for it, and its administration was supposed to be non-partisan. Anderson's opening gave Gardiner the opportunity to emphasize that he did not blame the depression and hard times on the Conservatives, but believed the difficulties that accompanied them were greatly aggravated by the policies of Conservative premiers at both the provincial and federal levels. The solutions lay in traditional Liberal policies: wider markets, freer trade abroad and, at home, reorganization in education, and relief and debt adjustment, all in the direction of local political control.[15]

The parties' several manifestos covered a good deal more than that. Manifestos were part of the party folklore inherited from national sources, which in turn had adopted British practices. Certainly in Gardiner's day a party was expected not merely to produce a manifesto, but a document that filled most of a newspaper page. It is improbable that a modern party would expect an electorate, trained to believe it was getting all the news of the world in a fifteen-minute telecast, to spend hours analysing manifestos. But at a time when the spoken word and its printed counterparts were the chief means of communication in politics, the manifesto played a role. It was supplemented by open forums made available to parties by newspapers, and by interminable pages of earnest or quarrelsome letters to the editor.

The Farmer-Labor manifesto was naturally based on the document now known as the Regina Manifesto, adapted for Saskatchewan in 1934. Anderson's was a personal document. The Liberals', written by Gardiner himself, began with the statement: 'The platform of the Liberal party, as amended from time to time to meet changing conditions, is the manifesto of the party to the people of the country.' Since the manifesto was much shorter than the platform, it was noteworthy that Gardiner chose to abridge it not by summarizing every topic, but by omitting some topics altogether. The Liberal manifesto was released on 25 May, Anderson's was published on 31 May, and Gardiner selected his offerings in the knowledge that the party was by then fighting two doughty opponents, not one. Thus mentions of such specific items as the redistribution of constituency boundaries, the price of gasoline, and the method of purchasing governmental supplies, with all of which the Farmer-Labor group campaigning in 1934 had had almost nothing to do, appear in the platform but not the manifesto. The text of the platform contained no section entitled 'Social Services,' but the accompanying summary of resolutions had a paragraph under 'Public Health and Social Services.' The social services have their own section in the manifesto and the reference is not entitled, as in the platform, 'Women's Activities.' A comparison of the platform and the manifesto offers a revealing indication of how Gardiner chose the weapons he found most useful in 1934.

All three manifestos had topics in common, for education, roads, agriculture, public health, unemployment, and municipal and farm debts concerned everybody, and any party that ignored them would have sounded like a visitor from a distant land. The proposed solutions varied, with the Farmer-Labor's naturally sounding the most radical. With the Liberal and Conservative platforms resembling each other, there were nevertheless two notable differences. Anderson allied himself with the policies of the federal Conservative government that had sought to help the prairies in an uncritical manner that Gardiner would never have adopted. He also proposed two more boards: to the Saskatchewan Relief Commission and the Education Commission which was to replace the minister, he planned to add an Advisory Economic Council and a Health Services Board. Anderson's manifesto, finally, was strikingly silent on one point: although during the campaign J.F. Bryant and others sought to stir up the Bryant charges again – as the Liberals did the Estevan Riot of 1931, for whose violent settlement they had no responsibility – Anderson did not make the Gardiner machine an item in his platform. Half a dozen almost fruitless investigations had rendered that useless.

All parties supplemented their various manifestos and platforms with broadsides and pamphlets, the Liberals spraying the electorate with over two dozen separate publications. Singly they were all vintage examples of Liberal campaign tactics of the period, severally citing statistics, emphasizing R.B. Bennett's promise to end unemployment, or creating slogans: 'A Merciless Mess of Mismanagement and the Way Out.' Together they offered evidence that the party's days of penury were over, and were notable for the amount of attention they paid to M.J. Coldwell, his platform, and his supporters. Gardiner was clearly not underestimating the rise of the left, and he fought it both as a separate phenomenon and as an alleged partner of Anderson's Co-operative Government.

Men calling themselves Farmer-Labor in the legislature could be proven to have kept that government in office on more than one occasion. At the same time – and while some Liberal supporters were arguing publicly that the Conservatives and the ccf were in silent partnership – Liberal pamphlets also separated the two opposing groups. A favorite theme was a triple-barrelled comparison, such as: 'The c.c.f. will take your earnings. The Conservatives will spend your earnings. The Liberals will increase your earnings.'

None of these slogans would have gone out over Gardiner's opposition. He knew that they were no more partisan or misleading than what was being said and written on behalf of other parties, for he conscientiously collected their publications. He also received copies of speeches made by their leaders, taken down by Liberal stenographers, which were of particular value because the lack of staff available to him as leader of the opposition had led to the virtual abandonment of any newspaper clipping service between 1930 and 1934. Gardiner also collected material on Social Credit; subsequent events suggest that he was taking Social Credit more seriously than were the Liberals in Alberta.[16]

Gardiner left nothing to chance. Radio addresses, leaders' tours, and public meetings were conspicuous, and designed to be so. But behind the scenes the usual detail was being attended to, merely speeded up for the election. The regular meticulous checking-out of voters' lists was going on, individuals were being quietly spoken to, pieces of paper bearing pertinent information were being passed around. Volunteer workers had to be deployed, and serious consideration given to having Saskatchewan's federal members come home to campaign while legislation crucial to the province was before the House of Commons.[17] Misleading newspaper reports had to be countered. An uncritical mention of the ccf in, of all places, a Sunday school leaflet, was looked into.[18]

Rumours are impossible to document, but there is at least some evidence that the Liberals were wooing Roman Catholics by spreading the word that the ccf may have been condemned by their bishops (what the bishops had said is not that clear),[19] and courting teetotallers by commenting on J.T.M. Anderson's failure to be one of them. When, after the election but before resigning, Anderson had the misfortune while not on government business to wreck a government car, a subsequent question in the House produced the answer that the insurance company had paid no claim partly because of 'certain peculiar circumstances surrounding the accident.'[20] The campaign of 1934 was a vast mélange of publicity, argument, bombast, and whispering.

Unlike 1929, when there had been multi-party contests in only thirteen seats, in 1934 there were only two genuine two-party fights. Forty-two three-way and seven four-way contests took place, and where in 1929 candidates willing to support a Co-operative Government won a majority, in 1934 they were, literally, wiped out. The Liberals won fifty seats and were runners-up in five; Farmer-Labor won five and were second in eighteen; the Conservatives won none and were second in twenty-seven, fewer than half the total.

The Liberal victory was neither so complete nor the Conservative débâcle so devastating as the seats won would indicate. As is usual with any electoral system which gives the whole seat to whichever individual polls the most votes, the relationship between seats won and votes polled was a tenuous one. The Conservatives won nearly 27 per cent of the vote for no seats, while the Farmer-Labor, with barely 24 per cent, won five. The Liberals' capture of fifty seats out of fifty-five was effected with 48 per cent of the vote. The Conservatives' vote held up particularly well in the major cities, but always in second position. The Farmer-Labor group was more successful with its Farmer sector than its Labor, and all five of its victories were in large rural constituencies, four of them on the province's western edge. Their winners did not include their leader, M.J. Coldwell, who shortly found himself unable to get leave-of-absence from the Regina School Board either to seek a seat or conduct the party from outside the legislature, a circumstance that may have profoundly affected the early history of the CCF.[21] Gardiner carried every poll but one in his own riding.

A man who has vanquished two parties and become the only leader to survive at the polls is likely to be in a cheerful frame of mind on election night. Gardiner listened to the results at the farm, and when victory was certain flew to Regina. There he was met by cheering crowds who lined the streets as a motorcade, complete with pipe band, took him to the legislative building. On the steps he stoutly refused to make a speech having, as he said, been speaking non-stop for six weeks. His victory, coupled with a similar win on the same day by the Ontario Liberals under Mitchell Hepburn, was celebrated in Ottawa by the parliamentary party. Alone among Liberals, Mackenzie King had a broken heart: word from the occult on the outcome in Ontario had been grievously wrong.[22]

If Gardiner was upset by any erroneous prognostications from beyond, he left no trace of it. On election night he was of course exultant, and after a few days of tidying up details, he took off for a holiday at Banff. En route he reported to King: 'My task of cabinet making will be greatly facilitated if I can be reasonably sure that you would be agreeable to acting upon a recommendation ... I think Mr. P.M. Anderson would make a first class King's Court judge.' King's answer was circuitous but an unmistakable no. But if federal patronage was not to be used for provincial purposes (which King gave as his reason) the reverse was not necessarily true. In his letter explaining his stand, King urged on Gardiner the desirability of finding 'some immediate appointment, should one be available, for ... the President of the Prince Albert constituency.'[23] And P.M. Anderson, a Regina member, remained an ordinary MLA, and was re-elected in 1938, after which he did get his judgeship.

Gardiner had experienced MLAs to consider for his cabinet, and one criterion by which he weeded them out was survival in the general election of 1929. A number of members had sat in the legislative in the 1920s, had been defeated or had not run in 1929, to reappear in the landslide of 1934. Gardiner did not take a single one of them into his new administration. The most notable of these was the veteran Taylor, who had sat for Kinistino from 1917 to 1925, when he did not run, and then won fame by trouncing the turncoat McIntosh in the celebrated by-election of 1933. Taylor was to stay in the legislature until he retired in 1944, but he did not reach the ministry. Charles Agar, who sat as a Progressive from 1921 to 1929, when he crossed the floor and won as a Liberal, was another veteran with a similar fate.

The cabinet Gardiner put together in 1934 was a nice mixture of old and new whose members with a single exception had one thing in common: they had never been defeated running as Liberals. Including himself, there were five hold-overs from his ministry of 1926–29, and all became members of the cabinet again: Gardiner, now sitting for Melville; T.C. Davis, still in Prince Albert; W.J. Patterson, now sitting for Cannington; George Spence, now elected for Notukeu, and S.J. Latta, still at Rosthern. Gardiner also had two freshmen appointed, J.W. Estey of Saskatoon, defeated in 1929, and J.G. Taggart of Swift Current. He also recommended C.M. Dunn, from Francis, a veteran organizer first elected in 1929, and J.R.M. Parker of Pelly, first elected as a Liberal in 1929, after having been defeated as a Conservative in the provincial election of 1917. In due course he was appointed Saskatchewan's eighth lieutenant-governor.

Gardiner was satisfied with his new ministry, for while it looked after only nine of his fifty members, it had a strong agrarian base to balance the city lawyers, Davis and Estey. The rural seats also contained several major towns, such as Gardiner's own Melville and Taggart's Swift Current. The geographic division was suitably scattered, with the weakest representation coming from seats west of Saskatoon, and from Regina and Moose Jaw. Gardiner, with himself and eight other ministers resident in Regina most of the year (and Moose Jaw just a few miles west), could not believe that the area had earned a high priority for representation in the cabinet; it was one reason why P.M. Anderson's election had posed a problem.

Truly, on 19 July 1934 Gardiner was riding high. He was fifty-one, in excellent health, with a happy family life. He loved politics, and he was back in power. Mackenzie King, seeing him less than two weeks after his return, wrote of Gardiner that 'he looks *remarkably* well, has filled out and has greater poise, is very happy, office seems to give men heart as well as strength.'[24] As an old athlete, Gardiner might have wanted to know what his chief meant by 'filled out,' but he would not have disputed the rest.

11

The Politics of Triumph

Gardiner's position in the Liberal party in 1934 was a strong one. He was personally undefeated in twenty years, and had gained a party-wide reputation as an expert at organization. He had delivered the national leader's seat in Prince Albert in successive victories. When he had faltered, as in the provincial election of 1929 and the federal one of 1930, it was at a time when the party generally was faltering. But Gardiner had also lost the only provincial election he had fought as premier, and taken the Saskatchewan party into opposition for the first time in its life. In 1934 he had dramatically shown another government the road to limbo, but that was a government that could probably have been beaten by a troop of boy scouts.

He stood out because his provincial rivals elsewhere had less attractive records. In the same year as Gardiner's triumph in Saskatchewan, King told his diary that his lieutenant in British Columbia, T.D. Pattullo, had 'gone mad' in assuming autocratic powers as if he were a Bennett, and he shook King's confidence again a month later when he was seen drinking at a banquet. Drinking was also exhibited by Hepburn in Ontario, whom King foresaw in April 1934 as 'a lightweight for a prime minister of ... Ontario.' Six months after Hepburn's victory, King dismissed him as an adventurer, one of those with little on his mind but the party machine and patronage. In Quebec, King felt, there was 'an autocracy that is a law unto itself.'

The Liberal leadership in Manitoba had all but gone underground in John Bracken's coalition government, although King expressed satisfaction with the 'friendly cooperation and near relationship of feeling' he found there. To the west the Alberta Liberals were in fearsome disarray, having been in opposition for over a decade with no reason to believe they had not become a fixture there. The Alberta leader, W.R. Howson, severely shook both King's and Gardiner's confidence in his political sagacity when in 1934 he proposed a summer conference of western Liberals at a time when, both in Saskatchewan and nationally, success in the next election seemed so certain that any public meeting of the party could only open the door to needless divisions over policies. Amid all these fiefdoms Gardiner alone seemed to have built a model of Liberalism and sobriety, and an observer would have had to go all the way to Nova Scotia to find anything resembling it.[1]

King, of course, blew hot and cold over his provincial colleagues, on occasion even speaking well of Hepburn. Gardiner himself was to fall from grace, and without ceasing to be a teetotaller. But in 1934 that day was far in the future, and Gardiner was still in a position to render indispensable services. One of these was to negotiate, as a Liberal, with a federal government that was to remain Conservative for another fifteen months, in such a way as to benefit Saskatchewan but not to commit or compromise the national party. Gardiner's first attempt involved federal-provincial relief policy, the first major problem he took up after forming his cabinet.

The last arrangement for relief between R.B. Bennett and J.T.M. Anderson had been based on terms which expired on 31 March 1934 but were continued on an interim basis while a new agreement was being prepared. The agreement, a detailed document which distinguished between urban and rural needs, gave all major initiatives to 'The Dominion,' and had the federal government pay for stated percentages of costs in most instances, whatever the totals might be. It thus committed the Dominion to signing the equivalent of several blank cheques.[2] There is no evidence that the province abused the provisions of the relief arrangements, but Bennett liked financial deals to be tidy, especially when the ultimate responsibility was his. Ironically enough, the Liberals in the Commons had earlier objected strongly to giving the government a blank cheque to cope with the depression, strongly favouring rigid parliamentary control of finance,[3] but Bennett's proposal in 1934 for that very principle did not please their leader either. Gardiner's views were summarized in King's diary: 'He would favour federal government taking over jurisdiction over factories and mines, for uniform labour laws, also social legislation, leaving provinces to take over many municipal matters.' But, King added, Gardiner 'is agreeable to accepting a lump sum grant in aid from Bennett.'[4]

That was what he got. It is virtually certain that Gardiner would have himself suggested a simple grant if Bennett had not, for he planned to abolish the Relief Commission created by Anderson, desiring a system under ministers in his own cabinet. The only points to argue turned on the amount of the grant and the purposes for which it could be used. The full terms of the new federal-provincial agreement for relief were not negotiated: the Dominion announced unilaterally early in August that it was shifting from paying stated percentages of costs to monthly grants for direct relief, and the task of any premier needing money was to get as much as possible. Gardiner made two trips to Ottawa to press for at least $225,000 a month, but as early as 14 August he had been told that Saskatchewan's share was $200,000 and the final agreement fixed on that sum to 31 March 1935.

The province was given a free hand in administering the grant, the agreement asserting only that the money was for 'discharging the Province's responsibilities connected with the relief of necessitous persons within its borders ... without any discrimination as to the race, religious views or political affiliation of the recipients.'[5] The provincial Relief Commission was closed down by mid-August of 1934, its duties taken over mainly by branches of the two departments: Agriculture; and Railways, Labour and Industries. About the same time Gardiner announced that the province and the municipalities would share equally in costs incurred beyond the federal grant for direct relief, while for indirect relief (for example, for seed and fodder), existing types of federal assistance would continue.[6]

The rapidity with which Gardiner was able to replace Anderson's relief administration demonstrated that he did not need a legislative session to implement some immediate goals. The turnover in 1929 had seen a large replacement of liquor-store vendors, hospital workers, jail guards, and other employees of provincial institutions, and Gardiner's government was not slow to follow its predecessor's example. The ebb and flow of government employees that began again on 19 July 1934 can be measured statistically for the early months, thanks to questions subsequently asked in the legislature, and its extent from the beginning can be guessed at by an undertaking Gardiner gave to the Canadian Legion in August that there would be no displacement of war veterans in the civil service. He was talking in net terms: dismissed veterans were often replaced by other veterans.

A sessional paper dated 14 February 1935 showed that twenty-one public servants had been put on indefinite leave since the previous July, two of them subsequently being given part-time jobs. Another paper of the same date revealed that since Gardiner had resumed office 23 civil servants had been superannuated, 86 had resigned, 8 had had their appointments cancelled, and 129 had been dismissed. (Employees of liquor board stores provided 63 of the dismissals, and Public Works another 32.) In the same period 404 new appointments were made, 83 of them of persons who had worked for the government before. Since Anderson's Public Service Commission had observed that 'The Commission trusts that permanency will be acknowledged by all concerned as inherent in the present Service organization,' it is of interest that 390 of the 404 new appointments made by the Gardiner administration in 1934–35 were to temporary positions.[7]

That was a reflection in part of Gardiner's conviction that few things kept a public servant more loyal than a temporary position, and the figures cited are an understatement. The information tabled in the legislature was 'exclusive of Justices of the Peace and Commissioners for Oaths,' and as the *Saskatchewan Gazette* for the period shows, these functionaries were replaced by the hundreds in 1934–35, along with agents for the attorney general, examiners under the Vehicles Act, and issuers of various kinds of licences.[8] The turnover in 1934–35, that is, matched that of 1929–30.

The temporary new positions could be defended on the grounds that the people were hired for what everybody hoped was temporary work: the administration of relief. The Saskatchewan Relief Commission had been outside the Public Service Act partly because its work was temporary, and its replacement by departments had, for example, meant the addition of 88 temporary employees to a new Bureau of Labour and Public Welfare in the Department of Municipal Affairs, and 54 in Agriculture to supervise the distribution of seed, feed grain, and fodder to municipalities for relief. Both enterprises were part of a minor realignment of cabinet functions: the two departments of Highways, and Railways, Labour and Industries, were abolished, railways being put under a new portfolio entitled Highways and Transportation, labour under the new bureau in Municipal Affairs, and industries under Natural Resources.

Gardiner's turnover in the public service has been cited as evidence that Anderson's valiant attempt to reform the civil service was simply reversed, and the clock set back. But the Liberals did not consider Anderson's achievement all that valiant, nor did the new government simply abolish the Public Service Commission. The re-reform of the public service was high on Gardiner's agenda, and he announced his plans in general terms while still sorting out the new administration of relief. From the first he talked of replacing Anderson's three-man commission with a single commissioner, in the interests of economy, but the commission was still to be independent.[9]

Changes in the civil service comprised only one of the policies Gardiner intended to present to the legislature; in 1934 he felt that he had not only a lot to do, but a lot to undo. Some of his plans, as with the negotiations for and reorganization of relief, or his reordering of ministers' functions, could be executed through the use of his powers as premier. Other major changes required legislation, and once his administration was settled into its new responsibilities, he devoted much time to the legislature's agenda. It was summoned as soon as Gardiner was ready, on 15 November 1934, and sat until the following 21 February, with a Christmas adjournment from 4 December to 8 January. The division of the session into two separate parts, one short and one long, and the selection of legislation for each, revealed Gardiner's priorities.

He himself found the new legislature unusual, for his huge majority meant not only a minute opposition, but one different from that he had faced in 1929 and after. The Anderson supporters, to a man, were gone; the new Farmer-Labor opposition consisted of five freshmen members, who could be challenged only about what they said, not about anything they had done. Nonetheless, the opposition bravely occupied the entire side of the House to the Speaker's left, making the fifty Liberals opposite look as if they faced some sort of tribunal.

The speech from the throne reflected Gardiner's retention of the provincial treasurer's portfolio. It called for action on

three well defined lines:
First: the financial position of our governing bodies, our agricultural and other industries, and our labouring people, must be improved and stabilized ...
Second: the agricultural industry of this Province must be re-established upon the experiences of the first generation in their attempt to build permanent homes ... [A] permanent plan should be established whereby seed may be provided and sown each year without becoming such a charge upon the Province as to make the ordinary financing of government almost impossible ...
Third: my Government is seized of the absolute necessity for the re-establishment of our position outside the Province.

The speech then went on to declare that all government expenditures in Saskatchewan must be kept within revenues (a comment on the large

Anderson debts), and added a ringing denunciation of the Conservatives' federal policies; calling for free trade 'in food products, in machinery, in clothing, in oil and other things necessary to the carrying on of our industry; the Federal Government must withdraw entirely from the field of direct taxation entered into during war years.' The speech emphasized the desirability of expanding Canada's trade with Great Britain, which was to become almost an obsession with Gardiner; and changes in the public service, education, municipal administration, 'and other matters of a general character,' including enabling legislation to permit the province's farmers to take advantage of the federal farm loans provisions. The teetotal Gardiner had also to promise a bill which would acknowledge that concurrently with the general election of 1934 the citizenry, when asked 'are you in favor of the sale of beer by the glass on licensed premises?' had acquiesced by 197,630 to 164,752.[10]

The first week of the session was taken up with routine matters, mainly the debate on the address, and was notable historically for the first official amendment moved by a CCF opposition. It summarized a good deal of what Gardiner considered the usual nonsense: the government should inaugurate a planned economy, mobilization of resources to provide security, socialized medical services, and an acceptance of 'Socialism as the basis of our economic activities, through which we will cooperate for the general good rather than continue to compete for profits.' It was defeated without a formal division.[11] During the campaign, interestingly enough, the man who was to become Gardiner's minister of public health, Dr J.M. Uhrich, had referred to a medicare scheme in such clear terms that Gardiner had agreed that the Liberals were 'more or less committed' to study the feasibility of state medicine and hospitalization.[12]

After defeating the Farmer-Labor program, the House settled into the government's agenda. Several bills concerning relief and debt adjustment were shortly on the order paper: the bill to abolish Anderson's Education Commission received first reading; the bill on the public service appeared 27 November. The relief provisions differed from Anderson's more in degree than in kind as Gardiner's administration also desperately canvassed every possible way of alleviating drought and depression without placing too onerous a burden on any single institution. The legislature amended existing legislation to permit municipalities to borrow money for seed grain, petroleum products, binder twine, and gopher poison. Citizens in danger of losing their property because of debts were given further extensions. The province revised its attempts to co-ordinate its own activities with federal and municipal authorities. A Debt Adjustment Board was created, with broad powers to delegate its authority to tribunals in each judicial district which in turn could delay and restrict legal actions by which property could be seized for any of several reasons. In all this, Gardiner's course followed Anderson's, with the important exception that where possible everything was brought back under the control of responsible ministers.[13] The Saskatchewan Relief Commission went, and so did the provincial Research Council and the Education Commission, while the minister of education was reinstated as a member of the Executive Council. The Public Service Commission was replaced, again in the direction of more ministerial influence.

Since the Public Service acts of 1930 and 1934 reveal so clearly the differences between Gardiner's and Anderson's theory of a public service (and by inference between Gardiner's and Coldwell's) some comparisons are necessary. Gardiner had never taken Anderson's statute seriously, for by the time it came into force on 1 June 1930, there had already been a large turnover of civil servants. But it was nonetheless a major piece of legislation that could affect the future. Gardiner's act, assented to on 4 December 1934, at a superficial glance reads like a re-enactment of Anderson's; in both documents the substantive clauses covering the management, grading, and classification of the public service are almost the same word for word.

There were, however, two crucial points of departure – one in the terms themselves, and one in their interpretation. Anderson's public service commission was more independent. Its three members were named in the statute and their salaries set forth. Gardiner's commission consisted of one person whose selection was left to the lieutenant-governor-in-council, which also determined his salary. The chairman of Anderson's commission was appointed for ten years, the other two members for five. Gardiner's commission was appointed for seven years. Any commissioner of Anderson's could be suspended by the executive, after which he could be removed only by a two-thirds majority of the legislature. A Gardiner commission could be removed by the cabinet on an address of the legislature, or suspended by the cabinet and replaced until the House took action, and in either case a simple majority was enough. The chairman of Anderson's commission was named in the statute. A chairman of Gardiner's was named by the executive. The commissions under both premiers were on paper independent, and took the same oaths, but Anderson's three-man board clearly enjoyed much greater opportunity to be independent than did Gardiner's single appointee. Anderson's commissioner was also considerably more energetic in pursuing the goals of a merit system in the public service than was the commissioner during Gardiner's second premiership.

The other difference in the two commissions came from the weight attached to clauses which were substantively the same in both statutes. Under Anderson's act no person could be appointed unless:

(c) a competitive examination under the provisions of this Act has been held and the person proposed to be appointed is the most successful candidate; or (d) having regard to the nature of the appointment, competitive examination is not required or may be dispensed with – under the provisions of this Act.[14]

The clauses in Gardiner's statute omit the last six words; and the public service commissioner during Gardiner's second administration held no examinations whatever. Gardiner still held, when pressed, that 'the competitive principle prevails in all cases as there are invariably many applicants for each position and the Commissioner chooses therefrom.'[15]

He was not asked on what basis the commissioner made his choice, and did not volunteer the information. The abolition of competitive examinations at a time of high unemployment was considered a reasonable economy, but the crucial factor in the choice of public servants then became the commissioner's interpretation of his functions. However independent he tried to be, the new system was plainly capable of degenerating into old-fashioned patronage, although there is no evidence that it did so in an avalanche after July 1934. The two reports the commissioner filed while Gardiner was premier were short, characteristically recording that 'some changes for better organization and efficiency were recommended and have already been carried out,' without even identifying the departments thus improved. Neither report contains any reference to the conditions of employment laid out at length in the act. Both reports consisted in the main of the required annual lists of temporary employees and the second noted that 'the drought conditions have accounted for a temporary increase "in personnel" consequent upon the extra volume of work.'[16] It should be added that as of 30 January 1935, of those on strength when Gardiner took office in 1934, nearly 95 per cent (2,888 individuals) were still employed, and of those a further 3 per cent (95 individuals) had been given notice.[17]

Having taken up the relief burden, abolished the relief and education commissions, and reformed the civil service, Gardiner's other priority during the first part of the legislative session was the statutory revision consequent on his cabinet reorganization and the creation of the Bureau of Labour and Public Welfare. Since the de facto changes had already been made, the Liberals' huge majority rendered the passage of the relevant acts routine. Much the same was true of the legislation after Christmas, which brought to ninety-four the total of public statutes introduced by Gardiner's second administration. The great majority of them were housekeeping provisions, variously designed to clarify, simplify, make more complicated, tidy up, revise in some direction discerned to be desirable, and otherwise alter things to keep the bureaucracy moving onward and upward. Most of them revealed convincingly how, regardless of drought, depression, changes of government, and other Acts of God, the inertia of motion keeps a government at work. The major enactments that preceded Christmas of 1934 consisted of innovations one might expect a new government to offer. The same could not be said of an act respecting slot machines or an act to amend the Steam Boilers Act, both passed early in 1935. In the speech Gardiner wrote for prorogation on 21 February 1935, he had the lieutenant-governor return to the priorities emphasized in the first part of the session. Nothing in the prorogation speech suggested that drought and depression had shaken Gardiner's faith in Liberal solutions to society's problems.

The session over, Gardiner settled into day-to-day governing, and the less routine business of preparing for the federal election certain to come in a few months. Planning for the distribution of seed among municipalities beset – and in some instances reduced to destitution – by their inability either to collect taxes or realize on assets seized in lieu of tax arrears, was probably the chief preoccupation of Gardiner's administration in the spring of 1935. But there were other equally pressing matters, most of them requiring collaboration with municipalities and school boards in the province (for local governments had to raise money to pay teachers too), and the federal authorities. The general poverty of all governments meant that issues that might in less strenuous times have been settled at the administrative level tended to gravitate upwards to the political. Gardiner would have been busy enough as premier, but as his own provincial treasurer he was brought into everything that cost the province money; and that involved him in communications with R.B. Bennett, which ultimately erupted into what Gardiner considered the most outrageous intervention ever by a federal government in provincial affairs. His public references to it included such terms as 'the most diabolical conspiracy ever perpetuated upon the people of any province or city'[18] – and that was said two weeks before events became critical. Throughout his dealings with Bennett, Gardiner regarded him as at best a distant warlord of uncertain temper, about whom from time to time he received dispatches from surly correspondents at the front, including his own leader.

Part of the tension between Gardiner and Bennett came from one quality they had in common: both were jealous guardians of what they saw as their responsibilities. On that score, as politicians often do, they appeared to understand and even respect each other. They could, and did, make deals, for example, over the handling of the various relief programs. Where they differed was at the borderline of their jurisdictions, where each had to make a judgment over not only his own responsibilities, but the other's. One difference of opinion was what lay behind the fatal event that entered history as the Regina Riot of 1 July 1935.

It is easy now to see how the Regina Riot could have been avoided. Better communications between the decision-makers at Ottawa and those they instructed in the west could have minimized the trouble. A delegation of authority to federal men on the spot in Saskatchewan, instead of a rigid centralization of control within Bennett's cabinet, could have led to a negotiated settlement between the opposing factions. At one crucial point, indeed, when the assistant commissioner of the RCMP in Regina, Colonel S.T. Wood, thought he had authority to proceed, he had all but reached agreement when his orders were changed. Had there been a precedent to settle who commanded the RCMP when the force was under contract with a provincial government, the circumstances that led to the riot might never have started to develop. But in the event there was a riot, and for days before it occurred Gardiner, among others, was freely using the word to describe what he feared was coming.

Like so many crises, the Regina Riot began simply. As part of its overall relief policy, the federal government had established a number of camps for unemployed single men, and the living conditions in them were not high. In return for food and shelter, the men not only did manual work without other remuneration ('work without wages' became a well-publicized complaint) but, in the words of one of them, 'the boys were denied the rights of citizens in the camps. They had no appeal to civil rights.'[19] It was a situation made to order for the kind of organizers whom conservatives always consider radical, and it was hardly surprising that a local of the Relief Camp Workers' Union came into being in one camp near Vancouver. The men prepared a list of seven demands, the main element a proposal of fifty cents per hour for unskilled workers and trade union rates for skilled. Since the only course available to them was protest, they planned and in due course carried out a series of peaceful demonstrations, in general trying to attract attention to their plight. When their early tactics failed, they decided on 29 May to hold an 'On-to-Ottawa' trek. On 3 and 4 June a large body of men, later estimated by sundry tallymen at between nine and thirteen hundred, left Vancouver by train.

From the start the men were technically trespassers, for they rode on freight trains without paying fares; but the railways made no attempt to collect any. On the contrary, the trains proceeded eastward in an almost circus-like atmosphere, crowds gathering at railway stations to greet the trespassers at several points. The railways began to treat the men as guests, not only laying on extra cars for them, but extending to them the same sort of courtesies as those enjoyed by customers. At Calgary the train was stopped at a point from which it was most convenient for the travellers to march to the Stampede grounds, which they did escorted by police on motor cycles. At Swift Current the men were given lunch by the city and kept overnight, and the municipal authorities were again host at Moose Jaw. The prime minister, R.B. Bennett, announced that the federal government would not interfere with the trek unless a provincial government requested it, so that Gardiner and his colleagues had no reason to expect anything else but that the trains would continue their triumphal passage through Saskatchewan.

Behind the scenes, however, steps were being taken that Gardiner always believed were part of a conspiracy, the plotters Bennett and the railways, especially the Canadian Pacific, who formulated a strategy to divide the men by easing the movement of some of them eastward. In the meantime the RCMP were dispatched from the Regina barracks to the west coast to look after dissidents who had stayed behind. On 19 June Gardiner told King that he had received reports of the RCMP in Regina practising with tear-gas. 'Both the government and CPR representatives here,' he wrote, 'told the same well-rehearsed story of a communistic movement across Canada which was to break all at the same time.' Even the clergy was involved: 'The only Tory preacher in town here was filled with the communist stories and got them off in his pulpit on Sunday night.'[20] What Gardiner saw was thus a double conspiracy, designed to quell communism, but at a site outside Alberta (Bennett's own province) in a province which had the only Liberal government on the prairies.

Precisely why the trek, after receiving nothing but co-operation from the day it left Vancouver, should have been stopped without warning or consultation in Regina, was never made clear. The royal commission which held the usual post-mortem came down heavily on the side of law and order, concluding that there was indeed a communist plot which the federal authorities were quite right to foil. But it did not convincingly show why the marchers were in effect lured to Regina and there halted.[21] The commission found that the railways, although their employees had been giving friendly co-operation to the trekkers, announced on 4 June that the trespassing was to cease at Regina. A week later the RCMP was instructed to stop the trek, and when some of the workers sought to proceed eastward by car and truck, the police were ordered to stop that too. The provincial government and the city of Regina thus found themselves, without consultation, co-hosts to some two or three thousand indigents (for the trek had grown as it progressed) who had nowhere to stay, and no way of going anywhere else.

Gardiner's initial policy (the royal commission later found that the provincial government had 'not been made aware of the potential dangers lurking in the trek') assumed that the workers were ordinary transients entitled to be treated like any other, and the hospitality shown the marchers in the Saskatchewan communities west of Regina had been with his government's assistance. In Regina the provincial government fed the marchers until, in Gardiner's view, the federal government assumed responsibility for their presence in the city, and that began when two federal cabinet ministers came west to meet a delegation from the men, as a result of which several of their leaders travelled east to present their demands to Bennett. The demands were refused on 22 June.

By that time Gardiner and Bennett had exchanged a series of blistering telegrams (which Gardiner generously shared with the public), at the heart of which was a question to which Gardiner never received a satisfactory answer: how can a province discharge its constitutional duty to administer justice in the province if command over the provincial police, an indispensable instrument, can without notice be assumed by the federal government? The question was not academic. Had the provincial government had command of its police the trek would not have been stopped in Regina and there would have been no riot. There might then, as the royal commission was to suggest, have been a riot somewhere else, but that assumed that the trek was the first action in a revolution that had to be stopped by force. Gardiner never believed that for a moment. While some of the marchers' leaders were in Ottawa, Gardiner and T.C. Davis met a delegation of seven others, and a transcript of the proceedings reveals a clear and frank discussion, in which the men (they called themselves strikers) reiterated that all they wanted to do was present their demands to Bennett. That had already been said in public, and underlined in instructions to the men by their leaders, who repeatedly urged 'No Hooliganism,' on the grounds that only orderliness would earn for the marchers the support of the public.[22] Those who met Gardiner and Davis pointed out that 'there had been no misconduct or disorder' thus far, and by that time most of them had been on the road and in Regina for roughly three weeks. All the talk of violence, the men averred, came from the other side, and one of them reported to the two ministers that they had heard 'reports with regards to the battle, and reports that the battle will be here. We do not intend the battle to be anywhere.'[23]

Those words, spoken a week before the riot, were not rhetoric, and Gardiner and Davis believed them. There was, unfortunately, a breakdown of communications which kept Gardiner out of what may well have been the last-ditch negotiations that might have avoided trouble. His conference with the marchers during their leaders' absence concluded with a somewhat unclear understanding that if, on their return, further talks with the provincial government were desired, Gardiner and his colleagues would be prepared to meet them, and also 'to discuss the matter with the Federal Government and railways further.' What happened was that on the leaders' return from Ottawa, the federal government stopped feeding the men and, according to Gardiner,

ordered them into an interment camp at Lumsden, thirty miles out of Regina. The men refused to go, and came back to our Government and asked us to assist in feeding them. We stated that they were now in the hands of the Dominion Government and the City, having entered into arrangements with them without consulting us, and that the police force were taking their instructions from Ottawa and not from us, and that we were not in a position to meet their requests.[24]

The men then decided that they now had no alterative but to disband, their only remaining condition being that they would disperse from

Regina under their own organization rather than go to Lumsden under federal auspices and be demobilized like a military unit. The men conceded that they would abandon the trek, that is, and asked only to be allowed to do it their way. Negotiations to implement their proposal with Assistant Commissioner Wood were proceeding on 1 July with sufficient success that the trekkers' request, which seemed sufficiently reasonable to Wood, was submitted to Ottawa. It was rejected out of hand. The next hours were graphically recorded by Gardiner who was at the farm when the crisis began:

Mr. Evans on behalf of the men telephoned me, and asked me to come to Regina and meet them that afternoon. I ... met the men in our own office between five and six o'clock. The buildings were locked that day on account of the holiday. I let all the leaders of the trekkers into the building with my own key and locked the door, and had them in my own office for an hour or an hour and a half. It was known to the authorities that the men were there. As a matter of fact they could have been arrested without any difficulty whatsoever at any time during that period. They stated to me that the Dominion Government had refused their request, and asked the province to take them out. They stated that they were prepared to go under arrangements made with us, because they felt satisfied if we made the arrangement we would carry it out. I stated to them that I would get the Government together if at all possible that night, and give them an answer about nine or ten o'clock ...

While I was waiting in my office for other members of the Government, about eight o'clock, I got word from down town that the men had been attacked in the market square, and that one man had been killed and many others wounded and sent to the hospital, and that a great deal of property had been destroyed. After the riot was over the men were interned in the exhibition grounds under a very heavy guard of mounted police armed with rifles.[25]

The Regina Riot Inquiry Commission, a provincial body set up by Gardiner's government, found that the first outbreak was an attack by strikers on police, not vice versa, that the strikers had obviously been preparing for days by stockpiling stones and making clubs, that the actions of the police from first to last had been impeccable while, in general, anybody giving evidence to the contrary was not to be believed. The single fatality was a Regina policeman, Detective Miller, while 'not a single person, either striker or citizen, has brought evidence before the Commission of an injury inflicted by the police ... except of a very minor character.'[26] The commission had initially shown some independence by demurring at federal objections to judges sitting on a provincial royal commission without federal approval, but it explicitly declined to say whether Ottawa had exceeded its authority by instructing the RCMP in Saskatchewan while it was under contract as a provincial force.

Since to Gardiner as premier that was one of the fundamental points at issue, it was one more point on which he found the commission's report unsatisfactory; but by the time the report was released he had left provincial politics, and made little public comment on it. Privately he stuck to his own account of the riot, with whose aftermath his own government had to cope. After he learned of the marchers' internment at the Regina exhibition grounds he asked on the day after the riot that those of his previous day's callers who had not been arrested be allowed to come to his office, and he also summoned Assistant Commissioner Wood. When Wood told him that he had instructions not to feed the men except at the Lumsden internment camp, 'I stated to him that we had not had a police force for the last few weeks and that we intended to have one within the next twenty-four hours, and that if he did not take instructions from us someone else would.' Gardiner followed that stern admonition with an ultimatum to Bennett, giving him 'two hours in which to move toward feeding the men.' When Bennett did not reply, the province resumed feeding the men, and all that remained was a mop-up.

With the federal authorities now out of it, the provincial government entered negotiations with the railways to send the trekkers home, and Gardiner and Davis, premier and attorney general, personally acted as station agents. On the credit of the province they sold tickets worth $40,000 on 'trains which we forced the companies to run out of Regina.' (The royal commission later found that the riot initially cost the province $31,257 and Ottawa $30,000, the province's share being returned to it after Bennett was defeated.)[27]

In later years Gardiner often reminisced about the Regina Riot, lumping it with the Estevan Riot of 1931 (when three miners had been killed after provincial intervention) as the sort of thing one had to expect when Tories were in power.[28] The key element was compulsion, and he considered it no coincidence that the other major prairie issue for the federal election of 1935 involved compulsion too. Bennett's struggles to market abroad what Canadian wheat was grown had been only modestly successful, the major achievement being the Ottawa Agreement of 1932 which provided some preference to Canadian products in Britain. His chief wheat salesman, John I. McFarland, was from 1930 chairman of the Central Selling Agency originally established by the farmer-owned wheat pools, and his appointment was made in response to pressure from the banks to which the pools were indebted. McFarland's experience was in the private grain trade, not the co-ops, and while not indifferent to price, he believed his primary duty was to sell grain rather than withhold it to keep a price up. McFarland's agency did not have a monopoly, but existed alongside the private trade.

Throughout his regime R.B. Bennett was under steady pressure from the grain growers to establish a selling board on the model of the Canadian Wheat Board of 1919, which was the exclusive agent for handling the crop of 1919 and any leftovers from 1918.[29] His response, just before the election of 1935, was a bill that would have created a compulsory selling agency not just for wheat but 'with power to take over all elevators in the prairie provinces and to exercise exclusive control over the inter-provincial and export movement of the various grains grown in the prairie provinces.'[30]

The bill, along with Bennett's labour and welfare proposals of 1935, must have startled his more conservative supporters, but it also seriously threatened to divide the Liberals. McFarland went west in February 1935, four months before Bennett's bill was introduced. Gardiner wrote King to report the fact and ask what, in effect, Liberal policy on wheat was. The party's chief voice in Manitoba, the *Winnipeg Free Press*, was a staunch supporter of the Grain Exchange, but its own editor agreed that 'in Saskatchewan there is undoubtedly a considerable body of farmer opinion which is completely prejudiced against' it.[31]

Bennett's comprehensive proposal for a compulsory board for all grains forced the Liberals to take a stand, but for some time it was not at all clear what the stand should be. King saw as early as 7 June that 'this is by all means the largest question that Canada has to face.'[32] Within his own party Bennett's proposal not only divided the business interests and western farmers, but the western farmers themselves. Gardiner told King on 10 June that he was prepared to oppose a compulsory all-grains board. But Jack Vallance, the member for South Battleford, told King that he might be defeated if he opposed the measure, having received a number of telegrams from his constituents that gave him that idea. King, believing that Bennett's bill would be opposed everywhere outside the prairies, where it had considerable support, had first to try to conceal the disunity among his followers, and then try to find a formula that displeased as few as possible.[33]

Gardiner played an overt role in what followed. While dutifully respecting the boundary line that kept a provincial leader out of his party's federal activities, he was able to make excellent use of what King achieved. With Bennett himself in the chair, a Commons committee recommended, and the House approved, that the board handle wheat only, and that the compulsory elements in the bill be not statutory but come into effect only by order-in-council. What started out as a proposal which could still be used in the election campaign as an example of Tory dictatorship, ended up, thanks to Liberal intervention, as a compromise which left every farmer (whether he wanted it or not) with a choice of two marketing devices. The central executive of the three prairie wheat pools, a champion of state marketing, said that the amended bill was as acceptable as the original proposal.[34]

Gardiner in June was too preoccupied with the events preceding the Regina Riot to make much of Bennett's proposals on wheat, but the federal Liberals happily took them in due course and made them a dominant theme in their campaign literature. Bennett's decision to put off an election as long as possible permitted the 1935 crop on the prairies, a considerable improvement over its immediate predecessors, to come in. The new Wheat Board set a price of 87 $\frac{1}{2}$ cents a bushel on top grade wheat, and when C.H. Cahan, Bennett's secretary of state, unwisely tried to gain some credit with an eastern audience by telling it that the board had initially recommended 8 or 10 cents more but the cabinet had not allowed it, the Saskatchewan Liberals put out a broadside on that. When Bennett himself sought to gain kudos for the Wheat Board, Gardiner's forces printed another pamphlet listing the main proposals of his bill beside the amendments pressed for by the Liberals. The wheat situation gave the particular approach needed to explain Tory iniquities to the Saskatchewan public, and it could be, and was, exploited to lead on to related topics: trade, tariffs, and reciprocity with the United States.[35]

Like Gardiner in 1934, the federal Liberals in 1935 had almost a surfeit of issues to employ against the Conservatives, but the Regina Riot and the Wheat Board gave them something special – issues they could hardly have improved on. Both were perfectly timed to take into a campaign that had to begin in the summer, for if no dissolution was sought the seventeenth Parliament would expire on 18 August. The Liberals were well aware that even with everything going against them, the provincial Conservatives under J.T.M. Anderson had still polled 27 per cent of the popular vote in 1934. The credit for handling the riot and the Wheat Board bill was not only useful against the Conservatives:

the credit all went to the Liberals, with nothing for the new unknowns, CCF and Social Credit.

Gardiner took the family to his boyhood home in Ontario for a holiday in July, and returned west to spend the rest of the summer in preparing for the election, paying a good deal of attention to the new groups. He knew enough of M.J. Coldwell's performances on the hustings not to underestimate him as a campaigner, but he had no idea of what Social Credit might be like as a rival. The summer of 1935 saw the new doctrine generating enormous excitement in the province to the west, as Gardiner knew, and he did not underestimate its potential. On 15 August, the day Parliament was dissolved, the press reported that for Saskatchewan's twenty-one federal seats the CCF had a full slate of candidates nominated, the Liberals twenty, and the Conservatives sixteen, but no other. A week later William Aberhart stunned the electorate by leading his Social Credit forces from none to fifty-six of the sixty-three seats in the Alberta legislature, the Liberals dropping from eleven to five. By the end of September there were seven Social Credit candidates in the field for the federal seats in Saskatchewan, and on nomination day twenty filed papers.

The Social Crediters were not the only imponderables in a campaign that was one of the most confused and confusing in Gardiner's experience. He had personally a great deal at stake, for in July 1934 Mackenzie King, expecting a general election in the autumn, had asked Gardiner 'if he would like to come to Ottawa in the event of our winning.' Gardiner, remembering his high hopes of 1926 when Charles Dunning had been chosen over him for the federal cabinet, had responded warily, saying that 'he felt he would owe it to Saskatchewan to keep on there for a while at least.'[36] By the summer of 1935 he had kept on for a while, and knew for a certainty that he could become Saskatchewan's man in Ottawa if he chose. Dunning was no longer a rival, having been defeated in Regina in 1930. W.R. Motherwell was running again, and that made him a rival of Gardiner in one sense, for he occupied the federal seat that included Gardiner's provincial riding and had the same name, Melville; a cabinet position for Gardiner might oblige him to run in an unfamiliar area. But Motherwell in 1935 was seventy-five, and had moreover so annoyed King by his support of Bennett's marketing legislation in 1934 that it was extremely unlikely King would again accept him as a confidential colleague. Gardiner's future in federal politics appeared assured as long as the Liberals won the election of 1935.

But if that was clear, little else was. The leadership of the Conservative party was in doubt on several separate grounds. R.B. Bennett's health was such that there were widespread rumours that he would step down before the election; but early in July it was announced that he would carry on. His public quarrels with members of his cabinet led to the defection of H.H. Stevens, minister of trade and commerce, who then created a new Reconstruction Party whose manifesto was published shortly after Parliament rose. It contained numerous proposals agreeable to westerners, and in Saskatchewan J.T.M. Anderson, who secured the Conservative nomination for Saskatoon, said thirteen of Stevens's fifteen planks were acceptable to him, although he was a Bennett man. The representatives of six Conservative constituency organizations in the province felt obliged to announce that they too would stay with Bennett, but it was apparent that the western electorate was not totally opposed to Stevens.[37] In Saskatchewan the Reconstruction Party fielded three candidates, all of whom were opposed by Conservatives. Two of them ran last in four- and five-way contests, but one was runner-up to a victorious Liberal.

If Saskatchewan Conservatives felt some uncertainty about whom to follow, there were parts of the province where the connection, or lack of it, between the CCF and Social Credit produced chaos. Given the meagre information available about Social Credit (and its founder, C.H. Douglas, was on record criticizing William Aberhart's own understanding of it[38]) the movement's triumph in Alberta on 22 August, followed by an eruption of nominations in Saskatchewan's federal seats where the CCF already had a full slate, could not fail to puzzle electors. With both parties freely criticizing capitalistic institutions and, at a time when debt was a major problem for many, talking of the need to socialize credit, it took a voter of more than average sophistication to tell the two apart. The province was flooded with proposals that would have Social Credit back CCF candidates, and the CCF leaders finally had to issue a formal statement that forbade the party's official candidates' acceptance of any alliance with Social Credit. A week later the stand was reportedly modified to suggest that each constituency be left free to make up its own mind; but when one candidate accepted a double nomination to run as CCF–Social Credit, the CCF provincial executive refused to endorse him. In Weyburn, T.C. Douglas, after accepting a CCF nomination, received Social Credit backing without seeking it.[39]

The local Liberals in Weyburn were also involved with Social Credit, for they allegedly offered $3,000 to the man whom Douglas had defeated for the nomination, if he would run as a Social Crediter to take votes from the CCF. Gardiner would not have approved of the overture had he known about it, for the Liberal line on Social Credit, frequently voiced by himself and King, was that the Tories were helping finance it as an anti-Liberal tactic. When some of Aberhart's followers moved eastward to aid the cause in Saskatchewan, Gardiner referred to them as 'the riff raff of Social Credit in Alberta,' in the province to join forces with the Tories in splitting the Liberal vote. Both Tories and Social Crediters stoutly denied that and Aberhart, who joined other party leaders in campaigning in Saskatchewan, let it be known that he could not accept Social Crediters who made alliances with any other party.

Gardiner was busy throughout the campaign with matters that would have needed attention whether or not there was an election. In September, as provincial treasurer, he released a report on his second government's first year in office which showed a satisfying reduction in expenditures and an increase in revenues. In August he announced, as a supplement to established relief programs, a comprehensive plan to resettle eight thousand families in northern arable lands. His government's negotiations with the federal authorities covered not only relief, but attempts to get the Regina Riot Inquiry Commission back to work after Bennett had challenged the use of judges without federal approval. Bennett claimed in September that the riot had been part of a plot to take him hostage while a Soviet type of government was established in Canada, but for other reasons the commission did not effectively get back to work until the campaign of 1935 was over.[40]

Gardiner in 1935 campaigned considerably less in Saskatchewan than he would have otherwise. He spent two weeks on the hustings in Ontario and the Maritimes in September, Mitchell Hepburn reciprocating by travelling west for the same time. In Gardiner's absence four of his colleagues deployed themselves around the province, T.C. Davis and W.J. Patterson taking northern ridings, J.M. Uhrich the northwest, and J.G. Taggart the south. A team of sixteen Liberal speakers, including Gardiner and King, took to the road in the latter half of September, the two leaders staying together but the rest scattering widely. Early in October, in a carefully arranged move, all provincial Liberal premiers spoke the same night, the newspaper coverage receiving a half page or more.[41]

Gardiner's leader said more than once during the campaign that if he had a personal choice the election would be fought on the single issue of responsible parliamentary government versus Tory dictatorship. Certainly in Saskatchewan, given a special fillip by the Regina Riot and the original Wheat Board bill, the issue received a good deal of attention. More familiar issues were also exploited, all of them old favourites. Wheat, imperial preferences, trade generally, tariffs, and transportation (the Tories were flirting with amalgamation of the major railways, the Liberals against it) came up day after day, while Bennett's celebrated New Deal, a mixed bag of labour and welfare legislations, was rarely mentioned. Even J.T.M. Anderson, who wrote frequent newspaper columns, made nothing of the New Deal. The multiplicity of parties may have been bewildering, but the issues were old friends to Gardiner. In his own final speech he spoke of the need to reform the British North America Act, and of the need for properly run civilian relief camps in which men would be paid for work performed. He closed with a final swipe at Social Credit, about which the Liberals were increasingly nervous.

The old machine, too, ran in well-worn grooves, only a few spots needing oil. In Regina a group of dissidents, upset over the nomination of D.A. McNiven whom they identified with the party's old guard, formed a Liberal Labor League which presented the local organizations with a platform it wanted adopted, and threatened to oppose McNiven if it were not.[42] Nothing came of it and McNiven was an easy winner. A different kind of problem had arisen earlier in Prince Albert where the Liberal candidate, Mackenzie King, put on his familiar mask as a poor man and refused to contribute financially to his own campaign. If the Prince Albert Liberals expected him to underwrite all manner of costs, King told Gardiner, 'I shall just have to seek nomination in some other riding, in which event I would wish to know immediately what I may expect.' Gardiner was shortly able to assure King 'you do not need to think anything more about it.' The fact remained that, despite his eminence, the Prince Albert Liberals always found King a less than ideal candidate.[43]

These problems aside, the Liberal organization came down to 14 October in excellent shape. Unlike 1930, when the province's twenty-one seats saw eight two-way and thirteen three-way contests, there were in 1935 no two-way fights and only two three-way; but seventeen constituencies had four candidates, and two had five. The Liberals had a candidate in every seat, as did the CCF and Social Credit (if one counted the double-barrelled nomination in Yorkton for each), and the Conservatives were only two short. Three Reconstruction representatives helped produce a record total of eighty-four candidates.

The election was a massive victory for the Liberals. Nationally the party, while marginally dropping in its share of the popular vote, rose from 91 to 173 seats, the largest majority in the Commons' history to that time.[44] The altered distribution of the vote over the 1930 pattern gave King all but eleven seats from Quebec east, with clear sweeps in Prince Edward Island and Nova Scotia. West of Quebec the Saskatchewan Liberals made the best showing, while the Saskatchewan Conservatives were, as in 1934, the all-round losers. Their popular vote dropped from 38 per cent in 1930 to less than 19 per cent in 1935; they held only one of the eight seats taken in 1930. Social Credit earned 18 per cent of the vote and two seats. The CCF won over 21 per cent of the popular vote and two seats. The Liberals, perhaps because of the upsurge of the two new parties, dropped from 46 per cent of the vote to 40 per cent, but their holdings of seats rose from eleven to sixteen. The winners as a group included some experienced men, some new: Motherwell, King, Coldwell, Tommy Douglas, and Walter Tucker. The losers also counted the famous: J.T.M. Anderson, Robert Weir (Bennett's minister of agriculture) and F.W. Turnbull, a distinguished Conservative lawyer who had been elected in Regina in 1930. The two new parties, it appeared, had split the anti-Liberal vote, not the Liberal.

For Gardiner, the federal election of 1935 was his second triumph in as many years. He had delivered the goods again, and the results removed the last possible doubt about whether he was going into federal politics. It was not just the sixteen Liberal victories in Saskatchewan that ensured that. Jack Vallance, who was the same age as Gardiner and had sat as MP for South Battleford since 1925, was the member of the Saskatchewan caucus at Ottawa whom both King and Gardiner had considered the 'most promising' cabinet material from the province;[45] but Vallance was defeated in 1935. The Gardiner luck was holding.

12

Arriving at an Unknown Destination

Or was it? Gardiner's position in 1935 was not unlike that in 1926, when he feared that if he did not move into federal politics he would be doomed to remain indefinitely in Saskatchewan. In 1935 he had to decide whether to go to Ottawa at once or face the possibility of never getting there at all. 'In many political matters,' he told an associate in another connection a few months later, 'the only time to act is at the moment.'[1] Thus in 1935 Gardiner argued that a delay in getting down to Ottawa might give some newly elected Saskatchewan MP the opportunity to demonstrate his qualifications as a potential minister, and give King the notion that a premier as sound as Gardiner should stay in his province.

Two basic motives moved Gardiner in 1935. He was ambitious, as his unbroken rise in Saskatchewan had revealed. As a good Liberal he believed in a progressive advancement, not just for mankind in general but for individuals. And in Saskatchewan he had conquered all; just as ambition took him westward in his youth, so in his prime he needed fresh challenges. As his friend T.C. Davis was to tell King, about both himself and Gardiner, 'provincial politics were a small arena and he had had enough of it.'[2]

At the same time, in the provincial arena Gardiner was the undisputed boss of both the government and the party. The federal move would once more make him somebody's lieutenant. His responsibilities would not include the whole landscape of a government's operations, but a single portfolio. One man likely to be in the King ministry would be Charles Dunning, whose departure into private business after his defeat in 1930 Gardiner had hoped was permanent. In 1935 Dunning emerged again as a colleague and potential rival. Gardiner would be a freshman minister in a cabinet of sixteen, and a freshman member in a Commons of two hundred and forty-five, instead of the veteran leader of a House of fifty-five. As a federal member he could not hope to maintain his control over his provincial power base. As a minister in a cabinet that did not include his old friend W.R. Motherwell he would at least be senior in one way to that old warhorse; but, as King observed wonderingly at the time, 'it would almost seem that Motherwell controlled him.'[3]

King wrote that when it appeared that the change in Gardiner's status was to include having to settle for a portfolio that was everybody else's leftovers. While King had let Gardiner know well before the federal election that he would like him to come to Ottawa, he had not hinted in what department, and the two had quite different ideas about what was suitable. Gardiner's qualifications, in King's eyes, were both positive and negative, and Gardiner himself probably did not know about all of them. King's diary reiterates his desire to exclude from his cabinet drinkers, lobbyists, and grafters, and Gardiner had a perfect score on all those counts. Unlike T.A. Crerar, the most prominent Manitoban elected in 1935, Gardiner had eschewed the Union Government of 1917 and had not turned Progressive thereafter. His energy, and loyalty to King and Liberalism, were well known, and he was also the right man 'to get Alberta, as well as Saskatchewan, into line.'

He had, in King's eyes, two weaknesses as a future colleague. His antipathy to Charles Dunning, who was wanted by King for a major financial portfolio because of his reputation in business circles, was something Gardiner made no attempt to conceal. King also wrote of Gardiner that 'he is not large-minded, and he has ambitions to be in touch with the big interests, and to create a machine.'[4] Any reader of King's diary might wonder how he defined 'large-minded,' and Gardiner would have been puzzled to learn that his leader suspected that he sought to be in touch with interests which throughout his life he saw as a potential enemy of Liberalism; and he had never thought of any Liberal organization of his as a machine, but an ordinary organization.

King, paradoxically, put his cabinet together in 1935 as precisely as if he were building a machine, and one in which Gardiner was by no means a large cog. Gardiner recalled in his old age that he and Ernest Lapointe discussed the whole cabinet with King, and that was true. But King's diary is clear that he also discussed it with several others, and Gardiner was not brought into the talks until cabinet construction was well under way. By that time the assignment of particular individuals was beginning to shape up with increasing firmness in King's mind, and Gardiner's personal shopping list was virtually obsolete.

Gardiner was taken aback when King, whom he saw first on cabinet matters on 18 October 1935, at the outset began to talk of Dunning and Gardiner's relations with him – a gambit which, King recorded, made Gardiner take on 'a very strong and defiant look.' Gardiner spoke ill of Dunning at some length, describing him as a man who 'had always taken the easy course ... [and] waited to see how things were going to go before he would take any part.' Gardiner cited Dunning's record, the latest unpleasantness in which was that he had only joined the western campaign in 1935 when the battle was already won, and had actually helped fund some candidates without telling Gardiner, thereby gaining both undeserved credit for Liberal victories and Liberals who were obligated to him. Gardiner found the opening negotiations over a cabinet post for himself cluttered up by the unexpected resurgence of a man he distrusted.

King privately agreed with most of Gardiner's strictures on Dunning, and told Ernest Lapointe, who 'seemed to feel that I felt that if Gardiner held out we would have to accept his views and not seek further to secure Dunning.' But King did not tell that to Gardiner, who assured King that he understood the complexity of forming a government and did not want to embarrass him over Dunning, 'though he [Gardiner] might have to reconsider his own position.' In the event, King protected Gardiner's western empire, partly by finding for Dunning a seat in the east, and partly by telling him he was to respect Gardiner's territory, an admonition Dunning appears to have accepted cheerfully. But Gardiner's difficulties over Dunning were not confined to their respective baronies. King wanted Dunning as his minister of finance, and that was Gardiner's own first choice of portfolio, followed by National Revenue and a planned new catch-all department that was finally a combination of Mincs, Immigration and Colonization, Interior, and Indian Affairs.

King has recorded with his usual detail the series of manoeuvres involving men, portfolios, provinces, and interests that preoccupied him for the six days from 17 to 23 October, when he announced his cabinet on the eve of Thanksgiving Day to give the nation something to be grateful for. Gardiner was more involved in the dealings than most of King's potential ministers for, ironical as it appears now in the light of the reputation he subsequently earned in Agriculture, in 1935 he did everything in his power to avoid it, and was full of suggestions about King's cabinet. Still, his recollections years after the events do not on many points accord with the diary kept at the time by King.[5]

Gardiner felt in 1935 that his education and experience made him a strong contender for Finance. King, while conceding that, not only believed Dunning's knowledge and experience made him yet stronger, but felt that Gardiner, leaving a premiership, would find it embarrassing to deal with the other premiers on financial matters, while he was less well equipped than Dunning to counter R.B. Bennett as leader of the opposition. Gardiner was sufficiently impressed that he withdrew his opposition to Dunning, a move which, since King was planning a cabinet of sixteen instead of Bennett's twenty-three,[6] considerably eased King's task of settling Finance at once.

King's initial inclination on 18 October was to offer Gardiner National Revenue, a portfolio he wanted filled by a low-tariff man, but Gardiner did not as a teetotaller want to be in charge of collecting excise taxes on liquor. Nonetheless, at first he preferred National Revenue over the proposed 'consolidation [of] ... immigration, colonization, lands, forests, mines, parks, Indians, territories, etc.' Gardiner began to feel differently the next day when King urged the proposed portfolio on him as one that 'touched all the western questions ... a department with great patronage,' which 'would keep him in the West and master of an empire there, while Dunning would be in the east.' By the afternoon of 19 October, however, Gardiner was telling King that W.R. Motherwell might wish him to take Agriculture 'rather than have it get into Crerar's hands'; but in the evening he also sounded out the possibilities of Railways and Canals, which King wished to couple with Marine. With nothing settled, Gardiner left for the west the same day, to see Motherwell, to arrange what he could about his own successor in Saskatchewan, and to seek a federal constituency.

Although there does not seem to have been any possibility of Motherwell again entering a King ministry, he was to play an eccentric role in the events of October 1935. As King's minister of agriculture in the 1920s, Motherwell had pressed to have transferred to Agriculture (from Trade and Commerce) the Board of Grain Commissioners, a regulatory body created in 1912 to ensure, among other things, that farmers were treated honestly by the grain elevator companies and merchants who weighed their grain at various points as it moved to market. The board, which had at peak periods over six hundred employees, had always been considered a proper responsibility of the minister of trade and commerce, since it was concerned not with the production of grain but its subsequent handling, and it had commercial counterparts in the department which looked after the quality of products other than grain. While it could be attached to almost any department – as the public archives and the supervision of race-track betting were for years under Agriculture – its closeness to the marketplace made Trade and Commerce seem the most logical place to have it. It was not a selling agency, but when a selling agency was created, in Bennett's Canadian Wheat Board Act, the minister through whom it reported was the man in Trade and Commerce.

Motherwell, re-elected for Melville at the age of seventy-five, saw one more chance to get the Board of Grain Commissioners into Agriculture. Gardiner had on 18 October told King that Melville was the federal seat he wanted and that he 'believed Motherwell would do whatever he wished,' which was to accept the lieutenant-governorship of Saskatchewan. But Motherwell once again became stubborn, using the only tool he had, Melville. King telephoned Gardiner in Regina on 21 October, to be told that it was Motherwell's belief that 'if Gardiner was going to leave the grain business to the eastern people [i.e., with the two relevant boards in Trade and Commerce] there would be no advantage in his letting Gardiner have his seat, as his real desire was to get control of the grain for the west.' Gardiner's response was to ask King for Trade and Commerce, which King thought should be given to a former minister with seniority and almost certainly an easterner. Gardiner raised again the suspicion that Agriculture was a minor portfolio, which King indirectly confirmed, although not to Gardiner, by telling his diary that 'the truth is, the little beggar is angling for one of the more important portfolios, and running the danger of getting out of his depth.'

King went on to record that, despite his doubts, he would discuss Gardiner's request 'with Dunning and others tomorrow.' But when tomorrow came, Gardiner telephoned to revive another alternative: simply transfer the Board of Grain Commissioners to Agriculture, as Motherwell had always wanted, and that would get him Melville at once. King, knowing that Dunning was convinced that any such change would be a mistake, stood firm: Trade and Commerce would keep the board, and Motherwell could keep Melville, which meant some other seat for Gardiner. There was one concession, which King was actually discussing with Dunning and Lapointe at the moment Gardiner called: the Wheat Board (the selling agency, not to be confused with the regulatory Board of Grain Commissioners) would be put under a subcommittee of the cabinet consisting of the ministers of agriculture, finance, and trade and commerce.

With that Gardiner had to be content. Having himself failed to get any of the portfolios he wanted and, when pressed, having chosen Agriculture over the new department that was shortly to be labelled Mines and Resources, he found himself on 22 October virtually faced with a take-it-or-leave-it situation. By that time almost everything was settled, and King was to announce his list of ministers the next day. Gardiner made one last attempt to get Trade and Commerce, but that was now firmly consigned to Ontario, while Agriculture and the new department were earmarked for the west. King's diary does not say that Gardiner agreed to accept Agriculture, and without that confirmation it is unlikely that Gardiner did. What the diary did receive, as one more drop of lubrication for Gardiner, was this:

I also told him that I would let it be known ... that I had asked him to take the Department of Agriculture, and was most anxious that he should; that I was keeping the portfolio unfilled, in order to give him a chance to confer with members of his government, and also with his following in the Legislature. He said if I would say that, it would help him very much.

Gardiner also had King's assurance that he could continue in cabinet to press for the transfer to Agriculture of the Board of Grain Commissioners (as, presumably, he could press for anything else not forbidden by law), so he could take to his supporters in Saskatchewan the offer of one portfolio, one-third of a committee supervising the Wheat Board, and a glimmer of hope about the Grain Commissioners. It was nowhere near what he had hoped for, and except for the expansion he was able to achieve for the department itself, it became no larger. When Gardiner left Agriculture twenty-two years later, the two boards were still reporting through the minister of trade and commerce.

In 1935, between what he was offered and nothing at all, Gardiner took what was offered. King announced his cabinet on 23 October, drawing attention to the vacancy in Agriculture and the reasons for it. That gave Gardiner time to placate those of his supporters who reportedly had hoped for something better, and shortly he was able to advise King that he had the unanimous consent of his caucus and constituency executive to accept the federal portfolio. At King's urgent request he went at once to Ottawa and was appointed a member of the Privy Council on 28 October 1935, five days after all the other freshmen ministers. Since the appointment of acting ministers, and particularly an acting prime minister, usually went by seniority, Gardiner's delay in being sworn in was to provide a source of minor irritation for years.

More pressing in 1935 were the choice of his successor in Saskatchewan, the designation of a new leader of the organization, and the search for a federal constituency. The first two of these were settled with relative ease. The caucus chose W.J. Patterson as party leader, chiefly because T.C. Davis did not want the job. Davis, both in 1935 and later, would have been Gardiner's choice, but he voted against himself and for Patterson, which gave a majority of one to Patterson, who voted for himself.[7] Unlike Gardiner, Patterson did not assume control of the organization, which he had never had even when he was minister of highways in 1926–27. The organization went to the minister of highways Gardiner had selected in 1934, C.M. Dunn, an MLA since 1929. There is little evidence to suggest Gardiner had been schooling Dunn to take over the organization pending his own departure, but Dunn was an experienced worker. His views on organization are implied in an admonition Gardiner sent him when Dunn had been running the organization for barely three months:

I think it would be an absolute mistake to place the organizers in Saskatchewan on Government pay, either in Saskatchewan or at Ottawa. If the Liberal Party cannot finance these two men they had better close up shop. We have had one demonstration of the fact that the people of Saskatchewan will not stand for a party organization paid with Government funds. Our main difficulty at that time was that we did not make the change early enough. When we were attacked on that basis our organization had been removed from the Government service two years earlier ... The Party organization should be made, as far as possible, to stand on its own feet.[8]

Finding a seat for Gardiner was more complex. Motherwell's decision to keep Melville deprived Gardiner of his own choice, for the federal seat included his farm and his provincial constituency, and he knew the area well. The district next best known to Gardiner (and it was one which showed Gardiner's youthful wisdom in moving around for several years as a school teacher) was Assiniboia, which occupied the southeast corner of Saskatchewan. There Gardiner had taught both school and Sunday school, played baseball, hockey, and football, and met people of varying backgrounds; his former students and fellow athletes were now all adults, many of them locally influential.

The problem with Assiniboia was that it was occupied by one Robert McKenzie, a ten-year veteran who had retrieved the seat from a Progressive in 1925, and kept it since. But McKenzie agreed to accept appointment to the Canadian Farm Loan Board, which vacated the seat. Gardiner had no trouble securing the Liberal nomination, although not by acclamation.[9] At a by-election on 6 January 1936, he was an easy winner over a former MP representing the CCF, William Irvine, by 7,282 votes to 3,717. M.J. Coldwell later recorded that while the Saskatchewan Conservatives, virtually wiped out in the successive elections of 1934 and 1935, did not nominate against Gardiner or officially support the CCF in Assiniboia, their lone MP, E.E. Perley (Qu'Appelle), 'gave Mr. Irvine his personal blessing and support.'[10]

Leaving provincial politics, and getting elected for the eighth time, involved little that was novel to Gardiner. The same could not be said of his responsibilities as the designated federal minister for Saskatchewan and Alberta, and as minister of agriculture. His roles of course overlapped, but he had duties as a territorial minister that had little to do directly with Agriculture. In a speech in Regina in 1936, one of countless attempts on Gardiner's part to explain what he and the Liberals were doing, he first described how his departmental obligations had to take precedence over the desire of people to have him address public meetings unceasingly. He then set forth his own agenda, in a passage which, besides revealing his background as a teacher, spelled out his roles as minister, western representative, MP, and Liberal:

One is the problem having to do with unemployment and the other is the problem having to do with the accumulation of debt. It is not my intention to deal with either of these questions insofar as they are related to the whole Dominion of Canada ... [I intend] to deal with debt adjustment and the necessity for relief as applied to the agricultural areas of Western Canada. After having done so it is my intention to discuss with you the marketing of farm products, including wheat, in order that I may point out what I consider to be the Liberal policies ... and also to indicate the extent to which those policies have been put into effect.[11]

That passage reflects Gardiner's conviction that style had to take second place to content when he was educating his supporters – a euphemism for which he sometimes substituted 'dragging them along' – which he saw as the greatest difficulty Liberal leaders had.[12]

In the speech Gardiner carried out his agenda in meticulous detail, canvassing the Liberals' handling of debt adjustment and possible alternatives, and the relevant distinctions between federal and provincial jurisdiction. He did the same with unemployment, pointing out that Saskatchewan was unique in that its 'ordinary' unemployment, caused by an absence of jobs, could be managed readily if it were not for the inability of fifty thousand farm families to pay hired men; the government's plan for that was to subsidize the placing of hired hands on individual farms. He reiterated the Liberal belief that the long-run solution to all the problems he was discussing was 'the freest possible exchange of goods,' and that led him into the marketing of wheat. Here he pointed out that exports of farm products had doubled over the previous year since the party took office, conceding (while digressing to criticize the CCF) that possibly Liberal policy alone was not entitled to full credit for rising exports and prices. He traced the history of wheat marketing from the open market, through the voluntary farmers' pools of the 1920s, to the compulsory pool sought by R.B. Bennett in 1935, assessing the relative merits and weaknesses of each. He made it clear that he had not as yet made his own decision on the best method, and said he was awaiting the report of the Royal Grain Inquiry Commission (delivered in 1938), whose chairman was Mr Justice W.F.A. Turgeon, a Saskatchewan native.[13] The speech ended on a note certain to appeal to western farmers: 'We are within sight of the end of the greatest wheat gamble ever perpetrated upon the producers of wheat in Western Canada.'

It was a typical Gardiner speech, partisan, full of both information and a willingness to accept responsibility for being in a government. He was not, as minister of agriculture, responsible for the Board of Grain Commissioners, and as only one-third of the committee supervising the Canadian Wheat Board he could be outvoted there. But he was one of those collectively responsible for the working of both boards, ambitious to make the responsibility more directly his. To that end he sometimes spoke as if his responsibility was greater than it actually was. He did not remind his listeners then that he had in fact tried and failed to get the Board of Grain Commissioners into Agriculture. Loyalty to the cause, if nothing else, precluded that.

Behind all these activities there was, of course, a phalanx of nameless public servants and interested people who were always entitled to at least some credit for what was done. Charles F. Wilson has recorded in his monumental *A Century of Canadian Grain* how acutely short-staffed in the mid 1930s the federal government was for the formulation of long-range policies.[14] In any event, Gardiner was never one to let public servants tell him what to do or say. Nonetheless, he knew as well as anybody the value of informed advice: he was, after all, constantly handing it out himself. As with any minister, there were branches in his department in which his interest was not large, and for them he needed all the help he could get.

The department's annual reports contained weighty paragraphs on such varied topics as the Federal Apple Maggot Advisory Committee, the Maple Sugar Industry Act, and Horse Club Policy, to all of which Gardiner dutifully gave his attention as a conscientious administrator; but (barring some crisis) they were hardly among his major preoccupations. The reports, tabled in the Commons months after the ending of the fiscal year they covered, took years to reflect the impact of Gardiner's energetic personality: like a glacier, the reports slid through assertions on experimental farms, sundry branches regulating dairies, cold storage, health of animals, seeds, entomology, fruit and vegetables, carrying along offices coping with economics and publicity, and the supervision of race-track betting. A reorganization of the department announced by Gardiner on 13 April 1937 did not reach the annual report until that covering the year ending 31 March 1939.[15]

For all that, the reports are an invaluable if uncritical source of information on the astonishing range of activities for which a minister accepts responsibility. They do not, however, necessarily reflect either the minister's zeal, or his real interests. The report for 1936–37, for example, reveals little of what Gardiner put in two memoranda addressed to the prime minister on 15 May and 7 November 1936. The first, in part a forerunner of the reorganization of the department he announced in 1937, was sent with a covering letter which began: 'Enclosed is a copy of the plan for a more active promotion of the marketing of farm products mentioned by me on a number of occasions in Council.' Towards the end it added: 'I believe the outstanding effort of the Department for the next four years should be to maintain, increase and expand our markets for agricultural products.' The department already had a small marketing section and the first annual report Gardiner signed, for a fiscal year that ended seven months before he became minister, cited studies on costs in creameries on the prairies, the collection of statistics on farmers' co-operatives, and nine research projects undertaken at the request of the Dominion Marketing Board.

Gardiner's memorandum of 15 May envisaged far more than that: the equivalent of a non-grain Board of Grain Commissioners, in effect, but in Agriculture rather than Trade and Commerce. Gardiner's new marketing branch took some time to develop, but his announcement in 1937 erected the department's small marketing branch into one of four main services (production, experimental farms, and science services were the other three), each with a director. Its main functions, which included investigation of marketing methods, of transport costs and facilities, and 'the placing of prospective purchasers in touch with sources of supply,' sounded as if Gardiner's new marketing division did indeed belong in Trade and Commerce. His colleagues by that time were beginning to learn that where Agriculture was concerned, Gardiner was a hard man to move.

The vigour Gardiner showed in churning up his department was revealed also in his memorandum of 6 November 1936 'on arrangements for handling the situation in the west down to the present.' This document, a follow-up to an earlier plan presented in August, recalled that the Liberals' 1936 strategy for the drought area had concentrated on trying 'to keep all the people in the area during the present year, their stock and equipment,' and went on to describe familiar plans (most of them having had their roots in Bennett's policies) for providing food, clothing, and shelter for needy persons, moving feed and water to animals, vice versa, and so on. Gardiner explained with his usual thoroughness how federal, provincial, and municipal duties were divided, and how each authority for each part of the plan was held financially accountable.

The most complex part of the November memorandum, which dealt with debt adjustment, is an excellent example of a problem which had little to do directly with the Department of Agriculture, but nonetheless came under Gardiner's responsibilities as one of the chief western ministers. His chronicle said in part:

... the second proposal was to complete arrangements with the Loan companies, Municipalities and Governments for a blanket debt adjustment down to two years ago ... I [have] had a map completed ... showing in red that part of Saskatchewan which has had an average crop per annum of less than six bushels to the acre over the last six years ...

The proposal made was that the Loan and Mortgage Companies should cancel all arrears of interest down to January 1st, 1935; that the Federal Government should cancel all relief and seed grain provided prior to January 1st, 1935; and that the Municipalities should cancel all taxes in arrears prior to January 1st, 1935.[16]

Concurrently with these plans at the federal level, Gardiner was hearing about finances from his old friend T.C. Davis, still attorney general of Saskatchewan, who wrote him three letters dated 28 August 1936. In one of them Davis reported on a conversation with the general manager of the Bank of Toronto. Davis told the bank executive frankly that Saskatchewan was 'living, virtually, from hand to mouth,' and reported further to Gardiner:

With the advent of Aberhart, the credit of the Western Provinces, if they had any before, was completely gone, and I told him that we were, therefore, forced to live on income, and that too large a part of our income had to go in the payment of interest on our bonded indebtedness ...

After some discussion, he said that, in his opinion, the proper thing for this Province to do, under the circumstances, was to announce our position to the world, and say that we were in a position where we could not pay interest, and that we were not repudiating our debts, or interest, or anything else, but simply could not carry on, and the minute we were in a position to do so we would resume payments.

Davis added that he was 'absolutely dumbfounded' at hearing such words from a bank executive, perhaps because the banker's suggestions so closely followed a plan already set forth by Gardiner, of which Davis summarized his own understanding in another of his letters of 28 August. Gardiner's reply confirmed Davis's views, and he was able to report in November 1936 that he had followed up the various negotiations by meeting the government of Saskatchewan on 15 September, and the mortgage interests on the 16th, as a result of which a general settlement was reached, the main parts of which covered 156 municipalities in Saskatchewan.[17] Gardiner could not in 1936 calculate with any precision how much the whole scheme would save the farmers of the province, but he did venture to suggest that the cancellation of obligations owed to governments alone would reach $75 million. Although Gardiner was acting as a national minister, he had to report that while taxes, and seed and relief costs, were being written off in Saskatchewan and some progress towards that end had been made in Manitoba, no action whatever had yet taken place in Alberta.[18] Unquestionably he would have agreed with one observation by T.C. Davis: 'This Province of Saskatchewan is the sheet anchor for sanity in Western Canada, and, therefore, the sheet anchor of Canada as a whole.'[19]

The federal minister for the sheet anchor was, in truth, a busy man.

Quite apart from his work as head of a department and the prime minister's right-hand man in the west, he was also a member of Parliament; his severest critics would have had to concede that he was not lazy. From the start he saw the House as a great forum, having as added attractions his old adversary M.J. Coldwell, and a Tory opposition, something he had been deprived of in Saskatchewan after 1934. Gardiner was too experienced a legislator to make himself conspicuous too early in the House of Commons; he was, after all, elected only as of 6 January 1936, whereas all but two of his fellows had been returned the previous October. Parliament met on 6 February, and he did not make a speech in the debate on the address in reply to the speech from the throne.

During that debate of wide-ranging speeches he made a couple of interjections, the first a nine-word supplement to a statement of R.B. Bennett, the second, a little longer, to correct courteously an assertion by the Conservatives' lone Saskatchewan member, E.E. Perley. On 18 February, without a word to suggest he was doing it for the first time, Gardiner began to pilot the agricultural estimates for the next fiscal year through the House, fielding a series of detailed and varied queries. For that he had with him, technically not in the chamber but nevertheless sitting before him in the centre aisle of the House, the necessary officials, and from the start he gave his assistants credit, with reiterated phrases like 'the department is inclined to think ...' For several weeks the only observation he made that took more than a few moments was a short speech to support and amend a resolution calling for a full inquiry into the prices of farm implements. Until nearly the end of March he quietly established himself in the House as a knowledgeable – and noticeably non-partisan – minister, whose grasp of his responsibilities was commented on favourably.[20] Then on 27 March he came out swinging.

The only opposition member who seemed determined to provoke Gardiner was R.B. Bennett, who, to be fair, did not single out the minister of agriculture, but indiscriminately did his best to aggravate everybody on the government side. Gardiner had no alternative but to single out Bennett when he moved second reading of a bill to make a final payment to farmers for 1930 wheat delivered to the provincial pools of the time. Bennett, as a westerner, a financier, and an expert on rail transportation, had been his own minister on wheat, and any review of wheat marketing that covered his years in office could concentrate on no other parliamentary figure. Gardiner and Bennett were certain to collide, and their first passage at arms was notable.

The occasion itself need not have produced a combat, for there was no serious difference of opinion between government and opposition about what the problem was, or the solution. In 1930, as part of an attempt to stabilize wheat prices, the government had taken a substantial quantity of wheat from the pools and kept it off the market down to the election of 1935, during which period the executive of the pools' central selling agency kept pressing for adequate compensation. Nobody denied that compensation would be proper, but under the pressures of depression, drought, and collapsing markets, negotiations were never brought to a satisfactory conclusion. In Gardiner's words the whole affair sounded simple:

On July 31, 1931, there were 76,375,000 bushels of 1930 pool wheat in the hands of Mr. McFarland ... Now what was done with that wheat? ... It was actually taken off the market, put into an account in order to stabilize the price to other people who were producing wheat throughout the length and breadth of Canada, and it is because these 76,000,000 bushels were taken off the market and kept off the market from 1931 to 1935 that the wheat pools have been claiming that they should have payment in connection with that wheat. The government is inclined to think their claim is well founded.[21]

Whether the policy had worked or not, Gardiner added, the fact remained that farmers who had delivered grain to the three prairie pools in 1930 had, in the interests of the government's desire to support prices, been kept at a disadvantage in comparison with non-pool producers.

Gardiner was entrusted with both the resolution that preceded a financial bill, and then the bill itself, and if he was selected so that the prime minister could assess his capabilities in the House, he must have obtained high marks. He presented a performance which, after a few weeks in the chorus and a couple of minor solos, demonstrated convincingly that he was ready for leading roles. He put his topic into perspective, surveying it in both analytical and historical contexts. He was well prepared and used his complex material with great skill, revealing in the process an encyclopaedic knowledge of grain policy. In the face of repeated taunts from Bennett he remained cool, countering the opposition leader to such good effect that, for minutes at a time, Bennett was on his feet too. For a freshman MP it was a remarkable show, a veritable tour de force of a kind to which Parliament was destined to become accustomed. It was also combative, and led Bennett to open his case with what he did not intend as a tribute: 'Mr. Speaker, for two hours and a half the chamber has listened to the most violent political speech that I have heard in it for many years about a matter that affects the welfare of every province in the Dominion of Canada.'[22] No matter; Gardiner's parliamentary debut had launched him as a national figure, and his opponents had been given notice never to underestimate him.

The same lesson, in other ways, was concurrently being borne in on his Liberal colleagues. In particular, as will be discussed later, Gardiner's subsequent exploitation of Bennett's Prairie Farm Rehabilitation Act of 1935 and his initiation of the Prairie Farm Assistance Act, to provide compensation to those with small crops or none, indeed, saw him emerge so successful a champion of western interests that he shortly (and unwittingly) contributed to a split in the Liberal party.

On only one major front during his early years in Ottawa did Gardiner suffer defeat, and it involved not the welfare of farmers but his own view of how to govern the grain business. Although he had failed to get the Board of Grain Commissioners transferred to Agriculture he had King's assurance that he could continue to press for the move, and it is possible that King underestimated how persistent his lieutenant could be. W.D. Euler, in Trade and Commerce, was naturally aware of Gardiner's desire to strip him of a major responsibility, and it did not help that he represented a constituency associated with the manufacturing of the same farm implements whose price western members were always wanting reduced. He had not remained loyal to Laurier in 1917. Both ministers were assertive spokesmen for their chief interests. From any point of view, Gardiner and Euler were an unusual pair to have in a situation where; as King admitted to the House in 1938, 'there has always been a question as to just where the jurisdiction of the Department of Agriculture ... ended, and where the jurisdiction of the Department of Trade and Commerce with respect to marketing and sale began.' He added that the departments naturally had to be in close contact, implying that their staffs tended to be critical of each other.[23]

King was commenting on what some opposition members saw as 'a sort of government crisis' involving Gardiner's and Euler's departments, in which the real protagonists were not officials but the ministers themselves. Euler had been in Parliament since 1917, a winner in six consecutive elections. He was in King's cabinet from 1926 to 1930, and after 1935 was in his third portfolio. For the rookie Gardiner it was his first brush with a cabinet colleague, and while of no particular significance in itself the episode was an indicator of things to come. It turned on a document which became celebrated as the Shaw Report.

A.M. Shaw was a former dean of agriculture at the University of Saskatchewan who had been appointed to the Canadian Wheat Board when the newly elected Liberals replaced its membership with their own appointees in December 1935, and while still on the board was seconded to Gardiner's staff in January 1937.[24] (The board, neglected by a government which had not made up its mind about what to do with it, was in a state of near disintegration at the time.[25]) Gardiner had assigned him to chair a committee on the marketing of agricultural products, and late in 1937 told Shaw, 'I would like to have the report out before Christmas.' The minister then left for an unforeseen trip west, neglecting to tell Shaw to make sure the acting minister of agriculture submitted it to the cabinet before it was released.

The report might have been innocuous enough had it not been for Gardiner's well-known ambition to assume responsibility for matters under the minister of trade and commerce. As it was, the report's findings about inadequacies in Canada's marketing of agricultural products appeared to reflect on Euler's management of his department. King was absent from Ottawa and unable to exercise his usual conciliatory powers, and by the time he returned relations between Euler and Gardiner had deteriorated seriously. As soon as the prime minister returned, Gardiner was quick to admit that he had been in error in not ensuring that the report went to cabinet, particularly since it contained inaccuracies. But the damage had been done. 'I thought,' King advised his diary, 'that Euler in this case was right in feeling that an injustice had been done him and officials, and that Gardiner was pressing matters too far.'[26]

The solution was straightforward enough. Gardiner agreed to replace the first edition of the Shaw Report with a corrected version, thus giving the opposition two separate documents to use as proof of a rift in the cabinet. In due course Gardiner read to the cabinet what 'purported to be a sort of agreement between Euler and himself' which sounded, as King said at the time, 'like a wedding march.' The dividing line between their functions was certainly impressive: the Atlantic Ocean, 'Gardiner's work to be confined on this side, and Euler, to the other, with the understanding that Euler would take one or more of Gardiner's men as advisers upon advertising.'[27]

The incident did nothing to improve Gardiner's chances of taking on the marketing of grain, but it did establish that the Shaw Report's strictures on Canada's agricultural marketing generally were not without foundation. As Gardiner said of his first trip abroad as minister of agriculture: 'I saw this sign, "Eat New Zealand cheese." Under those words was something about New Zealand butter. Out on the street I saw a bus going by bearing a sign, "Eat Australian lamb." Then I saw another sign, "Eat Australian butter." I walked all the way down to Canada House without seeing the word "Canada." '[28]

The Shaw Report may have occasioned a slip in protocol, but there could be no question that it was needed. It says much about Gardiner's determination to further the cause of Canadian agriculture that it was he, and not the minister of trade and commerce, who commissioned it. Gardiner always looked back at the Shaw Report with satisfaction just as he could, as the end of his first Parliament approached, look back on his successful negotiation of several relief policies such as debt adjustment, his legislation to encourage the marketing of grains through co-operative pools, to the Prairie Farm Assistance Act, and the proliferation of activities under the Prairie Farm Rehabilitation Act. These were major landmarks, supplemented by unbroken attention to a multitude of details: his correspondence was growing, and annually in the House of Commons he handled questions and comments on topics as diverse as bacteriological work and butter prices, corn borers and fruit storage, vegetable grading and hog grading, not to mention the pea moth and the potato beetle.

He had not, by the outbreak of war, fulfilled his own and Motherwell's ancient ambitions to get all of wheat marketing under Agriculture. But his star was rising, and it was clear that his star was going to be of a special kind. In a debate in 1938 on the report of a Commons committee on farm implements, Gardiner observed mildly 'that there is no good reason why the implement companies could not have reduced their prices instead of increasing them.' In the same debate he had to hear MPs from industrial constituencies in southern Ontario say, in one form or another, 'I believe the farm implement industry has been discriminated against.'[29]

It had been one thing, as a provincial leader in the west, to oppose opinions like that no matter who expressed them. It was a new experience to find people who expressed them not only in one's own caucus, but even in the cabinet.

13

Settling In

Gardiner's move in 1935 meant a major upheaval for his family, as federal politics always does except for the few parliamentarians whose homes are in or near Ottawa. The Gardiner children ranged in age from sixteen to four, growing up in a home whose life had been divided between the farm at Lemberg and the compact city of Regina. Ottawa was considerably more than twice the size of Regina, several days' drive from Saskatchewan. Although the farm was to remain a focal point for the family, and Gardiner returned to it so often that his cabinet colleagues commented on his frequent absences, Ottawa was nonetheless a watershed in the Gardiners' life. For the older children it meant new schools and new friends in an unfamiliar environment, and for Violet Gardiner it meant breaking a settled pattern that had begun when she first moved to Lemberg in 1916.

Gardiner too found much that was strange. Large though the agricultural belt of Saskatchewan was, it was for most of the year capable of being covered by automobile. Its population, following similar pursuits, had similar dislikes of tariffs, debts, and high freight rates, all of which could be blamed on central Canada. Its social organizations, whether called pools, law societies, teachers' federations, or churches, were variously grouped under leaders most of whom Gardiner knew personally, and he had a warm relationship with the president of the only university, Dr Walter Murray.[1] To leave all that to go to central Canada, to start anew to build up the vast network of individual contacts indispensable to a successful politician, working with colleagues with interests and views opposed to his own, was for Gardiner the kind of challenge he had always enjoyed.

Saskatchewan was barely five hundred miles from east to west, its main settled area in 1935 considerably less than that. Fifty-four of its fifty-five legislative members represented seats in the southern half of the province, the care of the entire north belonging to a lone Liberal who won 1,329 of 2,299 votes in 1934. (Gardiner, in his rural Melville, in the same election won 4,989 votes out of 8,423.) The relatively simple government could be supervised by a cabinet of nine. As the new federal minister of agriculture, Gardiner took on a department whose installations included three dozen experimental farms and stations from coast to coast, laboratories for the study of animal diseases on the same scale, and seed laboratories scattered from New Brunswick to Alberta. The department in 1935–36 had exhibits at sixty-four fairs and shows. In the same year its inspectors carried out 94,377 on-the-spot examinations of fruits, vegetables, and containers, and its publicity division answered 851,712 requests for information, while sending out several million releases which had not been asked for. Three hundred kits of educational lantern slides were prepared and sent out.[2] As a farmer Gardiner had himself been the recipient of some of these attentions.

If the last chapter has given the impression that Gardiner's new federal role was to consist in large part of public pronouncements as a minister and MP, it is important to make clear that what the public sees of the necessary activities of a successful politician is probably less than the proverbial tip of the iceberg. With rare exceptions, a politician becomes successful only through the expenditure of enormous amounts of time and energy by large numbers of people, and their efforts must be organized and financed. At all that, by 1935, Gardiner was an old hand indeed.

Campaign funds were among the few topics on which Gardiner did not keep systematic records which have survived. That was not because he thought there was anything wrong with political money, about which he wrote freely. Over a period of forty years, he said, he collected and spent four million dollars for the party, and from 1931 he was responsible for all the Liberal money raised in Saskatchewan. Collecting funds, he averred, entailed some of the most effective campaigning that could be done, and every Liberal who couldn't work every day during an election should at least contribute money.[3] Political money was, in Gardiner's view, so necessary that one simply took it for granted.

Gardiner also freely admitted that he raised money wherever he could get it which meant, since Saskatchewan was not noted as the headquarters of affluent financial and industrial interests, that he went elsewhere for it, and notably to Toronto and Montreal where, for a prairie farmer, he was remarkably successful. His own recollection was that he did best with the big oil companies, but he also had contacts with banks and other financial corporations, and on at least one occasion the party used him as an agent to deal with the CPR.[4]

Before 1935 his collecting of funds for his own affairs made it hard to justify any interference with his activities in the interests of the national party, although Charles Dunning made a point of noting that Gardiner ran an expensive campaign. After 1935 his private collecting continued and, as Reginald Whitaker has observed in his admirable study of Liberal finances, Gardiner not only expected Saskatchewan to remain an importer of party money from his own sources and national funds, but in his own collecting he competed directly with national collectors.[5] Gardiner agreed that money should not be accepted if there were any strings attached[6] although, as the party's chief national bagman of the time, Norman Lambert could not help but feel that there ought to be at least a positive correlation between contributions and patronage, especially in contracts. In 1947, in a different context, Eaton's appears to have refused a request for funds before a desired statement on party policy had been made.[7]

Gardiner's position was unique in the party's anatomy. In one sense he belonged utterly, a conscientious and devoted believer who gave all his energies to the cause; in the national organization itself, indispensable though he knew it to be, he remained, in the words of contemporaries, 'odd man out,' a 'lone wolf.' That was inevitable, given his strong convictions about the worth of the individual and the value of individual effort. He worked hard at implementing his own versions of liberalism and Liberalism, and expected other supporters of the party to do the same. When they did, Gardiner respected them and their efforts, even though he did not consider that his respect committed him to accepting in perpetuity whatever they did; he always reserved the right to keep on opposing wrong conclusions drawn from right premises. When some party supporters did not do their bit, he was likely to conclude not that they were lazy or inattentive, but bad Liberals. Real Liberals were workers.

That led him on occasion to say little about affairs in which he had a great interest but which, he was satisfied, were in good hands. For example, although the Royal Commission on Dominion-Provincial Relations grew directly out of studies by the Bank of Canada of the finances of Manitoba and Saskatchewan, Gardiner did not speak in the House on the announcement of its personnel nor, when the commissioners' impartiality was impugned by R.B. Bennett, did he leap to their defence, leaving that to the prime minister and Norman Rogers.[8] He played a minimal role in Saskatchewan's brief to the commission, leaving that, in keeping with his views on local responsibilities, to the provincial cabinet. When M.J. Coldwell commented on that 'excellent brief,' Gardiner did not take the opportunity to respond. However, he was simultaneously busy on what he considered his own fronts, and instances can be selected to show him in revealing roles. In Saskatchewan, of course, he was always as busy as an MP and minister of agriculture could be, but he had wider activities that taxed his skills as a politician and administrator: in the Prairie Farm Rehabilitation program (PFRA) for example, in Alberta, and in Ontario.

Almost unnoticed at the time among Bennett's last-minute flurry of social legislation, PFRA had as its general purpose the conservation of water on the prairies, and to that end provided subsidies to farmers who excavated dugouts to catch run-off, authorized the construction of dams, and in due course community pastures, wherever they seemed desirable within the areas designated in the act. It was by any standards an imaginative piece of legislation.

Because the drought was regarded as a temporary phenomenon, PFRA was initially a temporary cure. The statute provided $750,000 to be expended in the first year of operation, and $1 million for each of the next four years, by which time everybody hoped the need for it would have expired so the act could do the same. For that reason the staff was not brought under the civil service, and that gave Gardiner precisely what he needed to replace the Saskatchewan Liberal organization he had used with such skill since he took charge of it in 1922. His influence within it remained enormous, of course, for he was *the* federal minister for the province. But after 1935 the provincial organization was under other direction, and Gardiner believed that local affairs should be run locally. Provincial patronage was provincial, and to offset that Gardiner always insisted PFRA was purely federal. Early in its history he instructed one of PFRA's chief executives to consult Regina in regard to personnel only when told: where staff was concerned, 'I am not expecting that the Regina organization is going to have anything whatsoever to say.'[9]

Another reason was that Gardiner did not like what he was hearing about the post-Gardiner era in Saskatchewan. As early as April 1936 his old associate T.H. Wood wrote a long letter complaining that the pressure of petty demands in Regina was causing him to neglect his own business so seriously that he wanted out of the party's local executive. He concluded revealingly: 'I have thought about it for several days, just trying to think of somebody who might take over the job and do it in a way that there will be no scandal attached to it, and also somebody who has not got sticky fingers – they all seem to have them at the present time.' A few months later G.H. Danielson, MLA for Arm River, told Gardiner of the party's deterioration because of a group of self-seeking members who were even tolerant of the liquor ring the former premier had successfully fought off. Gardiner's reply was characteristic: 'I think this is a matter which you should place squarely before the caucus of the Party at Regina ... There is no time when an organization is completely free from the encroachment of groups such as you refer to. Those in charge must always keep such organizations at arm's length.'[10]

Gardiner's departure from the Saskatchewan scene was clearly permitting developments he would never have tolerated; but he could not have operated the Saskatchewan organization from headquarters in Ottawa. Besides, he needed a federal organization, and it is ironic that he found it in the very portfolio he had been so reluctant to accept.

The systematic way in which Gardiner went about building up PFRA is impressive. With most federal patronage he inherited long-standing traditions of a kind that are rarely taken into account as part of a culture. Thus the judicial bench, for example, had to include an understood percentage of Roman Catholics, and 'successive appointments, or appointments close together, could not be made from the same constituency, the same town, the same religious minority, the same ethnic group, the same law firm or the same family.' To those recognized protocols (the quota on Roman Catholics went back to territorial days) Gardiner added his own gloss: he would not recommend any Liberal who had ever flirted at any level with coalition with other parties, and he was loathe to recommend a judgeship for a constituency with a poor record in electing Liberals. Judgeships were rare, but all Saskatchewan MPS from largely rural seats had dozens of village postmasterships, and government members could obtain a vacancy in most of them by a declaration that the incumbent had been guilty of political partisanship. For Gardiner's own seat his files on postmasters alone included nearly 5,500 pages of correspondence relating to over sixty villages.[11]

In 1935 PFRA was new, and Gardiner had the rare opportunity of creating his own traditions. He followed several parallel courses, to enlarge its annual budget, to convert it from a temporary to a permanent institution, and to expand its powers. In 1937 the statutory ceilings on PFRA's annual expenditures were removed, and the administration empowered to spend 'sums not exceeding the amount appropriated by Parliament in each year' down to 1939–40. In 1939 that time limit was removed, and the minister's powers enlarged to permit him to enter into relevant agreements with any or all of the prairie provinces, and persons or companies in them; at first any transaction over $5,000 had to be approved by order-in-council, and that ceiling was in due course raised to $10,000.[12] By the end of his first Parliament Gardiner, having failed to obtain the Board of Grain Commissioners, had invented something better, and a minor portfolio was on the way to becoming major.

The key to his success with PFRA lay in his ministerial power to appoint 'such temporary, technical, professional and other officers and employees as he may deem necessary and expedient,' and the key lay in the word 'temporary.' Gardiner was too shrewd a politician, and too conscientious a public servant, to hire soil experts and engineers who would recommend or build dams or dugouts that would not hold water. To decide whether water was or was not being held took no great expertise, however, so that while the technical men were as good as any a merit system was likely to produce, the 'inspectors,' employed and paid on a per diem basis, could be almost anybody. They comprised a splendid band of political workers over whose correspondence there still lingers a slightly raffish air, men to whom Gardiner had to say from time to time, in effect, 'Do not use the PFRA letterhead for political letters,' or 'PFRA money cannot be used for party purposes.'

One zealous toiler once dedicated a pamphlet on Liberalism to Gardiner, advising him that he was working for two candidates concurrently. All of them helped organize cells of Liberals, reported to Gardiner on the faithful and the unfaithful, and generally promoted the cause in any way that occurred to them.[13] Undoubtedly some of them used tactics about which they did not trouble their chief. And atop this miniature bureaucracy were better-known Liberals: Jack Vallance, who held South Battleford as an MP for the party from 1925 until his defeat in 1935, was one chief executive; George Spence, briefly a Liberal MP in 1925–27, except for that as MLA from 1917 to 1938, and a provincial minister in five portfolios, was another. Several other candidates, both successful and unsuccessful, caught the eye of the parliamentary opposition as they enlisted in PFRA.

But PFRA was not a make-work project for party supporters: it was from the start an immense success, praised by members of all parties in the House, a regional program that quickly aroused jealousies elsewhere. At the end of its first five years it had completed over fourteen thousand small water projects, ten thousand of which were dugouts: that meant ten thousand contacts with individual farms. Any enterprise that conserved water was bound to find favour with western members, and its good works were so highly thought of that there were remarkably few complaints about it. Typical was a comment made years later by Ross Thatcher, in 1950 the CCF member for Moose Jaw: 'In my opinion the PFRA is accomplishing much in the prairie provinces, yet I wonder how at every election these PFRA trucks can run around working for Liberal candidates.'

On the other hand, PFRA was barely launched when Tommy Church, a crusty Tory from Toronto, complained, 'Ever since the present Minister of Agriculture has been in the house he has been getting preferred and special treatment for his province.' Not long thereafter J.F. Pouliot, MP for Temiscouata, said dourly of PFRA, 'We cannot get anything from the Department of Agriculture for the province of Quebec.'[14] In later years, reminiscing about the Gardiner organization, MPs were to recall that Liberal field workers for PFRA and PFAA used the preferred benefits of the two policies to intimidate electors into voting Liberal; but there were no such complaints about either in the early years.[15] Attempts to check out the later complaints have produced no evidence, only nostalgic opinions about the wicked old days.

The great beauty of PFRA to Gardiner was that it was an amenity that did not involve other ministers or departments. Its value to him could hardly be overestimated, for at a time when depression and war made automobiles and gasoline costly and scarce, Liberal workers could, as Ross Thatcher was to observe, always hitch rides on PFRA vehicles as they went about on their endless rounds. The chief limitation on both the PFRA and the Prairie Farm Assistance Act (PFAA) as political tools was that they were applied to defined geographical areas, and while the areas were large, Gardiner had outside them no comparable organization. Not all the PFRA workers themselves were content with their lot; for while the machinery became permanent, each individual worker had only temporary status until well after the war, and while the political workers were used to it, the technical men would have liked some security.[16] As with the subsequent alleged use of PFRA and PFAA to intimidate voters, that was the sort of detail of which the minister, judging from his papers, was not kept well informed. He did receive occasional complaints about the political uses of PFRA, and about the frustrations of the technical employees who were for so long kept temporary, but to him PFRA and PFAA remained a source of pride.

He did not feel the same of his assignment in Alberta, of which he wrote in 1938, 'I have been more disappointed with the efforts put forth in relation to political matters in Alberta during the past two years than with any previous experience I have had.'[17] For Gardiner, who was not given to grumbling about Liberals, that was a remarkable admission, and it stemmed from the growing recognition that, when King asked him to take charge of Alberta in 1936 because Alberta had only one Liberal MP and no minister, he had been handed an insoluble problem. The Alberta Liberal party was so different from Saskatchewan's that none of the devices that Gardiner had developed in his own province could work in the other. From first to last Gardiner's Alberta venture was a striking demonstration of how a successful politician, well schooled in the Liberalism he had grown up with in Manitoba and Saskatchewan, found himself all but helpless in the context of another community as close as Alberta. It might have led a man with more time for reflection to wonder if Liberalism had the universal applicability its proponents claimed for it.

Gardiner had for three decades been working within a well-disciplined party trying to solve problems which, however mixed the province's population, were fairly homogeneous throughout the area. The party was a success; and even its defeat in 1929, by letting Anderson's Co-operative Government struggle with the worst years of the drought and depression, turned out to have been a blessing in disguise. The Liberal party of Alberta had been out of office since 1921, and because the party had been in office federally for more than half the time since then, a split had developed between its federal and provincial wings to the point where they had separate organizations. This mystified Gardiner: 'Whenever there is a political fight on in Saskatchewan,' he told Alberta's lone Liberal MP, James MacKinnon, in 1936, 'we are all in on it.'[18] There were further divisions between northern and southern sections of the party and, because of the Alberta electoral system, a rural-urban split besides.

The urban sections of the party, particularly in Edmonton, were led by lawyers and businessmen, and since the only available patronage was federal, a steady procession of leaders to the judicial bench was inevitable. The turnover had been so great, indeed, that the party was constantly either breaking in a new leader or seeking his successor, and a by-product of that after 1935 was a growing sentiment that the next leader should be an urban lawyer only if nobody else was available. The search for a leader itself led to further divisions over whether the party should fight the messianic Aberhart as a straight Liberal organization or enter some kind of deal with willing members from the Conservatives and United Farmers of Alberta. The new leader finally chosen, E.L. Gray, seemed at first to favour the first alternative, then a variety of courses based on the second.[19] Inevitably, Gardiner was totally opposed to coalition in any form. More than once in the late thirties Gardiner reminded Alberta Liberals that coalition, as in 1917 and 1929, was basically a Tory plot: whenever Tories get into trouble they 'talk of unions or amalgamations of one kind or another.'[20]

In Alberta after 1935 a lot of Liberals were doing the same, partly because partyism itself was in bad odour in the province, to such an extent that some Liberals told him it was unsafe to nominate people using the party label. To Gardiner that was incomprehensible, in much the same category as the notion that the Bible is pornographic. There was only one way to fight Aberhart, and that was with straight Liberalism, and after 8 June 1938 he was able to point to the party's triumph in the Saskatchewan provincial election as proof. Before that, he used every device he knew to persuade the Alberta Liberals how to run a party. From the beginning he insisted on local autonomy, making no recommendations on patronage without Alberta advice; the channels of communication he used were MacKinnon for the north and, at first, Senator W.A. Buchanan of Lethbridge, for the south, MacKinnon in due course taking over the whole province.

The true basis of local organization, he told E.L. Gray was 'the primary meeting' in each polling division, which chose delegates to the constituency convention, which in turn had control over constituency matters; policy was laid down by the provincial or federal convention, and the constituency organizations had 'no right to change in any way whatsoever' a policy decision made at the higher level.[21] In pre-Gray days Gardiner had impressed on several correspondents, as he had told C.M. Dunn in Saskatchewan, the necessity of keeping the reorganized Alberta party free of the civil service. When a party member sent him a plan for using the prairie census of 1936 to gather, along with the usual statistics, private information on the political inclinations of the citizenry, Gardiner replied: 'I may say that much of the organization work done in the past in the West was done in the manner suggested, and it has been most valuable ... The most effective political worker is one who has no employment with the Government, and works for the cause because he believes in it.'[22]

If that sounds inconsistent with Gardiner's own deployment of PFRA (which, incidentally, was not nearly as useful in his Alberta operations as in Saskatchewan where the need for the plan was greater), it is important to note that in his letter he twice wrote 'most effective'; he did not say, nor did he mean, that party workers on the public payroll were ineffective. Gardiner frankly conceded that PFRA appointees were likely to have political inclinations. But they were casual workers for both PFRA and the party, and were not part of the provincial Liberal organization which was *the* party organization in Saskatchewan. As good Saskatchewan Liberals, most of them would as a matter of course throw their weight into any handy campaign.

One of Gardiner's basic techniques in Alberta was to build up a network of informants to whom he wrote, and heard from, frequently and at length. In that correspondence the role in Alberta of the National Liberal Federation in the thirties does not surface with anything like the clarity with which the NLF's secretary, Norman Lambert, perceived it in his diary. The diary conveys the impression that if Lambert had ever had to take sides in the ancient Motherwell-Dunning feud he would have been a Dunning man, and therefore not a Gardiner man. As early as 1932 Lambert had written, in a passage that would have astounded Gardiner, that Gardiner 'cannot be superceded [*sic*] just now; and will have to be carried along and used and influenced.' Later Lambert recorded an informant's opinion that Gardiner's organization for the federal by-election in Mackenzie in 1933 was 'most ineffective,' and that even Gardiner's old friend Jack Stevenson was uneasy about it.[23] These opinions are evidence of nothing, but coupled with other diary references to Gardiner, such as the campaign extravagance he was alleged by Dunning to have indulged in, they do suggest that Lambert had reservations about Gardiner. When their responsibilities crossed, as they did in Alberta after 1935, misunderstanding was to be expected.

Lambert's role in the party was a peculiarly thankless one, in which he appeared to be relied on to deliver campaign funds without compromising the party's relations with contractors, while at the same time receiving a minimum of credit and recognition; and he was also an experienced organizer. The kind of clash that might develop had already been foreshadowed in the Mackenzie by-election of 1933. Gardiner was the minister from Saskatchewan who knew all the local organizers, the chief of whom in Mackenzie was that practised guerrilla fighter,

Archie McCallum. Mackenzie was a federal constituency, and Lambert was the federal fund-raiser with, or so he believed, some responsibilities in federal campaigns. Who specifically, then, was in charge of Mackenzie? And when Gardiner's Alberta assignment added to his fiefdom another whole province with seventeen federal constituencies, who was in charge of Alberta?

Gardiner believed that his responsibilities in Alberta were the same as they were in Saskatchewan, and early in 1936 his man McCallum told Lambert that he was going to make a political survey of Alberta, not as a member of the Saskatchewan organization (which would never do) but as a federal man. McCallum told Lambert that James MacKinnon approved of the trip; but that was not MacKinnon's own understanding. Shortly it was decided that McCallum might properly survey Alberta and report to Gardiner but Lambert, because he really needed to know, pressed the question of his jurisdiction in Alberta. His understanding was that Gardiner spoke for the province in the House and was to handle recommendations for appointments, while organization rested with the National Liberal organization – in other words, himself. He was wrong, but his misunderstanding was not inexplicable: when Gardiner was assigned control of Alberta, including the organization, Lambert had not been told. In November of 1938, by which time Gray had dropped Gardiner as his mentor in provincial matters and was flirting with coalition, Lambert wrote of a talk with Gray: 'He said he intended to call Alberta executive together when he returned and make fresh start on co-operative movement to form an Alberta Govt Ass'n. He asked me if I could help with finances. I said that while my position re Alberta was clearly favourable to his independent action, I was bound to play the game with the policy of the federal Govt as expressed by Gardiner.'[24]

There is no evidence that Gardiner knew that the secretary of the National Liberal Federation was promoting, however obliquely, a form of non-partisan coalition in Alberta, and that was just as well since they were also colleagues in another non-departmental enterprise concerning a provincial leader, the premier of Ontario. Gardiner and Mitch Hepburn had shared an unusual experience: each had led his provincial party to victory on the same day in 1934. That was about all they had in common, but Gardiner recalled on his deathbed that he had at one time regarded Hepburn as an able young man with a great future in the party. He fitted what Gardiner told the Albertans they needed in 1937: 'a man who has always been a Liberal and knows why he is a Liberal; a man who is outstanding among Liberals.'[25] Alberta did not pick a man who met Gardiner's qualifications, and events were to prove that neither had Ontario.

The precise point at which Hepburn began to turn against the federal Liberal party is not clear, but it is plain that his antipathy was not against King alone. The observant Norman Lambert noted in 1933, that Hepburn was so irritated with Vincent Massey (then the party's president) for not placing him at the head table at a dinner that he 'would have nothing to do with V.M.'s Summer Conference, or anything else.' Months before the federal election of 1935 Hepburn told Lambert that 'he had never had a "break" from K[ing]., who had no "guts" ... if Stevens was taken on by the Cons. he w'd beat King.' After the election, in which he campaigned hard for the federal party, Hepburn was further put out at not being consulted, as Gardiner was, about the new cabinet, and because 'not one Hepburn man received an appointment to any position in the King administration of 1935.'[26]

He was not appeased when Gardiner campaigned for him in the Ontario election of 1937, praising him highly as a fearless leader of the right type. Not a man to leave a grievance unnurtured, Hepburn set aside his help from federal sources and picked up several national policies with which he was unhappy. Concurrently he made trouble for Lambert's attempts to collect money in Ontario, and ventured into Quebec with the same intent. He instructed the secretary of the provincial party not to invite any federal member to appear on behalf of his own followers.[27]

One of Hepburn's grievances grew out of Gardiner's successful championing of the west whereas, as he told Tommy Davis, 'everything the Ontario government had asked the Federal Government to do had been turned down completely and ... they had received infinitely better treatment from Mr. Bennett's administration.' In the same discussion Hepburn told Davis, as he told Gardiner, that he was 'quite prepared to wreck the Party, if this was necessary to defeat Mr. King,' but would throw his whole weight behind Gardiner if he were leader.[28] Gardiner dutifully reported these disloyal sentiments to King, who was not particularly pleased.[29] Even after Gardiner had done yeoman service in an attempt at conciliation, King noted that he had long 'watched with interest the eagerness of some of my colleagues to associate with Hepburn in a provincial campaign, and to identify themselves with him since.' King named C.G. Power, Ian Mackenzie, and Gardiner, assuring himself that while he did not doubt their loyalty, he would some day be succeeded, and 'Hepburn, having the machine in his hands, would probably be the successor or dictator.'

The suspicious King was being considerably less than just, for Gardiner's loyalty to his leader and the party had been repeatedly demonstrated, and indeed frequently noted by King himself. But the suspicion that Gardiner's involvement with Hepburn in the thirties included disloyalty to the prime minister was to linger. Yet the truth was simple enough: Gardiner and Hepburn met when the former was attending the Royal Winter Fair in November 1938, and they frankly discussed party affairs. Gardiner told Hepburn he would be reporting fully to King, but that did not prevent Hepburn from repeating his distrust of King, and his willingness to support Gardiner. Gardiner expressed his appreciation, reiterated his loyalty to King; and reported to him. Hepburn asked Gardiner to return to Toronto, which he did on 25 November: 'Mr. Hepburn ... told me that his reason for calling me back was that he was already convinced Mr. King was going to stay, that if he remained he would oppose Mr. King and that rather than break up the Liberal Party as suggested previously he was considering quitting.'[30]

Gardiner had not received Davis's letter when he wrote the words quoted above, but he already had evidence enough of Hepburn's unpredictability. Between Gardiner's two visits to Toronto, Hepburn had given an interview which clearly suggested that Gardiner had approached him as an emissary to offer concessions in the interests of party peace, none of which was true. 'I do not know the reason for the interview,' Gardiner said publicly, 'but presume it is the result of the usual round of rumours which are associated with any such controversy' as the Hepburn affair. It was the rumours, as well as the truth, that lingered: Gardiner had been an emissary of King's; he had not, but did approach Hepburn in a manner disloyal to King; he had misled Hepburn on King's views; and King on Hepburn's, and so on.

Gardiner's own version was that his conversations were 'an attempt on my part to be conciliatory,' in a discussion which was 'a natural one to develop between two Liberals' – the work of a good party man in a position of influence. But Hepburn's attitude hardened until in January 1940 he supported a motion of the Ontario leader of the opposition, George Drew, condemning the federal government's war effort. The motion passed, giving King the issue he needed for a sudden dissolution of Parliament. Had Gardiner's well-meant intervention in 1938 succeeded, he might not have had it.

Gardiner's non-departmental activities, like his work purely as a minister, naturally covered a good deal more than party problems in Alberta and Ontario. But the two sets of duties were inseparably mingled: just as a ministerial trip to the Royal Winter Fair let him talk with Hepburn in 1938, a party trip to Alberta could give him an opportunity to pursue departmental matters in Manitoba. Nor was all his work oriented towards the west: Nova Scotian apples and Prince Edward Island potatoes were agricultural products too, and he was particularly interested in the reclamation of the salt marshlands of the Maritimes, where the problem was based in part not on drought but its opposite. Nonetheless, his home base remained Saskatchewan, the province which produced most of the wheat that moved abroad, the lion's share of PFRA, and all of the Saskatchewan Liberal party.

It is part of the folklore of Gardiner's critics that after he left for Ottawa he remained in charge of the Saskatchewan Liberal party. There is no doubt that his influence in Saskatchewan remained enormous, for his departure left his successors 'bereft of imaginative counsel to a degree not evident before in Liberal administrations.'[31] It was also true that his advice remained valuable. But it could only be advice. Gardiner was a firm believer in local autonomy as a Liberal principle and, as he told James MacKinnon of Alberta, 'no one living at a distance can be arriving at conclusions which will be sound.'[32]

In Saskatchewan W.J. Patterson was the premier and C.M. Dunn the minister supervising the organization. The organization was a well-disciplined body requiring day-to-day consideration of minute details: there was no way that Gardiner, living most of the time in Ottawa, could control it. There was Liberal dissatisfaction with the party's direction after Gardiner's departure, and further proof of the absence of Gardiner's touch can be found in the provincial election of 1938. Gardiner's old seat of Melville had remained Liberal by acclamation in 1935, but in 1938 C.M. Dunn, of all people, lost it to one of the two Social Crediters elected in that year, and then in a by-election lost Humboldt, which had remained Liberal in the general election, to the CCF.

Dunn's double defeat in turn by the Liberals' chief opponents in Saskatchewan in 1938 offered Gardiner a striking indication that things were changing back on the ranch. He was aware, although not pleased, that in the first legislature to which CCF members (running nominally as Farmer-Labor) had been elected in 1934 the party had, by skilful use of parliamentary devices, established itself as a credible institution. The CCF may have had only five members, but they were also the official opposition, and they spoke knowledgeably and intelligently on every significant government issue, in addition to raising many of their own.

The Liberals had no experience of Social Credit at the provincial level in 1938, although the party had appeared out of nowhere to run a full slate of federal candidates in 1935. Gardiner had reason to observe them in Alberta, and his initial inclination, as part of his all-round antipathy to coalition, was to point out that Aberhart's government 'have not made half as bad a mess of running Alberta as the Anderson Coalition made of running Saskatchewan.'[33] Not even Anderson, however, had been catapulted from nowhere into office. In his first legislative assembly Aberhart survived petition by some of his followers to the lieutenant-governor requesting his replacement; irritated the lieutenant-governor (who seriously considered dismissing him) by snatching his official home away from him; and introduced a sizeable volume of legislation that was variously reserved, disallowed, or struck down by the courts. Gardiner was bemused by the gyrating Aberhart, but not to the point where he would overlook a chance to campaign against him when the Albertan invaded Saskatchewan in the spring of 1938 in an attempt to repeat his 1935 Alberta coup.

Gardiner felt obliged to say little publicly in Alberta, not just about the government but about the Liberal party, whose leading members seemed to regard patronage as an end in itself instead of merely a useful tool. In sensible Saskatchewan Gardiner was very much at home, and he campaigned as if he were still premier, which no doubt helped convince his opponents that he still controlled the party. It was a relief from his chores in Alberta, where he wanted to see an organization that would not even ask Ottawa for anything until it had won half the seats. At the moment it was such a mess that it couldn't even keep Aberhart at home.[34]

Concurrently with the Saskatchewan campaign, E.L. Gray was seriously considering going along with the lieutenant-governor's proposal to dismiss Aberhart, after which Gray would accept the premiership, a suggestion both King and Gardiner considered utterly mad.[35] Gardiner was also busy with his estimates in the House of Commons down to 25 May – the election was 8 June – so that his campaigning was foreshortened. It was not for that reason that the Liberals' share of the popular vote dropped from 48 to 45 per cent, and its seats from fifty to thirty-eight. The Conservatives, who held no seats, saw their 27 per cent of the vote in 1934 drop to 12 per cent, while the CCF though doubling its seats to ten, went from 24 to 19 per cent of the vote. The whirlwind week Aberhart spent in the province was not fruitless: two Social Credit MLAs were returned, and two successful Unity candidates completed the legislature's roster. The victory was highly satisfactory to Gardiner, and strengthened his hand in Ottawa. Less pleasing was the emergence of the CCF as an established party.[36]

There remained one other major matter that had to be settled in the thirties, and it took Gardiner back to the beginnings of his public life: he had to find a home seat. Unlike his leader, who had already sat for Ontario, Prince Edward Island, and Saskatchewan constituencies, Gardiner had no desire to move about. As a western tribune, he wanted to maintain a base in the west. He was fed up with Alberta. Manitoba already not only had a minister, T.A. Crerar, but one not known for his tolerance of Gardiner's work against the Progressives in the twenties. That left Saskatchewan. But Gardiner's farm and former provincial seat were miles to the north of Assiniboia; maintaining a base in one area while representing another meant a lot of uncomfortable travelling over roads which, when they were not covered with mud or snow, were usually dusty. Gardiner was familiar with Assiniboia, which had two permanent boundaries that could never be gerrymandered; but it was out of the way, far from the main movements of automobiles and trains. The town of Melville, which gave the federal and provincial seats their common name, was a division point on the Canadian National Railway, and the shops there were yet another focal point for Gardiner's attentions as minister.[37]

Melville had three distinct disadvantages, not least of which was that in 1938 the provincial portion of the seat had gone Social Credit. Gardiner's old partner in arms at Regina, T.H. Wood, warned him early in 1939 that, with war with Germany in sight, Nazi sympathizers were stirring up the German population, working through the Bunds – there was a cell even at Lemberg. Unlike 1914 and 1917, Wood reminded Gardiner, when the last war and conscription began, the Liberals in 1939 were in power, and he did not think the Bund was likely to direct German-Canadians to vote Liberal.[38] And Melville was occupied by Motherwell, whose obstinacy had sent Gardiner to Assiniboia in the first place.

Motherwell's retirement was favoured by many (though not, until 1939, by Motherwell), and there is at least a hint that local Liberals planned to offer the next nomination to Gardiner anyway. Assiniboia also wanted to keep Gardiner, enjoying the perquisites that go with having a minister. In protracted negotiations the party was able to work up a good deal of speculative publicity over Motherwell's possible retirement, Gardiner's choice of seat, and related matters. Some thought that Gardiner should run in the weaker seat with the hope of ensuring two Liberal seats instead of one, but veteran organizers were unclear on which seat he should choose. The kind of potential opposition he might face in either seat was also canvassed, for the unsettled electorate was being offered a remarkable variety of choices that included not only Liberal, Conservative, CCF, and Social Credit, but a composite generally called Unity which could be a coalition of almost anything. The entire operation, which required several hundred pages of correspondence, was a striking exhibition of precisely what a well-organized party does behind the scenes.[39]

In the event, Gardiner let it be known that he was willing to stand in either seat, and leave the choice to the party. On 3 December 1938 the Assiniboia executive acceded to Gardiner's request that he be released from seeking renomination in that constituency if he so decided. Then, since Motherwell was still the sitting member for Melville, Gardiner scrupulously kept himself out of public involvement in that seat's affairs until his nomination somewhere was settled. When Motherwell made his retirement official in June 1939, Gardiner at once declared he would seek the Melville nomination and he was chosen in a successful constituency convention on 7 July. One detail revealed by the correspondence is that Gardiner was then personally paying his own workers.[40]

That Gardiner and the Saskatchewan Liberals, at a time when Chamberlain was trying at least to postpone a war which the Canadian government considered inevitable, should spend long hours on a simple transfer from one constituency to another, might strike one as an ill-advised waste of time. To Gardiner, high policy and local organization were all part of an integral pattern. Mackenzie King constantly railed about the inadequacy of the organization his colleagues were providing, but he also seemed to believe that organizers and fund-raisers were a kind of lower-class citizen within the party structure: indispensable, but unlikely to be invited into the inner circle of policy-makers. Gardiner was a conspicuous exception, but chiefly because he was also indispensable as an experienced western leader whose duties included delivering King's own seat, Prince Albert.

There is almost no evidence in King's voluminous papers relevant to Gardiner to indicate that he had any clear idea of what Gardiner actually did. Gardiner was in due course to run head-on into King's belief that organizing and fund-raising were somehow menial tasks, but in 1939 it is doubtful if he was even mildly aware of it. King had for years been thanking and praising him for the strength of the party in Saskatchewan, and Gardiner at the end of the thirties was not far enough removed from his provincial past to realize that his own position within the western party was changing fundamentally. He had been accused of interfering in Alberta affairs, and he was personally, although not seriously, charged with interference even in Saskatchewan in 1938. The criticism then was not effective, for the province was also invaded by CCF and Social Credit leaders during the 1938 campaign, and Gardiner's activities did not particularly stand out.[41] What was to come – and it took Gardiner a while to grasp it – was criticism not just from opponents, but from fellow Liberals.

But who in 1939 would believe that a Liberal with Gardiner's record could be accused of interfering in the affairs of the Saskatchewan Liberal party? The theme he had tried on Liberals in Alberta – 'We are all in this together' – seemed to him an indispensable characteristic of Liberalism itself. To implement high policy you had to be in power. To be in power you had to have a seat in Parliament. To get a seat in Parliament you needed an organization. In running an organization no detail, however small, could be safely overlooked. The move from Assiniboia to Melville had to be done properly, just as the provincial campaign of 1938, the attempts to conciliate Hepburn, or efforts to revise the party in Alberta, or the deployment of PFRA personnel, had to be done properly.

To Gardiner it was as simple as that. The whole basis of his theory of political action was to be challenged by the war; but then, as he was soon to exclaim in one form and another: 'Liberalism was never established to run a war – it was established for the purpose of making war unnecessary.'[42]

14

A Politician at War

Gardiner's belief that Liberalism and war hardly went hand-in-hand did not make him anti-war. In 1935, when King believed that war in Europe soon was a possibility, he noted that Gardiner 'thought we ought to go into war.'[1] Gardiner's faith in the British empire (he never did become comfortable with the word 'Commonwealth') was such that he could not contemplate a Britain at war without Canada. Besides, it was safer to have any war there managed by Liberals rather than unreconstructed Tories, with their disposition towards restricting freedom even in peacetime.

Gardiner's imperialism was rooted in his upbringing and education. As a student he was a champion of the empire, which he saw variously as the embodiment of Christianity in practical affairs, the chief hope for free trade in the world, and the basis for national unity and progress in Canada. As a teacher he had used history as a way to further British institutions. Campaigning in 1929 against the combined forces of Conservatives, Progressives, the Orange Lodge, and the Ku Klux Klan, Gardiner repeatedly spoke of 'fairness to all under the Union Jack,' sure that British tolerance would triumph. When in his view it did not, he was profoundly shaken.[2]

He was fully recovered by 1939, however, and a trip to the United Kingdom in 1940 was to confirm the sense of pride he felt as a citizen of the empire. The war gave him an unprecedented opportunity to display that sense, whether he was speaking of young Canadians contributing their bit to the empire, pinning the wings on graduating RCAF pilots who included his eldest son, Edwin, or helping organize the massive increases in agricultural production needed to feed civilians in Canada and the United Kingdom, and members of the Allied forces everywhere. Gardiner was never an idle man, and some thought he worked too hard, at the wrong things. But nothing in Gardiner's career had prepared him for the colossal demands that organization for war necessitated.

To fit drastic changes in one's way of life into familiar methods is not easy, and in 1939 Gardiner was fifty-six, at an age when he might justifiably have been thinking of settled routines. At first, to be sure, the government of which he was a member moved into the war years considerably influenced by the attitude of 'business as usual' engendered by several years of power. By the summer of 1939, nearly four years after the last election, the prime minister had to think of the next, and on 10 July King circularized his ministers to ask their judgment on the wisdom of an autumn poll, the probable outcome of each minister's area, the state of local and national finances in the party, and allied matters. Gardiner favoured an election in the first half of October, predicting little change in Saskatchewan's representation of sixteen Liberals, two Social Credit, two CCF, and one Conservative. He saw almost no chance of Liberal losses in Saskatchewan, but did think 'there is some possibility of an increase,' while any losses in Manitoba should be offset by gains in Alberta. On finances he was explicit: 'It is costing about $6,000 a month to carry organization activities going on in Saskatchewan at present. This is being met from funds already raised. It is estimated that about one-third of the amount necessary to conduct a campaign in this province will have to be provided by the central office, or in other words by Senator Lambert, in addition to all that the local organization will be able to supply.'3

If Gardiner's assumption that Saskatchewan was a permanent importer of funds bothered King, as it sometimes did Senator Lambert, the prime minister does not appear to have said so. King's own seat was in Saskatchewan, and he was a thrifty man: any export of funds from the province might find him, as leader, expected to set some sort of example. What did preoccupy King was the possibility of a fall election, and as late as 4 August 1939, Gardiner responded to a letter of King's about the contents of a pamphlet 'in case there is a campaign.' Gardiner's proposals offer revealing insights into his thinking during that dark summer. At a time when trade channels, in anticipation of war, were closing down, he suggested: 'The Liberal Party believes that trade is the basis of industrial, commercial and agricultural development, and that Canada needs trade.' For external trade, he proposed that the party continue to promote reciprocal trade agreements, with particular emphasis on the disposal of surplus farm products in world markets. Internally, 'The Liberal Party is opposed to artificial price control and agreements in restraint of trade ... It will continue to encourage the formation of co-operative organizations of producers or of those controlling facilities to handle or process natural products.'

The pamphlet, Gardiner added, should probably refer to the aims of the 'Government' rather than the party. Agriculture might be better served by a separate section than by being subsumed under 'Trade.' He then drafted several clauses on how trade restrictions hurt agriculture, and what the government proposed to do to continue to rehabilitate devastated areas, reduce farm costs, and improve transportation. He ended with as clear a statement as he ever made on marketing:

The Government has made it possible, through legislation, for those who are marketing wheat to try out three methods of marketing which have been the subject of controversy for many years, namely,
1. The open market method,
2. The co-operative or pooling method,
3. The Government Wheat Board method.
These are now available, controlled or supported by the Government, to the western farmer and will be tested fully with a view to determining which one or which combination of them will obtain the best results for the farmer.[4]

Since Gardiner was frequently criticized as an opponent of the Wheat Board and a champion of the 'open market method,' it is significant that in a confidential letter in 1939 he made clear that he was neither.

A campaign pamphlet that was still in the drafting stage on 4 August 1939 was not going to be ready for use before the war began. The advent of war and the immediate absorption of Gardiner and his colleagues by new tasks ruled out an autumn election. Parliament was convened on 7 September for six days of sittings (the first of two short consecutive sessions in which Gardiner, uncharacteristically, spoke not a word), and then prorogued with the promise of another session before the next general election. The promised session was held, on the afternoon of 25 January 1940, by which time Mitchell Hepburn, the Liberal premier of Ontario, had supported the Conservative motion condemning the federal government's war effort, and thus given King a reason for testing the government at the polls.

Gardiner's predictions of 1939 did not hold up well: in his own province the Liberals, though increasing their share of the popular vote, dropped from sixteen seats to twelve, while the ccf went from two seats to five. In Manitoba and Alberta the party made spectacular gains in the popular vote, rising by 33 per cent over 1935 in Manitoba, and more than doubling in Alberta, and as a result gaining seats in both provinces. The circumstances of early 1940 were, of course, vastly different from those of the summer of 1939, but the showing of Gardiner's Saskatchewan forces did not enhance his chances of rising in the party. It did not help that Saskatoon, which had been taken handily by the Liberals in 1935, had fallen in a by-election in December 1939 to a virtually unknown United Reform candidate, who won the seat again in 1940.

It is never possible in a parliamentary democracy to separate politics from administration as if they were different entities, and to divide Gardiner's official work as a minister and his political work as a regional leader inevitably involves some simplification. The problems of separating politics from administration were, indeed, revealed by an actual attempt to separate them. In the election of 1940, and after, the Conservatives cried loudly for a 'National Government,' and many Conservative candidates ran with a National Government label. King's response in 1940, when the Liberals returned 177 members to the Conservatives' 39 (these figures represent straight party victories only), with representation from all provinces as compared with the Conservatives' elimination from three, was that Canada indeed had a national government, whose name happened to be Liberal. Partially to give credence to that claim, the Liberals issued to members a memorandum suspending partisanship for the duration.[5] The memorandum had a considerable impact on Gardiner.

As a minister Gardiner was of course part of a team, and his contributions, like those of his colleagues, cannot all be seen as the work of a single individual. His preoccupation with wheat, while the selling of wheat was located in Trade and Commerce, has already been cited. The proliferation of wartime responsibilities and agencies was to multiply that kind of cross-jurisdictional arrangement, often to Gardiner's utter exasperation. Consider the conflicts latent in arrangements such as the following. For wartime purposes the Department of Agriculture was responsible for the production of foodstuffs seen to be necessary, and for the allocation of production materials (e.g., seeds, but not wheat or feed grain seeds) between domestic and export markets; and for supervising the export of foods sold under contract, almost all of it to the United Kingdom. The domestic distribution and pricing of foods, on the other hand, was under an agency responsible to the Department of Finance, the Wartime Prices and Trade Board. Wheat was different: its marketing was still under an agency in Trade and Commerce. Farm labour, and manpower for industry and the armed forces (and in all three areas shortages became crucial) was under none of the foregoing, but the Department of Labour. The transportation of agricultural products (which included the moving of feed grains grown on the prairies to beef and dairy cattle in central Canada) involved railways under yet another branch of government.[6]

The complexity of the chronicle of Canada's wartime agricultural achievements suggested by that sample establishes another major point. Although, as Gardiner was wont to point out, agricultural products are rarely regarded as munitions of war, and are often omitted altogether from histories of wars, they are as indispensable as tanks and planes. Gardiner did his bit to correct the record. He continued to provide correspondents with lengthy accounts of his department's activities, and in wartime clearly felt a particular obligation to keep the House of Commons, and thus the public, informed in detail. In doing so he was merely extending for special purposes a practice he had always followed as a minister. 'In that connection,' he said of wheat policy in January of 1939, 'I wish to place on Hansard some information ...' He then went into a long statement that included eight tables covering several years of wheat acreages, world trade, and unemployment.

His speeches may not have been artistic, but they were clear, and their comprehensive nature, combined with his willingness to obtain more material if members wished it, were among the reasons why at the beginning of the war the minister of agriculture was a popular figure. Opposition members spoke freely in his praise. M.J. Coldwell, on 14 February 1939, observed that 'without seeming in any way derogatory of the Minister of Trade and Commerce,' he thought that Gardiner could give 'a better picture of the [wheat] situation than perhaps could be given by any other minister.' Two days later Coldwell congratulated Gardiner for a comprehensive and constructive statement on marketing, and E.E. Perley, the Conservative member for Qu'Appelle, echoed his words, both MPs of course reserving the right to disagree with the minister. Social Credit joined the chorus a month later when J.H. Blackmore, member for Lethbridge, commended Gardiner for his work on prairie farm rehabilitation.[7]

Gardiner's reputation was enhanced when he revealed how his

department had begun to organize for war not long after he took office. The speech in which he told the Commons about preparations for war was a typical Gardiner performance:

Before the war came, the government had reorganized the Department of Agriculture into four divisions, with a director over each division ... [and] it was not advisable at that time to suggest that it had any relationship with war ... The day war was declared, the principal officers of the department were called together to discuss the part to be played by agriculture in war activity. An agricultural supplies board composed of six members, four of whom were the four directors I have just mentioned, was established. The board, together with the department, commenced immediately to deal with agricultural situations arising out of the war ... to accomplish the following things:
1. To establish constructive direction for agricultural production;
2. To make available for export those commodities required by Great Britain;
3. To conserve essential supplies such as feeding materials, insecticides and fertilizers needed to meet the production of farm products in Canada, and
4. To assist in the marketing of surplus farm products.
   A conference between the agricultural supplies board and representatives of the provincial departments of agriculture was held at Ottawa on September 27 and 28, 1939. At that conference Great Britain's probable needs of Canadian farm products were outlined and stress laid on so planning war-time activities that the agricultural industry should not be thrown out of gear when the war ended ... At the close of that conference provincial delegates agreed to cooperate in work undertaken by the board, as the central directive agency, and undertook the responsibility, in cooperation with producer representatives and dominion field men in their respective provinces, of implementing such production programmes as might become necessary.[8]

Gardiner then put on record in pitiless detail the wartime arrangements so far established.

As needs arose, committees and organizations proliferated, some by fresh fiat and some by amoeba-like parturition. When it early became apparent that Canada was to be a prime supplier of the United Kingdom, partly because the North Atlantic sea lanes were short enough to reduce both fuel costs and exposure to enemy action, the wishes of the British government influenced Canadian organization. The British preferred to have a separate Canadian agency for each commodity dealt with in bulk; so just as the Canadian Wheat Board handled wheat, a Bacon Board was created in 1939 for pork products, joined in 1940 by a Dairy Products Board. A Special Products Board, established in 1941, negotiated contracts for a specific group of commodities. At the international level Canada had a stake in the agricultural activities of the Canada–United States Joint Economic Committee, and the Joint Agricultural Committee of Canada and the United States, which later ceased to function when Canada became a member of the Combined Food Board which had at first involved only the British and Americans. Gardiner was the Canadian member of the Combined Food Board, and the minister to whom the Canadian boards were responsible. Since he was ordinarily opposed to government by boards, as distinct from ministers, his wartime experience provided one more example of a politician obliged to accept procedures which he considered less than ideal.

Nonetheless, the wartime achievements of Canadian agriculture were formidable, and they were accomplished under the direction of a group of ministers (aided of course by able civil servants) who were increasingly overworked, overtired, and frequently distracted by crises which seemed all but irrelevant to their individual assignments. Gardiner, for example, had problems over securing manpower, and manpower was not under his jurisdiction. The dramatic confrontations over conscription for overseas service included events which he found hard to take seriously. Further distractions came from new wartime responsibilities. The war was barely ten months old, and Gardiner still building his part of the wartime administration, when the prime minister asked him to consider a second portfolio, National War Services. The new department was to be a wartime secretary of state's department, a catch-all for functions which did not clearly belong under other portfolios. And like the secretary of state's office, the Department of National War Services did not assume a high position in the ministerial pecking order.

Gardiner was not King's first choice as its minister, nor were Gardiner's ideas about the department, as it turned out, King's. The prime minister, before approaching Gardiner, discussed the organizing of a department of war services with James Macdonnell, who was not a member of Parliament but 'had had a great ambition to be a minister of the Crown.' (The offer to Macdonnell, a Conservative, was part of an unsuccessful attempt to lend a less partisan and more representative look to the cabinet, which King told the House about in general terms when announcing a reorganization in July of 1940.)[9] On consideration, Macdonnell did not feel equal to the task, and King then sent for Gardiner. What Gardiner was offered, in effect, was a portfolio with a broad national constituency rather than a particular regional bias, which carried the additional attribute of membership on the cabinet war committee. King's plans included Gardiner's relinquishing Agriculture. Gardiner, on 28 June 1940, was prepared to do whatever his leader wished, but did say that he would like his agricultural policies continued. To that end he favoured the transference to Ottawa of Saskatchewan's minister of agriculture, J.G. Taggart.

King expressed reluctance at bringing in somebody 'over the heads of our own men,' and shortly found that other ministers agreed with him. Since Gardiner had already recommended to King the name of W.J. Patterson, his successor in Regina, for the Senate, with Taggart likely succeeding to the provincial premiership, King suggested bringing Patterson to Ottawa at once, for Agriculture. Gardiner in turn opposed Patterson because Patterson 'had never had to do with a farm' and King accepted that. In the event, Patterson stayed in Regina, Gardiner for nearly a year kept two portfolios, and Taggart, who was already chairman of the federal Bacon Board, continued there and as a provincial minister.[10] Any anomaly involved in having a provincial minister, responsible to a legislature, chairing a board reporting to a federal minister responsible to Parliament was of no concern to Gardiner, and he shortly created a second. As part of his new portfolio he brought in as his associate deputy his trusted friend T.C. Davis, who had been appointed to the bench in 1939. Davis continued to hold his judgeship (though not sitting on cases) while deputy minister of national war services and, in due course, a member of the diplomatic corps serving abroad.

Gardiner would have preferred appointments to his new staff to be by order-in-council rather than by the Civil Service Commission; but a specific attempt to obtain that privilege for the staff in the information branch, on the grounds that commission categories did not fit what the department needed, failed;[11] Gardiner was formally appointed to the new portfolio on 12 July. The House of Commons had already been advised of the government's intentions, and some of the functions of National War Services, such as the establishment of a register of citizens, had been announced as necessities no matter what department was in charge. In announcing the portfolio King spoke first among its duties of 'the coordination of the activities of voluntary war organizations and services.' But more pressing was 'the duty of mobilizing and guiding the activities of thousands of our citizens who are seeking practical and useful outlets for their enthusiasm and patriotism.' The prime minister emphasized that the new minister would be expected to create immediately a nation-wide organization for the department's purposes, and went on to cite specifically national registration (an indispensable prelude to the implementation of the National Resources Mobilization Act) and 'the coordination of existing governmental information and publicity services connected with the war' as examples of what the organization would be needed for. Some of the department's functions carried with them the possibility of conflict with other departments, and within a year this contributed to Gardiner's return to Agriculture alone.

Gardiner was assigned National War Services partly because of his skills in organizing, which received praise from both sides of the House, and he threw himself into his portfolio with his usual energy. Even before he was appointed, Gardiner was describing plans to King on a letterhead purporting to be from the office of the minister of national war services.[12] The government wanted the results of the registration as quickly as possible, which was why the groundwork for it began before Parliament, guided by Gardiner, had passed the required legislation or he had assumed the office it created. Because of the nature of the department's work, Gardiner chose to have two associated deputy ministers, one from each of the two main language groups, and both T.C. Davis and his counterpart, Major-General L.R. LaFleche, were in Ottawa several days before they could officially start work. Members of Parliament, like the dual deputy ministership, were to play an unusual role in the registration; for, partly to pay lip service to the fiction that the war effort was non-partisan, and partly to encourage members' participation, the government turned to the electoral system for the registering of citizens, and Gardiner ran the registration like a general election.[13] Each MP was asked to recommend for his constituency a registrar, who was the equivalent of a returning officer, and a deputy registrar, and these officials set up registration offices in each of the polling divisions, enlisting unpaid volunteers to act as polling officials. Setting up the machinery took approximately the same time as an election: the needed legislation was passed on 12 July by which time several days' work had already been done, and the 'polling' took place on 19–21 August.[14]

The actual questionnaire prepared for the citizen was less impressive than the machinery. Since the chief purpose was to provide information for the mobilization of manpower for military, industrial, and agricultural needs, one might have expected a few relatively simple questions to suffice. The new department, anxious to avoid neglecting anything of potential use, canvassed all the departments for proposed questions, and ended up with a weird grab-bag of queries which might have satisfied many vested bureaucratic interests, but left Gardiner and his advisers with an impossible choice. How, without stepping on influential toes, did one select some questions for use and reject others? Acutely short of time, the minister could reject them all and start over, or accept them all; and the second course was the more politic. A few of the questions, given the nature of some questionnaires with which the social sciences have since favoured the world, might not now appear strange, but in 1940 they were bizarre. Men were asked eighteen questions, and women twenty, many of them with several sub-questions. Both sexes were asked if they could milk cows or handle horses, but only women were asked if they could drive a truck. All were asked, 'Is there any particular occupation in which you would like to be specially trained?' Even the prime minister was reportedly bemused when required to suggest what sort of thing, apart from his regular job, he could do well.[15]

The questions gave opposition members and the press a field day,[16] but the registration as a whole was an enormous success, marred only by a call to the citizens from Mayor Houde of Montreal, urging them not to register – for which he was promptly interned. Operated wholly by volunteers below the official level, the registration brought together the efforts of MPs, churches, factories, clubs, and other social organizations from coast to coast in an enterprise that was morale-building as well as productive. Over two hundred thousand unpaid workers registered virtually all permanent residents sixteen years of age and over, and the results were at once used for calling up young men for training. The second priority was given to identifying those with occupations relative to the production of war materials, and the third to locating those with farming experience but who were not at the time farming. Several Allied governments used the records to locate their own nationals in Canada. It was entirely, as Gardiner said, 'something of which every member can well be proud.'[17]

Gardiner continued to develop his new portfolio's duties in as many directions as its powers allowed. Registration was followed by an active role in the calling up of men requisitioned by the Department of National Defence. Apart from military purposes, National War Services co-ordinated the appeals of such fund-raising bodies as the Red Cross, hoping to reduce the appeals to one annually. The organization of women's groups was begun, and campaigns to eliminate waste and encourage salvage were undertaken. Gardiner took seriously the co-ordination of wartime publicity, arranging for 'as many ministerial press conferences as possible,' speaking tours, innumerable radio broadcasts, hundreds of posters, and millions of pamphlets. All of this Gardiner, as usual, reported to the House of Commons in detail.[18]

Gardiner also tried to use his new powers to move in a little more on the handling of wheat. He had been minister of national war services less than three weeks when the opposition gave him an opportunity to return to a favourite theme. Reminding the House rather sharply that the marketing of wheat was under Trade and Commerce, he said:

If there is in Canada one material resource that is of greater importance than any other, in order that this war might be prosecuted to a successful conclusion, surely it is wheat. Wheat is the outstanding Canadian product which will play a very important part in the prosecution of the war, and in taking care of the people when the war is over. Therefore, in so far as the new department is concerned, my interests in wheat have in fact increased, rather than diminished, and my responsibility in relation to wheat has increased rather than diminished.[19]

That statement of intent may have been offered too soon. Writing to the prime minister about the Department of National War Services early in 1941, Gardiner opened with the suggestion that 'I think it was your desire that it should become a much more important Department than it has turned out to be up to the present.' He cited two boards, outside the department, which had proven obstacles in developing the work of the division on human and material resources, one of them for again making impossible a projected program, the other one for surveying industrial development with post-war reconstruction in mind. The letter was plainly the work of a frustrated minister, and it concluded on a revealing theme: 'If it is the desire to have the Department of National War Services really function to do a job, then I think it should be given more authority and speeded up in connection with publicity and the utilization of material resources.'[20]

Gardiner's plea for more co-operation from other, larger, departments was read by a prime minister who was himself dissatisfied with National War Services, but not inclined to accept his minister's diagnosis. King told Gardiner on 27 November 1940 that he was prepared to let him keep two portfolios 'provided he devoted more time and thought to the War Services portfolio; that I thought there was the greatest opportunity there, but that thus far enough had not been made of it, particularly in organizing the women and seeing to industrial training etc.' That opinion, expressed almost casually between references to a possible Senate appointment from Saskatchewan, was not one with which Gardiner disagreed, but just three days later he told Senator Lambert that he had told the prime minister 'that War Services Department was being duplicated in too many places to be satisfactory.' Unfortunately for Gardiner, he was almost concurrently incurring King's displeasure in matters agricultural, and early in January 1941, after a trying cabinet meeting and a scolding by King, Gardiner offered to resign.

King, supported (he believed) by other ministers, considered that an excessive reaction, and it led to an outburst in his diary: 'He is adopting Euler's tactics of being unpleasant with every colleague who disagrees with him and trying to get his way by a ruthless forcing of the situation, sometimes in a very underhand manner.' Comparing Gardiner with Power, King added, 'Each has certain excellent qualities but each has very decided defects. Gardiner's run in a Hepburn-Hitler direction.'[21]

That absurd conclusion points up that King himself, while an experienced party leader and prime minister, had little first-hand knowledge of the problems faced by a minister given the specific tasks that go with a portfolio. Any minister worth his salt would push his department's interests, and if it meant arguing fiercely with other ministers, it was up to them to defend *their* departments' interests. King's involvement in such activities, except as an observer in his own cabinets, had been minimal. The Department of Labour, which he headed for two years from 1909, had twenty-four employees when he relinquished it in 1911; the Department of External Affairs, which the prime minister still held in 1941, had a staff of 293 in that year. In 1941 Agriculture had 3,110 employees and National War Services 1,079, and both had large domestic programs unlike anything King had ever faced.[22]

Having upset his leader over affairs in both his departments, Gardiner was beginning to find his position increasingly uncomfortable, and notably in National War Services. On 20 January the prime minister, apprised by T.C. Davis of a proposal to authorize $5,000 for prayer books to be used in a special wartime church service in Montreal, at once had visions of an uprising of 'Orange Lodges, Ku Klux Klans, etc.' The project had by that time been endorsed by Ernest Lapointe, P.F. Casgrain (who as secretary of state was responsible for printing), and Gardiner's department; but the combined acumen of Lapointe, Casgrain, Davis, and Gardiner (who was away) was not enough to convince

King. Bypassing Gardiner, and with the support of the cabinet war committee, he sent instructions directly to Davis to order the project halted immediately.[23]

Less than three weeks later Gardiner again took up the matter of co-ordinating publicity, unfortunately expressing views which ran directly counter to King's. Gardiner was strongly in favour of a centralized publicity organization instead of a weak one supplemented by publicity outlets in several departments. But the government's policy was precisely this one of decentralization. It had been based on a report prepared by Norman Rogers, who had concluded that there was no other practical way of getting around the desire of the departments 'to have publicity organizations of their own.' Gardiner continued to oppose the existing policy, buttressing his case with supporting memoranda from his advisers.[24]

It was Gardiner's opinion that he could not properly carry out his responsibilities as minister of national war services nominally in charge of co-ordinating publicity. 'I think it is an absolute mistake,' he told King in February, 'to have half a dozen publicity organizations in different Departments and at the same time a central publicity organization.' So round a condemnation of government policy was unlikely to pass unnoticed by a man as sensitive as King, especially since Gardiner, speaking of the energy and money wasted by a flawed policy on publicity, in the same letter said, 'if I were not a member of the Government I would probably be saying something about it.' Three weeks later Gardiner reported the co-ordination of publicity was 'proceeding satisfactorily excepting in relation to newspaper publicity,' which was of course a major aspect of the whole problem.

A few weeks later Gardiner and his staff produced what they considered a solution: a new branch of the department under a chief editor 'who knows the kind of thing which the public will read,' who would have a reportorial staff like any newspaper's. The staff would gather news from the departments, but the proposal included taking into the new office the publicity bureaus already existing in other departments, whose staffs could remain where they were but be directed by the chief editor. The latter would work with a representative of the press censor. The staffs, Gardiner thought, would need to be increased only if, in addition to telling the public what was going on, the government undertook 'to direct public thought to an objective which we have in mind.'[25] In other words, extra staff would be needed for overt propaganda but not straight reporting.

Gardiner's advice, which was supported by at least his English-speaking associate deputy, T.C. Davis, and his director of information, G.H. Lash, was rejected outright by King. King took the plan to cabinet on 14 May, and his subsequent diary reveals a considerable gap in understanding on somebody's part. 'The whole thing,' he wrote,

was the wrong way about ... I finally said I thought there should be a Ministry that could handle this thing by itself to the end of co-relating the media and bringing each single question in turn before the Cabinet. Council as a whole, and even Gardiner, acquiesced, Gardiner getting down at last to the position that we needed one good man to get the material in statistical and factual form. We gave him this authority but I let Council understand we were heading for a change.

The change was in the portfolio: 'Yesterday I spoke to Lapointe and Ralston about the possibility of taking Abbott into the Cabinet and giving him the War Services Department.'[26]

Gardiner did not know that, but the discussion in cabinet sent him some signals, and baffling ones at that. If a new division in an existing department was 'the wrong way about,' what was 'a Ministry that could handle this thing by itself?' 'One good man' was what Gardiner had proposed, and even named: W.L. Clark of the *Windsor Star*. 'Co-relating the media' was one of the things Gardiner had been trying to do, complaining to his chief about the obstacles in his path. But whatever King had in mind, Gardiner at once had T.C. Davis look into the changes in plans he thought were necessitated by King's objections to their proposal. Davis discovered that much of the information King sought was already being collected. J.W. Pickersgill received reports from the three branches of the Department of National Defence, and was trying to work out a similar arrangement in Munitions and Supply. 'The thought at once arises in my mind,' Davis told Gardiner on 19 May, 'as to whether or not this service should be duplicated.' Gardiner at once sent Davis's report to King, with a covering letter which repeated his deputy's speculation and offered another: would the prime minister be willing to let information from his office go to a bureau in National War Services? If so, 'all that's required is for someone such as you suggested to put the information in [a] form which can be utilized by members.'

Unless King's diary is misleading, Gardiner and Davis appear to have been caught in an inexplicable misunderstanding of the prime minister's desires. Because the information that Davis found being sent to the Prime Minister's Office included some that would have had to be kept confidential, he assumed (and Gardiner accepted) that its circulation would be restricted; but King, it turned out, was not talking about that kind of information. Because they assumed that circulation would be restricted, they concluded further that King meant the recipients to be people in selected categories. Gardiner referred to use of the information 'by members,' but Davis had an even smaller audience in mind. The second paragraph of his report to Gardiner read: 'I presume that the use of this material would be restricted to members of government as some of it might be of a confidential nature.' On his copy of the same memorandum the prime minister scribbled, 'NO – it is to get into leaflets that *all* can use.'[27]

As he was already considering possible successors to the minister of national war services, King had little patience for further attempts to straighten out the incumbent. Gardiner told Senator Lambert on 2 June that 'he had quit War Services himself because of impossible ambiguities.' The next item in Lambert's diary reads; 'Saw C.D.H. [Howe] afterward, and he said Jimmy had been fired.'[28] Gardiner might well have been fired if he had not resigned, but he did in fact resign.[29] The resignation was routinely accepted and announced in the House, together with the name of the new minister, Gardiner's old schoolmate, J.T. Thorson, who received at the same time enlarged powers for the co-ordination of publicity.[30] What would Gardiner's position have been in June of 1941 had he resigned from Agriculture when he was appointed to National War Services?

For Gardiner the departure from the latter portfolio, his first failure of the kind, was an ignominious ending to an enterprise that had begun with an instant triumph, the national registration. That early success may have been part of Gardiner's difficulties in National War Services, for after several weeks of pressure, the registration ended as suddenly as an election campaign, and what followed was not nearly as interesting, either in the uses made of the registration or the department's other functions. In wartime, the co-ordination of fund drives and similar co-operative ventures was indispensable, but that did not make it dramatic or exciting. Gardiner, accustomed to challenge, characteristically pursued the one issue in the department which offered challenge – the organization of publicity. His persistence this time led to his downfall. His own files suggest that, apart from national registration and bucking the various publicity establishments, he had not found a great deal to capture his imagination in National War Services, and for what he did find to do he did not think he received adequate support.

But there was plenty to do in Agriculture, where problems came in as regularly as crops, but more often. Within the party, his distinguished record in Agriculture, however, was to remain offset to some degree by his faltering in National War Services. The prime minister in 1941 was sixty-seven, and beginning to think about retirement. He wrote of Gardiner in January 1941, after the joust in cabinet referred to above: 'What he does not see is extent to which he is prejudicing his own future in the eyes of his colleagues who will have some say on the ground of who is to succeed myself.'[31]

In the party's inner circle the loss of the portfolio included a clear demotion: the minister of national war services was a member of the cabinet's war committee, but the minister of agriculture was not. Following so closely on the loss of seats among his Saskatchewan supporters, Gardiner's inability to fathom what King expected of national war services was another setback in his career.

15

War and Agriculture

Whatever evaluation might be placed on Gardiner's tenure as minister of national war services, there was no ambiguity about his effectiveness as wartime minister of agriculture. Here his achievements were indisputable. Of this fact he was confident, as were his supporters, many of the general public, and even some opponents. Years later, in the general election of 1958, of ten accomplishments he chose to list in an open letter to the voters of Melville, five dealt with wartime agricultural policies and two with such related pre-war activities as the reorganization of the Department of Agriculture in 1935 and the extension of PFRA in 1936; his experience in the National War Services portfolio he did not mention. From the public, either organized, as in the wheat pools, or, individually, support was frequently evident. There are few more poignant examples of it than a letter in 1942 (with a one dollar enclosure) for Gardiner's son Edwin, now stationed with the RCAF in England, from a farm woman who lauded Gardiner for his 'splendid job ... in giving [acreage] bonuses ... [which] has meant new life to us.'[1]

In the House, critics in the formidable contingent of Saskatchewan members present after 1940 – E.E. Perley, M.J. Coldwell, T.C. Douglas, and John Diefenbaker, for example – as well as opposition leaders such as Gordon Graydon and R.B. Hanson praised the aggressive organizing ability Gardiner displayed in formulating and carrying out new and complex policies to help the farmer.[2] There were complaints, of course, but because agriculture was not a frontline department in the prosecution of the war and because so many of its activities were intended to improve domestic conditions, criticism was less frequent and less severe than that directed at ministers responsible, say, for Defence or Munitions and Supply. Not that Gardiner courted approval – quite the reverse.

Believing that criticism was generally constructive, he welcomed debate; Arthur Meighen's return as Conservative leader he treated as harbinger of a revived opposition, one which under R.B. Hanson 'had been so weak that it was pathetic.'[3]

Thus the war years constituted the period of Gardiner's greatest success in public life. The programs by which Canadian agriculture achieved the stability and prosperity he had sought to give it since coming to Ottawa were firmly in place when hostilities ended. More important was the change in attitude evident among his colleagues in cabinet and in the House generally; it was now accepted that the federal government had a responsibility to aid disadvantaged agriculture. Initially, attention was concentrated upon the prairie farmer because of the hard times he had passed through in the thirties. Gradually, however, that cast of mind broadened to include other parts of the country, as demonstrated in the Maritime Marshlands Rehabilitation Act, passed in 1948.

The multitude of programs and initiatives made Gardiner for most Canadians the pre-eminent federal minister for any subject touching on livestock or crops, regardless of whether or not his responsibility actually extended to the matter in question. This was certainly the case with regard to wheat marketing which throughout his time in Ottawa was always the responsibility of the minister of trade and commerce; but it was also true with regard to a myriad of questions raised in the House which he would have to refer to appropriate colleagues.[4] Such universal recognition proved both his strength and his weakness: a strength in that it helped him raise agriculture to the status of a 'basic industry' from that of being a 'poor relation,'[5] and in so doing secured his reputation as a master politician; a weakness in that it isolated him in a complex and arcane world of subsidies, ceilings, floors, and supports, of acreage, bushelage, and deficiency payments, of quotas, parity prices, and participation certificates. It all became too much for Mackenzie King, who complained about the 'tedious' wrangles over agriculture, and for the growing number of MPs concerned about urban, industrial, and labour matters, subjects whose importance wartime policies and demographic movements accentuated.[6]

Before, during, and after the war, Gardiner's concern remained with agriculture; and it was to be his experience that while agriculture assumed greater political visibility as a result of his efforts, it declined in relative importance in the Canadian economy. The consequence of that contraction for his political power and ambition proved extremely damaging. He admitted, for example, that it helped deny him the leadership of the Liberal party in 1948, because 'those who represented interests other than agricultural interests ... preferred to have Mr. St. Laurent [who was] closely associated with their development over a long period of years.'[7] The war and its conduct at home were responsible more than anything else for these economic and social changes. In particular, the war with its combination of non-partisan politics and expanded bureaucracy was responsible for helping to undermine further the already faltering Saskatchewan Liberal organization. Thus, Gardiner's political world went into eclipse with the return to peace. But for the period between 1939 and 1945 his policy triumphs shone with exceptional brilliance, and it is to these that this discussion must now turn, after a final comment on Gardiner's personal life during the years under review.

Because this is a political biography, Gardiner's personal life enters only to the extent that it can be determined to impinge on his official actions. Such a concentration is defensible since the vast majority of Gardiner's voluminous papers deal with policy and party matters and say nothing about his private affairs. Indeed, his private life remained just that, notwithstanding his practice of citing personal farming experience when making a case for some agricultural legislation in the House or before a committee. Admitting the distinction between public and private life, it must nonetheless be said that for Gardiner the war was a time of personal tragedy. In 1942 his son Edwin was killed at Dieppe, and in 1944 Violet, his wife of twenty-seven years, despondent over the loss of their eldest child, committed suicide by drowning herself in an inlet of the Rideau Canal in Ottawa. Gardiner said his wife was as much a 'war casualty' as his son. Certainly the shock of the second loss could not have been less than the first, for it came unexpectedly at the height of the conscription crisis and soon after his unprecedently unsuccessful labours in the Saskatchewan provincial campaign. At the end of 1944, with wartime policies about to come to an end and with major post-war adjustments required, Gardiner found himself politically rebuffed and personally bereaved but with domestic responsibilities enhanced. He had a son in his sophomore year at Queen's University, a daughter recently graduated from Macdonald College, Montreal, and a second daughter at home in high school.

For a person whose political beliefs led him to abhor force, the loss of two loved ones in this war, and the death of two brothers and permanent injury of two others in the one before, brought about the only evidence of self-doubt Gardiner ever displayed. He began to wonder whether he should quit politics and devote himself to his family and to the farm. The immediate domestic problem, however, was resolved with the help of his sister-in-law and by the return home of his elder daughter, Florence. For the time being at least family life was restored to an approximation of what it had been and politics could go on. All of these events took place with scarcely a disruption to ministerial responsibilities, however – a fact which revealed both devotion to duty and a steel will.

The challenge presented to Gardiner by the war was two-fold: to continue the policies of rehabilitation which had not yet restored western agriculture to the economic condition it had enjoyed in the late 1920s, and to do so in a situation that was completely new. With the fall of France in 1940, Europe was closed as a market for Canadian exports, and grain farmers (as well as fruit, poultry, and dairy producers) became dependent for their prosperity on one customer – the United Kingdom. The closing of European markets meant that any lessons Canadian policy-makers might hope to learn from Canada's experience in the First World War were bound to be of no value. In 1914 traditional purchasers continued to buy agricultural products, only in greater quantities once their European supplies were cut off by the Germans. Canadian farm production, especially wheat, could meet the demand because it had just gone through a decade or more of expansion and it proceeded to do so through traditional channels until 1917. The Board of Grain Supervisors, created that year, exercised monopoly control of the 1917 and 1918 crops, thus establishing a precedent that whetted western appetite for central selling. By 1940 all of Canadian agriculture's customary practices were in abeyance. The West was still depressed, and a monopoly buyer and a market system that was no longer as open as in the First World War threw special responsibilities on to the federal government. Gardiner, as the minister most responsible, found himself having to develop policies with three broad objectives: to guarantee dependable supplies to one customer, to assure hundreds of thousands of producers a fair share of the market, and to promote adequate returns to farmers, large numbers of whom were experiencing varying conditions of economic welfare.

As a result, Gardiner's wartime agricultural policies were nothing if not complex. One way to appreciate both the reasons for their complexity and Gardiner's dexterity at handling the crises the policies were intended to meet is to briefly summarize the development of Canada's agriculture immediately prior to September 1939.

The pivotal institution in the handling of wheat after 1935 was the Canadian Wheat Board. R.B. Bennett had intended the board to have monopoly control over the marketing of grain but Liberal opposition in Parliament and trade opposition outside had seen to it that initially compliance to the board would be voluntary. That is to say, the grain exchange or open market continued to exist alongside the board and the farmer had a choice as to how he would dispose of his crop. The Liberals repeatedly made it clear that they considered the board temporary. It existed, they said, only because the intolerably low grain prices constituted an emergency for Canada's major export industry. For W.D. Euler, for example, then minister of trade and commerce and responsible for grain marketing, the board represented 'class legislation of the worst kind ... confined to one class in one particular section of the country.'[8] Gardiner believed the board interfered with open-market trading and brought the government into the picture when really the farmer, either individually or, better still, co-operatively, should be responsible. Simply put, Gardiner's policy was to return to the wheat pools of the prosperous twenties.

Yet despite the united views of these two principal ministers, the Liberals were never able to get free of grain. Indeed, their responsibility grew to the point where Gardiner became the industry's chief spokesman and defender in cabinet and Parliament. The reasons for this 180-degree shift reveal distinctive features about western agriculture which Gardiner was the first to appreciate and to accept as the necessary bases for long-term policies.

Except as a temporizing expedient, the voluntary board had little to recommend it: western farm opinion, expressed in petition and by delegation, was universally and permanently against it and in favour of a monopoly board. The Liberals, philosophically opposed to government enterprise, grew frustrated with an institution that accumulated losses, because farmers patronized the board only when the open-market price fell below the board price. This situation, where neither the makers nor the users of a policy were satisfied, had both political and climactic explanations. In its attempt to withdraw from direct involvement in the grain trade, the Liberal government in 1936 had appointed the Royal Grain Inquiry Commission, with W.F.A. Turgeon as chairman, to investigate alternative methods of grain marketing. Two years later the commission reported in favour of returning either to the open market or to a pooling system, but only under 'normal conditions,' which it recognized did not exist in 1938. Indeed, in 1937 the western grain producer had received the worst blow in his history: the average crop yield in the prairie provinces in 1928, the year taken as the best normal standard, was 23.2 bushels per acre; for the whole of the 1930s it was 11.6, and for 1937, 6.4, with the Saskatchewan average that year a scant 2.6 bushels per acre.[9] Now, to those other factors of production denied to the western farmer since 1929 – capital, arable land, working equipment – was added seed. With the last in danger of disappearing, no government could abandon the board. The following year produced bountiful harvests in major grain-producing countries, thereby reducing the price of wheat from $1.50 to 60 cents a bushel. Thus the western farmer's income, which an improved harvest seemed ready to boost, was to be cut again. The time to restore a completely open market did not seem propitious.

It was Gardiner who saw the way to break free of the cycle of depressed prices and surplus crops. In 1938, after intense debate in cabinet between those wanting a low price – Euler and J.L. Ilsley, then minister of national revenue, were the leading advocates – and those wanting a high price – Gardiner and King were the chief spokesmen – cabinet agreed to the board's making an initial payment of 80 cents a bushel. This price was a good 15 to 20 cents above the world figure and represented something never seen before in Canadian public policy: the federal government trying to rectify an income shortage in one sector of the economy by means other than relief payments. Gardiner had initially favoured 87.5 cents but had accepted King's proposal of 80 cents, with a total cost to the treasury of $61.5 million. Opponents to the bonus summoned laissez-faire economics to support their contention that regional assistance was detrimental to the nation and its citizens' interests, and greeted with disbelief the retort that the protective tariff was just such assistance to Ontario and Quebec. King interpreted the argument more simply as one of east versus west and personally favoured aid for the west after what it had gone through. Although representing Prince Albert, King made his argument in national terms, as Gardiner was always to do, and it was a position which earned the prime minister Gardiner's lasting respect, whatever other disagreements the two men might have.

Within the dominant political party of the period and against potent intra-party opposition, arguments for regional equity had won over appeals to political principle. But the solution, in Gardiner's opinion, was less than ideal. By early 1939 he was warning that 'marketing legislation alone will not solve the problems of the wheat growing areas,' and he continued to argue that high wheat prices were not the final answer to the west's problems.[10] Higher prices benefited those with average or better-than-average crops; they did nothing to help those with crop failures. If government was to be involved – a commitment to which Gardiner was moving by the end of the blighted decade – then its objective should not be to reward the successful alone but to aid the disadvantaged and in so doing create stability for the industry as a whole. The method was to separate wheat marketing (the duty of the board) from income guarantees. It was this second matter which underlay the creation of the Prairie Farm Assistance Act (PFAA). The act stipulated that the minister might make special payments to prairie farmers in designated areas where crop yields were abnormally low or when the average price of wheat fell below an established floor. As with PFRA, inspectors were recruited, usually on a casual basis and therefore outside the Civil Service Act, to determine which farmers were eligible for assistance. The act became one of two pillars of what Gardiner saw as a permanent wheat policy. The other pillar in fact consisted of twin pieces of legislation – to promote co-operative marketing of wheat on the one hand and of all other agricultural products on the other hand – which in the event never assumed practical importance.

All of this legislation was accomplished in the first session of 1939, but not before terrible rows in cabinet over fundamental issues. Gardiner was almost alone in favouring a lower price for wheat and higher assistance payments; against him were ranged other western ministers (Crerar, for example), those financially and philosophically conservative Liberal ministers like Euler and Ilsley, farmer delegations who opposed lowering the price of wheat from 80 to 60 cents, which in practical terms was what would happen if Gardiner got his way, and a restless western Liberal caucus. King, as usual, sought to accommodate, and he succeeded, by getting agreement on a 70-cent price but with a reduced assistance payment, a five-thousand-bushel limit on deliveries by any one producer, and extension of the Wheat Board's jurisdiction to Ontario and Quebec wheat farmers.

The Liberals' grain policy in the pre-war years illustrates how, despite their desire to dislodge themselves from this responsibility, each year they became more entangled in the fortunes of the industry. Gardiner's contribution to this complex progression of policy was to secure from his colleagues acknowledgment, grudgingly given by all but King, that grain was an essential industry, farming an endangered way of life worth saving, and the west a region deserving equal partnership with central Canada. In a major contribution to the debate on PFAA, Gardiner committed his government and the Liberal party to a position that later events proved more revealing of his values than those of his colleagues:

What we think is most important is to put the greatest possible number of families in comfortable circumstances upon the farm lands of this dominion. Believing that, we think that any policy for the marketing of farm products should be based upon the idea that sufficient returns should come to the individual families to make it possible for them to maintain themselves with the ordinary comforts and give proper education to their families. The objective of this government has been and will continue to be to set up as many homes as can possibly be maintained on farms in the prairie section of western Canada. We believe that to do so will assist in solving our labour problem, our railway problem and every other national problem.[11]

Gardiner thought of agriculture not so much in terms of the individual farmer as he did of groups of farmers and their families. There was a pronounced historical consciousness in his view of politics, the one constant being the importance of agriculture across space (between and within countries or regions) and over time (from one generation to the next). He referred repeatedly to the federal government's obligation to those farmers it had encouraged, while Ottawa still controlled the west's natural resources, to settle on quarter- and half-sections, particularly in the semi-arid Palliser Triangle; it was those people who had opened the west and made the nation, and the empire, prosper. A malign conjunction of events following the transfer of resources in 1930 did not absolve Ottawa of its duty. Parts of the prairies were overpopulated as a result of federal policies, while all farmers had 'a claim of right' to assistance, even if it was only help in moving to better land and their old farms returned to grass. As well, he never tired of issuing warnings about the dismal consequences for the nation that would follow if young people refused to stay on the land, which he prophesied would happen without the kind of help the PFAA provided.[12]

Although wartime policies were necessarily contingent and often temporary, Gardiner never lost sight of his long-term goals. Stability and security lay at the base of what he called his 'national policy for agriculture.'[13] Adverse conditions before the war and the war itself established a sequence of immediate imperatives – first prairie rehabilitation and then a complicated balancing of wartime aims – that delayed realization of his permanent objectives. In fact, the war presented a unique challenge; for while it helped to restore prosperity it also aggravated the contrast between the farming and non-farming sectors of the economy. Cash farm income increased but not as fast as income in other sectors, with the result that the west continued to lag behind the rest of the country. Liberals, including the prime minister, as well as opposition spokesmen, warned that if equity between regions and between sectors of the economy was not achieved during the war, it would never happen. Instead there would be two classes of citizens – the favoured and the disadvantaged. Gardiner agreed, but with characteristic optimism saw the war as offering an opportunity to make 'our western country ... [of] much greater importance than in the past.'[14]

It would be difficult to underestimate the challenge the wheat economy presented to the minister of agriculture in the first year of the war. After a decade of drought and depression, the 1939 harvest proved to be the second largest in history. Anticipating increased European demand, the farmers sowed more wheat for their next crop and harvested 514 million bushels, an increase of 100 million over the year before. But by this date all of Europe was closed and the British government, the sole purchaser, had indicated as strong a need for meat and dairy products as for wheat. This was unwelcome news to grain farmers whose herds had been depleted by drought and feed shortages during the thirties. The week the Germans overran the Low Countries wheat futures fell from 90 to 60 cents, with a full 10-cent drop on 18 May. Multiple problems ensued. What would happen to the prairie farmers' income now? Where would the back-up of wheat, already 300 million bushels before the 1940 harvest, be stored? Who would pay for its storage? Who was to tell the farmers to stop growing so much wheat after a decade of disastrous crops?

The same month the market collapsed, James A. MacKinnon, from Alberta, was named minister of trade and commerce, a position he was to hold until 1948. Neither a farmer nor a grain trader, MacKinnon from the outset lacked Gardiner's recognized claim to speak for the wheat industry. As one Gardiner confidant soon noted: '90% of the people are of the opinion that you are wholly responsible for the handling of the wheat.'[15] MacKinnon's perceived weakness as a representative spokesman boosted Gardiner's political stock just at the critical moment of a major innovation in policy, so major in fact that Gardiner later referred to it as the beginning of 'a reconstruction of ideas' following the end of the phoney war.[16] That policy – the wheat acreage reduction program – could not have been put in place without Gardiner's authority to shepherd the initial regulations through the House. Legislation would be introduced the following year, but regulations were necessary in the spring of 1940, for in this matter the politicians were captives of the growing seasons.

Seed had to be planted, but for the first time Canadian wheat farmers were to be paid for planting something other than wheat: $4 an acre if they put land into summer fallow and $2 an acre if into coarse grains, that is oats and barley. An added inducement to shift crops was the introduction of a maximum total delivery of 230 million bushels for wheat. These two proposals would reduce pressure on elevator storage as would a third: that farmers be paid to hold grain on the farm. For the first time delivery quotas, which limited the number of bushels a farmer could bring to the local elevator, were introduced. Quotas were to become a permanent feature of the Canadian grain trade, but in 1940 they constituted an innovative departure from tradition as well as a valuable means of recording grain stocks, which in a pre-computer age proved indispensible to planning. A final provision for the 1941 crop was the introduction of a two-price system for wheat, the domestic price being inflated by a processing tax to be paid by millers and the proceeds to accrue to the farmers. The package Gardiner had worked out, based on an advance payment per bushel of 70 cents, gave the farmers a total income of $325 million. This figure proved to be the most important feature of the wheat reduction program, for it was recognized by the Liberals as the rock-bottom income the prairie farmers must have. Ultimately, this acknowledgment of a required basic total income, which over the next four decades was to triple in value, helped transform permanently the perception farmers and the federal government held of each other.

Gardiner's method of winning assent to this unprecedented policy was of a piece with earlier practices honed in Saskatchewan, where he always consulted with interested parties before proceeding to introduce or revise legislation. This time consultation meant meeting with the wheat pools, the newly resurrected Canadian Federation of Agriculture (both in its prairie regional guise and with its national officers), and with officials from the Saskatchewan Liberal party, who endorsed his plans, and whose favourable response was then embodied in a resolution passed by the Saskatchewan legislature. Such a broad base of support was necessary to the success of a policy that depended on voluntary compliance. The minister of agriculture was not telling the farmers what to do but was indicating, in the strongest possible terms, what the government wanted them to do. In the event, the government's wishes carried the day: a 24 per cent reduction in acreage led in 1941 to a 42 per cent reduction in wheat harvested. But wheat acreage reduction did not end the problem; instead, it created a new one, although this Gardiner took in stride, philosophically telling a key Regina Liberal that 'so many things will happen between now and the end of the war ... that we will wonder why we ever thought anything which we passed through earlier was difficult.'[17]

The new problem was an old one back again: the income of wheat farmers could not keep up with that of industrial workers or even of other farmers. By 1941 total farm income almost matched the 1926–29 average ($921 million versus $966 million), but wheat farmers, of whom in 1941 Gardiner reported to the House, there were only 'a few more than in the 1926–29 period,' were only half as well off as fifteen years before ($210 million as against $405 million).[18] Moreover, wheat acreage reduction did not help those on the semi-arid southern prairie who could grow nothing but wheat. On top of that, because the rest of the wartime economy was moving so fast, there was talk of wage and price control. The stage was being set for one of Gardiner's early passages at arms with Donald Gordon and his officials of the Wartime Prices and Trade Board (WPTB): to wit, if price ceilings were to be set, were they to be placed on wheat when its price was depressed because of exceptional market conditions and its producers' incomes comparably low? Gardiner was to engage in many battles with the prices board, both because the board's policies, intended to cut inflation, ran counter to his overriding desire to see agricultural prices improve, and because the board's method of operations, personnel, and attitudes did not conform to his beliefs of how responsible government should work. In each instance Gardiner's position was that of the 'working democrat,' a description a colleague applied to him some years later but which was earned before and during the war.[19] In his opinion, when agriculture was not overlooked, it was looked down on. This was a practice he had intended to change since coming to Ottawa, and in the early war years he was determined that the wheat farmer who produced a commodity Great Britain absolutely needed should not be asked to make that contribution alone or at an exhorbitant cost. Equally, he was convinced that whatever policy the farmers should have could not be formulated 'by a few men sitting in offices.'[20]

Gardiner's answer to the income shortfall was another bonus, this time for $20 million, which when taken with all other payments would give the grain farmers in 1942 $200 million in exchange for wheat deliveries of some 200 million bushels. The farmers' long-sought goal of one dollar wheat seemed to have arrived, but not without controversy on all sides. The wheat pools argued that the combination of payments constituted a sly attempt to keep the price of wheat down, a charge repeated in the Saskatchewan pool's internal election campaign in 1941 when, as Gardiner presciently noted, 'the Wheat Pool has organized the whole of the province ... as though it were a general election.'[21] His mentor, W.R. Motherwell, vigorously attacked all such transfers as politically inspired, since they gave the minister the power 'to clutch the throat of the voter at election time.'[22] The old Liberal was not alone in spying Gardiner's departmental interest in promoting subsidies and the like but his suggestion proved to be no alternative: a higher price for wheat would mean more wheat and that was the least favourable result for Gardiner or the Wartime Prices and Trade Board. An increased and a secure farm income was Gardiner's goal in war and in peace. When a large delegation from the west descended on Ottawa to protest low wheat prices and a possible ceiling on them going higher, Gardiner was in his element when called upon to meet them. He assured the farmers that he agreed with them, that the government's long-run objective was a higher price for grain but that some farmers on less fertile land were better off under his scheme of subsidies and bonuses than they could ever be with higher wheat prices and that in any case the wartime economy could not tolerate the price level they wanted.

This initial joust with the prices board over wheat evaporated when it was agreed that no ceiling would be placed on the domestic price for wheat (in fact, the initial payment set for August 1942 was increased to 90 cents a bushel) because most wheat was destined for export. In any case, by 1942 events had moved on and the market for grain had turned around once again. Now there was an extensive demand for feed grains to provide the livestock necessary to fulfil the meat contracts with Britain and to replace domestic fats and oils lost as a result of Japan's conquest of Asia. Feed grains in fact became the key to increasing the supplies of most foodstuffs. By 1943 acreage sown in wheat had declined by 42 per cent over 1940, while that in feed grains had increased by 72 per cent.

For the first time in the west's history more coarse grains were grown than wheat.

Every payment to farmers had to be fought for in the face of alternative and pressing wartime expenditures sought by fellow ministers. Gardiner, however, was equipped for the task. He was, said Mackenzie King, 'so set in his own way that he is almost without a supporter ... but is terribly tenacious' and it was this 'hard pressure' for whatever immediate issue possessed him – fluid milk bonuses, PFAA, freight differentials – that led Grant Dexter to ascribe the physical 'ruin' of the minister of finance, James L. Ilsley, to Gardiner's tactics.[23] A combative personality combined with a resolute defence of the farmer may partly explain Gardiner's prominence. But there was a functional explanation as well.

Agriculture was central to Canadian politics; only in wartime did its pivotal position become clear. Controls on farm production, though indirect, touched wholesale, processing, and consuming levels of the economy. Agricultural subsidies became part of the government's price control administration because farm incomes had to be boosted while prices were controlled; and the demand for farm labour, more crucial in an era when mechanized agriculture had only begun and at a time when energy supplies were curtailed because of the war and equipment depleted after a decade of deprivation, brought the needs of primary producers face to face with those of industry and the military. All of this activity occurred at the same time that agriculture had to increase production to meet the combined demands of greater domestic consumption, expanded armed service requirements, and special British wartime needs.

British purchases of food were made under contracts 'which specified the minimum and maximum amounts to be taken, the prices to be paid, the period of delivery, and the grade or quality.' The first agreement, in 1939, was for bacon, while other major ones followed: cheese, butter, eggs, evaporated milk, beef, and lamb. Until 1944 the contracts usually lasted for a twelve-month period, but later some ran for two or more years.[24] For the farmer the advantages of this form of trading meant assured markets for a volume of production and a contract price which acted as a floor price. For Gardiner, whose goal was to guarantee a fair and stable return to agricultural producers, the lure of the contract proved equally strong and continued into the post-war period, vanishing only after a prolonged and unhappy experience with the Canada–United Kingdom Wheat Agreement, from 1945 to 1950. The contracts joined PFAA, the wheat reduction program, and wartime subsidies generally in preparing public and governmental opinion to accept a post-war system of price supports, which was realized in the Agricultural Price Supports Act of 1944.

Fulfilling the contracts challenged Gardiner's talents for organization and administration. The establishment of the Agricultural Supplies Committee (later Board) was described in the preceding chapter but at its creation, in September 1939, no one, not even Gardiner, could have anticipated the breadth of its future activities. One of the most complete and lucid accounts of this and companion boards in the Department of Agriculture is to be found in an exceptional series of meetings of the Standing Committee on Agriculture and Colonization in June 1943, before which both Gardiner and his senior officials appeared.[25]

The general responsibilities of the board were to direct agricultural production and to purchase and distribute supplies to promote that production. Illustrative of its activities were subsidies to Nova Scotia and British Columbia apple producers whose principal export market disappeared when the British government in 1939 declared fresh fruit a low-priority import. Federally assisted experiments at dehydrating apples, so that the fruit might be shipped more economically, proved moderately successful. But even with this boost in exports, four thousand apple 'families' still received payments which, according to Gardiner, on average far exceeded the amount paid to 250,000 wheat farmers.[26] Of equal importance was the freight subsidy program, which grew out of the wheat reduction scheme to direct farmers into growing coarse grains. Under the board's supervision, freight assistance would still make it possible to sell meat and dairy products under the price ceiling. It was, in other words, a bonus to eastern farmers given at the time western farmers received the acreage bonuses. Of $30.6 million paid out in freight assistance between 1941 and 1944, two-thirds went to Ontario and Quebec farmers. Gardiner, who kept cattle on his family's farm near Lucan, Ontario, attested to the program's efficiency, when he told the House he had shipped grain east from Abernathy, Saskatchewan, to feed his Ontario cattle at no cost to himself.[27]

The Agricultural Supplies Board was one of several wartime bodies under Gardiner's authority: bacon (later meat), dairy, and special products boards were established in 1939, 1940, and 1941 respectively with, for example, powers to regulate exports within their area of concern, to determine price differentials, and to set storage amounts and conditions. The main difference between the Agricultural Supplies Board and the others was that it could spend money to help production, as it did in assisting the construction of dehydrating equipment. None of the boards bought goods; rather, each acted to see that the terms of the contracts that affected them were carried out. Their cumulative impact on Gardiner in wartime politics was to enhance his authority in either of two ways: they acted as a countervailing power to assertions of control by the Wartime Prices and Trade Board; and their very complexity encouraged members of all parties to look to him to preserve the traditions of responsible administration.

The deputy minister of agriculture, G.S.H. Barton, assured the standing committee that he understood why 'there should perhaps be some confusion in [their] minds ... in respect to these boards because we have quite a few of them.' All boards possessed the power to make what he called 'operative regulations,' because this was needed in the uncertainties of wartime, but all regulations were subject to ministerial approval. Gardiner's reputation as a dominant minister who characteristically would assume 'full responsibility for all the [actions] which I have recommended to the house' and who would never disavow any policy as 'merely a recommendation of officials of the department,' came to his aid now.[28] In the uncertainties of wartime administration, the members trusted him.

The Agricultural Food Board was established in March 1943 within the Department of Agriculture as part of an attempt to rationalize the ad hoc division of responsibilities which had evolved between the department and the WPTB. Chaired by the deputy minister of agriculture, the Food Board's major innovation was to concentrate responsibility for the payment of all agricultural subsidies under one authority – in this instance Gardiner. In the context of interdepartmental politics, this new alignment of authority constituted a victory for Gardiner and a set-back for Ilsley and Donald Gordon in their attempts to keep the control of wartime price levels to themselves.[29] Politics notwithstanding, from the perspective of how best to maximize production in the third year of the war, the transfer of responsibility made sense, for as the war progressed the need for control on all fronts grew. As Gardiner would explain, it was always possible to control one product, say bacon or ham, but what then happens to the production and consumption of a substitute, like beef? Or, if Great Britain wanted all of Canada's cheese (which she did in 1942), what happens to butter if dairymen move to cheese? Price supports might be necessary to guarantee butter supplies, but for reasons of timing or location they might not achieve the result wanted. Seasons and regions became crucial factors in determining adequate supplies; adequate information on which to act equally so. It was for these reasons that food rationing was eventually introduced. Though never one of Gardiner's responsibilities, he accepted rationing as necessary, for it helped him to determine Canada's basic food needs and on the basis of that knowledge release as much food as possible for Great Britain.

It was not the war that made agricultural production a complex matter to supervise; thanks to a constitution which made agriculture a concurrent power, it was already that when the war began. In the dairy industry, for instance, grades and standards were set by the provinces, although according to the chairman of the wartime Dairy Products Board, standards were 'fairly uniform' among the several jurisdictions. Members of the Standing Committee on Agriculture and Colonization, all of whom were farmers, greeted this information with indignation. They found the defence that this was just 'practice' a most unsatisfactory explanation for the provincial milk boards adding yet another layer to wartime administration. Gardiner and his department, however, took advantage of the normally close relationship existing between the two levels of government. The chairman of the Agricultural Supplies Board, A.M. Shaw, expressed the federal position succinctly when he explained that 'the provinces were responsible in a large measure for production; they always have been, and they have very good organizations for handling that industry in the provincial governments.' Indeed, the relations were so good in some instances, British Columbia for example, that the federal department paid the provincial Department of Agriculture for the use of a British Columbian civil servant to oversee the shipment of products from the province.

Outside of an exceptional organization like PFRA, the federal department, unlike the provinces, did not have strong field services. It was this disparity in manpower and expertise, and the consequent lack of information, that encouraged the federal department early in the war to summon the first of many federal-provincial agricultural conferences to help regulate production. By 1943 at least nine conferences had taken place. They were attended not only by officials from both levels of government but by Canadian Federation of Agriculture representatives and members of the farm press. Annual meetings, continued after the war, providing Gardiner with a major platform from which to pronounce his department's accomplishments and gauge agricultural opinion. Near the end of his federal career, he compared the conferences 'more or less [to] a party caucus ... behind closed doors ... [so as to] get free expression of opinion.'[30] However described, the meetings became another part of the machinery Gardiner created to join farmers to the federal government, machinery whose reciprocating parts carried opinion to Ottawa and policy back to those on the land.

The standing committee meetings in 1943 could be seen in a similar light, for they offered support to Gardiner's administration of wartime policies and in so doing provided useful ammunition in the continuing battle to advance agriculture's cause. In 1943 Gardiner attended seven of the thirteen hearings and his presence was almost palpable, although his interventions were rare. And yet at the end of this exceptionally thorough exploration of the department's wartime activities, it was the WPTB which emerged scathed, with a Liberal describing the prices board as the 'holy of holies,' a CCF member demanding (unsuccessfully) that a representative from the prices board appear to give evidence, and a Conservative obliquely suggesting that because of the prices board 'there has been a lot of interference with the Agricultural Department.'[31]

The federal-provincial annual conference and the standing committee provided two vantage grounds from which Gardiner could press his campaign on behalf of the farmer. The popular media was a third. In March 1943 he wrote an article for *Maclean's* magazine in which he described the economic burden Canada's farmers had had to bear when their pre-war markets were lost, either in Europe because of Hitler or in the case of the United States because of Ottawa's decision to close the border so that needed supplies might be guaranteed to Great Britain.[32] A draft copy of the piece, routinely sent to the Prime Minister's Office, profoundly disturbed King's aide, Jack Pickersgill, who advised his employer that the article 'contains a most serious indictment of the price control policy as applied to agricultural products. If published without qualification, every organized group of farmers would be able to point out that the Minister of Agriculture himself admitted that the costs of keeping down food prices was being borne by the farmers, for the benefit of the consumers. It would probably result in farm pressure on the price ceiling which could not be resisted.' Two parts of the draft, Pickersgill added, 'are a direct incitement to a campaign for higher prices or increased subsidies. What is completely ignored is the fact that all prices are effectively controlled in Canada: what the farmer buys is kept down as well as what he sells (in fact more thoroughly).' Pickersgill concluded by offering to have a reply prepared to Gardiner 'suggesting that due emphasis be given to the other side of the farm picture.'[33] In the event, the letter drafted for King's signature was considerably milder than Pickersgill's memorandum, but it made the same point in diplomatic language.

The article eventually appeared in amended form to take partial account of these criticisms, but Pickersgill's interpretation of the original draft was close to the mark. For Gardiner, protecting the farmer meant raising or, better still, removing the price ceiling on agricultural products. Grant Dexter explained at the same time Gardiner's political technique and his predicament, when a few months later he quoted a conversation he had had with the minister: 'He [Gardiner] is urging every farm leader he meets to get out and kick the ceiling. He can't do it, on account of the fiction of cabinet solidarity. He thinks to continue the ceiling is suicide.'[34] The immediate beneficiaries of this policy were the Department of Finance and the prices board but, as Dexter also reported, in the long run the minister feared the government would lose, for there were no safe Liberal seats left in the west. Of equal concern to Gardiner, however, was the detrimental effect of the policy on the farmers both in the short and in the long run: 'I do not think that the holding down of prices to those who are producing food can be justified by anyone anywhere unless they can guarantee that they are going to be able to keep prices from going down later on. That will be found a much more difficult problem than putting a ceiling on prices.'[35] Here again, the need for support, for stability to the farmers' income, dominated his thinking, as it had ever since coming to Ottawa in 1935. This was the continuing thread to his agricultural policy, which he perceived as dividing into three periods: the first (1935–40) characterized by concern for rehabilitation and development, the second (1940–45) by marketing matters, and the third (the post-war years) by the transition of agriculture into an assured prosperous sector of a national economy characterized by new industrial growth.

Important as conferences, committees, and the media were in promoting Gardiner's objectives, the principal forum remained the House of Commons. Whether defending his estimates, or in throne or budget debates, or in the passage of wartime bills, Gardiner never avoided an occasion to make a clear statement of agricultural policy in layman's language. So, too, his candour about the administration of agricultural policies: he was proud of the fact that his expense accounts had consistently been among 'the highest ... among ministers of the government,' and he claimed that no inspector in his department 'would be worth his salt if he did not have a high expense account.' The opposition's response was 'to complain about his not spending enough' and to begrudge wartime restraint as revealed in the decline of Agriculture's appropriation, from $13 million in 1940 to under $9 million in 1943. Few were inclined to disagree with Gardiner's own positive assessment of his performance: 'There were not many opportunities for putting forward the case for agriculture of which I have not taken advantage.'[36]

On balance, it was an extraordinarily skilful and sustained performance. It confounds Gardiner's reputation as an outsider or a lone wolf who was scrappy in his dealings with colleagues and opponents alike, and demonstrates a level of effectiveness he achieved then which he never equalled later. Gardiner's success lay partly in his very isolation from his colleagues. He liked to operate on his own, to consolidate as much power as possible in the department or amass regulatory power under PFRA and PFAA. And the war, with its imperative to organize all aspects of national life, rewarded his desires in two ways: it multiplied the opportunities to accumulate power through such measures as the wheat acreage reduction and feed freight assistance programs, for example, and it turned the attention of his colleagues in other wartime directions. Entries in King's diary make plain that agricultural matters, if not peripheral, were secondary, though no less irritating for that, to the preoccupied prime minister. And their importance decreased as the war dragged on and military questions grew more pressing.

But there was another reason for Gardiner's success. Unlike his colleagues in the cabinet war committee, where he sat only while minister of national war services, his labours were more reminiscent of peacetime politics because they were more familiar to the members of the House. To the extent that the equation of agricultural products to munitions of war held true, it was an equivalence readily understood and welcomed by a House 20 per cent of whose members were themselves farmers. In addition to food supplied to combatants, it was literally true that crops were munitions: milkweed for a synthetic rubber pilot plant in Ontario, fibre flax for airplane fuselages and parachute cords, new strains of coarse grasses to hold the sand along runways thus protecting aircraft engines. These, plus the development of agriculturally related machinery to replace that formerly imported, or the experimentation with seeds, many biennial and none native to Canada, required the cooperation of individual farmers, their organizations, departments of agriculture in Ottawa and the provinces, and university researchers. It was a tremendous achievement, one which members of Parliament could share with the minister, and one which encouraged them to support him over and over again in his battles with the prices board or with the Department of Munitions and Supply to have agriculture's contributions recognized. As the head of the Agricultural Supplies Board told the Standing Committee on Agriculture and Colonization, eggs were 'just as important as a tank or aeroplane' and, consequently, new egg stations deserved the benefit of accelerated depreciation just as much as any other manufacturer of war material.

The war marked the zenith of Gardiner's career as an administrator and as a minister. He was never again to occupy so decisive a position in public affairs, first, because agriculture's relative importance in the national economy continued to decline even while the prosperity of its individual producers improved, and secondly, because the delegation of emergency powers which made such prominence possible could not last indefinitely. Of this last reality Gardiner was acutely aware: 'Our country,' he reminded laymen and leaders, 'is a federation and the authority to take possession of farm products for delivery to anyone rests largely with the Provinces.'[37] Wartime conditions had fostered a successful marriage of personal ambition and agricultural policies; the trick was to keep that alliance fruitful in the absence of war.

With peace threatening attrition of his ministerial power and a return to low agrarian incomes, Gardiner responded by taking programs framed to deal with the unusual conditions of the first half of the decade and adapting them to ensure agricultural stability in its second half. On balance, the attempt proved disappointing. The effect of legislation such as the Agricultural Prices Support Act was limited and not particularly useful to farmers.[38] A more telling measure, however, was the fate of the Canada–United Kingdom Wheat Agreement, for that agreement touched the largest sector of the nation's farm industry, a sector in which Gardiner during the war had clinched his reputation as the wheat farmers' premier spokesman and its most accomplished politician. Modelled on the successful wartime foodstuffs contracts, the Anglo-Canadian wheat agreement garnered scant praise for Gardiner, who must be considered its chief proponent and defender, despite MacKinnon's continuing responsibility for grain.

The issue of the contract that seized Gardiner's attention and which, characteristically, he continued to explain until the end of his days, was the failure, as he saw it, of the British government to keep the spirit of the undertaking.[39] The four-year agreement set wheat prices for the first two years of its operation but only floors for the last two; a 'have regard to' clause for the crop years 1948–49 and 1949–50 suggested, to

Gardiner at least, that the British ultimately would take into account any discrepancy between the world price and what they paid for Canadian wheat after 1945. When world prices shot up, as they did after the war but also after the conclusion of the agreement, Gardiner expected some compensation. Recompense was never made, although the British government did eventually forfeit the last $65 million of a Canadian loan which was then distributed to the farmers at the end of their crop year.

Over his long career Gardiner's forte lay in clarity of purpose, forceful advocacy of goals, and energetic and personalized administration, and the Anglo-Canadian agreement seemed to capitalize on these strengths. It offered the opportunity in peacetime to realize his first objective of agricultural security: 'quantity is just as important as price,' he later said in defence of the agreement.[40] Moreover, the agreement was long term, in the mode of the later wartime contracts, and was the result of personal discussions between Gardiner and British officials. In other words, the substance and procedures appeared familiar, with the resemblance approximating a form mutually beneficial in the past to him and his constituency. Once concluded, the agreement set exactly the kind of tangible production schedule (600 million bushels over four years) which Gardiner could use to mobilize the farmers through the collaborative machinery fashioned during the war. At a time when post-war trading relations still appeared obscure and international market arrangements were yet to be determined, the bilateral agreement was simple, concrete and, in Gardiner's estimation, reasonable, since it provided insurance against the return of the hungry thirties.

Why then did this contract prove so unrewarding? Gardiner would say the question was wrongly put, that the farmers did all right, and would have done better had British officials kept their word. But whatever he might have said, from the incubation of the plan until its conclusion, almost no one else agreed with him. The Canadian Wheat Board, the organized farmers, his cabinet colleagues, nearly everyone remained uneasy about such a long-term, high-volume commitment. It was a measure of Gardiner's persuasive determination, of MacKinnon's political weakness, and of the government's uncertainty in the wake of the 1945 election results, that Gardiner carried an unenthusiastic majority before him. In his arguments for the contract he played upon an old wartime theme – that even if the price was initially low Canada had an obligation to Britain, one which the British would appreciate and honour, financially, at the end of the contract.[41] The British, whom he eulogized in countless speeches and on behalf of whom he had rallied farm and non-farm Canadians in 1940 and after, proved untrustworthy, although Gardiner frequently allowed that the Labour government's socialist ideology more than any other reason explained this lapse in good faith.

The Canada–United Kingdom wheat contract undermined Gardiner's reputation for astuteness. Whatever its immediate worth to the farmers, the contract had long-run effects for Canadian agriculture. Because the government had concluded so mammoth an undertaking, it was necessary to renew once again the monopoly position of the Canadian Wheat Board. That board, which at the beginning of his federal career Gardiner had intended to abolish, had now become, as in the 1930s, essential to the realization of his primary objective – the security of the grain farmers' income. By the end of the contract period, the board had no more vociferous defender than Gardiner. The failure of the wheat contract had a more directly personal influence on the man who had fought so hard for it. After 1950 Gardiner turned his attention away from international markets and concentrated once more on domestic, even regional, questions. In particular, he looked forward to a rejuvenated prairie west through the building of a South Saskatchewan River dam. Wheat markets and wheat production were not separable issues – they never were for Gardiner – but the intensity which had characterized the securing of markets for farm products ever since the beginning of the war now ended and Gardiner returned to his original concern – the securing of the west in Canada. The tools available to him were political and administrative, but the war had tempered Gardiner's political power at the same time as it had elevated his administrative dominance.

16

A Less than Perfect Organization

The Liberal government's public declaration in 1939 to set aside war-time partisan differences proved fateful to so partisan a politician as Gardiner. After a quarter-century of combating coalitionists, independents, and co-operators, as well as out-and-out opponents, Gardiner was neither intellectually nor emotionally disposed to bury political animus just when a major battle was about to begin. At its start, no one could know the course or outcome of the war, although little foresight was needed to predict another division of opinion over conscription. The argument that national unity required a political truce carried slight weight with a campaign veteran who believed that politics was fought on policies and that elections decided issues. As past differences over strategy to fight the Progressives had indicated, Gardiner did not share the prime minister's love of compromise. King's style of leadership, when joined to the memory of Union government and its aftermath, explained his unwillingness to see that experiment repeated. Gardiner's leadership style, best exemplified, he believed, in his honourable defeat in 1929, was influenced by the same event. But where King saw the 1917 coalition the consequence of disreputable partisanism, Gardiner put the emphasis elsewhere – on the willingness of those who had deserted Laurier to abandon their party.

This contrast in political styles stemmed partly from a difference in individual personality: Gardiner scrappy, tough, and confrontational; King elusive, soft, and accommodative – though no less ruthless for that. But the contrast was also traceable to the different offices each held: the one prime minister, the other his subordinate. King did not see Gardiner as a good potential leader of the party; in his opinion, Gardiner lacked sufficient vision for the top job. This was a standard, and imprecise, criticism King directed at several ministers. Whatever its validity with regard to the others, in Gardiner's case the charge was not totally unfounded. For him, political decisions were both simpler and more sequential than they were for Canada's first minister. The difference in their qualifications was the difference between micro- and macro-political skills, and Gardiner definitely excelled at the first. Superabundant energy, great persuasive powers, resilience in the face of set-backs – these qualities rendered him a formidable adversary. But for their optimal impact they required the attraction of a clear goal as, for example, in PFRA, the wartime food contracts and, later, the unsuccessful campaign for the South Saskatchewan River dam. The same was true when Gardiner turned his talents to organizing and winning elections; then the aims of Liberalism, whose appeal he never tired of extolling or measuring in votes won or lost, provided the concrete objective. The more abstract the goal, the less congenial the challenge, a self-truth which later contact with United Nations' bodies revealed to him: 'I feel much more at home working at my job as Minister of Agriculture here where one can at least see the results of efforts put forth ... I like to see something happening.'[1]

Gardiner's niche then was Agriculture, a sanctuary he made, in Bruce Hutchison's words, 'a kind of semi-soverign power.'[2] And it was this quasi-autonomy that rendered him so effective a proponent of agriculture in wartime Ottawa. Less controllable because more independent than perhaps any other minister, Gardiner was the *bête noir* of the new and powerful bureaucrats who flooded the capital after 1939 but who failed to breach Agriculture's defences. Along with distinctive specialized policies, the department's chief protection was its minister's command of a formidable party organization, centred in Saskatchewan but with significant impact periodically in the other prairie provinces. Decades later, Canadians have generally forgotten that until the 1951 census Saskatchewan was the country's third most populous province, sending twenty-one MPs (against Ontario's eighty-two and Quebec's sixty-five) to the House of Commons in 1939. It was this fact, and Ontario's perversity in voting Tory, that regularly informed Gardiner's election calculations: 'Just so long as we can elect Liberals in the Maritimes, in Quebec, and in Saskatchewan, we can keep on winning Canada.'[3]

His personal political code and the Liberal party's high stakes guaranteed that the decision to suppress partisan differences for the war's duration would not be welcomed by Gardiner. There were other reasons for concern. The Liberal party was as near to being a 'perfect' organization as human ingenuity and energy could make it, after thirty-five years of nurturing.⁴ The adjective, which was Gardiner's, implied an organization ceaselessly in motion: raising funds 'which [might be] only fairly successful as a[n] election collecting effort but as a political activity was most successful' or marking voters' lists, for 'the trying to find out is the most important part of it, as it is bound to result in canvasses being made,' or drafting polls, 'a most important part of organization.' T.H. Wood, one of Gardiner's principal informants on the provincial scene, echoed these sentiments, when he recalled, early in 1944, how perfect it once had been: 'We never stopped introducing some new idea, either weekly or monthly, that kept the organization rolling and never let it stop.'⁵ But by then the comment was invidious, for the political news from Saskatchewan had grown grim, with Liberals telling Gardiner on the one hand about 'this CCF hot bed' and on the other that 'we are going to loose [sic] the Province.'⁶

Thus, to suppress partisan activity ran counter to political nature and political practice and, by the war's onset, contrary to political sense in Gardiner's judgment. In Saskatchewan, the Liberals faced a disturbingly stubborn CCF whose economic and ethnic appeals they might refute on the hustings but whose electoral attraction continued unabated. For, unlike earlier challengers to Liberal dominance in the province, the CCF emulated Liberal organization methods and thoroughness. The socialist challenge, already real, appeared more threatening if local Liberals, obeying Mackenzie King's decision, vacated the field. Wartime agricultural policies compounded the dilemma, for they were unfamiliar and complex and had to be explained to the western farmer. This was one of the party's traditional roles – to mediate between governor and governed. It was also one that Gardiner, the former teacher, personally relished and encouraged other Liberals to copy but with decreasing success as the war lengthened. The need for the party increased as protests by organized farmers mounted at the government's wartime prices and incomes policy. The effect of a moratorium on partisan activity thus extended far beyond electoral matters, undermining as it did the federal government's principal advocates throughout the region.

Gardiner's reluctance to see the Liberal organization unwound was not matched by Saskatchewan's provincial Liberal ministers. They jumped at the chance to call a halt to politics. Although patriotism may have had something to do with the belief that party competition was unseemly in wartime, practical considerations underscored the wisdom of a truce. The Saskatchewan Liberals were exhausted, 'worn out' a Gardiner correspondent was later to recall, after a decade of drought, depression, bankruptcy, and third-party challenges.[7] The opportunity to rest was too enticing to resist and W.J. Patterson, the premier, succumbed almost immediately to Mackenzie King's proposal, going so far as to suggest to Gardiner that the Union government precedent of the last war might be the answer in this one. It was not a recommendation to tempt Gardiner, who believed instead that a modest amount of politics might be good for people, taking their 'attention a little away from the difficult [war] situation.'[8] The fact that Gardiner's successor in Saskatchewan could make such a suggestion, and to Gardiner personally, indicated another, more fundamental problem for Liberals in Saskatchewan: the provincial leaders did not share the federal minister's passionate belief in the Liberal cause and they were so gauche as to indicate as much. There was a leadership problem – a compound of apathy and lukewarm commitment to principle. A third part of the mixture can only be stated negatively: there was an absence of political finesse.

One did not have to be as intense a Liberal as Gardiner to express alarm at one correspondent's description of political conditions in Saskatchewan in 1942: 'Everybody has gone on a holiday since you and Mr. Davis left the Govt.'[9] In what once had dominated them most – the maintaining of up-to-date party lists, the appointment of competent supporters to government bodies, the promotion of their own and federal government policies – the Saskatchewan Liberals no longer demonstrated much interest.[10] The disruption in local communities caused by the war was part of the reason, for it made regular party organization much more difficult to maintain, especially in a largely rural province. Hundreds of thousands of men and women had enlisted or gone into war industries and had left the province. The return of comparatively good economic times deprived the party of a pool of willing workers from those left behind. And there were competing endeavours, such as national registration, salvage, war savings and recruiting campaigns, and the Red Cross, temporarily of higher visibility, for those with the skill and experience to fill them. Bill Bird, Gardiner's organizer in Melville until 1945 and later provincial organizer, noted the effect of nine loan drives on politics: '[They] made it difficult to interest anyone in politics ... most of the Victory Loan people here are Liberals and key men at that and have not had time to do much for us till now.'[11]

These competing activities diverted the attention of Liberals at the very time the government's interventionist policies and multitude of wartime regulations began to irritate the public. These non-partisan alternatives competed for scarce organizing ability and, dependent as they were on massive publicity, added to an avalanche of wartime pamphlets which forced the Liberals to revise their methods of communicating with the voters. 'Practically no one reads the *Liberal*,' Charles Dunn wrote Gardiner on the eve of the Saskatchewan election. And Dunn, now out of office but for a time successor to Gardiner as the minister responsible for party matters, ought to have known.[12] The gap between voter and representative, which Gardiner took such care to bridge, yawned ominously in Saskatchewan during the last year of the war. The result, Gardiner noted, was that 'people are not voting on policies ... [but] on things that hurt for the time being.' Cryptically phrased, they were against the government because 'they blew out a tire, and it took too long to get another one.'[13] As unreasonable as that attitude might be, Gardiner could at least understand it, for Liberalism too opposed regulations except in unusual circumstances, such as the prosecution of war. What particularly offended him was when the CCF joined the chorus of critics, for in his opinion that party was willing 'to regulate every human individual in the country' and therefore it had no justification in 'objecting to our regulating beef steaks.'[14]

Whether Saskatchewan was unusual in the number of complaints aimed at wartime policies and regulations it is impossible to say. But there is no doubt that there was a distinctive prairie problem when it came to explaining them. The west was unusual in that economic questions dominated its thinking. Through settlement, boom, bust, war, depression, drought and, after 1939, war again, the index of well-being lay in land prices or wheat prices or the numbers of residents on relief. It took a monumental abberation, like the Klan in the twenties, to jar such attitudes, and then only temporarily. Gardiner recognized, with frustration, that the Second World War did not possess this rare capacity. He was told repeatedly by Saskatchewan informants that in the west 'one would hardly know that there was a war.'[15] With few war industries in their midst but with a rapid decline in unemployment through migration, plus improved economic conditions and only moderate casualties compared to the First World War, many westerners viewed the government's war policies with suspicion, puzzlement, and even hostility.

Confusion and lack of understanding of his government's policies thus plagued Gardiner throughout this period and provided a recurrent theme for his correspondence; there was no shortage of critics, both outside and within Liberal ranks. Even had the CCF abandoned organizing altogether, conditions were such that support would have continued to flow to it. The wartime realignment of traditional grain farming coupled with conservative prices, although supplemented by bonuses, upset the industry's hundreds of thousands of producers. Even with advances of 90 cents a bushel plus acreage payments, Gardiner himself recognized that the grain farmers had reason to complain and that, unlike most Canadians, they possessed a potent weapon with which to demonstrate their displeasure.[16] By the early 1940s, the Wheat Pool, the premier voice of organized agriculture on the prairies, had turned against its former Liberal allies. Once that happened, it hardly mattered who was for them, since the CCF could tap that aggregated opposition at the first opportunity.

This occurred in 1943 in a federal by-election in Humboldt, a seat the Liberals had held for nearly twenty years. The CCF won on a platform critical of wartime regulation, the government's handling of wheat, and Saskatchewan's failure to do as well out of the war as other provinces.[17] Liberal 'machine-bashing' once again became the order of the day in the House of Commons, and Gardiner characteristically took advantage of the opportunity to refute in meticulous detail the charge that the government had used PFRA employees and their cars, burning rationed gasoline, for the benefit of the Liberals.[18] But the legendary thoroughness of a Gardiner-run campaign was evident in Gardiner's annotations recorded alongside selected poll results: 'Radical CCF,' 'Conservative,' 'CCF on Wheat,' 'Railway Labor Troubles,' 'Liberals [sore],' and then, 'All these towns pressed about regulations etc.'[19] Notwithstanding the lively exchange in the House, Gardiner, who treated by-elections as a serious test of a government's policy, could not ignore the decline in Liberal support, from 53 per cent of the votes cast in 1940 to 36 per cent in 1943. He blamed the defeat on the provincial Liberals' apathy, but most of all he attributed it to the CCF's coming of age. Its supporters had principles they believed in and on which they would not compromise, and they volunteered their abundant energies to convince the voters that these principles were sound. In other words, they acted the way Gardiner thought Liberals should act.

CCF and pool opposition was to be expected, but provincial Liberal criticism of federal policies proved more difficult to tolerate. According to Gardiner's way of thinking, the role of local Liberals was to support their federal brethren. At this stage of his political career, the idea that a provincial wing of the party could be in opposition, let alone permanent opposition, to its federal wing was still a repugnant concept. Moreover, in the war years in Saskatchewan it made no sense. The lack-lustre performance of the provincial Liberals and the overwhelming influence of federal agricultural policy on the provincial economy suggested to Gardiner that the Saskatchewan troops should get on side if they were to take any credit for improved conditions.[20] In his mind still, organized Liberalism started at the federal top and extended down to the provinces. That did not mean that provincial parties were less important than federal ones; rather they were telescoped parts of one organization which could not be expected to function if one part failed to work. Therefore, results like those from Humboldt and reports, such as the following from a local organizer, profoundly disturbed him: 'I have never experienced, such a complete breakdown of morale, amongst normally reasonable, and sound people, as I have witnessed, in the several weeks I have been meeting our liberals.'[21]

Equally disturbing was the provincial Liberals' treatment of Saskatchewan's ethnic population, more particularly the 14.5 per cent who, according to the 1941 census, were of German extraction but whose wartime experiences at the hands of their British-Canadian rulers unsettled all 'non-English' residents. From the time of Saskatchewan's creation in 1905, the Anglo-Saxon proportion of its population was the smallest of any province in Canada (for example, according to the 1941 census 44 per cent as opposed to 72 per cent in Ontario); half a century before the word or policy became popular, Saskatchewan was Canada's original multicultural community. And the Liberals early in their history had learned to tailor their appeal to this heterogeneous population, and by so doing had helped incorporate large numbers of immigrants into the Canadian political system. Since before the First World War, Gardiner had played a part in this endeavour, as the tens of thousands of pages of his papers reveal. He had better reason than most of his cabinet colleagues to be sensitive to the effect of government policy on Canada's different racial groups. Arguably, it was the Saskatchewan experience and Gardiner's early, almost daily, contact with the foreign-born that explained his strong belief in democracy and reform, and his lack of prejudice about race, class, and religion.

However, his liberal values did not make him an advocate of the melting-pot or of unhyphenated Canadianism. Had he adopted such a view his political task in Saskatchewan would have been easier, for the non-English of whatever ethnic origin would have become interchangeable representatives of all. But Gardiner was as alive to the province's kaleidoscopic nationalities as he was to the Scottish and Canadian parts of his own heritage. The political implications of this more discriminating attitude, at a time when the European relatives of Saskatchewan's 'different nationalities ... are fighting against one another,' deepened as the war progressed.[22] Quite clearly, and in addition to his own personal sentiment, conscription for overseas service constituted a land mine as far as harmony among Saskatchewan's multi-ethnic population was concerned.

Evidence of the danger was apparent in the dark days of 1940: on the matter of anti-German sentiment, T.H. Wood described how 'every member of the Government is going goofy right now' and, as an indication of the problem, the premier warned Gardiner that 'to make an appointment of a German to the Public Service at the present time would cause a storm of protest.'[23] Attributing this particular hysteria (at Balcarres, on the brow of the Qu'Appelle Valley, there were demands for a home guard, a hundred rifles, and two machine-guns) to the Nazi Blitzkrieg, Gardiner reminded Patterson about similar outbursts in the First World War and predicted that 'many people will be more or less ashamed of their actions when the war is over.'[24] But in the mean time it became one of his jobs to chasten, chastise, and counsel Liberals in their dealings with the foreign-born, for at every turn the opportunity to offend was great.

National registration was an early example and in that enterprise the government in Regina was told that all Canadians should be made to see that they had a personal stake in its successful completion; for that reason those doing the registering should not be exclusively British in background or from the Canadian Legion. Indeed, all wartime patriotic campaigns offered the non-English the chance to support the war effort without regard to party and outside of the flammable question of military enlistment. Gardiner's watching brief extended even to relations with his federal colleagues, especially a minister like the postmaster general (W.P. Mulock). Even in wartime Mulock was still under pressure when appointing local postmasters; but now a new twist began to appear – whether a candidate was of German or Austrian extraction. Arguing that all candidates were Canadian regardless of ethnic origin, Gardiner fought against a selection being made on such a criterion and went so far as to reject 'a comparison of that kind [being] made in a report.'[25]

Wartime appointments at the highest federal level were informed by similar considerations, as witness the fate in 1943 of Gardiner's campaign to have Dr J.M. Uhrich, a member of Saskatchewan's Liberal government since 1922, named a senator. This time Gardiner's will did not prevail, a fact which definitely indicated that after eight years in Ottawa he was still Saskatchewan's junior minister. Mackenzie King wrote in his diary that he rejected Uhrich 'because of his German associations and accent etc. and the use that could be made of it all by the Legion.'[26] As usual, the story was more complicated than this terse comment would suggest, but undoubtedly questions of race and religion ran through it. Uhrich had pressed his case with Gardiner early in 1940 on the grounds that he had stood aside from the provincial leadership back in 1935 because of his Roman Catholic religion and the events of 1929. As a result, he argued, he was owed something and since he was not a lawyer, it could not be a place on the bench. Gardiner supported Uhrich's appointment all the more warmly when King indicated his preference for J.F. Johnston, a former Unionist and then Progressive MP. Johnston's return to the Liberal fold, which recommended him to King, disqualified him for Gardiner, especially when Uhrich had remained a party stalwart. It is worth noting that during Gardiner's twenty-two years in cabinet, only four Saskatchewan senators were appointed, since at this time appointments were still for life.

The Uhrich matter hung on for three years, first as proposals were made to find him some other position in the Department of Health and Welfare, on the Farm Loan Board, the Railway Commission, or the Tariff Board, and then until after the by-election in Humboldt, where those of German origin constituted the second-largest ethnic group after the British. Uhrich eventually received his reward – he was appointed lieutenant-governor of Saskatchewan in 1948 – but not before a renewed discussion of his suitability, this time on the grounds of religion.

Dr Uhrich represented a rare phenomenon in Canadian and even Saskatchewan public life, at least until the end of the Second World War: he was a non-English, non-French, Roman Catholic elected figure of outstanding ability. The federal government possessed, through its appointment power, the means of acknowledging achievement and throughout Gardiner's career rewards were distributed with fine attention to Canada's original religious and racial divisions. Gardiner fought to expand the base of potential recipients to include the many, concentrated in western Canada, who were neither English nor French, and thereby to broaden the interpretation of Canada. Otherwise, he argued, the government could 'experience considerable difficulty ... [for] we are sticking to and depending absolutely on individuals who have very little in common with the people whose votes we are expecting at election time.'[27] But the war, with its heightened concern to assure racial and religious harmony, made progress in this direction slow; one of the casualties was Dr Uhrich's Senate appointment.

Nowhere did the partisan truce work its effect on traditional politics more quickly than in the realm of everyday patronage and appointments. For on the one hand Liberals no longer would be the sole beneficiaries of federal largesse, while on the other hand the numbers of rewards mushroomed as the federal establishment swelled in response to the emergency. Within days of war's outbreak Mackenzie King had pronounced on the nature of the change:

I had tried to make it plain in Parliament that, so far as business in war time correspondended [sic] with business in peace time, we would proceed as we ordinarily would, – contracts being subject to tender, and appointments made of those in whom we had special confidence, but the extent to which appointments were to grow out of organizations, new committees, and the like, we would have to deal with men and women of all parties. I said if we did that, and brought in outstanding men of different parties, entrusting them with work, we would find that, at the time the elections came on, these men would come to be as part and parcel of ourselves.[28]

The best construction to be placed on such self-denial was the one King gave: non-Liberals would become believers through working alongside Liberals. Over time, however, as the voters turned against his government, the prime minister grew less confident of the power of example, while it is fair to say that on this subject Gardiner never shared his leader's enthusiasm. He was opposed on philosophical grounds, while on the basis of organizational experience, he doubted the experiment could be made to work. But even he did not anticipate the coming administrative revolution or appreciate its implications for the methods of political organization of which he was a master. Ultimately, it was to matter less that some Tories and CCFers deliberately received favours, so as to calm partisan waters, than that partisanship frequently was ignored altogether in the awarding of contracts or the appointment of personnel by the agencies created to administer wartime controls.

The administrative response to wartime needs upset the 'perfect organization' Gardiner had spent two decades tuning. Afterwards he was unable to restore the organization to its pre-war condition, in part because the administrative disruption had proved so great, but also in part because the temporary dislocation had fed other wartime changes, such as the growth of the CCF, which proved a permanent check on re-establishing Liberal dominance.

Gardiner possessed the politician's suspicion of boards and commissions, since whatever their origin their purpose was to moderate or remove the political element. For him, claims to expertise or objectivity unsullied by politics constituted a recipe for non-responsible government. Others, in different circumstances, shared this view. For example, Ernest Lapointe early on became incensed at recruitment policies of wartime commissions, because they were based on personal knowledge and nothing else. 'This,' he concluded simply, 'cannot do.' In the west, Gardiner echoed this criticism: 'As far as I know, they pay no attention to the central prairie section of Canada at all in choosing their staffs for any of these Boards.'[29] Equally as serious as the boards' failure to recognize the regional dimension in Canadian politics was their disregard for popular government. Midway through the war, T.H. Wood told Gardiner that the government's unpopularity stemmed as much from the way its policies were being administered by wartime agencies as from the policies themselves. In a word, there were too many lawyers making decisions. Boards were chaired by judges who had been trained as lawyers and they chose other lawyers to sit with them. Labour, small business, and farming interests appeared to be excluded, or at least not given the same privileged access as the bar. The problem was compounded, Wood argued, by the general inadequacy of lawyers as 'executives.' This was not their forte; instead, they 'delegated all their work,' and because they did not have access to politically sensitive officials like deputy ministers, they selected 'the heads of these various institutions which they once represented or had business connections with, to head the various boards that have been established to run this war.' Sweeping as the indictment was, Gardiner did not demur. Rather, with characteristic bluntness, he expanded on it, describing the personnel of boards and commissions as 'dictators within their own field [who] resent anyone having anything to do with it.'[30]

The grounds for Gardiner's complaint became legion as the war progressed. Only a couple need be mentioned here to indicate the unfamiliar terrain which the extra-governmental bureaucracy now presented him. First, there was the scale of the operations. In Regina alone, the Wartime Prices and Trade Board office encompassed a vast array of responsibilities, none of which had challenged Gardiner's assertion of political control before September 1939. These included rentals, publicity, retail foods, services, credits, meats, oils, transit, tires, employment, office managers, salvage, consumers, rationing, trades policies, and more. Liberal workers who ran restaurants and abused their sugar ration were punished by cut-backs; party organizers who blew a tire had to put their cars on blocks because they could not get a replacement; farmers who used their trucks to drive to a picnic were threatened with fines for unauthorized use of vehicles, and so on. The list lengthened, Liberal patience grew short. Thousands applied to fill positions at Regina and in eight sub-offices; Gardiner had no role to play in their selection nor did he have any say in the appointment of fifty to sixty administrators or fifteen to twenty controllers in the regional office of the Department of Munitions and Supply. Secretaries were hired where they could be found, the relatives of opponents as likely to be employed as the scions of Liberals.[31]

The party apparatus immediately under Gardiner had to adjust as best it could to what in fact was a new organizational structure. Contacts in the new agencies became essential, and when that was not possible or too slow to achieve, Gardiner's private secretary would go personally to the 'Priorities Office with the application forms' that had to be authorized in Ottawa to help some Saskatchewan resident. But because so much of the wartime administration was decentralized, it became necessary at times to turn the old party organization on its head and have key men in the field discover the latest agency policy.[32] Gardiner was neither accustomed to nor appreciative of the adjunct role he was required to play in these matters.

A second complaint, directly related to the scale of operations, was the failure of the wartime agencies to mould themselves to the society they served. For example, it was not long before complaints were heard about their inadequate racial and religious composition. As the head of the Knights of Columbus in Regina noted, there was 'not a key man in the War Time prices setup [in the four western provinces] who was a Catholic.'[33] Lack of consultation with local people and officials was another criticism. The party organization with its multiple layers of contact required the languor of peacetime for maximum effectiveness. But the luxury of unlimited time no longer existed, as the exasperation of one harried post office bureaucrat dealing with a routine patronage inquiry made clear: 'Present-day difficulties, with curtailment of staff and increased work due to the war, have created such a situation in this Department that the time occupied in dealing with such cases as this can be ill afforded.'[34] If departments had to adjust their routine to deal with the emergency, the agencies never had a choice and, as a consequence, contracts were let without tender to persons unknown to the Liberal establishment. The score of RCAF airfields which came to dot the prairies after 1940 appeared without Gardiner being given notice as to location, contractors, or suppliers.

For the party the crux of the problem was the appearance, almost overnight, of an autonomous organizational structure immune and often insensitive to the effect of its policies on intricate and mature party relations. Even admitting the necessity for rapid decisions, wartime agencies still threatened party organization, because they were subject to none of the popular and traditional controls that hedged party activity. Parties, previously condemned as machines driven by personal ambition in search of public power, proved comparatively more accessible than the government-created administrative agencies which operated without recourse to public opinion. The former depended on a network of personally transmitted information from the poll through the constituency to elected officials. The latter acted according to dictates from above, in Ottawa, and in the process disrupted the normal flow of community intelligence. In these circumstances, T.H. Wood had cause for lament: 'I still do not know how we are going to run a political organization with as little information as is available at the present time.'[35]

Gardiner was more pessimistic still. The government had created a Frankenstein's monster of an organization, peopled it with Tories, and forsworn any control: 'There is no sense in talking about building up an organization in Saskatchewan to help elect Liberals if we are going to at the same time finance out of the Treasury of Canada another organization, to see that everything we do is belittled and criticized all over the place.'[36] There were other fears as well. The success of an agency such as the WPTB would rest on what it had prevented – ruinous inflation, for instance. However, the political appeal of that achievement would be easily offset by the voter's daily experience with regimentation. Or again, the WPTB dealt with big business and big unions, neither of which were native to Saskatchewan. The Liberal party's old constituency, composed of small businessmen and independent farmers, whose support the CCF was already undercutting, might evaporate as the Liberals became identified, thanks to the efforts of wartime administrators, with interests traditionally unsympathetic to the west.

On a larger front, the most contentious issue the government had to face after 1939 was whether there should be conscription for overseas service. In the determination of this question, Gardiner played only a minor role in cabinet and in the House. The Saskatchewan election in June 1944 and Violet Gardiner's death in October removed him from the scene of some of the most heated debate on that subject. Which was not to say that he did not hold strong opinions on the matter; he did. Rather, King did not look to him to take a leading part in the debate. From the start of the war Gardiner remained unequivocally opposed to conscription; in his opinion it was morally wrong, practically inefficient, and politically dangerous. Until his death he never recanted. No true Liberal, he believed, could advocate compulsory service, and any who did usually proposed it 'be done to someone else.'[37] In any case, compulsion was impractical because voluntary enlistments took more than half the eligible men and women and large numbers of those who did not join were needed to service those sectors of the economy (agriculture was the prime example) heavily dependent on labour. Any government which sought to determine who should go and who should stay was bound to act less efficiently than a process of voluntary choice; and it stood to earn the hostility of its citizens into the bargain.

Pro-conscription arguments were freighted with appeals to patriotism and morality. This was a rhetoric Gardiner never used and he heard it with suspicion and, occasionally, anger: suspicion because he believed the rhetoric often disguised Tory purposes, and anger because he thought it only thinly veiled anti-foreign and anti-French sentiments. His central grievance lay with the operation of selective service, which was 'all tied up together' with wage and price controls, and for that reason the subject is raised in this discussion of non-partisan wartime administration.[38] In conformity with the prime minister's decision to devalue partisan politics during the war, Gardiner had appointed draft boards in Saskatchewan 'composed entirely of Tories.' It was a decision he came sorely to regret: 'Our National War Services Boards in 1942 drafted almost everyone off the farm in the foreign speaking areas whom they could for any excuse take. The result is that in these areas we find old women, as old as seventy years, pitching hay and young girls, thirteen and fourteen years of age, assisting with the haying.'[39]

The boards had decided that 'too many English speaking people had gone into the army and the foreign element should be made to fight.' It was the kind of autocratic decision such bodies were prone to make because, he said, they operated under the empire of one idea. The self-righteous intolerance of conscriptionists offended Gardiner's liberalism, for in pursuit of their ends they abused the rights of others. This conviction and a personal distrust of the military, whose generals he believed had worked to bring about a political crisis for the government, led him into public controversy.[40] Gardiner accused General G.R. Pearkes of acting on behalf of the Tories while in uniform and, since he was about to retire, Gardiner suggested he consider running for them. Criticism of this charge came from the expected sources, the Legion for example, to which Gardiner replied that he needed no lessons on sacrifice or loyalty.

Gardiner nurtured a deep-seated suspicion of the military. The horror of the trenches in the First World War and the disaster at Dieppe in 1942 were due, he said, to a 'war-mongering type of officer,' who if given his head would cause social disruption at home as well as carnage on the battlefield.[41] Civil authority must remain superior if the country was to stand united. Conscription therefore was a political question before it was a military one. This was King's position, and it was Gardiner's. The prime minister worried about how Quebec would respond to conscription. Gardiner shared his concern, but he alone among his colleagues feared how it would be received by the non-English population in the west. Contrary to the draft boards' interpretation, it was not a question of loyalty or the lack of it but rather that large numbers of westerners saw their place in Canada as different from that of Ontarians or of Quebeckers. The following excerpt, from a letter written by Gardiner at the war's conclusion, summarizes his view of Canadian demography and relates it to conscription.

Saskatchewan and Alberta people are naturally different from those in other parts of Canada. A very large percentage of them left Europe sometime within the last fifty years to get away from war, and they never are satisfied that any government in this country should send their sons back to Europe to fight. I have a great deal of sympathy with them. They and their ancestors have seen their families wiped out periodically for hundreds of years. They finally come to the conclusion that they are going to get away from it all and come to a new continent where they do not have wars, and they are no more than established here until within one generation they are required to go back to Europe twice and fight. They naturally resent this, and even though they do not say much about it, it has considerable to do with their voting ...

There is a very considerable percentage of Anglo-Saxon people who feel very much the same way. When General de Gaulle was here a short time ago I had the privilege of sitting alongside his Secretary who could speak a little English.

He said to me 'I understand that your son was killed overseas.' I said 'Yes, he was killed at Dieppe, and fifty miles away two of his uncles who were about the same age during the last war are buried in France. Two who came back have been in hospital most of the time since the last war.' I said to him 'We have pretty much made up our minds over here that if you people on the continent of Europe start another war, the rest of the world ought to draw a ring around you and let you fight until there are none of you there. We shouldn't be required to make Europe a graveyard for our families on this side of the ocean in order to stop your madness from spreading to other parts of the world.' There is more of that kind of feeling in the central west than anywhere else, probably because we are located in the centre of the continent and therefore do not come into contact with peoples who are moving back and forth across oceans to the same extent as others do.[42]

Nine days after the Allied invasion of Europe in June 1944, Saskatchewan voters went to the polls in the first provincial election since 1938, the legislature's life having been extended as a wartime measure in 1943. The outcome was a stunning defeat for the Liberals: their popular vote went down ten points to 35 per cent and their seats reduced to five from thirty-eight; the CCF, with its vote up from 19 to 53 per cent, captured the remaining forty-seven seats in the legislature. This spectacular collapse was the culmination of preceding erosion which stretched back to pre-war days. Consequently, Mackenzie King recorded the outcome as 'no surprise' and, instead, blamed Hepburn in Ontario for giving the CCF their big chance and compared, unflatteringly, Patterson's image as 'heavy, lethargic, and less idealistic' to T.C. Douglas's high ideals and active leadership. Understating the case, he concluded that 'the Liberals have gone a little to seed there,' noting as proof that 'Gardiner has lost a certain hold,' partly because 'he is looked upon too much as a machine politician.'[43]

The disaster presented the Liberals with an occasion for introspection and certainly every one of King's complaints had some basis in fact. The Liberals in Saskatchewan had gone indeed to seed, a condition Gardiner traced to their universal apathy: they did 'nothing between elections' and never went 'near the public.'[44] C.M. Dunn agreed that 'half of them seem afraid to talk, or don't care,' but he attributed the real reason for their massive rejection to a more disturbing cause: 'The great mass of the people [believe] the Liberal Party is ... on the side of big business ... and has no longer the coinage to be the champion of the common man.' A realignment of voters had taken place, so that, for example, small businessmen, farmers, the non-English had shifted allegiance. Thus many of the CCF supporters had become 'what the Liberals should be.'[45] If by machine politician, King meant his minister's old habit of attending to the most minute electoral detail, then in 1944 Gardiner stood guilty as charged, although only he and very few others on the scene had committed that offence. Wartime controls had made an organizer's life not a happy one and Gardiner could be found in the spring of 1944 intervening on several fronts to get the right man in the right place in time for the election. In these labours the Patterson government proved worse than useless as an ally.[46]

Gardiner and Dunn both claimed to see another malign force at work; Gardiner elliptically called it 'the old issue of 1929 ... accentuated by the war,' but Dunn more idiomatically described it as 'a growing bitter feeling against anything French or Catholic.'[47] Whether, as Gardiner believed, this emotion had 'changed more votes than any one other thing,' there was no disputing heightened racial and religious tension in Canada or that Saskatchewan, with the most heterogeneous of provincial populations, had felt this distinct current of change.

In the aftermath of the returns, the key questions were how permanent the change would be and, regardless of the answer to that, what the defeat meant for the approaching federal election. Several years earlier, when prairie residents had begun to oppose the federal government's wartime economic policies, Dunn had prophetically observed that 'if anything should happen to us provincially it would be just too bad for our federal candidates later on.'[48] Now the improbable had happened and Gardiner, placed in charge at the end of 1943 of what he described as 'all the activities in relation to any election which may be held Federally,' faced an immense challenge even for a politician of his resourcefulness. He had to bring the Liberal party successfully through the next difficult federal campaign, while at the same time being deprived of the traditional sanctuary Saskatchewan had offered during all but five of his thirty years in public life.[49]

The Saskatchewan results might have been interpreted as sufficient reason to disqualify Gardiner in his new role as minister responsible for national organization. But they did not, and for reasons that revealed the respect others held for his organizational ability. If Gardiner with his reputation for thoroughness in these matters could not hold back the CCF tide, what hope was there for Liberals elsewhere? He was needed all the more now that the CCF had proved such a threat. Moreover, Saskatchewan was CCF territory; the socialist opponent might prove less formidable in other provinces where Gardiner could exercise his customary magic. Furthermore, it was argued, the federal government's progressive social policies, for example, family allowances, would blunt more decisively the driving edge of socialism than had the Patterson government's timid legislative response. In short, the federal sphere in 1945 was considered more conducive than the Saskatchewan arena had been in 1944 to the complete exercise of Gardiner's legendary talents.

Certainly Gardiner threw himself into the campaign with all his customary vigour, beginning with the appointment to key positions of men in whom he had confidence. For example, Allan G. McLean, a Saskatchewanian and later national secretary of the National Liberal Federation, was placed in charge of electoral organization. Through such contacts, Gardiner could begin to restore across the country the network of partisan communications that had atrophied during the course of the war's partisan détente.[50] But the essence of the ministerialist organization lay in the reminder King had given his ministers in September 1943: 'The duty of ministers of every province [is] to be responsible first and foremost for the organization of their own province, and for all Federal organization collectively.'[51] Thus, it was the job of each minister to pay attention to the minutiae of constituency complaints and to patronage distribution within his province.

In 1945 none of the ministers looked for an easy win. 'God knows,' wrote Bill Bird, 'we are doing every thing we can to put it over.'[52] But public exasperation after six years of restraints, fear that the future would mean a return to conditions of the thirties once the war ended, and anger over conscription made it a hard fight. The Liberals won, but they slid from their 1940 standing of 181 seats to 127 in a House of 245. Nowhere was the slide more precipitous however than in Saskatchewan, where they lost ten of their twelve seats, while the CCF picked up thirteen for a total of eighteen. Nor was the race tighter anywhere than in Gardiner's own seat of Melville, which he won by a majority of twenty-eight out of 20,320 votes cast in the province's only two-way fight. That contest was to lead to CCF accusations of vote tampering in one poll, which in turn led to the creation of the Melville Inquiry Commission, headed by the province's chief justice, J.T. Brown. Mr Justice Brown concluded his investigation by finding that tampering had indeed taken place, but with the intent to discredit the Liberal candidate. Had the scheme succeeded, he intoned, 'it would have had the much desired effect of defeating an outstanding member of the Government of Canada and an outstanding leader of the Liberal party in Western Canada.'[53]

The Liberals had survived the political trauma of the war but clearly had not emerged unscathed. Gardiner, especially, sustained permanent injury to his political reputation and prowess. The rest of the decade was spent trying to recoup the losses of 1944 and 1945. Along the way, he was to make a bid for the one great position in public life he never held – national Liberal leader. His failure here and the extent to which events during the war had deprived him of his old political dominance set the tenor for his remaining years in public life.

The report of the chief electoral officer for the general election of 1945 hinted at the nature of the post-war problem in Saskatchewan, for it revealed a highly competitive but substantially contracted organizational base on which to reassert a political claim. At the war's end, in eight of the country's constituencies, voter turnout reached or exceeded 90 per cent of the eligible voters. Seven of these constituencies were in Saskatchewan. Voter turnout for the province in 1945 averaged 85 per cent, substantially higher than in federal elections during the previous two decades. But while the participation rate was going up, the number participating was coming down. Of the nine provinces, only Prince Edward Island joined Saskatchewan in having fewer eligible voters in 1945 than in 1940, but even PEI had more eligible voters at the war's end than a decade earlier. Saskatchewan, however, had 5,785 fewer eligible voters in 1945 than in 1935. Gardiner had been aware of the decline ever since the census of 1941 which placed the province's total population at 895,992 compared to 921,785 in 1931. Indeed, it was information such as this in the larger wartime context of enlistment and of interprovincial shifts of population which had led the government to postpone decennial redistribution until after the war.[54] In 1946, the same year that intercensal figures showed a further slump of Saskatchewan's population to 832,688, a cabinet committee of which Gardiner was a leading member formulated a new scheme for redistributing Commons seats, a scheme whose principal attraction was to minimize a province's loss of seats. As it was, only Manitoba and Saskatchewan failed to benefit, and their losses were restricted to one seat a piece. As an exercise in placating regional unhappiness, the 1946 redistribution earned Gardiner credit with the prime minister and with the Liberal caucus. It was a role he would have to play even more adroitly when the 1951 census returns became known, for Saskatchewan's decline continued remorselessly, although it was to bottom out and then reverse so that the year Gardiner died it surpassed by 3,396 souls the 1931 total.

Even before receiving the gloomy federal returns, Gardiner foresaw the magnitude of the task ahead. To Sam Latta, who had latterly been the province's commissioner of publications, libraries and archives who the new CCF government lost no time in dismissing, he confessed: 'I had hoped that we might be spared the task of again starting out to build up the Liberal organization in Saskatchewan from the bottom.'[55] Although the federal election results underlined the futility of his hope, Gardiner showed no signs of depression. On the contrary, the reverses seemed to spark his boundless energy into new demonstrations of power. As a severe interpreter of the belief that responsibility in a political party lay with the leaders, Gardiner assumed that it was his job to help the party when it was down. As with earlier challenges in his career, the end was clear – to beat the CCF provincially and federally – and the means, in his mind at least, equally direct.

Only an exceptional man, at the age of sixty-four, would traverse the prairies in springtime 'by driving part by car and taking the train and finally travelling by jigger for one and one half hours during the night.'[56] Such singular energy moved all before it, especially when that consisted of a moribund Liberal organization. First, there was the need for a new leader. In 1946, W.J. Patterson stepped down after a decade of travail, leaving the legislature three years later to become a member of the Board of Transport Commissioners and then, in 1951, lieutenant-governor of Saskatchewan. A leadership convention followed, in which the only other Liberal MP from Saskatchewan, Walter Tucker, ran against a former provincial minister, E.M. Culliton. While adopting a stand of public neutrality in the contest, Gardiner thought 'everything possible should be done to have Mr. Tucker chosen.'[57] Critics explained the minister's preference by saying that Tucker was malleable; Gardiner said he was progressive. In the post-war years it became one of his articles of faith that to succeed electorally in Saskatchewan the party must adhere to a 'radical Liberal' position, by which he meant among other things attacking monopolies of all kinds and defending co-operatives against big business. There was another distinction between the candidates which received only muted expression: Culliton was a Roman Catholic and Tucker a Protestant. But in light of Gardiner's past and recent experience, that in itself would have been enough to tip the scales.

For the first time since 1916 the provincial Liberals chose as a leader a man without a seat in the legislature. In fact, Tucker kept his House of Commons seat until 1948, at which time he was elected to the provincial legislature in the Saskatchewan general election. As a result, the federal and provincial parts of the telescoped party organization, which had made the Liberals so redoubtable a force in Saskatchewan, began to separate. The significance of this fact was lost on Mackenzie King, who talked so often about the failure of others to appreciate the need for good organization: 'Any one,' he told St Laurent, 'could be found to take the leadership in the province.'[58] In fact, of course, no one could be found to lead the Liberals back to power in Regina during the remainder of Gardiner's years.

New candidates were as important as a new leader. Throughout his career Gardiner equated good organization with strong candidates. His own intense constituency activity established an ideal few others could meet but which nonetheless became their model and the standard by which they would be judged. Good candidates did not emerge unassisted. It was the duty of key men, including himself, to be on the look-out for promising material, recognizable in those who 'knew everyone in the seat,' who were good speakers, and who, in rural constituencies, had 'associations with the farm.' Gardiner's letters are filled with references to individuals he believed had 'what a candidate needs in as great a degree as it can usually be found in anyone.'[59] The decision on the right candidate, however, was too important to be left to a local constituency alone and it was too important to be decided by a contest which could divide a local party.[60] On the scale of candidate values in this period, constituency representativeness came after loyalty to the party's leader and a willingness to do battle with the enemy. As the years in the provincial wilderness lengthened and as the schism between him and the provincial party deepened, Gardiner changed his mind and began to give top place to policies and 'the organization put behind them' as criteria for success. But that was a decade into the future.[61]

It was perhaps inevitable that some Liberals and Conservatives in the province should consider the possibility of joining forces to oust the CCF. Gardiner's response was equally predictable after a lifetime of fighting such proposals. He voiced specific objections as well. Three-way fights were preferable to two-way contests, he argued, because regardless of which old party fought the CCF, progressive Tory and Liberal elements would be attracted to the CCF, while the conservative elements left behind would dominate the anti-socialist alternative. This result did not conform philosophically to his view of Liberalism, while tactically he called it futile, since there were more progressive- than non-progressive-thinking people on the prairies. Again, citing his axiom about the need for a party to control election machinery, he would point to the absence of any example of an effective coalition in which at least one of the participants had not had this control. Even proposals to nominate a single anti-socialist candidate in selected constituencies met his rebuke, for he argued that it was impossible to keep competition alive once the principle of independence had been compromised.[62] In fact, in Saskatchewan in 1948 four coalition candidates were nominated, while in the cities a sharing of candidates took place. Although one of the coalition candidates won, Gardiner complained that ten seats were lost due to these 'foolish arrangements.'

His determination to see the Liberals restored in Saskatchewan dictated his relations with the local party just as much as it did with the socialists, and occasionally with similar demonstrations of tough talk. Among the subjects that caused hard feeling was the use of federal patronage. Out of power, the Saskatchewan Liberals depended on the national government for the rewards that help keep a political organization alive. But now to the list of traditional qualifications – age, religion, location, and so on – was added loyalty to Gardiner's strategy for rebuilding the party. Of this consideration, he was quite candid: 'It is not my intention to make recommendations ... from among those who have been on the executives in constituencies where they have seen to it either that coalition candidates ran or that Liberals were prevented from running.'[63] By the end of the decade and with Mackenzie King gone, Gardiner's control of the patronage tap was absolute: 'I took the position a while ago that I was not going to worry too much about areas that do not stick too closely to the cause of Liberalism until such time as they get back into the fold ... I hope we have had our lesson in Saskatchewan on this matter.'[64]

That may have been understandable from his point of view, but the strategy and its single-minded application irritated and eventually angered Liberals in the province. Gardiner, for example, believed that appointments should not go to defeated candidates, that to do this rewarded political weakness as well as age, when what was wanted was a reinvigorated party. That meant appointing sitting Liberals and then re-electing other Liberals to fill their places. The result would be younger, more effective appointees, younger, more effective MLAS. If this counsel were followed, Gardiner argued, the party would 'get back to the position we were in at one time in Saskatchewan, which had something to do with the strength of the Liberal Party there.'[65] As sensible as this proposal might be, it did not answer the provincial Liberals' problem of being overrun with defeated candidates and nowhere to put them. Moreover, this advice originated in Gardiner's experience in provincial politics which had formally ended more than a decade before. For this reason his schemes, regardless of their intrinsic worth, were resented in some quarters of the Saskatchewan Liberal party.

Criticism of Gardiner and his tactics abated in the face of the provincial election results in 1948: from five seats in 1944 the Liberals jumped to nineteen although, thanks to coalition experiments and a short-lived Social Credit revival, their popular vote sagged another four points, to 31 per cent, until that time an all-time low. With the CCF seats down to thirty-one, from forty-seven in 1944, the scales appeared to be coming more into balance and Gardiner, who had fought insistently, relentlessly, to restore the Liberals, basked in deserved praise. Those who had counselled co-operation with other parties were chastened, and the more generous of them admitted their error, though few more succinctly than an old Liberal who wrote: 'You were right and I was wrong.'[66] The federal results, the following year, were even more reassuring: from their two seats out of twenty-one in 1945, the Liberals shot up to fourteen out of twenty (under the new redistribution). This time their popular vote climbed as well, to 44 per cent, the highest since 1930. The Gardiner electoral magic had returned. The decade which had begun in war and with a partisan truce had ended in peace and with the greatest federal victory recorded while Gardiner was minister of agriculture. The Liberals were not in power in Saskatchewan, but the future looked brighter than at any time in recent memory.

The elections of 1948 and 1949 appeared to restore the political certainty which had eluded Gardiner for ten years in and out of war. In fact, they marked the end, not a new beginning. The political world Gardiner had controlled for so long was about to change and would pass from view in the fifties. Political workers, political practices, political understandings would disappear, forcing Gardiner more clearly than ever into the role of regional lieutenant. Though he had always spoken ardently for the west, he had never limited his ambition to that of regional politician. When given the chance, with King's retirement in 1948, he would seek the Liberal party's greatest gift.

17

Region and Nation

Mackenzie King said ambition drove Gardiner to seek the Liberal party leadership in 1948, ambition so overweening, complained the prime minister, that Gardiner actually 'work[ed] to secure the position ... for himself.'[1] Looking back, Gardiner maintained that he had a different motive: to challenge party orthodoxy, which said Liberal leaders should alternate between 'French and Anglosaxon Canadians.' Such practice he viewed as detrimental to the party's interest because 'there are more Canadians now who are neither than there are of either'[2] and because it excluded large numbers of western Canadians, thus betraying the tradition of national Liberalism that stretched back to Laurier.

Gardiner sought the leadership midway through his Ottawa career, as anyone who knew him should have expected he would, and not only for the reason he later gave. In fact, in his speech to the leadership convention, he expressed as much concern about guiding Canadian economic development as he did about its political future. Only later did the Liberal party's handling of French-English relations come to occupy his attention. As a consequence, the leadership contest limited Gardiner's political fortunes in the post-war period and adversely affected Liberal sympathies in the west.

To take the last matter first, Gardiner's failure in 1948 underlined a truth about Canadian politics which more than a decade of his legislative victories for agriculture and the west had disguised: if central Canadians were united on a position, prairie Liberals must inevitably lose. This was all the more probable in a democracy of numbers represented by a delegate convention which was less susceptible than Parliament to Gardiner's talents of argument and persuasion. The outcome, said one disgruntled prairie supporter, constituted 'a defeat for the West.'[3] Exaggerated though this sentiment might have appeared then, it remained prophetic: for how long and by what means could the Liberals keep the farmers' allegiance, once the party had signalled a shift in interest away from its agrarian base outside of central Canada? For Gardiner personally, the convention marked an end to a political advance begun in 1914. From this point on, Agriculture was clearly the only portfolio he could expect to hold, a certainty which disappointed him but never caused complaint. King was right: Gardiner possessed ambition, but not of the hungry sort the prime minister meant to imply. On the contrary, his ambition, evident from the time he was a youth, took the form of a fearful dedication to work. It was just this bootstrap theme which Nathaniel Benson developed in his biography, *None of It Came Easy*. Indeed, Benson had taken on the project with a life modelled after Lincoln in mind.[4] But the idea proved congenial to the biography's central character as well; a year before the convention and on the occasion of his being sworn to the Imperial Privy Council at Balmoral Castle, Gardiner summarized his remarkable career in customarily blunt language: 'I have lived by relief and I have dispensed it to others.'[5]

King and members of the ministry, as well as bureaucrats, failed to distinguish between Gardiner's tenacity in advocating whatever policy possessed him at the moment and what they saw as a self-serving promotion of his own interests. The prime minister at least should have known better, for while Gardiner could be brutal in pressing Agriculture's case, never did he act in a manner that was unethical, underhanded, or discreditable. On the contrary, his loyalty to King and his colleagues had been tested more than once and found true. While persistent in promoting his department, he above all ministers was the master of the frontal attack. As King's diary bears witness and as Gardiner himself once said, he would never seek to curry favour with the leader or to intrigue against a colleague.[6]

Nonetheless, he did want to become leader because of the unique importance he attached to leadership. Leaders, he believed, determined not only the effectiveness of political institutions but also the values of the people they served. Whether or not one admired them – Bismarck, he thought, had created a servile nation of the Germans but Ben Gurion an industrious and egalitarian citizenry in Israel – he quoted approvingly Carlyle's dictum that 'real history is contained in the biographies of its great personalities' because, as he said on another occasion, it is they 'who inspire the building of nations and establish beliefs in lasting ideals.'[7] Thus, leaders were responsible for the nation's welfare, and because parliamentary representation could be made accountable through the political parties, that responsibility was enforced by the people. If leaders make history, then it was inevitable that Gardiner should seek to be chosen leader at the first opportunity, and this came in 1948.

He had several reasons to believe that he would win the leadership contest: among them were his organizational labours for a quarter-century on behalf of King and the party, his principled defence of religious toleration in 1929, his opposition to conscription after 1939, and his stout advocacy of Parliament against an acquisitive bureaucracy fed by war and the welfare state. To these perceived strengths could be added one more achievement – his battle to teach the federal government and Parliament to accept responsibility for redistribution policies on behalf of disadvantaged Canadians. Unlike the other candidates at the convention, St Laurent and Power, Gardiner spoke for an occupationally defined constituency, several hundred thousand strong in all parts of the country, who had benefited from policies he had advocated since 1935. For a time at least, he had wrought a change in official attitudes toward agriculture, from considering it as solely a matter of profit and efficiency like any other industry to realizing it was a complex way of life dependent for success upon the farmers' social, economic, and personal security. Because he knew a world different from that of the rest of the ministers, he resisted more strenuously the counsel of the bureaucrats, symbolized best in the policies of the Wartime Prices and Trade Board, who paid heed to agriculture's costs but not its worth. Gardiner's persistence in promoting political values in answer to calls for administrative convenience frustrated the public servants. But even they on occasion allowed admiration to temper impatience: 'What an audacious man,' Mitchell Sharp once exclaimed. 'How many cabinet ministers are there with this sweep of mind?'[8]

In the immediate post-war years scope for his political skills lay at hand, since consensus on future policy had yet to emerge. Confident that wartime food contracts pointed the way for peacetime agriculture, he pressed cabinet to approve a series of renegotiated agreements with the United Kingdom, the most crucial being the long-term contract for wheat. In addition, the recent emergency had conferred on the federal government both the tools and a commitment to realize national objectives which Gardiner now wished to see marshalled on behalf of post-war ends. An example of his conviction could be found in his copy of the *Proposals of the Government of Canada* presented in 1945 to the

Dominion-Provincial Conference on Reconstruction. There he scrawled across the paragraph devoted to 'federal assistance for transportation facilities of national importance' the injunction that 'development rather than availability of finances should govern. Development in certain directions will produce finances.' But in the debate over Canada's economic future, he spoke for the less popular side. Neither his colleagues nor their senior advisers, whom he dubbed 'brains trusters' without political judgment, shared his enthusiasm for orienting trade along the familiar horizontal axis of the pre-war days.[9] Instead, they favoured C.D. Howe's vision of new vertical ties through United States investment which would pull Canada closer to its powerful neighbour.

Gardiner did not stand alone in viewing this second option with suspicion. Another Saskatchewanian now in Ottawa, John Deutsch, equally distrusted the trend in government thinking: 'The West [will] pay the bill,' he privately predicted, for ' "integrating" the economy of Eastern Canada with that of the United States.' But as a minister, Gardiner could go further in resisting the tide. Nothing so exemplifies the autonomous power he still exercised than the frustration and anger his actions and opinions could elicit from public servants. If any measure of his influence were needed, it lay in their belief that he was the 'one man [who has] caused all this trouble' for Canada's new post-war economic policy.[10]

Thus, while Gardiner wanted the leadership so that he could pursue a course of economic action he thought essential for Canada's future, he had opponents in Ottawa who for the same reason wanted to stop him. Gardiner's principal strength lay in his energy and the thoroughness of his party and administrative organization. In a pre-computer age these advantages provided him with an unparalleled network of information which he intended in 1948 to transform into a base of delegate support. But the foundation of the one organization proved insufficient to the needs of the other. Gardiner's sturdy independence, never a quality prized by his colleagues, steered him away from the very connections and centres of power he needed in his appeal to the delegates. His failure to participate in such major wartime and post-war debates as, for example, those on family allowances, veterans' administration, reconstruction, old age pensions, and national defence, robbed him of the authority in 1948 to speak to large segments of the electorate.

Even before the convention was called, it was possible to see in matters great and small evidence of his eroding prominence. For instance, in 1946 King met with several of his ministers (St Laurent, Claxton, Ilsley, and McCann) as well as with the deputy ministers of Finance and National Revenue to discuss the line to be taken with the provinces in the new age of federal-provincial relations then unfolding. The only member of his cabinet who at that time was a past premier and who had maintained an exceptionally close oversight of his own and adjacent provincial governments was Gardiner, and he was not consulted. Less substantial perhaps, but indicative still of Agriculture's displacement in the galaxy of federal portfolios, was the department's physical removal to the Central Experimental Farm from the Confederation Building, built to house its officials some twenty years before. The office of the auditor general and the Department of Labour, who had shared space with Agriculture, continued in place when Finance arrived to occupy Gardiner's old structure at the foot of Parliament Hill. Finance, in turn, had been forced to vacate the East Block of the Parliament Buildings to make way for the arrival of External Affairs.[11]

Despite the economic arguments he presented then or his administrative and political successes of an earlier time, Gardiner could not break free of the stereotype a majority of the delegates held of him as a machine politician. As a result, he was considered an anachronism in his own party, a reputation which proved a positive obstacle to his selection. That was King's view in the months before the convention and, if the prime minister's diary is to be believed, the view of some prominent westerners, such as Walter Tucker, as well.

Despite his unfavourable opinion of Gardiner's qualifications for party leader, King did not dismiss the challenge his energetic minister posed. In fact, Gardiner's candidacy upset his own plan to orchestrate the succession in favour of St Laurent. While the prime minister never publicly expressed his preference in this matter, he devised a scheme to demonstrate Gardiner's lack of support among the group who knew him best – the cabinet. At the convention held in Ottawa in August 1948, five federal cabinet ministers (Howe, Brooke Claxton, Lionel Chevrier, Douglas Abbott, and Paul Martin) allowed their names to be proposed as leader, and then each in turn withdrew. Although none declared his support for St Laurent, the delegates correctly drew this conclusion from the pantomime. At its end, three candidates remained – St Laurent, C.G. 'Chubby' Power (formerly a minister in the King government and long-time critic of Liberal policies), and Gardiner. St Laurent was running as the 'understood' successor to King, Power on a matter of principle, and Gardiner because he wanted to be leader. In his fight for the leadership Gardiner anticipated later candidates for the office, resisting the then prevailing attitude of treating leadership succession as a coronation, and instead campaigning hard and long for support from delegates. In the event, he failed – St Laurent won on the first ballot with 848 votes, while Gardiner received 323 and Power 56 – but not before he had injected some uncertainty and controversy into a ritual which would otherwise have been placid.

One interpretation was given for the convention's more than two-to-one support for St Laurent as the next Liberal leader. Its essence was captured in the title of an article written soon after the event by James H. Gray: 'Machine Politics Triumphs and St. Laurent Succeeds King.'[12] What constituted a machine therefore appeared subject to different interpretation, depending upon one's vantage point east or west of the Laurentian Shield. Machine or not, Gardiner claimed to have secured the support of the agricultural areas of Canada he had depended upon: all of Saskatchewan (Tucker included, to King's disgust),[13] three-quarters of Alberta, two-thirds of PEI, and the farming sectors of Ontario and British Columbia. The dominance of metropolitan Winnipeg and the long memories of the Grain Exchange traders explained his weakness there, said Gardiner. The determining fact, he concluded, was that 'the decision was made by those who represented interests other than agricultural interests.'[14] More important, and more obvious, was that this support had been insufficient for victory. Thus Gardiner learned at first hand what the statistics of the Department of Agriculture had revealed for some time: there were more Canadians who were not farmers than who were.

It was characteristic of the man that once he had taken his stand and the delegates had made their choice, he said no more about the matter and returned to politics. Chubby Power had predicted that Gardiner would be a good loser because he was 'a strong party man'; and he was right.[15] To the new leader he proved as loyal as he had been to the old, although he considered St Laurent's political vision and skills inferior to King's. For his part, St Laurent found Gardiner's 'narrow, almost sectarian' partisanship distasteful, although such differences in political style never led to personal antagonism or to open breaches over policy.[16] Likes and dislikes did not enter into his calculations – which is not to say he did not have personal preferences, but only that it was the party's welfare, as he saw it, which determined any course of action. For without the party, nothing was possible. Rarely, in the thousands of letters he wrote, did he waste time speculating about the motives or the intentions of his colleagues. In this regard, his attitude stood in contrast to that of his tireless critics who professed to see the fell hand of Gardiner the manipulator or machine politician behind his every policy or action.

Gardiner's political style may not have changed as a result of the convention's decision, nor did his position as minister of agriculture, now in the St Laurent government, but everything else had. The transfer of leadership signalled the beginning of a readjustment in the balance between region and nation that had been deliberately set by Gardiner and King in the late 1930s. The readjustment was toward the centre, a perpetual tilt in the federal system that Gardiner had sought to right for nearly fifteen years. Now, as Liberal concerns turned to the metropolitan and industrial areas, he had to argue ever more aggressively and frequently on behalf of the region with which he was most closely identified. At the same time, to burnish his political reputation he looked to his old base, Saskatchewan, where a reversal in Liberal misfortunes would give him what he most wanted. In either case, the last decade of his career was the one succeeding generations have most identified with him – that of regional lieutenant, the prairie proconsul for Ottawa's Liberal governments. The rest of this chapter will examine his activities in three lights: party, policy, and national development. Each of these are at odds with this popular view of Gardiner's contracting influence and faltering grasp on national and regional politics.

Gardiner lived in a monotheistic political world where the Liberal party represented the force for good, with its several parts intended to work toward a common end – improving the life of the average Canadian. This article of faith gave him strength to assume the burden of persuading others – electorates, governments, and members of his own party – of their duties. His hard intensity led King on one occasion to describe him as 'rigidly Liberal' and it was the same curious mixture of traits which led others to find him intransigent and meddlesome.[17] But whether or not his principles found favour, no one could dispute the force of conviction which lay behind their constant repetition.

Personally rebuffed in national politics for a perceived narrowness of interest, he redoubled his efforts after 1948 to lead a political counter-reformation in Saskatchewan, thus earning even more assuredly the regional label his critics had used to indict him. Yet, to him, the need for senior guidance was indisputable: two successive provincial defeats (an unparalleled occurrence in Saskatchewan), a decline in reliable political loyalties as evidenced by renewed bouts of coalition fever, and a retreat from reform in the face of CCF and socialism all proclaimed the nature of the problem. The stakes were higher and the danger greater than just the outcome of one more election, however. The decline of the Liberals in Saskatchewan presaged to him a decline of national Liberalism even if the federal party continued to win a majority of the seats in Parliament:

Liberalism is a national doctrine and can only benefit from having a Liberal Party in Saskatchewan if the objective of the Party is to have the strongest possible voice in affairs in Ottawa ... Either the Liberals or the Tories can win in Canada no matter which way the Saskatchewan seventeen constituencies vote and, therefore, there may be a tendency toward letting the West do what it likes, so long as it does not vote for either one party or the other. If it does that it will have no effect upon national matters whatsoever.[18]

His greatest fear was the growth of political indifference on the part of the national party. If this were to happen, the cost would be high to both region and nation. Arguably, the so-called machine politician believed less than most that politics was about elections, still less that elections were the measure of politics. The sweep of his vision, which made him a national politician, stretched from the business of the cabinet back to the daily events in every one of his constituency's polls.

But this integrated conception of politics had already begun to ebb where once it had flowed so vigorously. In Saskatchewan he now spied 'the old Manitoba form of democracy,' by which he meant an unhealthy reverence for constituency opinion to the detriment of the party as a whole. Thirty years on, when the mechanisms as well as the demands for rank-and-file participation have progressed far beyond his most pessimistic prediction, Gardiner's model party hierarchy strikes the observer as even less timely than it did the grass-roots prairie Liberals of his day. Gardiner had always held a trustee view of representation, if one remembers the scorn he poured on the direct democracy theories of the Progressives a quarter of a century earlier. Accordingly, while members might properly discuss and even argue positions within the party, 'bickering' (his term) must stop once agreement was reached. In the normal course of events, as he saw it, constituencies did not initiate policy; they reacted to it. And their reaction must always be the same: 'to stand by the decision which has been reached by those who are in higher authority, even though [they] feel [it may] be wrong. After all, those who are put in the position ... have ... more of the facts before them.'[19] Because he expected women's and youth groups within the Liberal party to play the same missionary and educational role as constituency associations, the Saskatchewan organization traditionally made only minimal provision for those groups to act collectively too.

Primacy in all party matters rested within the federal sphere. Organizationally, this meant that once 'the federal seats [are] fully organized and working, then it does not make much difference who runs in the area in most of the provincial seats they will be elected.' Electorally, the thrust was the same, for 'no one ever won an election in Saskatchewan without talking Federal politics.'[20] When this order to priority was recognized, when the fate of all was seen to rest on the action of each, then the Liberal party would be invincible. Or so went the theory. The clarity of Gardiner's purpose and the absence of any similar conviction among provincial Liberals meant a dynamo occupied one level of the political scene and a vacuum the other. It also guaranteed that a series of protracted rows would punctuate the tranquillity presumed to reign over Gardiner's ideal scheme.

Practice, conforming to theory, meant initiative always lay with Gardiner. Encouragement and praise as much as advice or practical criticism flowed in a steady stream from him to a succession of provincial Liberal leaders, beginning with Walter Tucker in 1948, then A. H. McDonald from 1954 to 1959, and finally Ross Thatcher, who did lead the Saskatchewan Liberals to power in 1964, two years after Gardiner's death. In this flood of correspondence, Gardiner seemed never to entertain a doubt about the validity of his opinion on how best to find and train candidates, raise funds, or organize campaigns. Moreover, in typical fashion, nothing was too trivial to escape comment, even to the location of federal and provincial filing cabinets in the party's two-room headquarters in Regina.[21] In light of the prominence he attributed to leaders, it was not unexpected that Gardiner should willingly play Polonius to the Liberal troika of the fifties; nor was it surprising that they should resent this smothering attention.

Practical as well as personal reasons prompted Gardiner's actions. By the early part of the 1950s very few members of the Liberal caucus in the provincial assembly possessed legislative experience, certainly not enough to provide ballast for a sustained and effective opposition. In contrast, Gardiner had once, for more than twenty years, been active in provincial politics, on the back as well as the front benches and on both sides of the chamber. Thus, he proved generous to a fault in wanting to share this experience. The need for it was cruelly apparent in the face of a dynamically energetic CCF government under a leader, T.C. Douglas, whose platform capabilities were worthy of Gardiner alone among Saskatchewan politicians as an opponent. Gardiner's martial conception of politics, which equated the hustings and the chamber with battlefields, required of party commanders personal conviction and strategic gifts that few politicians possess. Certainly, neither Tucker nor McDonald demonstrated they had these abilities. Ross Thatcher succeeded where they failed, but not by following Gardiner's advice. Indeed, in the late fifties the former minister, as he then was, grew increasingly agitated at Thatcher's motives, which were 'to get rid of Socialism and ... not [be] particular as how it [was] done,' and by his methods, especially the work of certain supporters and fund-raisers, which Gardiner believed would drag down the new leader and 'the Liberal Party I have been associated with all my life.'[22]

Another reason Gardiner thought his advice valuable derived from his experience with the Saskatchewan electorate. Although not disposed to abstract thought, and scornful of theorists – among whom he numbered academics, bureaucrats, and parlour socialists – he believed he had divined the nature of prairie voters from prolonged, first-hand acquaintance. The truth he wished to impart was that prairie voters were less ideologically motivated in their actions than he was. Long before analysts had tried to decipher the bases of partisan allegiance, Gardiner had isolated what he saw as a fundamental feature of the Saskatchewan electorate: 'There are quite a number of people in Saskatchewan who are neither traditionally Liberal or [sic] traditionally Tory. Many of them came to this country from elsewhere. Their politics has been mostly of the kind which supports a government because of what they can get out of it. When we are in they support us – when the CCF are in they support them ... We, therefore, always have trouble with those people when we are in Opposition.'[23] The ease with which prairie voters had transferred loyalties through the range of partisan choices – Liberal, CCF, Progressive, and Social Credit – would be demonstrated once again in the Tory tide of 1958 which would swallow up Gardiner as well; alone among his contemporaries, however, he recognized the link between this electoral volatility and the region's recent settlement. The ethnic factor, never far removed from settlement questions, remained alive to him in the fifties but appeared fleetingly in his correspondence with provincial leaders. Ethnicity traditionally bulked large in patronage matters, and in this period provincial Liberals had no patronage to dispense other than that which Gardiner agreed to share with them. This was infrequent, meagre, and another source of discontent between federal and provincial Liberals.

It is not possible to discuss in detail the complex relationship which evolved between Gardiner and the provincial leaders through the decade between 1948 and 1958. Nor is it necessary, except as these reveal aspects of Gardiner's character as a politician. Background to the period may be found in the relevant election returns; that is, in the two provincial contests (1952 and 1956) and the three federal ones (1953, 1957, and 1958). Provincially, the Liberal popular vote climbed from 31 per cent in 1948 to 39 per cent in 1952, and then dropped to 30 per cent in 1956, while the number of seats won followed a reverse pattern: nineteen, eleven, and fourteen. The difference in the two sets of results was explained by the presence or absence of Conservative or Social Credit candidates. Federally, Liberal seats and votes declined together during the decade, from fourteen seats in 1949 to five (1953), and then four (1957) and finally none (1958) and from 44 per cent of the vote in 1949 to 38, 30 and, lastly, to 20 per cent. Thus, not only were Gardiner's hopes of restoring the provincial Liberals dashed, but his own political base became endangered as federal support crumbled too.

The integrated party system he envisioned no longer functioned as he intended, if in fact it existed any longer for anyone but himself. A separation between federal and provincial Liberal fortunes was occurring which he accepted neither in theory nor in practice. Instead, he blamed Tucker, in particular, for what was happening. It was axiomatic for Gardiner that Liberals defended Liberals. Thus, candidates or supporters took advantage of every opportunity, be it by-elections, public meetings, or private conversations to promote and defend the party. If this held true for followers, how much more did it apply to leaders. And yet, under Tucker's leadership, Gardiner complained, the provincial Liberals did 'not defend [federal] policies and get people to understand why they are there.'[24] Since he believed federal matters were of predominant concern to voters – for example, the Wheat Board's actions directly, and adversely, affected every western farmer in the 1950s – the provincial party could only avoid its duty by abdicating responsibility and, in the long run, hurting itself. This is exactly what his informants in Saskatchewan said was happening there and elsewhere: 'A pattern has been developing for some time ... that seems to indicate that people believe it is an advantage to have the provincial government opposed to and fighting with the federal government. If this is correct it is a pattern that will prevent any possibility of building a nation in Canada.'[25] Gardiner could not have agreed more and, had he known it, would have been angered by a letter Tucker wrote the same day to a Manitoba

Liberal in which he expressed the opposite opinion: 'I said this was a Provincial election and saw no point in arguing about Federal matters.'[26] Gardiner disputed the idea Liberals could win seats 'by agreeing that any other party [was] as good' and yet, to his mind, that was what provincial Liberals did when they refused to support Liberal policies.

Next to having a provincial Liberal leader with whom he did not agree, a worse possibility would be having no leader at all. This occurred late in 1952, when Tucker decided to resign after six years as Saskatchewan leader and return to federal politics. Gardiner was appalled at the prospect, first for the practical reason that a successor he could work with would be hard to find and, secondly, for the symbolic reason that the leader's resignation would signal the collapsing fortunes of the Liberal party. After lecturing Tucker on his duty – 'There are some things in which leadership must be given by the party as a whole represented by its leaders' – he hinted that if Tucker would hold on, he, Gardiner, might return to lead the provincial Liberals after the federal election, expected the following year.[27] Both arguments failed and Tucker, agreeing to act as provincial leader until a successor was chosen, resigned his provincial place, then sought and won a federal seat.

In fact, a new leader was not chosen until November 1954. This hiatus so incensed Gardiner as evidence of disloyal behaviour that he never forgave Tucker and worked actively to prevent him becoming president of the National Liberal Federation when rumours to this effect circulated in 1958.[28] The lame-duck interval from 1952 to 1954 allowed an increasingly damaging debate to grow over Gardiner's role in the provincial party. The debate was fed by the minister's obvious desire to see selected a provincial leader who was sympathetic to the federal cause. Once again it was the institution of the leadership convention which provided a forum for the exposure of intra-party tension and once again, as in 1948, it allowed opposition to Gardiner's wishes to prevail. Sensible to the potential split his candidacy would have on the party, he declined to run; his son, J. Wilfrid Gardiner, for the last decade the party's local man in Lemberg, did run, although Gardiner professed to see this bid as only an initial foray into politics. Of the four other candidates for leader, two, L.B. Thomson and A.H. McDonald, were treated as surrogates for the more personal rivalry surrounding the minister. Thomson was Saskatchewan director of PFRA and McDonald, a recognized Progressive Conservative and former coalition candidate in the 1948 provincial general election, was described by Wilfrid Gardiner as 'definitely Tucker['s] man.'[29] The party situation in Saskatchewan had grown so delicate that seven federal cabinet ministers in succession turned down invitations to speak at the convention, a rebuff Gardiner explained away as the result of the prime minister's general rule that ministers should not take part in local conventions. Gardiner himself eventually spoke at the banquet but not before McDonald and J.W. Simmie, another candidate, had tried to get the prime minister or the president of the National Liberal Federation to intervene and keep him away. For his part, Gardiner saw to it that the 170 delegates to which the federal constituencies were entitled did not attend, thereby trying to defuse claims of federal interference. As well, he wrote (but did not circulate) a five-page apologia of his Saskatchewan career.[30]

Intra-party tension continued after McDonald's selection, despite protestations of loyalty to the new leader by Gardiner. One might say, especially because of them. If McDonald indeed represented the non-Gardiner alternative, then every affirmation of support for him from Ottawa fed local fears that his autonomy was threatened. Thus, demands multiplied for a complete separation of federal and provincial party affairs.[31] Gardiner responded to this refrain by interpreting it as the most recent campaign 'of the only political machine we ever had in Saskatchewan.' It was the 'they' who in the twenties and thirties had tried 'to do a job on myself,' who had done 'a real job on Brownlee,' and who would now 'knife' McDonald were he not careful. This group of 'thugs' had tried 'many times to frame me but I always saw them coming.' If all this sounded familiar, it was, and would be repeated one more time, after Thatcher was selected leader in 1959.[32] Dissent did, of course, exist; Gardiner was not imagining it. But the demand in the 1950s to separate federal from provincial politics was a very different challenge to his authority than the one thirty years before which had tried first to bribe him and, when that failed, to discredit him through the local press. Perhaps it was inevitable, for one who put such intense emphasis on loyalty, to treat all dissent the same. Inevitable or not, Gardiner's uniform response to criticism limited his ability to moderate it.

Thus, in the last decade of his career as a minister, Gardiner's supremacy in organizational matters, even in his home province, was seriously challenged. In itself, as he recognized, challenges were to be expected, even welcomed as a means of keeping the party alive. Of concern here was his inability to find a formula to accommodate the party's own conflicting interests. A seasoned politician so deft at devising solutions to meet a host of national and international demands seemed impotent before internal partisan disagreement. Clearly, it was not enough to say again and again that an integrated party was the model to follow, when the ideal did not match Canadian political reality in the 1950s. Gardiner himself was aware that federal-provincial relations were running counter to the hierarchical relationship he preached. In the throne debate in 1949, he had struck out at conventional wisdom which said the tax rental agreements favoured Ottawa because they promoted 'centralized control.' On the contrary, he argued, they 'centralized [provincial] criticism' on the federal government.[33] He resented the transfer of federal money to the provinces because it subsidized increased initiatives by those governments at the political expense of local opposition parties. If wartime administration had undermined the Liberal party by depriving it of substantial patronage, then the post-war fiscal agreements were having the same debilitating effect but by a different route.

During the 1950s Gardiner's attention was divided among three types of policies. First, was the the extension of existing legislation, as, for example, when the principles of PFRA were applied to farmers in British Columbia and the maritime provinces where the need was to control flooding and drain water rather than to conserve it. Secondly, were matters of a specific nature, exemplified in the outbreak in Saskatchewan of foot and mouth disease in February 1952. That emergency taxed Gardiner and his officials, for in a matter of weeks, four thousand cattle, sheep, swine, and poultry had to be destroyed, with compensation negotiated, while quarantine zones were established and embargoes placed on exports. The whole episode, investigated by the Standing Committee on Agriculture and Colonization between 30 April and early June, provided an instructive commentary on the Department of Agriculture's capabilities in peacetime. Following over four hundred pages of minutes and evidence, the committee offered a four-paragraph report which concluded that officials from the Health of Animals Division had 'followed the well-defined plans laid down through long experience.'[34] Last, but as always, the policy of predominant concern was grain.

In the 1930s the imperative had been to rescue ravaged prairie agriculture, in the 1940s to adjust production to meet wartime needs. Now, a new problem, surpluses, proved equally troublesome and in need of urgent attention. Despite bromides from Gardiner and C.D. Howe, the minister of trade and commerce responsible for the Wheat Board, that fat years were preferable to thin ones, the glut of grain proved to be both intractable and pervasive. Gardiner did not exaggerate when he wrote that 'although we have nothing to do with handling wheat in this

Department, I get more correspondence complaining about the fact that wheat farmers cannot get money than I do about anything else having to do with agriculture.'[35] That the chief commissioner of the Wheat Board was the recipient of this complaint underlined the central position of the board in this whole period. Simply stated, the board monopolized the collection and marketing of wheat to a degree found in no other major Canadian industry. Quotas to control the flow of grain from farms into the local elevators, absolute jurisdiction over the elevator and railway companies to regulate the passage of that grain to tidewater terminals, and a monopoly on sales to foreign customers were ingredients of what in short-hand parlance was called 'orderly marketing.' Although Gardiner supported the concept, he had only slight influence over its practice, since the board was a quasi-autonomous body. Nonetheless, orderly marketing in conditions of surplus created chaos back on the farm, as stocks of grain piled up because elevators were plugged and farmers' incomes plummeted because they were prevented either from making deliveries or from trading wheat for the needed goods and services of local merchants. This latter prohibition the board defended as necessary if the grower was to receive maximum value for his wheat when it was eventually sold. Farmers' discontent mounted, and with it pressure on agriculture's most visible champion, Gardiner, securely established in the public mind as 'the real fighter for the farmers' cause' and 'the West's ... most stalwart supporter at Ottawa.'[36]

Gardiner found himself, however, in the unhappy position of defending particular board policies he did not support and was unable to change. To repeated requests for a more sensitive response to the farmers' plight, he received from the board replies couched in language he was not used to hearing: 'I would advise you ...' or 'as you are aware ...'[37] The timing of board announcements, too, caused him grief, as in July 1953 at the end of the official crop year and just before the federal election, when the board altered delivery quotas. The change, he euphemistically claimed, 'upset the people in thinking straight' while it reaffirmed his own dislike of non-responsible bodies: 'Too many such organizations across the country [and] elections would be entirely determined on what they did or did not do.'[38] Cabinet did not emulate the board's inflexibility when other industries – textiles, for example – sought special treatment. This contrast did not escape unnoticed by westerners who, although insensitive to the nice distinction between what regulatory agencies could or could not do, were alive to perceived discrimination of their region alongside others – textiles, the case in point, being centred in Quebec.[39]

Pressed to come up with some answer to the cash shortage, Gardiner characteristically reverted to his own farming experience for advice: feed excess grain to livestock and sell the animals or, again, avoid new equipment purchases and use second-hand machinery. But as sensible as these suggestions were, they scarcely constituted a policy response to the problem, while all around proposals flew from farmers, their organizations, and the opposition parties for deficiency payments or two-priced wheat or a supplementary income injection comparable to the $65 million payment made at the conclusion of the Canada–United Kingdom wheat agreement. To all of these Gardiner said no, although he expressed approval for schemes to provide bank loans guaranteed against farm-stored wheat and for an ambitious system of government storage facilities. Howe rejected the latter proposal as too 'broad' and substituted for the former a scheme of bank loans at 5 per cent interest.[40] The loan proposal followed an intense round of meetings of almost all farm organizations, first among themselves and then with provincial and federal government representatives (including Gardiner and Howe). At none of these had a rate as high as 5 per cent been discussed, although this was half a per cent lower than ordinary personal loans. The response throughout the west, in the words of one western Liberal, was as if a bomb has exploded. The proposal was described, even by established farm opinion, as unacceptable, an irritation, amazing, disturbing, and causing resentment.[41] Moreover, when the government proceeded with the special loans and made the banks the judges of which farmers were eligible, further complaints reached Ottawa about inconsistent and even Draconian administration, as the banks put applicants through what John Diefenbaker called a catechism.[42]

Some farmers complained that the loan forms were too complicated. A scheme which made thousands of wheat farmers, with bulging granaries but empty pockets, fill out forms that had to pass a bank's inspection (rather than the more conveniently located credit unions, who were not included in the scheme), and pay for the privilege of doing so, could never be popular. Gardiner himself told Howe that the government could not justify a proposal by which the banks took all of the interest, and suggested instead a 50 per cent rebate to the farmer when he delivered the wheat.[43] The interest provisions of the bank loan legislation remained unchanged, although the bill itself experienced a difficult passage through the House of Commons, where at one point the government lost control because only 36 of 110 Liberals were present for a vote on a CCF amendment. As a measure of Liberal interest in the west, the bank loan episode did irreparable harm to the Liberal cause.

Whether the prediction by one correspondent that the loan plan would 'mean in the end the downfall of the Liberal Government' was an accurate assessment is hard to prove.[44] The Liberals did lose the next election, but the process whereby their support among western farmers evaporated was more complicated than the prediction suggested; the disillusionment was more devastating too. Evidence of the shift taking place could be found in the Saskatchewan Wheat Pool's annual submission for 1957 to the federal government. That document pointedly observed 'the harsh fact ... that the great, prolonged boom in the Canadian economy has passed the farmer by.'[45] Echoing Gardiner's argument, nine years before at the leadership convention, the submission drew painful comparisons: 'We are assuming that the high levels of commercial and industrial activity and the large investments of foreign capital in Canada may have been beneficial to a majority of Canadians. But we do wish to point out that the farm group in Canada has ... been victimized by them.' In particular, the influx of foreign capital, which had driven up the price of the Canadian dollar, had required the western grain farmer to cut the price of his wheat if he was to compete in the international market.

More fundamental still than a disproportionate share of national income was the change in the balance of political forces which determined it. A feeling was abroad, said one westerner, that 'the federal government does not seriously pay much attention to the problems of any province except the ones who, by the power of their votes, can make or break a government.'[46] Implicit here was a critical comment on Gardiner's waning influence. The Canadian electoral map had not substantially changed. There had always been more people in the St Lawrence heartland than anywhere else in the country. What had disappeared was the federal commitment, crystallized in the late 1930s, to restore and maintain standards through government policies. At the beginning of his federal career, the force of Gardiner's arguments and personality had set this earlier change in motion. But twenty years later, having made successive claims for the west upon the country's resources, the brilliance of his arguments had grown dull with repetition, while a new audience sat in cabinet unfamiliar with their predecessors' commitment and in need of convincing once again.

The barometer of the changed environment could be found in Gardiner's tireless but ultimately fruitless advocacy of a dam on the South Saskatchewan River. From the day he arrived in Ottawa in 1935, Gardiner had had in mind the construction of a dam to provide a secure source of water and hydro-electric power in the parched and sparsely populated region of central Saskatchewan. Extensive geological investigation was needed before a site could be found for so huge a project, but in 1950 it had been determined that a dam of the size required could be built at Outlook, on the South Saskatchewan River, 160 miles upstream from Saskatoon. The structure (at completion in 1968, it was described as the world's largest earth-filled dam) would create a lake 185 feet deep at the dam and 145 miles long ('three quarters as long as Lake Ontario,' Gardiner used to boast). The lake would supply water to irrigate 500,000 acres and to generate 475 million kilowatt hours of electrical energy each year.

No other proposal so encapsulated his view of the respective needs and duties of the west and the federal government in the area of national development or indicated so accurately the eclipse of his power to effect the policies he wanted. By the fifties his fervour in its cause had become a liability: his promises were too fulsome and repeated too often, while for his colleagues the dam had become too much the pet scheme of an enthusiast. A steady stream of documents, films, and representations favourable to the scheme rained down upon his fellow ministers from the Department of Agriculture, while in the House his legislative sallies were peppered with references to the dam's inevitability. In the tumult surrounding second reading of the TransCanada Pipeline bill in 1956, the first of his few interventions was greeted by Stanley Knowles with the quip: 'Now, we will hear about the Saskatchewan dam.'[47] Elsewhere, Gardiner had confessed to the intensity of his sentiment and attributed it to the fact that 'I have lived all these issues, and therefore probably place greater emphasis upon them than others may.'[48] But the opposition's jibe, intended to deflate one more minister in that famous debate, anticipated the nub of Gardiner's subsequent argument for the pipeline. To him, both the pipeline and the dam were works of national development which a Liberal government should be proud to sponsor.

The dam had another defence as well, one which explained Gardiner's passion and also underlined the reason for the growing separation from his colleagues: the dam represented, he said, 'the final act of rehabilitation in Saskatchewan.'[49] The PFRA, PFAA, and earlier but smaller river projects in Alberta, now joined by the Saskatchewan dam, would exculpate the federal government from responsibility for past policies detrimental to the West – thoughtless settlement in the Palliser Triangle area and alienation of twenty-five million acres of prime land to the CPR were two examples – while it would recognize the west's extraordinary contribution to Canada and the empire in two world wars. If the dam was built, he calculated a total transfer of federal funds for rehabilitation in the neighbourhood of $300 million, and concluded that the compensation going to the prairie provinces would be roughly equal to $12 per acre for land lost in the construction of the first transcontinental railway. Thus, this argument for the dam drew its force from Gardiner's belief that, just as much as the measures of the 1930s, the dam was a matter of national importance. But what he accepted as a given the rest of the government wanted proved.[50]

Gardiner's self-assurance stemmed directly from his political and economic nationalism: that is, he believed the dam of national importance because it would guarantee a healthy, prosperous agricultural community in the west which would be of benefit to all of Canada. It is important, however, to emphasize that his outlook derived from no pastoral utopianism. Rather, he believed that Canadian agriculture and Canadian industry were interdependent and because the west was the least populated region in the country, expansion must take place there. He asserted that the requirements of a farm family on eighty acres employed between three and five workers in industry. The pivotal position of the South Saskatchewan River dam rested in its creation of hydro-electric power to support the necessary industrial development in the heart of the most agricultural of regions. Gardiner's vision, depicted on innumerable occasions over a thirty-year span, saw farmers and industrial workers working literally within sight of each other, the one sector providing cheap food, the other cheap manufactured goods.[51]

'White power' – by which he meant hydro-electric power – implied a revolution in Canadian political and economic life, for it permitted 'decentralized industry,' a goal he had espoused since entering federal politics. Decentralized industry would diversify and strengthen the west's economy at the same time as it promoted a greater balance to Confederation which had from the very first been tilted toward the central provinces. That readjustment would be assured, Gardiner thought, because the new west would be the magnet to attract hundreds of thousands of immigrants. The region would be restored to, even surpass, its former importance before the drought and depression of the 1930s. The economic benefits of a revitalized agriculture based on prosperous independent farmers should have added attractions for

Liberals: it would undercut the movement to bigger farms but fewer owners, a condition Gardiner called corporate farming and scathingly equated to a new 'Feudalism,' and it would defuse the socialists' arguments that planning and public ownership were the only alternative to check centralized political and economic control in Ontario and Quebec.[52]

The dam was one of several great development schemes Gardiner nurtured in the thirties, forties, and fifties. Two others, about which he wrote and spoke but not nearly so often as the dam, included the need for improved highways, particularly for a transcontinental road link to serve the industrial expansion he foresaw in the west, and the need for a railway running from Churchill, across the northern sections of the prairie provinces, through the Peace River country all the way to Prince Rupert on the Pacific Coast.[53] Although he never elaborated these projects, they too, like the dam, were seen as being of national importance and requiring the initiative of the federal government to make them realizable.

With regard to the dam, the sticking point was always the federal government's reluctance to become involved. Until his death he believed that 'if King had survived three years longer,' the dam would have been built. There is no evidence that King ever gave assurances to this effect, but his support for Gardiner's efforts to extend PFRA earned him the undying appreciation of his minister, who believed that King at least understood the magnitude of the west's problems and accepted the federal government's duty to help. With St Laurent it was a different matter; there was 'not the same understanding of western needs ... and the educational work required delayed actual construction for 10 years.'[54] It was not for lack of trying that he failed. Amassing thousands of facts on water storage and hydro-electric potential for schemes from the Murray River in Australia to the Missouri in the United States, or holding the prime minister captive in a motor launch in the middle of a Qu'Appelle Valley lake while he explained yet again the virtues of a dam, Gardiner was indefatigable in using whatever opportunity came to hand to press his case.

But after 1950 opportunities arose less frequently, while resistance mounted at the pressure being applied. In 1951, after more than a decade of feasibility studies and engineers' reports, a royal commission was appointed to examine the data and to answer, so the prime minister said, any lingering doubts about whether the federal government should become involved in the project. Gardiner opposed this move in caucus, for it threw the whole scheme into question; much better, he thought, if a decision were made now on whether to go ahead with the dam or abandon it. A favourable decision, even if to be implemented at some indefinite date in the future, would have satisfied him. Now the years of persuasion and education were to be shoved aside for the uncertainty of one more investigation. Nonetheless, he made virtue of necessity, telling Walter Tucker: 'I have been here long enough to know that when you want to get a thing done you had better proceed in accordance with the wishes of others.'[55] In fact, the decision to refer the matter to a royal commission proved to be the death of the dam under a Liberal government.

The royal commission's report and its reception provide a classic example of the use of a royal commission to buy time when there is no agreement on a course of action. Those who wanted a dam included the CCF provincial government, every farm organization in Saskatchewan, and Gardiner; those opposed were the governments of Alberta and Manitoba who feared the effects of a dam on water flows and levels in these provinces; while in between sat most of the federal cabinet. Gardiner's frustration with the actions of the prairie provinces, which he believed demonstrated a victory for narrow over national vision, was interlaced with anger at Manitoba, where a Liberal government appeared to rule in name (technically as Liberal-Progressive) but not in spirit.

The royal commission, which reported in January 1953, came down neither for nor against the dam but inconclusively observed that 'construction of the project should be considered only in relation to its timing in such a way as to *minimize* its real cost and to avoid increasing inflationary premises in the economy.' Gardiner's exasperation overflowed, as was evident in his annotated copies of the report's draft and final versions. Either in the margin or scrawled across the page, his red pencil figuratively tore through the text. Alongside its ambivalent conclusion, he sharply noted: 'Nothing of this nature would ever be undertaken if this principle followed,' while over a particularly abstruse passage on the legal rights of provinces, he wrote one of the very few if not only oaths in all his correspondence: 'Damn nonsense.' But his ire was directed most at the commissioners' failure to accord the electric power potential of the dam the importance he gave it and instead to concentrate on its irrigation features: 'The power could be much more important than the increased acreage to irrigation'; 'markets produced through industrial development could be much more valuable'; 'have left out greatest benefit of all namely the use of water for industrial development; irrigation is the least of the benefits.'⁵⁶

Quick, biting, and negative as his response was, the damage had been done as far as convincing the prime minister and everyone else in cabinet about the worth of the dam. For the next four years, he continued to discuss with the provincial government aspects of the dam's development but, repeatedly, agreement between him and T.C. Douglas was dashed by a watchful prime minister. St Laurent proved wary of both Gardiner and the socialists, for they shared a common objective: to get the federal government to admit that the dam was of national importance. But if such admission were ever secured, St Laurent knew that the federal government could never back away from completing the structure and at considerable cost to the federal treasury.

It was ironic that on this issue Gardiner, the self-appointed nemesis of socialism in Saskatchewan, should have found support in the opponents' camp. More than ironic, it indicated how regional issues had come to twist traditional partisan loyalties. Not that Gardiner would ever consider breaking with his party over this or any other issue. But in 1954, 1955, and 1956 he was reminded by his leader that personal desires could create political difficulties; in St Laurent's favourite phrase, he was 'quite disturbed' by Gardiner's actions.⁵⁷ Although the prime minister never overtly rejected the dam as a matter of national importance, he implied as much in the run-up to the campaign of 1957: 'I do not think it would be advisable to have any sign of pre-election activity on our part that did not mature into a firm decision authorized by appropriate legislation to go on with the undertaking and, as this does not seem likely unless and until we have something concrete for the Atlantic region, I am afraid our gestures would be looked upon as intentionally misleading.'⁵⁸

Clearly, the dam did not fall into the same category as the St Laurent government's other great national endeavours, for example, the St Lawrence Seaway, the TransCanada Highway, or the Canso Causeway. Inevitably, this failure of the west to measure up, now even in terms of need, became another cause for lament. The dam, wrote Allan McLean, later national director of the National Liberal Federation but then still in Saskatchewan, was 'a symbol of the extent to which Saskatchewan feels its economic inferiority.'⁵⁹ Gardiner had become another, a political symbol. The prairies' most aggressive defender no longer counted for as much in national attention or decision-making as he once had, although he still sat at the cabinet table.

Without the support of the national leader, which he believed King had given or which Sifton had once received from Laurier, the Liberals coasted into decline in the west. Gardiner sought to reverse the direction by harnessing the energies of the provincial party to meet federal goals. Alternatively, he tried to put a brake on those federal policies, and their administration, that irritated as well as impoverished the western farmer even while the rest of the country enjoyed the last of the post-war boom. But dissentient provincial Liberals and indifferent federal Liberals thwarted his efforts. The more regional his advocacy became, the less persuasive its effect. By 1957 he and Howe remained the only ministers from the government King had formed in 1935. But Gardiner, with twenty-one years of provincial experience before that, had established a political record, which would be extended another nine months in the new role as a federal opposition member.

18

Defeat and Retirement

Had Gardiner been leader of his party and prime minister in 1957 and had the election results that faced St Laurent faced him, Canadian political history would have to be rewritten, for he would not have resigned before meeting Parliament. The returns gave the Liberals 44 per cent of the popular vote to the Progressive Conservatives' 39 per cent but with 105 to the Tories' 112 seats in a House of 265. The CCF with 25 seats and the Social Credit with 19 seats (plus four 'others') thus held the balance. Gardiner thought the third parties, as in Saskatchewan in 1929, should be put to the test of publicly supporting one or other of the major parties. If their choice fell on the Conservative leader, John Diefenbaker, then they should be seen to have been responsible for turning the Liberals out. Although he pressed his case in cabinet before an indecisive prime minister, St Laurent eventually succumbed to other advice (from Lester Pearson, for instance) and resigned. Gardiner nonetheless, and without citing evidence, attributed the decision to a discredited source – Manitoba Liberals – via a distrusted route – the Senate.[1] The result, Gardiner never tired of complaining afterwards, was that 'for the first time we have a government which came into being when the House was not in session without being able to demonstrate that it had the support either of the greatest number of votes for its supporters, or the support of a majority of those elected to the House of Commons.'[2] He argued that severe penalties would follow this error in political judgment, and the 1958 election disaster apparently bore out the prediction, for in reply to Liberal appeals for support the voters answered, as Gardiner said they would: 'You put him in, now give him a chance.'

The strategy of forcing the parliamentary parties to take responsibility for defeating the government could be interpreted as one more scheme by a diehard wishing to cling to power. And so it was, as Gardiner would have been the first to admit; but it was more than this and of a piece with his whole political career. What else was politics but the getting and keeping of power to achieve a purpose? In his view there was nothing craven in seeking to win; far less could be accomplished if one lost, while to give up without a fight smacked of weak and confused purpose.

Gardiner's response to the 1957 débâcle revealed as clearly as any event in his public life the different layers which together comprised his political world. To begin with, elections were not about winning, although because of his unusual success in this regard, observers might be forgiven for confusing what Gardiner saw as a means for the end itself. That is, he took electoral success as necessary if the Liberal party and Liberalism were to triumph, but victory or defeat in themselves were hollow. The lesson of 1929, he said shortly after that tumultuous election, proved that 'one cannot afford to be wrong even if it means defeat to be right.' He continued to express this sentiment thirty years later after the federal deluge: 'A party cannot afford to be wrong when it goes out. If it is it will never come back.'[3] Thus, in the first and last instance elections centred on issues, not votes. Candidates and their supporters therefore should not pander to voters but instead should put reasoned arguments before them. And they should do this not just at elections but at all times. Gardiner was proud of the fact that he returned regularly to his constituency every summer and at holidays, and also during the session, frequently taking the transcontinental train on Wednesday nights and returning to Ottawa by early the following Tuesday morning, thus keeping before electors current political issues.

As a general principle he tried to convince other ministers to follow his example, but MPs from the west, he thought, had a special reason to adopt the practice. There, in addition to a federal system which placed matters of local interest in the hands of the provincial governments and the geographical distance from Ottawa, recent and precarious settlement had fostered an apolitical climate where immediate economic concerns superseded political discussion generated by distant national debates. His own policy successes, for example, PFRA, PFAA, and the food contracts, had brought the federal government closer to the people of the region than at any time in the west's history. But these policies compounded the communication problem because they were new and too complex for busy and preoccupied farmers to understand easily. An extreme example of the situation prairie MPs faced could be seen in

Gardiner's explanation of the origin and evolution of PFAA to a western correspondent nearly twenty years after the event. In answer to his assertion that he had written the act, the correspondent replied: 'I should have known you were ... [its] author. But ... since we had no radio, many important facts escaped us, for we were too tired usually to read, and in fact could not afford to subscribe to newspapers.'[4]

By 1957 conditions had changed and the appeals which once had found favour now were rejected. But the Diefenbaker sweep in that year and the next disguised how fundamental was the break with the past. The year after Gardiner died the Liberals returned to power in Ottawa but never recovered as a force in the west. National Liberalism ended at the same time Gardiner retired from public life. In the west the clearest evidence of the transformation lay in the state of the party. It divided in practice, if not in principle, between federal and non-federal parts. A condition which had existed before the creation of Saskatchewan and Alberta in 1905 had broken out again in 1919 in response to the Progressives' challenge, had become endemic in Alberta after 1935, and had threatened to do the same in Saskatchewan after 1950. It was, as well, the spectre Gardiner had sought to rout for over half a century. Accumulated dissatisfaction with the federal government, which had become synonymous with Liberal party, coincided with the approaching economic boom of the 1960s and a growth in provincial pretensions. Gardiner's political world, whose features were moulded during the period of great western and national development at the beginning of the century, went permanently into eclipse. And after 1958 no similar commanding personality seemed ready to try to stop the decline.

As happens in a system of free elections, the end to Gardiner's career came abruptly, moderated only by the nine months in opposition between the two general elections. In 1953 he had won 50 per cent of the vote in Melville, but in 1957 40 per cent and in 1958 less than 30 per cent. The perquisites of ministerial office disappeared first, in 1957, and then those of an elected member in 1958. In the last contest Gardiner came third, trading places with the Conservative candidate who had trailed in 1957 but won in 1958. This outcome provided one consolation, since he admitted he would have 'felt badly had [Melville] voted CCF.' Back-to-back elections did not attract a man of his age and he considered stepping down as a candidate; but the parlous condition of the Liberal party after 1957 and the groundswell of support for the PCs made that alternative impossible in 1958. Defeat, however, came as no surprise, he wrote on a questionnaire distributed by Liberal party headquarters, after the Liberals had 'turned the Government over to Diefenbaker' the year before and then selected a new leader 'not because of his well known ability but because he was Anglo-Saxon.' Saskatchewan voters, and particularly the ethnically heterogeneous voters of Melville, would not turn out a government led by a prime minister from Saskatchewan and replace it with a party that limited its leadership choice to English or French-speaking Canadians.

Gardiner never looked upon politics as a means of material rewards and rejected as suitable political timber anyone who did. But he more than most active politicians had reason to appreciate the provisions for free travel which elected office conferred, for the party organization depended upon this source of indirect support to mount effective campaigns. In the last four years of his life he continued to campaign for the provincial Liberals and do a variety of other political tasks, but on a pension of $3,000, adjusted downwards to take account of his old age pension, practical considerations limited his ability to meet every request for help.[5] As it was, he was forced on occasion to borrow from the bank against expected remuneration for expenses from local associations. He cut his style of travel to fit the funds, in consequence spending long hours on buses and waiting in terminals. Not that he was at all enfeebled: in the winter campaign of 1958, for example, in typical industrious fashion he took to a snowmobile to complete his constituency speaking engagements.

Characteristically, the departure from office and then from Ottawa was carried out with dispatch but minimal lament. It was, he wrote the deputy speaker of the House of Commons, 'a rather trying experience to know that this is not to continue' after twenty-two years behind the same desk and 'in the same chair at the Council Table.' It had, he concluded, been 'a wonderful experience.'[6] The general election of 1958, the thirteenth occasion since the by-election before the First World War that Gardiner had presented himself to his constituents and the only one he personally lost, was held on 31 March. On 9 April, Allied Van Lines handed him a bill of lading for his movable possessions in Ottawa contained in seven barrels, two boxes, five tea chests, twenty cartons, and seven crates; the declared value was $5,000, the length of haul 1,713 miles, and the destination the farm at Lemberg.

Part of the reason Gardiner accepted the voters' decision with equanimity was that he could at last go back to the farm he had been improving since he took it over from his brother during the First World War: 'It was always my plan to come back to the farm as soon as I was set free from a life which I deliberately set out upon at the end of my university term.'[7] Farming became his way of life long before he became the country's chief minister of agriculture. It informed his ideas, his values, even his language, as a reading of Gardiner's correspondence and speeches in and outside of the House demonstrates. As well, it gave him an intimate knowledge of the problems and attitudes of the nation-wide constituency of farmers, thus providing him with the assurance and authority needed to mobilize the weight of government and Parliament on behalf of this community. To suggest that he was only a gentleman farmer, as T.C. Douglas once did, was to earn a scathing rebuke from one who joyed in the belief that he was a doer, a practical man, struggling against theorists, among whom he numbered the socialists, who, in his opinion, had never earned a cent by the sweat of their brow.[8]

Except for the removal of his gall bladder in 1949, Gardiner enjoyed exceptionally good health throughout his career. Even following an operation in 1959 for cancer of the colon, after which he had a colostomy whose care and function he described in characteristic detail to others, the old pace scarcely slackened. His industry, combined with his age, became a subject of pride to him, especially after the operation:

I fenced the half section for purebred shorthorns. I did not do all the work myself. We dug post holes with a tractor. I supervised the work, pulled much of the wire off old fences and stretched most of it on our two miles of fence – 5 strands.

I next painted the house which has been there as you know for over 50 years and never was painted before. I did that without any help. I have been supervising and helping with the haying and harvest after having directed the cultivation of close to 600 acres of cultivated land and have marketed close to $6,000 worth of livestock including 10 pure bred bulls ... I am sure you will conclude I could be sicker.[9]

Thus, the last years of his life were happy and active ones. In his domestic affairs he could enjoy some relaxation now. He had married for a third time in 1946; his wife Maude was a long-time acquaintance and the widow of an old Saskatchewan Liberal loyalist, Dr Hugh Christie. Between her grown-up children and his own, some living nearby, there was always immediate family for company. In 1959 the University of Saskatchewan at its golden jubilee convocation conferred on him an honorary doctor of laws. On that occasion he was presented to the chancellor of the university by Mr Justice E.M. Culliton, a former member of the Patterson government and the unsuccessful contender for the Liberal leadership in Saskatchewan in 1946. The words of that presentation could not have been more opposite to Gardiner's career had he written them himself: 'While he will best be remembered in Canada as a champion of the farmers' cause, throughout the Western World he will be remembered as the man who made an outstanding contribution to the allied victory in the Second World War through his efficient and energetic direction of the mobilization of the food resources of Canada.'[10]

If retirement from public life brought personal contentment and honours, it also allowed more time for contemplating the past and, especially, the loss of his son Edwin who, he said, had intended to take over the farm: 'As we get older we miss him more and more.'[11] Gardiner visited Edwin's grave in France on three occasions after the war and maintained an active correspondence both with a local Normandy family who tended the grave and with the family of the other Canadian pilot who had died with Edwin when their Spitfires had collided while in pursuit of a German fighter plane. Indeed, the last letter in the Gardiner Papers is from that young man's parents, who expressed the hope that Gardiner, 'a thorough gentleman,' should recover from what in fact was to be his final illness.[12] Gardiner did not recover but died on 12 January 1962. But he remained alert until the end, allowing himself to be interviewed for several days over the period of the New Year about his political life by Una MacLean Evans, whose taped interviews with him give invaluable insight into his political credo.

Those interviews, as well as his correspondence with old colleagues, make it clear that while retirement brought personal satisfaction, that feeling did not extend to the political scene around him. He disapproved of the direction in which the party was moving under Lester Pearson. It was less a matter of what Pearson and his advisers did than their failure to act at all. He and C.D. Howe agreed that the Liberal opposition after 1957 appeared unnecessarily defensive and humble about the record of the King and St Laurent governments. On the contrary, the old ministers thought the legislative accomplishments after 1935 worth championing. On the question of party organization, and particularly organization in the west, Gardiner saw the Pearson Liberals as bereft of ideas or plans to recoup the party's fortunes. It was a measure of his continuing inventiveness, even when his career had ended, that he began to speculate about major organizational changes. Gardiner believed the cause of the election disasters rested in the lethargy of the provincial parties. It was in the provinces, therefore, where rebirth must start. If that proved impossible because provincial Liberals insisted on being parochial then, he argued, 'we should give some thought to setting up organizations in each Province based on the Federal constituency areas.'[13]

Nothing came from these speculations in terms of Gardiner's own involvement in the formation of national party policy after 1958. Instead, he came increasingly to look upon himself as one of yesterday's men, an image magnified by the persistence of his belief in a degree of party loyalty others no longer seemed to share. As of old, he continued to attend 'the fiftieth and sixtieth wedding anniversaries or the funerals of many of my old friends' and more than once found himself the lone representative of officialdom from an earlier political generation.[14] To drive 170 miles at 20 degrees below zero to attend a funeral of a Liberal stalwart in a Manitoba seat which had for decades sent a Liberal to Ottawa and to find no other ex-minister present, and then to drive home again was not a unique instance. It was party and political loyalty which prompted him and Maude to drive from Lemberg to Montreal for C.D. Howe's funeral in December 1960 and then to get right back into the car and return to Saskatchewan. Such devotion to people and a cause was no idiosyncratic trait but had become concentrated with the passage of time as Gardiner's keystone value – the mortar laid in 1917 when a majority of prominent prairie Liberals had deserted Laurier, and then hardened during the long struggle in the twenties and thirties to stem the defection of Liberals to the banners of Progressivism, socialism, and other non-Liberal 'isms.

It was this unshakeable adherence to political values, reinforced by a superior knowledge of his portfolio, that led parliamentary friend and foe alike to express regret at his departure from public life. David Croll, now a senator but a long-time Liberal acquaintance, predicted with more accuracy than he might have wished that 'it will be a very long time before we see your kind again on the scene,' while Douglas Harkness, Gardiner's Tory successor as minister of agriculture, hit the same note when he remarked that 'the House of Commons will be a much less interesting place with you absent from it.' He also admitted: 'I shall miss you.'[15] Such warm tributes from strong but independently minded politicians for another of their kind provided Gardiner, the principled politician, with the greatest compliment he could have expected or desired at the end of his extraordinary career.

Epilogue

A quarter of a century after Gardiner's death, and particularly in western Canada, criticism is often heard about inadequate representation in Parliament, about the inability of westerners to get their opinions heard. Such language implies that politicians are vessels to be filled with regional or other discontents which they then pour out in national debate. That was never Gardiner's view: for him, the politician interpreted particular, local matters in terms of the larger interests of party and nation. As a result, leaders must be active, not passive. Here was the source of his boundless energy, and of his Liberal nationalism. Here, too, was the basis for his disillusionment with St Laurent. From Gardiner's perspective, and from that of the west, St Laurent appeared passive. His failure to act on the dam was one piece of evidence, but in later years Gardiner cited others and made an invidious comparison between the national leaders he had served: 'I am afraid,' he told Paul Martin, 'if I had brought that [PFRA] legislation to the council in St. Laurent's time it would not have passed ... I had to make a special plea to Mr. King to get it through Council but when he put it through he stood by it at every opportunity ... I am now convinced that in the interest of Liberalism and Canada I should have done what you threatened to do on health. I should have resigned when he would not take my recommendation on the dam.'[1]

The job of a cabinet minister was to advance arguments on behalf of policies which he determined to be of benefit to those he represented and which at different times and in changing circumstances might be regional or national, occupational or religious in nature. The constant requirement was for the minister to be on his feet, figuratively and often literally, at every opportunity: in the House, on the hustings, in cabinet,

at caucus, and before the constituency. Nor was this as straightforward
as it sounded, for while the forum in one instance might be the House,
the intended audience could easily be elsewhere: the press, local voters,
farmers generally or, as was often the case with Gardiner, his fellow
ministers seated alongside him. That was the opinion of Gardiner's
wartime deputy minister of agriculture, J.G. Taggart, who noted how
his chief would use House debates to press his ministerial colleagues in
a policy direction he favoured but they resisted: 'He seeks to commit the
Government and if he makes a speech containing a definite promise – a
speech not challenged by his colleagues – it must be regarded as a
government commitment on the cabinet solidarity theory.'[2] Gardiner's
mastery of detail in a department whose concerns more members of
Parliament than cabinet ministers understood made him as formidable
and exasperating an advocate within his own party as within Parliament.

But it was at the cabinet table where the decisions were finally taken.
The arguments might be sharp or prolonged or bitter, yet once a
decision was reached, Gardiner believed it deserved the same commitment as the discussion that had preceded it. Cabinet decisions must be
defended totally and without apology. Disloyalty was a high crime in
Gardiner's book: loyalty from top to bottom, in government and in
party, win or lose, was the core of his political faith regardless of his own
desires: 'There is never a week goes by at Ottawa, and there never was
a week went by in Saskatchewan during all the time that I was in
Government there, even when I was Premier, that things were not done
which I did not agree with fully, or left undone which I did agree with.'[3]

His ministerial style, which frequently tried the patience of Mackenzie
King and St Laurent, was explained by his interpretation of the function
of cabinet. Cabinet was not a court of equity, where abstract principles
of fairness were applied, or a grand seminar composed of 'high class
thinkers' who determined what was best for the nation. Such concep-
tions were too bloodless to fit his passionate view of adversial politics
and too similar to socialist experiments with policy-making, since in his
mind they subverted government's responsibility to Parliament. One of
his favourite topics for a public address was 'The British System of
Parliamentary Government,' whose central theme warned politicians
against abdicating responsibility to 'bureaucrats,' advisory boards, or
other non-elected agencies. To the extent that politicians did not follow
this advice, he predicted a new 'autocratic' age to come.[4] This view of
cabinet, and of politics, was unashamedly majoritarian: 'Our system of
government assumes that when the people have voted a majority into

office they are established there from four to five years under a system which makes it possible for them to function in spite of what the minority may think.'⁵ Parliamentary government, he argued, was the best system at making it possible for voters to be heard and their demands transformed into policies. Certain preconditions must be met, however. Leaders determined policy after hearing rank and file opinion, and rank and file opinion never publicly dissented from the leaders' interpretation of what they heard. Instead, the test of acceptability was the response of the electorate in general elections, in by-elections, in regular consultation with constituents, and in the House of Commons where those who made policy faced the electorate's representatives. The House of Commons was not a revising chamber, nor its committees and members sources of policy initiation. What cabinet did do, legislative or administrative bodies should not be able to undo, barring of course that great declaration of want of confidence in a government – such as had brought down Gardiner's government in the Saskatchewan legislature after the 1929 provincial election, and such as he argued to his dying day should have determined the fate of the St Laurent government in 1957.

Gardiner's faith in the institutions of what he repeatedly referred to as 'representative, responsible government' depended upon the existence of two, and only two, political parties. Hence his lifelong hostility to coalitions and to third parties, because these experiments detracted from the vigorous advocacy of policies which the division of mankind into 'stand patters' and 'reformers' made inevitable and ultimately beneficial. For political competition was natural and Liberalism, at least in North America, where no dominant class or caste held sway, was the preferred value: 'I am so constituted,' he once said, 'as to be constantly looking for ways to improve what we have.' That made him, in his description, 'an advanced Liberal' who from his earliest days aligned himself with 'the people vs. the bank or the people vs. mortgage companies or the people vs. the railways.'⁶

If the two-party system maximized opportunities to help the mass of the people against the interests, it also offered the best chance to promote regional equality. Despite his identification in the public mind, then and later, with the west, Gardiner did not look upon himself as a regional politician with the limitations upon ministerial activity such a label implies. Both the demands of his portfolio and the ambit of his partisan activity extended far beyond the west. Nonetheless, he possessed special prairie responsibilities which he believed could best be promoted through one or other of the major parties, in his case the Liberal party. Third parties, by contrast, he believed, were prisoners of one idea, usually an economic heresy of some description, and from this narrow base they could not expand. Gardiner never tired of lecturing Liberals, and others, about the need for political parties to include, not exclude, people and ideas. If they followed this advice, he guaranteed they would be both more tolerant in spirit and successful in elections. The prairie west seemed particularly susceptible to the appeal of third parties, and their presence in the legislature even in small numbers frustrated him in the job he was trying to do: 'There is always someone building up some new organization in some part of the West which results in sufficient members sitting in a corner by themselves.'[7] The conclusion he drew was that little positive could be accomplished through third parties, while the centralism from which Canadian politics perennially suffered was reinforced yet again:

I have learned long ago that the western provinces have seen to it that they are not listened to too much in other parts of Canada. Nobody is going to be scared very badly here by a suggestion that the five Liberals in Ottawa from Saskatchewan now, including myself, might be kicked out the next time. The people of the western provinces have kicked out so many Liberals and put the representatives of some crack-pot party in their place that there are a lot of people in Canada who do not think it makes very much difference what we think. That makes me very bitter sometimes.[8]

Critical of third parties and coalitions, Gardiner remained uncritical of almost any other aspect of the political institutions he had mastered over forty years in public life. Of Senate reform he seldom spoke, of the alternative ballot he remained suspicious. And rightly so, in light of his belief that politics was about action and the taking of responsibility: 'It is not the intention of an election to provide a House so evenly divided under the different points of view which people hold as to make it impossible for anyone to carry on under any given policy.'[9] Even the defeat over building his cherished dam he translated in time into a victory. The decision by the old enemy, now in power, demonstrated to him 'the suitability of our representative, responsi[ble], democratic system operating under a federal form of government to the needs of a growing country. The opposition was convinced by what the PFRA organization had advocated even before the government which was responsible for raising the funds was prepared to act upon the recom-

mendations of the responsible Minister'[10] In cabinet his ministerial colleagues may have been unresponsive, in the Commons the Liberal back-
benchers may have sat mute, but on the other side the opposition had
listened.

Nothing could demonstrate more clearly the relationship he believed
should exist between cabinet and Commons or the primacy he attached
to the educative function of politics and political leaders. The dam was
to be built not because the Progressive Conservatives were led by a
westerner or because the PC caucus held more westerners than the
former Liberal caucus. Although of significance, these changes were of
less importance in Gardiner's scale of values than the case for the dam
having been convincingly argued in Parliament. Politics was about persuasion, its tools, facts, organization, and oratory. His cause was Liberalism, a philosophy detractors said could be twisted to suit its exponent's
immediate partisan ends but one few claimed was solely regional in
content. The more recent view that legislatures and executives are
unrepresentative when segments of electoral opinion are not translated
into equally strong voices in Parliament or cabinet he would find per-
plexing. Political, indeed national, unity grew, in Gardiner's opinion,
out of partisan sympathy organized behind acknowledged leaders. The
leaders' authority was derived from their achievements and political
skills, not from their geographic origin.

Enough has already been said to indicate Gardiner's clear-headedness
in matters of party politics. Contrary to the criticisms that surrounded
and trailed after him, politics, as he saw it, was about more than elections
and elections about more than votes. The strands of the skein that joined
the early to the later years and Saskatchewan to Ottawa were few but
distinct, some reflecting concern for individualism and openness, others
for centralism and control. But in both a vertical party organization
under a leader was placed in the service of a heterogeneous and evolving
society. The patronage that so exercised non-Liberals was distributed
so as to reward the loyalty of the few who performed the 'drudgery'
which kept the organization responsive to the many. By modern standards the stakes were small: some judges and inspectors, even fewer
senators, but many postmasters and rural mail contractors; public relations was virtually unknown and the hiring of party workers discouraged. On the other hand, advertising was spread thin but wide. Such
was the foundation for Gardiner's political and departmental longevity;
one which nonetheless helped him, he said, to 'so regulate and guide
developments as to keep returns high while agriculture passed through

the greatest and most costly revolution in methods ever experienced in this country at least.'[11] Gardiner did not say, nor did he appear to recognize, that the same revolution helped undermine the political organization that had made the revolution possible.

To speak of a revolution was no immodest boast. By any measure, dramatic changes in farm conditions had occurred between the time Gardiner entered and left the federal government. Consider, for instance, the arrival of new fertilizers, herbicides, and pesticides or the innovations in tillage, seeding, and harvesting practices or, even more basic, the widespread introduction of electricity to farm operations (the woman who did not know that Gardiner was the author of PFAA had not possessed a radio, but the majority of those farmers who did, including W.R. Motherwell, still used battery sets during the war). Again, compare the value of Saskatchewan's wheat crop which between 1916 and 1951 never exceeded $500 million, and the value of the same crop over the next twenty years when it exceeded that figure on nine occasions. Greater productivity accompanied increased mechanization in the more prosperous and salubrious post-war years.[12] Higher output involving fewer labourers could not help but disrupt a system created in horse-and-buggy days or the society it supported. And the consequent migration from farm to town led to a decline in services which in turn accelerated the unsettling of the countryside.

In a number of homely ways the social impact of the revolution bore in on the minister's office. When in 1955 his special assistant, Claude Schaller, tried to discover the name of the school at Lockwood, Saskatchewan, where Gardiner had taught for a term in 1910, so that a copy of *None of It Came Easy* could be sent to its library, he was informed that the building had been moved and the school district incorporated into a larger unit, for the simple reason that 'there are no children of school age in the District at the present time.' The same year, which was the golden jubilee both of the province and of Gardiner's arrival in Saskatchewan, brought growing complaints about deteriorating rural mail service as the post office found it increasingly expensive to serve a dwindling but dispersed population. Rather than going forward, one complainant grumbled, 'it has gone back fifty years.' Throughout the decade a group of Saskatchewan history enthusiasts, led by J.L. Phelps (with whom Gardiner jousted on other occasions over agricultural matters), successfully pressed the federal department to contribute periodic support to the province's Western Development Museum and by so doing to acknowledge, no doubt inadvertently, the quick passage of the era that had given birth to Gardiner's political world.[13] The province, too, recognized this transition under way by inaugurating an exhaustive investigation into all aspects of the vanishing way of life: the Royal Commission on Agriculture and Rural Life. A museum and an inquiry symbolized the shift taking place in respective federal and provincial responsibilities: the federal government, which had moulded the west through its nation-building activity – the railroads, retention of natural resources, the tariff, immigration – was contracting in influence, while the province, the provider of improved and expanded local services – paved highways, consolidated schools, and extended health care – grew ever more vigorous.

In Saskatchewan rural change directly and adversely affected party organization. But in Ottawa reverberations from the changes in western agricultural practices disturbed the old patterns of policy formulation put in place by Gardiner after 1935. Mackenzie King once confided to his diary that with regard to his cabinet ministers, the office made the man.[14] Whether true of others, this complacent judgment was patently untrue of Gardiner. He had arrived in the capital determined to raise Agriculture into the front rank of portfolios from what he judged to be its previous adjunct, support role to the provinces. And he succeeded, not just in terms of the policy benefits that flowed to the farmers, but in terms of the respect accredited agricultural concerns in the late thirties and onwards. One of Gardiner's greatest triumphs as minister was to impose order on agriculture's constituencies and to promote himself as their representative and spokesman in government. He devoted as much energy to moulding farm opinion as he did to transmitting it and in this endeavour, as in cabinet, he revealed himself the consummate politician. Because the courts had thrown up barriers to federal control in the production and marketing of farm products, Gardiner determined that 'a well-informed and guided farm population' should voluntarily reach the right decisions.

Voluntarism, an essential ingredient of Liberalism and in opposition to state control, took the form of nurturing the Canadian Federation of Agriculture, restored in its modern form in 1937, by establishing a privileged relationship between it and the Department of Agriculture: 'I and my officials discuss every important matter [with the CFA] concerning agriculture before action is decided upon.' The annual federal-provincial Farm Conference, attended by representatives of government and agricultural interests and in which the CFA played a visible and vocal part, 'was operated ... more or less like a party caucus ...

behind closed doors ... [so as to] get free expression of opinion.'[15] Through the annual meeting in Ottawa with Gardiner and his officials, the Farm Conference delegates helped legitimize the ministry's policies. But most importantly, when the delegates returned to their farms and offices they educated their fellow farmers and citizens in the worth of federal agriculture programs. Gardiner had created machinery to join farm and federal government, whose reciprocating parts carried agricultural opinion to Ottawa and official policy back to those on the land.

Though the relationship with the CFA was profitable to both principals, Gardiner never limited government's relations with the farming community to the CFA. He believed that if a politician or an administrator was to have influence he must act: join, petition, debate, but do something. He himself belonged to all the major and some of the minor farm groups, and when other Liberals would ask what their response should be to requests for help from the more radical organizations, like the Farmers' Unions, Gardiner's advice was always the same – join them, give them information, help them communicate with government. If one did not do that, then the field would be vacated to undesirable (that is, non-Liberal) influence; in the fifties he blamed western Liberals for neglecting this duty of a politician and, in consequence, turning over the farmers' organizations to the CCF, thus abandoning the Liberals' reputation as 'champions of the common man.'[16]

Farm organizations within the different sectors of agriculture had a history of fragmentation and rivalry. To avoid becoming an ally to one side and antagonizing the other, he instructed the department staff to show no favouritism but to give assistance to all. That being said, the CFA, because of its broad base of support, was treated as agriculture's senior spokesman, its opinion sought on appointments to committees and boards that advised the minister, its officers given privileged audience with the prime minister and cabinet. Those others who sought similar access had to make do with less formalized recognition, perhaps a meeting with prairie ministers or with some prairie MPs, because, as Gardiner observed: 'Our form of representative responsible government [does] not lend itself to the American Block system.'[17]

The symbiotic relationship between organized agriculture and its federal minister admirably served the purposes of each as long as the conditions which gave rise to it, or conditions having a similar effect, persisted. But the origins of the relationship rested in a period of uncertainty which had sparked Gardiner's quest for income stability before,

during, and after the war. By the 1950s, surpluses had replaced scarcity
and institutions such as the Canadian Wheat Board, to which Gardiner
had become a convert, no longer won universal acclaim for their policy
or operation. An evaluation of the board's policies over the last three
decades is beyond the scope of this book and in any case would require
an undertaking comparable to C.F. Wilson's mammoth study of the
grain industry in the first half of this century. What must be acknowledged is that after 1943 the board, as agent of the federal government,
assumed monopoly control of wheat; as a consequence, in the eyes
of the farmer the federal government alone, and uniquely, became
responsible for a crucial industry. The political implications of that
change for the Liberal party, and indeed for the west, were incalculable.
Every complaint about wheat – its price, handling, or sales – was now
directed at Ottawa; every remedy expected to emanate from there. The
primacy the board gave to guaranteeing stability and security freed
the farmer, even encouraged him, to look to diversification of crops.
Gardiner, never the minister responsible for the board but nonetheless
the pre-eminent western spokesman in cabinet, felt the winds of change
more forcefully than any of his colleagues, even C.D. Howe, the minister
of trade and commerce.

The simplicity of the old relationship between the wheat pools or the
CFA and the government broke down in the 1950s, as leaders of the new
and more aggressive commodity and livestock groups sought to enter
the circle of those who determined policy.[18] Gardiner, as witness or
party to the formation of every western farm organization of this century
and sensitive to the damage a dissentient group could cause an established organization, pressed the federation to adopt an open-door policy
toward the farmers' unions. He also lamented the absence of 'the proper
kind of farm organization in Canada today,' by which he meant something analogous to the old farm institutes that had stood ready to
give practical advice.[19] Organizational rivalry did not abate, however.
Indeed, in the same period the surpluses of the 1950s presented the
board and the government with a policy quandary which they proved
incapable of solving and which therefore dampened support for the
Liberals from even established farm organizations.

A footnote to this discussion of agricultural change concerns the reaction of the Canadian business community to these events. One effect of
the closing of the Winnipeg Grain Exchange to wheat trading was to
separate Canadian business in the fifties from the country's primary
industry and from the region in which it was located. It was one of

Gardiner's favourite themes to wax on the close attachment in Canada between city and country: the days of the pioneers were as yesterday in the history of the nation and the leaders of finance and commerce were only one generation removed from the farm. Perhaps true, and no doubt useful in sustaining his thesis that the west needed industrial expansion and the South Saskatchewan River dam would make it possible; but the connection he posited held scant meaning in the post-war years for the brokers of Bay Street or St James Street.[20] C.D. Howe's analysis, in a speech to the Junior Investment Dealers' Association in 1952, proved both more perceptive and more prophetic than did Gardiner's homilies. After opening with an apology for explaining why his audience should be interested in the subject of the Canadian wheat crop, he proceeded to note that an explanation would not have been necessary fifteen or twenty years before. Your predecessors 'would have been fully alive to the relation between the marketing of the western grain crop and the financial position of many Canadian businesses and, for that matter, several Canadian governments. The price of wheat, and the prospect for the western crop, were watched in those days as closely as many of you today watch the quotations on the Toronto Stock Exchange.'[21]

If the chronology between the frontier and the fifties amounted to a matter of a single generation, then Gardiner could hardly escape its immediate effects either. In the year leading up to the 1957 general election he admitted as much, confessing that he experienced difficulty controlling the local situation, because his organization creaked along with everyone 'nearly as old as I am.' Of the younger generation, he agreed with the opinion of a local key man that they 'do not have the same tenacity as that which dominated the pioneers, politically and otherwise.'[22] And technological innovations disrupted more than just agriculture. The arrival of the diesel locomotive on the prairie division of the CNR, he was told, 'is resulting in a number of changes as far as the running trades are concerned and a serious reduction in the number of employees' in Melville, the largest town in his constituency. In the rural parts of the prairies more disturbing still was the introduction of television, which preceded the government's defeat by only a couple of years. A cousin, writing in 1955 from Clearwater, Manitoba, where Gardiner first put down prairie roots, relayed news of the advancing revolution, telling him that some relatives who ran the local hardware store had 'started up' the first set in the town.[23]

It would be convenient to argue that television spelled doom for the type of political organization Gardiner had mastered, by encouraging electors to respond as passive spectators rather than as local activists. And that may even be true, but it is doubtful it could be proved; and in any event the loss of the election so soon after the appearance of television makes assertion of cause and effect in this particular instance improbable. Less speculative, however, is the effect broadcasting regulation had on party politics; for scattered throughout Gardiner's papers and extending back to the late 1930s is correspondence concerning the award (or alteration) of radio and later television licences. While the intricacies of each application are not of concern here, two general points arising from them are of significance for evaluating Gardiner's political skills in a changing world. First, he was never at ease with new or evolving technology; as late as 1955 he told the minister of national revenue, who was responsible to Parliament for the CBC: 'I still do not understand broadcasting sufficiently well to be able to make representations on [x's] behalf.' And he understood the formal politics of it only slightly better, since in the same letter he admitted he was unsure whether he should be writing to the minister of national revenue or to the minister of transport (the licensing authority). Secondly, he always subordinated the technical considerations to the older, and in his mind eternal, questions of politics, which broadcasting merely raised in a new guise.[24]

For instance, radio and television were subject to regulatory supervision, initially by the CBC and later by the Board of Broadcasting Governors. In either case, the regulators remained, to his disgust, 'a law unto [themselves] and completely outside the sphere of political influence.'[25] Technological regulation, like economic or any other kind, continued to affront his sense of political responsibility. At the same time, and not unrelated, such bodies sorely troubled his life. The licensing of a French-language radio station provided one example, for it affected an historic minority within the province, engaged the sympathy of Quebec members of Parliament outside, and threatened, he always feared, to bring about what one correspondent called 'a recurrence of the 1929 incident.' For these reasons, he even allowed himself to 'doubt ... whether it was a good thing to set up French radio stations in Saskatchewan ... I have always anticipated that we could easily experience a lot of difficulty which would affect us in many parts of Canada unless we are very careful.'[26]

Gardiner was anything but anti-French. His whole career had been devoted to promoting tolerance of all minorities, but he had always spoken especially warmly of the importance of Quebec's contribution to Canada's rise as a nation. Added to this was his personal appreciation for France and its people, represented by the villagers of St Aubin le Cauf near Dieppe, who had faithfully tended the grave of his son Edwin. Thus, the reservations he expressed here stemmed from another source: the belief that old issues, like French-English or Protestant–Roman Catholic relations, 'never die' but only lie dormant waiting to be roused by opponents of the Liberal party if the Liberals acted so as to give them the chance.[27]

The policy of the 1970s and 1980s known as bilingualism had not yet emerged fully blown in the last years of his life. But such harbingers of its birth as he saw upset him because they contradicted his view of Canada as a nation and especially the place of the west in Canada. On this point his argument in 1957 had scarcely altered from that of a decade earlier at the leadership convention, when he rejected the practice of alternating leaders between English and French Canadians. The consistency lay in Gardiner's view of himself as part of a living tradition whose substance comprised British parliamentary institutions and a respect for individual freedom. The triumph of process and procedure guaranteed nationhood in a country having 'no common ideals, no common literature, nor yet a common language, no common custom about which to build.'[28] His cast of mind was not such as to analyse or question these beliefs, but he did not desert them either. Indeed, his political experience provided confirmation for the belief that 'we never settle anything in politics' and thus for placing his faith ever more firmly in effective remedies. On the matter of race and toleration, for example, it is worth recalling that this was the subject of his maiden speech to the special session of the Saskatchewan legislature in September 1914, the issue of principle fifteen years later in his government's defeat, and the matter which exercised his emotions as much as any, another fifteen years on, in the conscription debates of the Second World War.

Because of his liberalism, because of his nationalism, and because of the area of the country from which he came, Gardiner had special reasons for feeling strongly about ethnicity and politics. For him, politics was the pre-eminent vehicle for overcoming cultural distinctions; it should moderate not elevate the stigmata of language and creed. But by 1957 division was just what Gardiner thought the Liberal party was set upon accomplishing:

About two weeks before the end of the campaign a report came over the radio to the effect that it had been stated at one of the Prime Minister's meetings in Quebec that it might not happen in our time but the time would come when everyone holding an important position would have to be bilingual ... They have sown a new form of nationalism which put[s] more emphasice [sic] upon the nationality of the candidate than upon his Liberalism. I have had several Ukranians [sic] come to me since the election and ask what we think they are. They say we and our children only wish to be known as Canadians so far as our political alignments are concerned ... Liberalism should be the first necessity for a candidate.[29]

Thus bilingualism struck at the root of Gardiner's beliefs and practices. Had he lived to see it, he would not have been surprised at later opposition in the west to the terms of reference of the Royal Commission on Bilingualism and Biculturalism which spoke of 'two founding peoples.' He had raised similar objections himself: how to reconcile the implications of bilingualism with the demands for recognition of a multicultural society, which the west had been ever since the turn of the century? His patronage files bulged with correspondence pressing the case of individual Ukrainians (Catholic and Orthodox), Poles, Germans, and Russians, along with an even greater number of letters on behalf of English- and French-speaking, Protestant and Roman Catholic suppliants. In the small and contained world of two dozen or so judgeships and senatorships, which were the prestige appointments sought as evidence of ethnic recognition, room for manoeuvre was limited indeed: 'If all the figures in relation to nationality are going to be brought into consideration of the question, it will be impossible to just look at the question on a purely statistical basis.'[30] How then to be 'fair to all minorities whether of religious or national origin'? He accepted the understanding made in Saskatchewan's early days which provided for French Catholic representation on the province's courts. Its extension to other nationalities (and other positions), however, proved extremely sensitive, so much so that despite sixteen years' pressure from Ukrainians, no appointment from this ethnic group to the provincial bench had been made as late as the 1957 general election. When early in his prime ministership John Diefenbaker made just such an appointment, Gardiner dismissed the action as 'playing for the Ukranian [sic] vote.'[31]

Gardiner's attribution of Tory pandering to the ethnic voter could be interpreted as no more than the sour, reflex response of a vanquished opponent. But in fact it revealed the deep-seated, even philosophical, unease of a majorities man in the face of cultural – that is, minorities – politics. It was also explained by his belief, equally representative of Gardiner's traditional way of thinking, that such appointments did not work electorally. 'The more we have attempted to do ... the less we have seemed to have the support of any of them. It may be that what we ought to be doing is congratulating all those who have come to us from other countries ... and place much greater emphasis upon the nature of our institutions and opportunities of our country and the fact that they are free citizens of a free country and can only lose that freedom by giving undue consideration to the claims of any group.'[32]

But even had the practice garnered votes, it was not congenial to his individualist values. Again, a paradox exists between Gardiner's reputation as a superlative machine politician and his life-long advocacy of democratic ideals. He distrusted reformers and proponents of systems just as he disliked those who asserted their superiority, be they academics, bureaucrats, military officers, or spokesmen for established religions, classes, or language groups. Here was the source of his devotion to party politics and his rejection of claims to authority that did not have at their base popular approval and acceptance. The test of an opinion or a policy lay not in claims that it was wise or sound or desirable but whether the voter accepted it. Reasonable politicians would place only sensible alternatives before the electorate, although they might still have to exhaust themselves persuading the voters that the proposals deserved support. Ultimately, however, the people alone must make the choice. If they erred and made the wrong choice, as in Saskatchewan in 1929, the politician had to live with the result, although he might continue to fight to change it. The Klan election was pivotal to Gardiner's political experience, for whatever view of human nature he brought to that campaign, he emerged from it convinced that the individual elector needed to be kept informed and made aware of policies if he was not to succumb to destructive ideas. Any policy or practice which discouraged participation therefore earned his rebuke, and into this category fell bilingualism and symbolic representation.

Thus, when pressed to take a direct hand in promoting the participation of women in the party, Gardiner rejected what in more recent times has been called affirmative action: 'I quite agree ... that there should be more women associated with all of our organization. I am inclined to think, however, that it is the wrong approach to try and secure it working from the top down. I think that the women through[out] the country ... ought to see to it that women are appointed to attend all kinds of meetings.'[33] Those women who thought otherwise might say his reply lacked sincerity and that the participation ethos he invoked disguised a masculine disregard for their contribution to politics. Given his age and background, it was unlikely that Gardiner's views on the status of women generally would be anything but traditional. Nevertheless, two qualifications to that assertion as it related to politics need to be made. First, it should be recalled that he had encouraged women's participation in the Saskatchewan Liberal organization soon after female enfranchisement; and secondly, in this matter his attitude was identical to the response he gave other groups seeking to enlist his direct help.

For Gardiner politics was about winning support from individual voters; the intricate and intensive party organization with which his name is identified made no sense otherwise. Of course, groups entered into the calculation. No one as sensitive as he was to ethnic and occupational interests could act differently. But the choices he presented to the voters of Melville or of Saskatchewan, the west, and the nation were couched in a language intended to appeal to their individual reason and good will. As he trusted his own personal experience in preference to 'statistics' which in his view, provided only 'a very flimsy basis upon which to establish conclusions,' so, too, he trusted 'the average of the decisions of 750,000 farmers having full information ... [rather] than to insist on all farmers following the opinion of a few so-called specialists.'[34]

It was these individual electors who provided the bedrock of the party organization he created. The success of that organization lay in its openness to public opinion, as one last example illustrates. Long before concern about the economic and cultural domination of Canada by the United States had become an issue in federal politics, Gardiner's informants relayed to him public unease at Canada's becoming 'a little Belgium,' a disquiet he in turn communicated to the prime minister. In reply, St Laurent expressed shock at the idea and opined that 'something [is] pretty seriously wrong with our government publicity.'[35] Here, as before, Gardiner's maligned organization proved a more sensitive barometer of public sentiment than the government party the prime minister led. Part of the reason, evident again in this instance, lay in the prime minister's ready recourse to publicity to make the Liberal case. That was not Gardiner's way; his response was to counter constituency opinion face to face. The flatness of his prose and its didactic delivery belied the cardinal characteristic of his personality: a total commitment to politics. He was a voracious listener, an indefatigable worker, and, contrary to appearances, a passionate politician. Above all else and throughout four decades in office, he believed absolutely in the power of politics to do good.

Appendix

Memo re Organization*

I note you have been selected as the candidate to contest your constituency in the next Federal election. As Minister from the Province of Saskatchewan, I am sending this memorandum to each candidate setting forth a form of organization which I think should be set up in every constituency. I feel quite certain that if such an organization is set up we will win most of the constituencies in Saskatchewan at the next election.

(1) You have already had set up at your convention an executive and an executive committee and I presume the executive has been given authority to add to the executive committee. The President, Vice-President and Secretary-Treasurer are usually looked upon as the active officials in connection with constituency organization and that is no doubt true of your set-up.

Some constituencies have a full-time paid organizer and others do not, but whether you have a full-time organizer or not I think the constituency should be divided into zones. I would say there should not be more than twenty polls in a zone and not less than half a dozen. I should be inclined to think that unless you have a very competent person to handle twenty polls the number should not be greater than ten. Some local man who lives in the zone should be selected as the organizer of the polls in that zone. If he is not already on the executive committee he should be added to it.

The duty of the zone organizer should be to set up a committee in every poll

**Gardiner Papers, 47605–9

which is consulted about the appointment of Deputy Returning Officer, Poll Clerk, and particularly Inside and Outside Scrutineers.

There should be a small list committee set up in every poll. This committee should be composed of two or three most reliable persons who meet in camera and keep their own counsel. The duty of the Poll Committee should be to check and report upon every voter in the poll.

I am having four copies of the list for each poll as compiled for the last election sent to you at once. Place three copies of this list for each poll for which he is responsible in the hands of the organizer for a zone and he in turn should place two copies of the list for their own poll in the hands of the members of the list committee. Keep one copy for your own records and have the zone organizer hold one for each poll in his zone for his records.

These list committees should be asked to hold a meeting immediately the lists are turned over to them, which should be at once, and at this meeting revise the list by striking off those who have gone away or died and adding on those who have come to the poll or who have come of age to vote. They should then mark the list as they are convinced the voters would vote, placing all those of whom they are not certain on the 'Doubtful' list. They should then proceed to make themselves certain of as many as possible of those marked 'Doubtful' and verify their opinions of the others, and hold another meeting a month later at which they will go through the same operation.

They should continue to hold these meetings at least once a month until the election is announced, and when the election is announced they should hold these meetings once a week.

Either the constituency organizer or you as the candidate should bring these zone organizers together once a month until the writs are issued and once a week after the writs are issued in order to obtain a report. They should all be at the same meeting and make their report in the presence of the others so that each zone organizer will pick up any worthwhile suggestions which the others can make as a result of their experiences. The reports at these meetings should only be in numbers. The opinions of individual voters should not be discussed in meetings excepting in the small list committee of the poll.

You as candidate, or the organizer, should total up the results of these reports at each meeting and be able to determine what the result of the election would be if it were held the next day. The work done by this committee should be in camera and not discussed in relation to individuals outside the meeting. The list as finally compiled should be checked with the enumerator's list as soon as it is available and enough of the new lists secured to supply workers with complete lists before election day. A copy of the list as marked should be in the hands of the outside scrutineer at the poll to be used as the basis of the activities at the poll on election day. Those drawing votes should follow the directions of the outside scrutineer.

This checking of the lists and the report to the candidate should be made the basis of all organization work carried on in the constituency.

(2) Each constituency has already been asked to set up a finance committee and this finance committee has been asked to select a group of wellknown Liberals who are anxious to see a Liberal organization maintained in the Province of Saskatchewan and suggest to them that they make a worthwhile contribution to help defray the expenses of running a central office at Regina.

It is expected that each constituency will raise $2,500 for this purpose.

I would suggest there should be a representative of each part of the constituency on that committee, and each individual member should be made responsible for having his area canvassed at as early a date possible. It is essential that these funds be available in sufficient time to permit of the organization setting up a plan of work which is to be done prior to the issuing of the writs.

It should be understood that this appeal is made in such a way as to not interfere with any appeal which is going to be made for funds to carry on local activities in the constituency.

It should also be understood that some of the most effective campaigning can be done while raising general funds to cover local expenses. It should not be necessary to do any campaigning in connection with the amount which is to be sent into the central office. The persons interviewed with regard to that should be known and working Liberals. Such funds as are sent to the central office should be sent to the Chairman of the Finance Committee, Mr. C. M. Dunn of Regina. They may be addressed to Mr. C. M. Dunn at the Liberal Office located at 315 McCallum Hill Building, Regina.

Mr. Ross Thatcher had a collection taken up at each of his meetings following his nomination and secured approximately $700 during the first month. If each candidate would have this done his financial difficulties would be solved. Take up a collection at every meeting you hold unless you feel you can finance your own campaign.

(3) I have found it most useful, and I think you would as well, to have the largest possible group of local speakers available for meetings. There is at least one person in every town or village who rather enjoys putting forth his point of view with regard to matters in which he is interested. This is particularly true if he is interested in promoting Liberalism. The younger he is the more anxious one should be to get him working. My practice has been to go over my constituency and find all the people of this kind, young and old, who are available, and give them a certain area to cover. I have followed the practice of taking them out with me for two or three meetings when I am in their district, asking them

at a second meeting to take any of the material out of the speech which I deliver the first night and add to it anything they think will be helpful and when they are well equipped to do so turn them loose in the seat to hold meetings or to attend the meetings of the Opposition. In other words, to carry on an active propaganda campaign.

The meetings to be held in the different zones should be arranged by the zone captain or organizer mentioned above. In my opinion, from now until the writs are issued there should be constant holding of house meetings of a semi-social nature at which there will be an hour given up to a discussion of political issues. A few school-house meetings should also be arranged where young speakers can be coached by older campaigners.

I am suggesting that all of this work be done at the earliest possible date.

The central office at Regina will be equipped with staff to reply to any inquiries you may wish to make in order that information with regard to broadcasts, literature, speakers, or any other thing you may desire information on may be got to you at as early a date as possible. Address your correspondence to the Secretary, Saskatchewan Liberal Association, 315 McCallum Hill Building, Regina.

James G. Gardiner
December 1956

Notes

Canada, *Debates*	Debates in the House of Commons
CAR	*Canadian Annual Review*
GP	Gardiner Papers, Saskatchewan Archives
JGG	James G. Gardiner
Journals	*Journals of the Legislative Assembly of the Province of Saskatchewan*
KP	King Papers, National Archives of Canada
NAC	National Archives of Canada
SP	Saskatchewan, *Sessional Papers*

CHAPTER 1 THE WAY IN

1 GP, Notes for *None of It Came Easy*, 33733

2 Nathaniel Benson, *None of It Came Easy* (Toronto 1955), GP, 33633–849. For the purposes of this biography all references to *None of It Came Easy* are to Gardiner's notes for it, not the published text.

3 Ibid., 1–269. The publisher's report is in 394. The novel has been published under its original title in the Prairie Books Series of Modern Press, Saskatoon, edited by Norman Ward.

4 KP, MG26, J1 vol. 131, King to JGG, 27 Feb. 1926, 111767–72

5 A good example is a letter to King which begins: 'My Prime Minister I have taken this way to tell you that I heard your splanded speach over the fone [radio] and I heard none liked it thay laughed when I said that the greatest speach that I leasent over the fone but there was nothing to laughed at.' Ibid., Mrs J.C. Gardiner to King, undated 1944, vol. 360, 311923

6 The material for the next several paragraphs comes almost entirely from Gardiner's notes for *None of It Came Easy*, supplemented by an undated mimeographed biographical summary which may have been prepared to hand out to delegates at the Liberal convention of 1948. See KP, MG26, J4, vol. 275, C189420–2.

7 GP, 407–8

8 KP, MG26, J4, vol. 275 (undated mimeo), C189421

9 GP, 'My personal experiences associated with the birth of Saskatchewan,' 33138–48

10 Ibid., 7 June 1913, 396; and undated, 400, reports by W.E. Stevenson

11 Ibid., 'Teaching of History to Grade VIII and Higher Pupils,' 415–27

12 Ibid., JGG to O.J. Sherloski, 26 Dec. 1933, 17171

13 Ibid., 'Party Government,' 433

14 Ibid., 'Nominating Convention,' Cupar, 1913, 491

15 See especially V.C. Fowke, *Canadian Agricultural Policy: The Historical Pattern* (Toronto 1946), and *The National Policy and the Wheat Economy* (Toronto 1957); W.A. Mackintosh, *Agricultural Cooperation in Western Canada* (Kingston and Toronto 1924).

16 GP, JGG to W. Eggleston, 22 Apr. 1937, 42674–6

17 Ibid., 390–2

18 Ibid., 'Essay on Protection,' Mar. 1910, 339–40; 'Economic Functions of Government,' Mar. 1911, 365ff, 311; Glenbow Alberta Institute, interviews of Gardiner by Una Maclean Evans, 29 Dec. 1961–6 Jan. 1962 (hereafter Glenbow Tapes), tape 1

19 GP T.W. Lawlor to JGG, 4 May 1926, 4919

20 Ibid., undated, unfoliated, 'General Regulations,' file 1-1-e

21 Ibid., 'Economic Functions of Government,' 6 Mar. 1911, 381

22 Ibid., 'Who is the True British Citizen?,' 508–9, 'The Churches Duty to the State,' 517–8 (both undated, but in Gardiner's college files)

23 Ibid., 'Party Government,' 430–1

24 Saskatchewan Archives, Walter Scott Papers, Scott to J.B. Gillespie, 4 Feb. 1911, 39240

25 The files on the case are in ibid., 545–685, 851–71.

26 Ibid., J.B. Gillespie to Scott and return, 26 Nov. to 16 Dec. 1913, 37238–44

27 GP, 33813–14

28 Ibid., 33815–16; JGG to J.W. Gardiner, 14 Feb. 1955, 42727–34

29 The plan and three drafts are in ibid., 478–91.

30 See ibid., 295, 480–1.

31 Ibid., 33799

CHAPTER 2 BACK-BENCHER

1 See *Canada Year Book*, 1932, ch. IV; J. Howard Richards and K.I. Fung, *Atlas of Saskatchewan* (Saskatoon 1969), sections 2 (Historical Geography) and 3 (Population Geography).
2 *Journals*, 1912–13, Appendix, *SP* 23
3 See Statutes of Saskatchewan, 1906.
4 David E. Smith, *Prairie Liberalism: The Liberal Party in Saskatchewan, 1905–71* (Toronto 1975)
5 Scott Papers, W.T. Diefenbaker to Scott, 21 Aug. 1908, 38719
6 Ibid., Scott to W.L. Lawler, 1 Sept. 1908, 38742; Scott to T.H. Garry, 31 Aug. 1908, 38749
7 Saskatchewan Archives, Motherwell Papers, F.J. Robinson, form letter dated 13 Jan. 1908, 12536
8 Saskatchewan Archives, Calder Papers, G.B. Johnston to Calder, 16 Aug. 1915, 6371
9 Ibid., C. Rasmussen to Calder, 17 Aug. 1911, and return 22 Aug. 1911, 3885–6; Scott Papers, petition to Scott, 20 Aug. 1908, 38707; Scott to G. Schaeffer, 31 Aug. 1908, 38710
10 Calder Papers, Calder to J.T.M. Anderson, 7 May 1922; and return 22 May 1912, 4059–62
11 Scott Papers, Scott to J.H. Thomson, 20 Aug. 1908, 38538
12 Ibid., Scott to A.D. Davidson, 20 May 1909, 38952
13 Ibid., Scott to candidates, 19 Aug. 1908, 38998
14 See Calder Papers, e.g., Sydney Fisher to Calder, 26 Feb. 1913, 6321; J.H. Ross to Calder, 19 Jan. 1912, 6120–2.
15 Scott Papers, Scott to S. Young, 3 Oct. 1908, 38827
16 GP, 33818
17 *Fifth Census of Canada*, 1911, vol. II: 328–9
18 See Calder Papers, Calder to M. Wallis, 16 June 1914, 6352–3; GP, 33818–21.
19 GP, 33820
20 *The Canadian Liberal Monthly*, July 1914: 131
21 Calder Papers, Calder to B. Alexander, 7 Feb. 1912, 4033; to W. Whyte, 6 June 1911, 5594; T.H. Mawson to Calder, 19 June 1913, 5608; Calder to R.W. Crowe, 23 Oct. 1916, 5582
22 GP, 1608
23 Ibid., 64366
24 Ibid. The novel is 1178–338.
25 Ibid., 872–83

26 *Journals*, vol. XIII, 1917: 767; vol. XV, 1918: 49, 52, 54
27 GP, 1330–42
28 See Norman Ward, *The Canadian House of Commons: Representation* (Toronto 1950), 227, and ch. XII, 'The Franchise.'
29 *Journals*, vol XV, 1918–9: 49–50, 54–5. A substantial part of the debate, including Gardiner's speech, is contained verbatim in GP, 1413–83.
30 Ibid. 1404, and 1372–412 passim; *Journals*, vol. XV, 1918–9: 36, 39–40
31 GP, 1346
32 Ibid., 1613–30, especially 1622–4 and 1630
33 Ibid., 1575, 1500
34 *Journals*, vol. XII, 1916: 114
35 Ibid., 100–1
36 The official record is in the main in ibid.; see index entries beginning 'Bradshaw Charges.' An excellent narrative is in J. Castell Hopkins, *CAR*, 1916: 696–710; 1917: 742–3.
37 Smith, *Prairie Liberalism*, 54
38 Statistics calculated from Saskatchewan Archives Board, *Saskatchewan Executive and Legislative Directory, 1905–1970* (Regina and Saskatoon 1971); Gardiner's files on the election are in GP, 908 ff.
39 See F.W. Anderson, 'Some Political Aspects of the Grain Growers' Movement, 1915–1935' (MA thesis, University of Saskatchewan 1949), with particular reference to Saskatchewan.
40 Scott Papers, 37884
41 GP, 1171
42 Glenbow Tapes, tape 3
43 Statistics from M.C. Urquhart and K.A.H. Buckley, eds., *Historical Statistics of Canada* (Cambridge and Toronto 1965), 618–20; Saskatchewan Archives Board, *Directory of Members of Parliament and Federal Elections for the North-West Territories and Saskatchewan, 1887–1966*
44 See *Journals*, XVII, 1920, SP, 56–9.
45 Glenbow Tapes, tape 1
46 KP, JGG to King, 1 Mar. 1920, 46504–6; reverse, 5 Mar. 1920, 46507–8
47 Scott Papers, Scott to A.K. Maclean, 20 Oct. 1911, 37727
48 GP, 4553; the whole complex story is well told in Smith, *Prairie Liberalism*.

CHAPTER 3 THE ASCENT CONTINUES

1 KP, JGG to King, 8 Sept. 1921, MG26, J1, vol. 60, 52172
2 GP, W.R. Motherwell to JGG, 5 Jan. 1922, 2268–9

3 Ibid., Motherwell to JGG, 17 June 1922, 2278
4 KP, King to JGG, 13 Mar. 1922, MG26, J1, vol. 73, 62293–5
5 David E. Smith, *Prairie Liberalism: The Liberal Party in Saskatchewan, 1905–71* (Toronto 1975), 92
6 Saskatchewan Archives, SGGA files, box 211, J.B. Musselman to R. Mc-Sweeney, 3 Apr. 1922
7 GP, JGG to King, 8 Sept. 1941, 43359
8 Glenbow Tapes, tapes 1 and 3
9 Queen's University Archives, Dunning Papers, Dunning's private secretary (unidentified) to JGG, 23 July 1929
10 *Annual Report of the Department of Highways of the Province of Saskatchewan, 1922–3*: 7–8
11 Statutes of Saskatchewan, 1923, ch. 8
12 GP, speech to SARM, 7 Mar. 1923, 4195–210
13 Dunning Papers, JGG to Dunning, 26 June 1924
14 GP, Dunning to King, 4 Jan. 1923, 2174–5
15 Ibid., Conference with Trades and Labour Congress, 25 Nov. 1925, 4512
16 Ibid., JGG to Motherwell, 9 June 1922, 2282
17 Ibid., Motherwell to JGG, 25 Apr. 1922, 2057–9
18 Ibid., JGG to King, 15 Nov. 1924, 2192–3; also in KP, MG26, J1, vol. 100, 84872
19 GP, Statement by C.A. Dunning (undated) 1922, 4566–8
20 Ibid., W.M. Grant to JGG, 15 Nov. 1923, 3295–6; same, 19 Nov. 1923, 3301; JGG to H. Pettoke, 19 Nov. 1923, 3307
21 Ibid., JGG to R.H. Hall, 5 Jan. 1923, 3035 and 17 Jan. 1923, 3031; reverse, 8 Jan. 1923, 3029–30, and 15 Jan. 1923, 3033
22 Ibid., A.J. Kenyon to JGG 19 Jan. 1923, 3944
23 Ibid., JGG to Hall and reverse, 15 July 1924, 3017–21; 28 July 1924, 3023–5; 31 July 1924, 3022
24 Ibid., 'Present at the Progressive Convention at Saskatoon, August 5, 1924,' 3959–62
25 KP, JGG to King, 1 Mar. 1920, MG26, J1, vol. 54, 46505
26 Ibid., undated, 4252; *Directory of Saskatchewan Ministries, Members of the Legislative Assembly, and Elections, 1905–53* (Regina and Saskatoon 1954)
27 GP, JGG to C. Stewart, 21 Sept. 1925, 2794
28 W.L. Morton, *The Progressive Party* (Toronto 1950), ch. 6, 'The Disintegration of the Federal Progressive Party, 1923–25'
29 KP, King to JGG, 10 July 1926, 111785; reverse, 22 July 1926, MG26, J1, vol. 131, 111790
30 GP, JGG to King, 18 Dec. 1923, 2179

31 Ibid., Motherwell to JGG, 5 Jan. 1922, 2268–70

32 See Norman Ward, *The Canadian House of Commons: Representation* (Toronto 1950), 45.

33 GP, Motherwell to JGG, 30 Sept. 1922, 2297–304; reverse, 20 Oct. 1922, 2305–9; same again, 19 Feb. 1923, 2353; Isobel Cumings to JGG, 1 Mar. 1923, 2357–8; JGG to S. Moyer, 27 Oct. 1924, 3620–1

34 See Morton, *The Progressive Party*; V.C. Fowke, *The National Policy and the Wheat Economy* (Toronto 1957); F.W. Anderson, 'Farmers in Politics, 1915–1935' (MA thesis, University of Saskatchewan 1949); *CAR* esp. 1921–6.

35 GP, JGG to Motherwell, 30 Apr. 1925, 2523–4

36 Ibid., JGG to King, 15 Nov. 1924, 2192–3; 26 Nov. 1924, 2194; reverse, 9 Dec. 1924, 2196. Also in KP, MG26, J1, vol. 100, 84871–3

37 GP, JGG to King, 10 Jan. 1925, 2201–2

38 Ibid., Motherwell to JGG, 20 Jan. 1925, 2500–1

39 See *Proceedings, National Liberal Convention, 1919*, 203–9.

40 Canada, *Debates*, 1922: 2529–30

41 GP, JGG to Motherwell, 9 June 1922, 2282–3; reverse, 17 June 1922, 2276

42 See ibid., JGG to Motherwell, with enclosure, 9 Feb. 1923, 2335–8; reverse, 12 and 14 Feb. 1923, 2339–43; JGG to Motherwell, 14 May 1923, 2381; JGG to King, 18 Dec. 1923, KP, MG26, J1, 73084–5.

43 Ibid., King to JGG, 22 Jan. 1924, MG26 J1, vol. 86, 83086

44 *Journals*, 5 Mar. 1924; 69–70

45 KP, JGG to King, 14 Apr. 1924, MG26, J1, vol. 100, 84859

46 Ibid., King to JGG, 18 Apr. 1924, 84860

47 See *CAR*, 1922: 240–3.

48 *SP*, 1924–5: 147–54

49 See Ward, *The Canadian House of Commons: Representation*, especially 226–32.

50 Manitoba Archives, Dafoe Papers, Dafoe to Sir Clifford Sifton, 26 Oct. 1926

51 GP, Stevenson to MLAS, 15 May 1923, 3806–8

52 Ibid., JGG to Motherwell, 9 Nov. 1922; and reverse, 14 Nov. 1922, 2321–4

53 Ibid., JGG to I.M. Monsees, 27 Feb. 1925, 3636–7

54 Ibid., R.J. Wells to A.P. McNab, 5 Feb. 1925, 3895–6; JGG to R.J. Wells, 10 Feb. 1925, 3894; *SP*, 1925–6: 23–41

55 GP, JGG to Motherwell, 25 Feb. 1924, 2421

56 Ibid., JGG to J. Bureau, 9 May 1925, 3291–2

57 Ibid., JGG to Motherwell, 16 Mar. 1925, 3276–7

CHAPTER 4 REACHING THE FIRST SUMMIT

1 Glenbow Tapes, tape 4, 1 and 3 Jan. 1962; see R. MacGregor Dawson,

William Lyon Mackenzie King: A Political Biography, I, *1874–1923* (Toronto 1958), passim.

2 KP, King to JGG, 8 June 1925, 97643; 30 Oct. 1925, 97659; 3 Dec. 1925, 97661

3 GP, JGG to King, 30 Nov. 1940, 43343–5

4 KP, King to JGG, 15 Jan. 1926, 111721; JGG to King, 18 Jan. 1926, 111724; JGG to Haydon, 18 Jan. 1926, 111722; same, 19 Jan. 1926, 111737; JGG to King, 26 Jan. 1926, 111747; King to JGG 5 Feb. 1926, 111751; same, 16 Feb. 1926, 111764

5 Ibid., Haydon to King, 23 Nov. 1925, with enclosures, especially 98532

6 Ibid., King to Dunning, 25 Jan. 1926, 111143

7 See H. Blair Neatby, *William Lyon Mackenzie King*, II, *1924–1932: The Lonely Heights* (Toronto 1963), 91ff.

8 KP, King to Dunning, 6 Feb. 1926, 111150

9 Ibid., JGG to King, 15 Feb. 1926, 111753

10 Ibid., JGG to King, 19 Feb. 1926, 111761

11 GP, JGG to Motherwell, 3 Feb. 1926, 2638; 15 Feb. 1926, 2640–1

12 KP, Haydon to King, 23 Nov. 1925, 98535

13 Ibid., King to JGG, 22 Feb. 1926, 111762–3

14 Ibid., King to JGG, 17 Feb. 1926, 111768

15 Dafoe Papers, Dafoe to Sir Clifford Sifton, 26 Oct. 1926

16 See Norman Ward, 'A Prince Albertan in Peiping: the letters of T.C. Davis,' *International Journal* 30, no. 1 (Winter 1974–5), 24–33.

17 Dafoe Papers, enclosure with J.W. Dafoe to Sir Clifford Sifton, 16 Dec. 1926

18 See David E. Smith, *Prairie Liberalism: The Liberal Party in Saskatchewan, 1905–71* (Toronto 1975), ch. 4; Keith A. McLeod, 'Politics, Schools and the French Language, 1881–1931' in Norman Ward and Duff Spafford, eds., *Politics in Saskatchewan* (Toronto 1968), 124–150.

19 Statistics from V.C. Fowke, *The National Policy and the Wheat Economy* (Toronto 1957), 72–5, 200; *First Annual Report of the Department of Railways, Labour and Industries of the Province of Saskatchewan for the twelve months ending April 30, 1929*, 15; M.C. Urquhart and K.A.H. Buckley, eds., *Historical Statistics of Canada* (Cambridge and Toronto 1965), 588–9

20 *Census of Canada, 1931*; vol 8: Agriculture, LXXIV, table XXIX

21 SP, 1927: 153–69

22 See Roger Graham, *Arthur Meighen*, II, *And Fortune Fled* (Toronto 1963), 379–477; Roger Graham, ed., *The King-Byng Affair, 1926: A Question of Responsible Government* (Toronto 1967); Neatby, *The Lonely Heights*, especially

chs. 8, 9. See also, Eugene Forsey, *The Royal Power of Dissolution of Parliament in the British Commonwealth* (Toronto 1943).

23 See GP, 'Address delivered by the Leader of the Opposition in the Saskatchewan Legislature during the Federal Election of 1930,' 19250.

24 Norman Ward, ed., *A Party Politician: The Memoirs of Chubby Power* (Toronto 1966), 113

25 GP, T.C. Davis to JGG, 26 Nov. 1952, 62016–7

26 KP, JGG to King, 31 Aug. 1926, 111798

27 GP, JGG to J.H. King, 15 Mar. 1926, 5163

28 Dafoe Papers, Dafoe to Robert Forke, 1 Feb. 1926

29 Ibid., Dafoe to Sifton, 16 Dec. 1926

30 GP, JGG to Motherwell, 10 Apr. 1926, 7720; see also James G. Gardiner, *The Politician, or the Treason of Democracy* (Saskatoon 1975), 186.

31 KP, King to JGG, 3 Mar. 1928, 129739

32 GP, JGG to Robson, 21 Sept. 1927, 8313

33 KP, King to JGG, 20 Aug. 1926, 111796–7

34 Ibid., JGG to King, 11 Apr. 1927, 121702–3

35 GP, H.A. Robson to JGG, 2 Apr. 1927, 8291–2 (italics in original)

36 KP, JGG to King, 22 June 1927, 121710–1

37 GP, JGG to Robson, June (indecipherable) 1927, 8298

38 Ibid., JGG to Robson, 21 Sept. 1927, 8313

39 Ibid., Robson to JGG, 26 Nov. 1927, 8304

40 KP, JGG to King, 17 Jan. 1928, 129730–5

41 Ibid., King to JGG, 3 Mar. 1928, 129737–41

42 KP, Dafoe to King, 2 Mar. 1929, 136837–8

CHAPTER 5 THE USES OF POWER

1 GP, N. McKay to JGG, 10 May 1928, 12212

2 Ibid., JGG to G.G. Harris, 23 June 1928, 6927; 19693 (undated speech)

3 Ibid., list dated 31 Dec. 1926, 5788–92

4 Ibid., 'Political Addresses, 1915–1925,' 1485, 1504

5 Ibid., e.g., clipping from *Regina Leader*, 21 Oct. 1928, 5800; JGG to S. Moulton, 3 July 1929, 9996–8; a full public description by Gardiner is in *Regina Leader*, 23 Oct. 1928.

6 Glenbow Tapes, passim; see also GP, clipping from *Regina Leader*, 23 Oct. 1928, 4799–4804; JGG to Harry Sifton, 26 Nov. 1928, 8691–3; JGG to C. Stuart, 22 Aug. 1929, 10115; speech at Davidson Picnic, 7 Aug. 1928, 11415;

JGG to K. Mayhew, 27 Apr. 1955, 62896; JGG to T.C. Davis, 1 Sept. 1959, 64342–4.

7 Glenbow Tapes, tape 1; see also John G. Diefenbaker, *One Canada: Memoirs of the Right Honourable John G. Diefenbaker, 1, The Crusading Years* (Toronto 1975), 64, 130.

8 GP, JGG to J.P. McIsaac, 19 Oct. 1936, 50755; JGG to L.E. Purdy, 6 Apr. 1940, 52557–8

9 *Journals*, 29 Jan. 1929: 128

10 Ibid., 1931: 303. See Norman Ward, 'The Press and the Patronage: An Exploratory Operation,' in J.H. Aitchison, ed., *The Political Process in Canada* (Toronto 1963).

11 David E. Smith, *Prairie Liberalism: The Liberal Party in Saskatchewan, 1905–71* (Toronto 1975), 169–70

12 Escott M. Reid, 'The Saskatchewan Liberal Machine before 1929,' *Canadian Journal of Economics and Political Science* 2, no. 1 (1936); reprinted in Ward and Spafford, eds., *Politics in Saskatchewan* (Toronto 1968)

13 GP, JGG to A. Hunt, 15 Mar. 1926, 5136–7

14 Reid, 'Saskatchewan Liberal Machine.' See Canada, *Debates*, 1975: 4685, where Reid's article is referred to as 'the Meisal study in the Queen's Quarterly.' The same member cities David Smith's *Prairie Liberalism* as an authoritative source on Gardiner's Prairie Farm Assistance Act and the accompanying organization. The book says nothing about either.

15 GP, undated, 19173

16 *SP*, 1928–9: 62

17 *Report of Public Service Inquiry Commission* (Regina 1930), 2

18 Ibid., 10–12, 12–13, 22–4, 31, 35–6, 40–4, 44–5

19 Smith, *Prairie Liberalism*, 169, especially n. 52

20 GP, JGG to W.S. Campbell, 30 Apr. 1936, 49869

21 Glenbow Tapes, tape 1

22 GP, JGG to C.M. Dunn, 4 Feb. 1936, 42543

23 *Report of the Royal Commission to Inquire into Statements made on Statutory Declarations and Other Matters* (Regina 1931), 68, 63, 84

24 Ibid., 93

25 Smith, *Prairie Liberalism*, 174

26 J. Castell Hopkins, ed., *The Canadian Annual Review of Public Affairs* (Toronto 1930–1), 256

27 See *Journals*, 1930: 198–9; and 1934: 31–2. The case, *Rex v. Mitchell*, does not appear to have been reported.

28 *Report of the Royal Commission ... on Statutory Declarations*, 68–9

29 Diefenbaker, *One Canada*, 136, 139
30 GP, JGG to Motherwell, 28 Feb. 1924, 2423–4
31 See ibid., JGG to E. Lapointe, undated copy of letter sent also to W.R. Motherwell, 30 Nov. 1926, 7625–8; memorandum of interview with Commissioner Staines of RCMP and Hon. Ernest Lapointe, 22 Mar. 1927, 5816–19; T.C. Davis to JGG, 3 Nov. 1958, 42462; JGG to Davis, 10 Dec. 1958, 42463.
32 Glenbow Tapes, tape 1
33 See Frank W. Anderson, *Saskatchewan Provincial Police* (Calgary 1972).
34 Diefenbaker, *One Canada*, 130
35 *SP*, 1928: 75

CHAPTER 6 THE LOSS OF POWER

1 Winston S. Churchill, *Great Contemporaries* (London 1937), 7
2 *SP*, 1925: 147–54
3 See Keith A. McLeod, 'Politics, Schools and the French Language, 1881–1931' in Norman Ward and Duff Spafford, eds., *Politics in Saskatchewan* (Toronto 1968), 124–50.
4 GP, JGG to Norman McKay, 27 Feb. 1928, 6290; *CAR*, 1928–9: 468; 1929–30: 494; 1930–1: 267
5 GP, JGG to C. Endicott, 20 June 1929, 9863–5
6 A critical history of power development is Clinton Oliver White, 'Saskatchewan Builds an Electrical System' (doctoral thesis, University of Saskatchewan 1968).
7 See Norman Ward, ed., *A Party Politician: The Memoirs of Chubby Power* (Toronto 1966), 18–25.
8 The main files on the Klan in the Gardiner Papers are between 8161 and 13792. The chief writings using them are the following MA theses at the University of Saskatchewan: William Calderwood, 'The Rise and Fall of the Ku Klux Klan in Saskatchewan' (1968); Patrick Kyba, 'The Saskatchewan General Election of 1929' (1964); Gordon Unger, 'James G. Gardiner: The Premier as a Pragmatic Politician, 1925–1929' (1967); see also Patrick Kyba, 'Ballots and Burning Crosses – The Election of 1929' in Ward and Spafford, *Politics in Saskatchewan*, 105–23.
9 GP, JGG to H.D. Ranns, 29 Aug. 1927, 12036–7; 15 Feb. 1928, 12091–4; J. Cox to JGG, 27 Feb. 1928, 12142
10 Ibid., JGG to J.L. Nicol, 11 Feb. 1928, 12076–84
11 KP, JGG to King, 23 Aug. 1927, 121723–4
12 *Canadian Jewish Review*, 15 June 1928, clipping in GP, 13791–2

13 GP, 'Memo' to *Saskatoon Star*, 28 May 1928, 13627; undated address signed 'Mark My Word,' 9723

14 Ibid., JGG to J.L. Nicol, 11 Feb. 1928, 12082

15 Ibid., 12076–7

16 Ibid., notes for speech used in North Qu'Appelle constituency, 28 May 1928, 11396–402

17 There is no transcript of the debate, but it was covered in several newspapers. A good account is in *Saskatoon Star*, 30 June 1928 (clipping in GP 13746–8).

18 GP, ibid., 'Chaplain' (anonymous) to JGG, 21 Jan. 1929; reverse, 26 Jan. 1929, 6322–4

19 *SP*, 1928–9: 69–70

20 Ibid., 1925: 68

21 Ibid. 151

22 The literature is well documented and analysed in George C. James, 'Constitutional and Political Aspects of Federal Control of Natural Resources in the Prairie Provinces 1870–1930' (MA thesis, University of Saskatchewan 1975).

23 Bram Thompson, 'A Statement to the Electors on the Natural Resources Issue,' *Regina Leader*, 25 May 1929, unnumbered clipping in GP; James, 'Natural Resources,' 67–84

24 Thompson, 'Natural Resources Issue'

25 Canada, *Report of the Royal Commission on the Transfer of the Natural Resources of Manitoba* (Ottawa 1929)

26 KP, *Conference with Saskatchewan re: Transfer of Natural Resources, February 19, 1929*, C90400–18

27 See White, 'Saskatchewan Builds an Electrical System,' especially 124–67.

28 Ibid., 118–19

29 *Report of the Saskatchewan Power Resources Commission* (Regina 1928)

30 GP, Speech at Craik, 17 Aug. 1928, 11420–33; *Regina Leader*, 15 Aug. 1928, unnumbered clipping

31 GP, JGG to Dunning, 25 Oct. 1928, 9106; JGG to H. Danielson, 17 Nov. 1928, 8686; to H. Sifton, 26 Nov. 1928, 8691–3

32 Saskatchewan Archives Board, *Directory of Saskatchewan Ministries, Members of the Legislative Assembly and Elections 1905–1953*, 74

33 GP, speech (undated) by J.T.M. Anderson, 10356; JGG to T. Taylor, 12 Dec. 1928, 8234; *Winnipeg Tribune*, 4 Apr. 1928, unnumbered clipping

34 GP, speech at Davidson, 7 Aug. 1928, 11413; ibid., clipping from *Regina Leader*, 6 May 1928, 6174–5. See also GP, section X, series II, no. 3, *The Saskatchewan Liberal Handbook, 1929*.

35 *SP*, 1928–9: 256–8

36 Ibid., 267–8. The entire speech is on pages 257–68, and Davis's is pages 269–72.
37 Ibid., 256
38 *Saskatchewan Liberal Handbook, 1929*, 14. See also Kyba, 'Ballots and Burning Crosses'; McLeod, 'Politics, Schools and the French Language.'
39 *Journals*, 1928–9, 15 Jan. 1929: 80; the Liberal view is in GP, section X, series 11, no. 5, 'Blockade Tactics of Tory Member blocks his own Inquiry'; see also JGG to T.H. Barnes, 18 Apr. 1929, 9485.
40 *Regina Star*, 30 May 1929, GP, unnumbered clipping
41 See *Regina Leader*, 23 Oct. 1928, GP, unnumbered clipping.
42 E.g., GP, JGG to Mrs T. Sutherland, 30 Mar. 1928, 8254; Mrs W. Cameron to JGG, 27 Oct. 1928, 8808; and pamphlet at 18038–52
43 GP, JGG to B. McGregor, 22 Apr. 1928, 9333
44 Ibid., JGG to J.H. Speers, 29 Apr. 1929, 9251
45 See ibid., A.W. Ingram to JGG, 20 May 1929, 9091–3.
46 Queen's University Archives, Dunning Papers, JGG to King, 3 June 1929
47 See GP, I. Cummings to JGG, 8 June 1929, 9802.

CHAPTER 7 AN UNEASY SUCCESSION

1 See Peter A. Russell, 'The Co-operative Government in Saskatchewan, 1929–1934; Response to the Depression' (MA thesis, University of Saskatchewan 1970), appendices A, B, D, where all three platforms are reproduced.
2 *Regina Star*, 20 June 1928, GP, unnumbered clipping
3 GP, JGG to King, 7 June 1929, 9554; 8 June 1929, 9553
4 Dafoe Papers, Dafoe to H. Sifton, 13 June 1929
5 GP, JGG to King, 7 June 1929; JGG to T. Wood, 10 Jan. 1933, 17912; statement to press 21 Jan. 1933, 17922
6 Ibid., King to JGG, 13 June 1929, 9942
7 *CAR*, 1928–9: 469–70
8 KP, King to JGG, 17 June 1929, 137647–8
9 Roger Graham, *The King-Byng Affair, 1926: A Question of Responsible Government* (Toronto 1967), 15
10 *CAR*, 1928–9: 470
11 GP, T.C. Davis to JGG, 22 June 1929, 9594–9
12 *SP*, 1929: 59–61
13 GP, JGG to A. Shinbane, 28 July 1929, 8356–61
14 Ibid.; the Price Waterhouse report is at 18867–75; see also *SP*, 1929: 30.
15 *SP*, 1929: 30
16 GP, 10593

17 Ibid., King to JGG, 21 Aug. 1929, 10522–5
18 *Journals*, 1929: 10–11
19 GP, Davis to JGG, 27 Aug. 1929, 10547–50; his deputy's memo is dated 17 July 1929, 10562–6.
20 Ibid., draft of speech on nominations of Speaker, 1929, 10544–6
21 *Journals*, 1929: 10–11; *Saskatoon Star-Phoenix*, 4–11 Sept. 1929
22 *SP*, 1929: 1–24, 25–40, 41–56, 57–8
23 GP, JGG to W.H. Newlands, 6 Sept. 1929, 10508
24 *Saskatoon Star Phoenix*, 7 Sept. 1929
25 Dafoe Papers, Dafoe to H. Sifton, 13 June 1929
26 *SP*, 1930: 164–78, 200–15, especially at 203 and 166; The Saskatchewan Farm Loan Board, Auditor's Report and Financial Statistics, 31 Dec. 1929 (copy in Saskatchewan Archives), 20. The board's history is chronicled in Susanna June Green, 'The Origin and Operations of the Saskatchewan Farm Loan Board, 1917–1951' (MA thesis, University of Saskatchewan 1951).
27 *Auditor's Report*, 17
28 *Journals*, 1930, p. 191; *SP*, 1930: 201
29 *SP*, 1930: 530–58. The reports themselves are *SP*, 41 and 42 of 1930
30 George E. Britnell, 'Public Ownership of Telephones in the Prairie Provinces' (MA thesis, University of Toronto 1934), especially 90–116 (copy in University of Saskatchewan Archives).

CHAPTER 8 A FIRST TASTE OF OPPOSITION

1 KP, JGG to King, 9 Sept. 1929, MG 26, J4, vol. 72, 137657–9
2 E.g., GP, JGG to A. Haydon, 21 Feb. 1932, 17578
3 Ibid., Dunning to JGG, 18 Sept. 1929, 17487
4 Ibid., JGG to J.W. Estey, 28 Oct. 1929, 14330
5 All relevant references are in Norman Ward, 'Gardiner and Estevan, 1929–34,' *Saskatchewan History* 27 no. 2 (Spring 1974), 60–5.
6 GP, Andrew Haydon to JGG, 25 Nov. 1929; JGG to Haydon, 1 Dec. 1929, 17566–70; KP, MG26, J4, vol. 123, JGG to King, 27 Jan. 1930, 148234–7
7 GP, JGG to Mrs L.M. Norman, 5 Jan. 1931, 17990
8 *SP*, 1930: 160, 138
9 See SP 54, 1930, 'Return to an Order of the Legislative Assembly dated March 14, 1930'; 49, 1930; ibid., 20 Mar. 1930. See also ibid., 1930: 137–8.
10 J.T.M. Anderson, *The Education of the New-Canadian: A Treatise on Canada's Greatest Educational Problem* (London and Toronto 1918). The references are, in order, to pages 93, 7–8, 32, 130–1, 171, 154.
11 GP untitled speech, 7 Mar. 1923, 4217–9

12 Ibid., JGG to W. Brown, 15 Jan. 1934, 17252
13 Russell, 'The Co-operative Government in Saskatchewan'; and 'The Co-operative Government's Response to the Depression, 1930–1934,' *Saskatchewan History* 24, no. 3 (Autumn 1971), 81–100. The files of *Saskatchewan History* contain numerous other relevant articles. See also George E. Britnell, 'Saskatchewan, 1930–1935,' *Canadian Journal of Economics and Political Science* 2, no. 2 (May 1936), 143–66; H. Blair Neatby, 'The Saskatchewan Relief Commission,' *Saskatchewan History* 3, no. 2 (Spring 1950), 41–56.
14 *CAR*, 1932: 259
15 GP, JGG to I.F. Fitch, 17 Dec. 1932, 17856; JGG to J.W. Hedley, 16 Dec. 1933, 17090
16 Benson, *None of It Came Easy*, 159–60
17 GP, A. Murray to JGG, 7 June 1929, 9664–6; JGG to Murray, 12 June 1929, 9661–3; JGG to H.D. Leitch, 12 June 1929, 9668
18 Ibid., JGG to Motherwell, 15 June 1929, 9576–8; to C. Endicott, 20 June 1929, 9863–5; to J. Fowler, 20 June 1929, 9874–5; to A. Shinbane, 20 June 1929, 10077–9; untitled speech, 19647–53
19 *SP* 103, 7 April 1934
20 GP, JGG to the Editor, *Witness and Canadian Homestead*, 19 Sept. 1929, 14250–4; see also untitled speech, 19365–74.
21 Ibid., Diary entry for 23 Sept. 1924, 1823
22 Ibid., JGG to J. Mainil, 21 Feb. 1934, 17359
23 Ibid., JGG to M. Sutherland, 4 July 1929, 10084–8; to King, 14 Sept. 1929, 17579; to A. Bergquist, 19 June 1933, 16368; to S. Kanee, 26 Apr. 1933, 15834; to J.A. Ross, 1 June 1933, 16300–1, memorandum, 'Why Young Liberal Clubs,' 46084–5
24 Ibid., JGG to M. Sutherland, 30 Mar. 1928, 8254; Sutherland to JGG, 19 Dec. 1932, 15295–6; JGG to W.H. Ross, 28 Mar. 1936, 51388–9; to H.A. Mackie, 24 Dec. 1926, 51242–4. See also pamphlet, 'How Liberal Women Can Assist,' 18032–4.
25 Ibid., JGG to C.F. McLellan (?), 5 Oct. 1932, 15130
26 Ibid., JGG to J.W. Brown, 21 Aug. 1933, 16641
27 Ibid., JGG to H.A. Mackie, 24 Dec. 1936, 51242–4; Britnell, 'Saskatchewan', 150; JGG to W. Spedding, 24 Aug. 1932, 15076; message, 'To the People of Saskatchewan,' 15085–6; to A. Federko, 8 May 1933, 16060; to G.A. Stephens, 1 June 1933, 16255
28 See ibid., JGG to N.B. Williams, 4 Dec. 1930, 14775; to King, 25 Nov. 1933, 17722; to C.F. McLellan (?), 5 Oct. 1932, 15130; to J. Jardine, 26 Sept. 1933,

16714. See also, on organization, JGG to W. Barrie, 22 Aug. 1929, 9792–3; to H.A. Mackie, 24 Dec. 1936, 51242–4.

29 Ibid., P.B. Hopkins to JGG, 6 May 1933, 16058

30 Ibid., 'Platform Resolutions of the Saskatchewan Liberal Party adopted at Provincial Liberal Convention held at Moose Jaw, June 15–16, 1931, and by the Central Council of the Saskatchewan Liberal Party on September 27, 1932, and January 18, 1933,' 20061–280; 'Supplementary Platform Resolutions of the Saskatchewan Liberal Party adopted by the Council of the Party, January 9–11, 1934,' 20081–2

31 Ibid., 'The Policies of the Liberal Party in Saskatchewan as Formulated at the Liberal Convention of 1931 and explained by James G. Gardiner, Leader of the Party,' 19468–76

32 Ibid., JGG to H. Wells, 20 June 1929, 10157; see also JGG to King, 1 Aug. 1931, 17645.

33 Ibid., JGG to C. Stewart, 14 Mar. 1930, and to Euler, same date, 14471–4; varied correspondence, 15629–33; to S.N. Fowke, 29 Mar. 1933, 15871–3; KP, MG26, J1, vol. 196; King to JGG 25 Mar. 1933, 166327–8; JGG to King, 3 Apr. 1933, 166330

34 GP, JGG to W. Kerr, 17 July 1933, 16506

35 King Diary, 29 July 1933, 291

36 GP, 19249–55

37 Ibid., JGG to J. Fowler, 20 June 1929, 9874–5; to King, 11 Aug. 1930, 17601–2

38 KP, MG26, J1, vol. 174, JGG to King, 19 May 1930, 148246

39 Ernest Watkins, *R.B. Bennett* (Toronto 1963), 139

40 GP, JGG to T. Wood, 26 Dec. 1933, 17176; King to JGG, 22 Oct. 17684

41 See Norman Ward, *The Canadian House of Commons: Representation* (Toronto 1950 and 1963), 45–6; John C. Courtney, 'Mackenzie King and Prince Albert Constituency: The 1933 Redistribution,' *Saskatchewan History* 19, no. 1 (Winter 1976), 1–13.

42 KP, MG26, J1, vol. 196, JGG to King, 3 Apr. 1933, 166330; GP, Motherwell to JGG, 11 Apr. 1933, 17762–4; F. Totzke to JGG, 12 Apr. 1933, 15934; JGG to H. Mackay, 19 Apr. 1933, 15969; to F.W. Anderson, 27 May 1933, 16201; King Diary, 26 July 1933, 286. See also Courtney, 'Mackenzie King.'

43 KP, King to JGG, 25 Mar. 1933, 166327; GP, JGG to C. Endicott, 11 Nov. 1933, 16854

44 KP, JGG to King, 3 Apr. 1933, 166330

45 GP, JGG to T. Sutherland, 18 June 1933, 16340

CHAPTER 9 A GOVERNMENT IN DEPRESSION

1 *Journals*, 1930: 9–12

2 *SP*, 10–11 Feb. 1930: 162–3

3 *CAR*, 1932: 263; 1934: 275. See H. Blair Neatby, 'The Saskatchewan Relief Commission, 1931–1934,' *Saskatchewan History* 3, no. 2 (Spring 1950), 41–56; Peter A. Russell, 'The Co-operative Government's Response to the Depression, 1930–1934,' ibid. 24, no. 3 (Autumn 1971), 81–100.

4 *CAR*, 1934: 276

5 *SP*, 10 Feb. 1930: 147

6 Ibid., 146–7

7 *CAR*, 1932: 261

8 *Journals*, 1931: 291, 298; *SP* 79, 1934, 'Return to an Order of the Legislative Assembly dated March 7, 1934, on a motion by Mr. Patterson'

9 Figures calculated from *Journals*, 1929–34, passim

10 GP, Davis to JGG, 21 Jan. 1930, 14347–50; 29 Oct. 1936, 41289

11 *Journals*, 1930: 198–200; 1934–5: 31–2

12 Ibid., 1930: 173–4; 1931: 49–50

13 GP, JGG to T. Wood, 10 Jan. 1933, 17912

14 Ibid., letter to editor signed by Gardiner and Coldwell, 27 Feb. 1933, 30787–9; see also stories from *Leader Post* for 6 Jan. 1933, etc., in papers at 59586–91.

15 GP, JGG to E. Simington, 30 Jan. 1933, 15528

16 Ibid., same, 5 Jan. 1934, 17298

17 J.M.T. Anderson, *The Education of the New-Canadian* (London and Toronto 1918), 27, 29–31

18 GP, JGG to W. Knowles, 17 Dec. 1932, 15260

19 Ibid., 'Convention to Wolseley for Wolseley – Qu'Appelle,' 10 Aug. 1933, 19530–7

20 Ibid., JGG to Tom (Wood?), 20 Aug. 1933, 16637

21 The statement is in ibid, 30787–9; see also 59586–93 and 17922–4.

22 Ibid., 'To the People of Saskatchewan,' 15085

23 Quoted in *CAR*, 1932: 260

24 GP, undated note signed J.M. Uhrich, 42995; JGG to King, 4 Sept. 1932, 17668–70; untitled memorandum, 42997–43001; T.C. Davis to JGG, 15 Sept. 1932, 17815; C. Stewart to JGG, 6 Jan. 1933, 17874–6

25 Ibid., untitled memorandum by W.J. Patterson, 10 Nov. 1932, 42996

26 *CAR*, 1933: 240

27 GP, Anderson to JGG, 7 Nov. 1932, 17833

28 Ibid., JGG to Anderson, 11 Nov. 1932, 17835–6; W. Murray to JGG, 3 Mar.

1930, 14465; Anderson to JGG, 19 Nov. 1933, 17839–43; JGG to Anderson, 29 Dec. 1932, 17864–70

29 Both papers are quoted in ibid.

30 Ibid., JGG to T. Wood, 17 Dec. 1932, 17855

31 Ibid., Anderson to JGG, 19 Dec. 1932, 17860–1

32 Ibid., Anderson to JGG, 19 Dec. 1932, 17860–1; JGG to Anderson, 29 Dec. 1932, 17864–70; Anderson to JGG, 12 Jan. 1933, 17881–2

33 Ibid., JGG to Anderson, 29 Dec. 1932, 17869

34 Ibid., Anderson to JGG, 12 Jan. 1933, 17882

35 Ibid., W.F. Kerr to Anderson, 25 Jan. 1933, 17899–900; Anderson to JGG, 28 Jan. 1933, 43029

36 Ibid., JGG to E. Simington, 30 Jan. 1933, 15528–30

37 Ibid., Anderson to JGG, 8 Feb. 1933, 15561–2; JGG to Anderson, 9 Feb. 1933, 15563

38 *Journals*, 1933: 27–33; letter from Gordon Barnhart, Clerk of the Legislative Assembly of Saskatchewan, 28 Jan. 1977

39 GP, JGG to A. Grant, 17 Dec. 1932, 17845

40 *CAR*, 1933: 240; McIntosh's statement to the press is in *Saskatoon Star-Phoenix*, 22 Nov. 1932.

41 Quoted in GP, JGG to Anderson, 29 Dec. 1932, 17864. See also *Journals*, 16 Mar. 1932: 45, 79, 82.

42 Saskatchewan Archives Board, *Directory of Saskatchewan Ministries, Members of the Legislative Assembly and Elections*, 1903–53: 89

43 KP, MG26, J1, vol. 196, JGG to King, 24 May 1933, 166338–41

44 GP, 'Radio Address by J.T.M. Anderson, March 7, 1934,' 19865–71

45 *CAR*, 1934: 274; George E. Britnell, 'Saskatchewan, 1930–1935,' *Canadian Journal of Economics and Political Science* 2, no. 2 (May 1936), 145

CHAPTER 10 TRIUMPH

1 GP, JGG to Ray, 24 Dec. 1933, 17160; to J.W. Reid, 23 Dec. 1933, 17153; JGG to Aberhard 23 Dec. 1933, 17154; Aberhart to JGG, 6 Jan. 1934, 17247; JGG to A.M. Dafoe, 15 Jan. 1934, 17271–3

2 Ibid., JGG to K.R. Jackle, 18 Apr. 1933, 15938–9; to L.F. Bailey, 18 Dec. 1933, 17122; to S. Sinclair, 4 Dec. 1933, 17034; to Dr A.M. Young, 25 May 1933, 16159–60

3 See Lita-Rose Betcheman, *The Swastika and the Maple Leaf* (Toronto 1975), especially 125–8; Doris Shackleton, *Tommy Douglas* (Toronto 1975), 110.

4 GP, *Platform Resolutions of the Saskatchewan Liberal Party adopted at Provincial Liberal Convention Held at Moose Jaw*, 15–16 June 1931: 20061–80

5 Ibid., JGG to G. Spence, 10 Jan. 1933, 17879
6 *Journals*, 1934: 7–11
7 Ibid., 31–2, 124–6
8 See *Saskatoon Star-Phoenix*, 17, 22 Mar. 1934. The relevant legislation is Saskatchewan Statutes, chs. 3 and 36, 1934.
9 *Saskatoon Star-Phoenix*, 21 Mar. 1934
10 Ibid., 15 Mar. 1934. See also *CAR*, 1934: 277ff.
11 *Journals*, 1932: 307–8
12 *Saskatoon Star-Phoenix*, 2, 17, 18 May 1934
13 Ibid., 22 May 1934
14 Ibid., 13 June 1934
15 Ibid., 1, 3, 17, 18 May 1934
16 The main pamphlet collection for the early 1930s is in GP, especially series II, VI, and VII. See also XII, series II, 273.
17 KP, King to JGG, 6 June 1934, MG26, J4, vol. 163, 170721–3
18 GP, A.M. Young to JGG, 16 Mar. 1933, 15777; JGG to Young, 24 Mar. 1933, 15776
19 See *Saskatoon Star-Phoenix*, 5 Mar. 1934.
20 *Journals*, 1934–5: 178–9
21 *Saskatoon Star-Phoenix*, 22 Aug. 1934. All election statistics calculated from Saskatchewan Archives Board, *Saskatchewan Executive and Legislative Directory 1905–1970*.
22 King Diary, 20–26 June 1934; 209ff
23 Ibid., 31 July 1934: 321; KP, MG26, J1, vol. 200, JGG to King, 25 June 1934, 17026–8; King to JGG, 12 July 1934, 170732–6
24 King Diary, 30 July 1934: 320

CHAPTER 11 THE POLITICS OF TRIUMPH

1 King Diary, MG26, J13, vol. 26, 26 Mar. 1934: 81; 25 Apr. 1934: 123; 11 Apr. 1934: 104; 1 Dec. 1934: 497; 12 July 1934: 279; KP, King to JGG, 8 Sept. 1934, 170742–3; Howson to King, 2 June 1934, 171035–6; JGG to King, 9 Oct. 1934, 170745; series between Howson and King from 30 Aug. 1934 to 27 Dec. 1934, 171050–66
2 The basic agreement is in *SP*, 34, 1934–5.
3 Norman Ward, *The Public Purse* (Toronto 1962), especially ch. 10
4 King Diary, MG26, J13, vol. 76, 30 July 1934: 320
5 *SP*, 34, 1934–5
6 Ibid; and *Saskatoon Star-Phoenix*, 20 July – 31 Aug. 1934

7 *SP*, 49, 52, and 53, 934–5; *Report of the Public Service Commission of the Province of Saskatchewan for the Eleven Month Period June 1, 1930 to April 30, 1931*

8 See e.g., *Saskatchewan Gazette* 30, no. 21, (15 Nov. 1934); no. 22 (30 Nov. 1934); no. 23 (15 Dec. 1934).

9 *Saskatoon Star-Phoenix*, 31 Aug. 1934

10 *Journals*, 1934–5: 3–5; *Saskatchewan Gazette* 30, no. 16 (31 Aug. 1934), 3

11 *Regina Leader Post*, 26 Oct. 1934

12 *Journals*, 1934–5: 20, 22

13 Saskatchewan Statutes, 1934–5, passim

14 Ibid., 1930, ch. 7, s.31; 1934–5, ch.4, s.34

15 *Journals*, 1934–5, 16 Jan.: 153; 28 Jan.: 159

16 *Report of the Public Service Commission from December 11, 1934 (the date the Public Service Act came into operation) until the end of the Fiscal Year, i.e. April 30, 1935* (*SP* 7, 1936); ibid. for the fiscal year 1 May 1935 to 30 April 1936 (*SP*, 13, 1937)

17 *Journals*, 30 Jan. 1935: 162

18 *Regina Daily Star*, 13 June 1935

19 GP, 'Report of Conference between Premier Gardiner and Hon. T.C. Davis and The On-to-Ottawa Marchers,' 24 June 1935, 20404–17: 11

20 KP, MG26, J1, vol. 205, JGG to King, 19 June 1935, 176493–4

21 *Regina Riot Inquiry Commission*, 1935 (2 vols.), *Report dated April 23, 1936*

22 A comprehensive file of newspaper clippings on the Regina Riot is in GP, X, series III, 102–8.

23 Ibid., 'Report of Conference ...'

24 Ibid., JGG to R.C. Marshall, 8 Feb. 1938, 51271–5

25 Ibid.

26 Regina Riot Inquiry Commission, 1935, *Report*, 288

27 GP, JGG to R.C. Marshall, 8 Feb. 1938, 51271–5; to T.C. Davis, 28 Dec. 1955, 33459–61; Regina Riot Inquiry Commission, *Report*, 303

28 E.g., GP, speech entitled 'Ontario Provincial Election, 1937,' 46184–5

29 See G.E. Britnell and V.C. Fowke, *Canadian Agriculture in War and Peace, 1935–50* (Stanford 1962), ch. 3; V.C. Fowke, *The National Policy and the Wheat Economy* (Toronto 1957), especially chs. 13 and 14.

30 Fowke, *National Policy*, 264

31 KP, MG26, J1, vol. 205, J.W. Dafoe to King, 29 June 1935, 175622–4

32 King Diary, MG26, J13, vol. 78, 7 June 1935: 401

33 Ibid. 10 June 1935: 410; 12 June 1935: 417; 19 June 1935: 432

34 *Saskatoon Star-Phoenix*, 11 July 1935

35 GP, X, series II, 42–51, contain a representative sample of pamphlets.

36 King Diary, MG26, J13, vol. 76, 31 July 1934: 321
37 *Saskatoon Star-Phoenix*, 27 and 30 July, 1935; *Winnipeg Free Press*, 23 July 1935
38 *Winnipeg Free Press*, 10 June 1935
39 Ibid. 8 Oct. 1935
40 *Saskatoon Star-Phoenix*, 24 Sept. 1935; *Regina Daily Star*, 22 Aug. 1935; *Saskatoon Star-Phoenix*, 23 and 24 Sept. 1935; *CAR*, 1935–6: 312
41 *Regina Leader Post*, 11 and 16 Sept. 1935; *Edmonton Bulletin*, 9 Oct. 1935
42 *Regina Daily Star*, 18 and 24 July, 1935
43 KP, MG26, J1, vol. 205, King to JGG, 7 May 1935, 176465–6; JGG to King, 14 May 1935, 176467; various interviews with Hon. C.J. Davis
44 The electoral data in this paragraph are derived from Howard A. Scarrow, *Canada Votes: A Handbook of Federal and Provincial Election Data* (New Orleans 1962).
45 King Diary, MG26 J13, vol. 76, 31 July 1934: 321

CHAPTER 12 ARRIVING AT AN UNKNOWN DESTINATION

1 GP, JGG to J.B. McBride, 24 Aug. 1936, 50581
2 King Diary, MG26, J13, vol. 78, 12 Dec. 1935: 1119
3 Ibid., 19 Oct. 1935: 792
4 Ibid., 21 Oct. 1935: 812. King's account of his cabinet formation in 1935 runs from 17 to 23 Oct.
5 Nathaniel Benson, *None of It Came Easy* (Toronto 1955), 163–4
6 NAC, *Guide to Canadian Ministries since Confederation July 1, 1867–January 1, 1957* (Ottawa 1967), 51–60
7 King Diary, MG26, J13, vol. 78, 12 Dec. 1935: 1119
8 GP, JGG to C.M. Dunn, 4 Feb. 1936, 42542–3
9 Ibid., untitled nomination speech by Gardiner's seconder, Assiniboia, 1935, 34602–3
10 NAC, Major James William Coldwell 'Memoirs – No. 20 (a),' MG27, 111 C12, vol. 58, 3
11 GP, 'Address delivered by Honourable James G. Gardiner to the Young Liberals' Service Club at Regina, Thursday, September 30, 1936,' 64408–31
12 Ibid., JGG to A.L. Brown, 4 Feb. 1937, 55615–7
13 *Report of the Royal Grain Inquiry Commission* (Ottawa 1938)
14 Charles F. Wilson, *A Century of Canadian Grain: Government Policy to 1951* (Saskatoon 1978), especially 488ff
15 GP undated memo entitled 'Reorganization – Department of Agriculture,'

43068–9; 'Reorganization of Department of Agriculture,' 13 Apr. 1937, 43091–2; *Reports of the Minister of Agriculture for the Dominion of Canada for the Year Ended March 31, 1935*
16 GP, Memorandum on arrangements for handling the situation in the west down to the present, 6 Nov. 1936, 25849–57
17 Ibid., T.C. Davis to JGG, 28 Aug. 1936, 41271–80 (three letters); JGG to Davis, 2 Sept. 1936, 41281–2
18 Ibid., Memorandum on arrangements, 6 Nov. 1936, 25856
19 Ibid., Davis to JGG, 28 Aug. 1936, 41274
20 Canada, *Debates*, 1936, especially 65, 166, 172–3, 269ff, 408, 658ff, 702–4
21 Ibid., 1549; and 1440ff, 1467ff, 1532ff, 1609ff, 1629ff, 1690ff. See also Wilson, *Century of Canadian Grain*, 519–22.
22 Canada, *Debates*, 1936: 1553
23 Ibid., 1938: p. 55–6
24 Ibid., 1938: 756.
25 Wilson, *Century of Canadian Grain*, especially 497ff
26 King Diary, MG26, J13, vol. 83, 16 Dec. 1937: 876–7; KP, MG26, J1, vol. 234, JGG to King, 15 Dec. 1937, 201416–8
27 King Diary, MG26, J13, vol. 83, 16 Dec. 1937: 877; ibid., vol. 84, 11 Jan. 1938: 36
28 Canada, *Debates*, 1938: 162
29 Ibid., 1938: 2424, 1344

CHAPTER 13 SETTLING IN

1 See, e.g., GP, JGG to W. Murray, 6 Mar. 1926, 5194–5; Murray to JGG, 3 Mar. 1930, 14465; Murray to JGG, [24] June 1940, 57006–7.
2 Canada, *Report of the Minister of Agriculture for the Dominion of Canada for the year ended March 31, 1936,* passim
3 Glenbow Tapes, 3 Jan. 1962; GP, 'Address to Federal Candidates in Saskatchewan,' 63542–5 (undated)
4 Glenbow Tapes, tape 2; Queen's University Archives, Norman Lambert Papers (Collection 28), box 9, Diary for 18, 26 July, 2, 26, 29 Aug. 1933 (hereafter Lambert Diary)
5 Reginald Whitaker, *The Government Party: Organizing and Financing the Liberal Party of Canada, 1930–58* (Toronto 1977), 127
6 GP, JGG to W. Tucker, 1 Oct. 1947, 59731
7 Ibid., W. Tucker to JGG, 26 Sept. 1947, 59722
8 Canada, *Debates*, 1937: 921–3, 2204; 1938: 29–30, 58–9, 121, 204–5
9 GP, JGG to J. Vallance, 10 Oct. 1936, 44766

10 Ibid., T.H. Wood to JGG, 23 Apr. 1936, 44816–8; G.H. Danielson to JGG, 14 Jan. 1937, 41235–6; reverse, 25 Jan. 1937, 41237–8. See also (signature illegible) to JGG, 15 Mar. 1939, 56134–7.

11 Norman Ward, 'The Politics of Patronage: James Gardiner and Federal Appointments in the West, 1935–57,' *Canadian Historical Review* 58, no. 3 (September 1977), 294–310

12 See Statutes of Canada, 1 Geo VI, 1937, c. 14; 3 Geo VI, 1939, c. 7; 4–5 Geo VI, 1940–1, c. 25; 11–12 Geo VI, 1948, c. 25; 15 Geo VI, 1951, c. 58.

13 E.g., GP, JGG to J. Vallance, 10 Oct. 1936; to H. Roberge, 11 Jan. 1957, 63761; Roberge to JGG, 7 Feb. 1940, 56723–4

14 Canada, *Debates*, 1950: 1995; 1937: 2302; 1941: 3425

15 E.g., ibid., 1975: 4865–8

16 Several undated conversations, particularly with Dr Harold Moss, Saskatoon. See also Ward, 'Politics of Patronage.'

17 GP, JGG to J.P. McIsaac, 14 Sept. 1938, 50843–4

18 Ibid., JGG to J. MacKinnon, 21 Nov. 1936, 50946

19 See Norman Ward, 'Hon. James Gardiner and the Liberal Party of Alberta, 1935–40,' *Canadian Historical Review* 56, no. 3 (September 1975), 303–22.

20 GP, JGG to J.P. McIsaac, 19 May 1937, 50775–6; JGG to H.H. Parlee, 2 June 1936, 51318

21 Ibid., JGG to E.L. Gray, 18 Dec. 1937, 50393–8

22 Ibid., JGG to W.S. Campbell, 30 Apr. 1936, 49868–9

23 Lambert Diary, 20 Sept. 1932; 27 July 1933

24 Ibid., 28 Sept. 1938; 21 Nov. 1938

25 Glenbow Tape, 2; GP, JGG to R.M. Edmanson, 1 Feb. 1937, 50231–3

26 Lambert Diary, 19 Jan. 1933; 9 Mar. 1935; Neil McKenty, *Mitch Hepburn* (Toronto 1967), 74

27 McKenty, *Mitch Hepburn*, 85

28 GP, T.C. Davis to JGG, 10 Dec. 1938, 41405–7

29 King Diary, MG26, J13, vol. 85, 21 Nov.–17 Dec. 1938: 902–1017

30 GP, 'Statement of Mr. Gardiner re visit with Honourable M.F. Hepburn,' 13 Dec. 1938, 42940–3

31 David Smith, *Prairie Liberalism: The Liberal Party in Saskatchewan, 1905–71* (Toronto 1975), 230

32 GP, JGG to MacKinnon, 24 August 1936, 50881–2

33 Ibid., JGG to J.P. McIsaac, 19 May 1937. See Norman Ward, 'William Aberhart in the Year of the Tiger,' *Dalhousie Review* 54, no. 3 (Autumn 1974), 473–9.

34 GP, JGG to P. Rideout, 11 May 1938, 51368–71

35 See King Diary, MG26, J13, vol. 83, 19 May 1938: 371–3

36 Smith, *Prairie Liberalism*, ch. 6; M.C. Urquhart and K.A.H. Buckley, eds, *Historical Statistics of Canada* (Cambridge and Toronto 1965), 632

37 GP, JGG to C.D. Howe, 17 Dec. 1936, 31671–2. A file on the CNR at Melville begins with 31596.

38 Ibid., T.H. Wood to JGG, 24 Mar. 1939, 45024–6. Further Bund correspondence is in ibid., A. Barthel to T.C. Davis, 15 Apr. 1939, 45039–40. See also Jonathan F. Wagner, 'The Deutscher Bund Canada in Saskatchewan,' *Saskatchewan History* 31, no. 2 (Spring 1978), 41–50; Lita-Rose Betcherman, *The Swastika and the Maple Leaf* (Toronto 1975).

39 A file on the move from Assiniboia to Melville begins in GP, 52029.

40 Ibid., especially JGG to E.W.F. Harris, 14 Nov. 1938, 52094–7, Harris to JGG, 3 Dec. 1938, 52128; JGG to Harris, 9 Dec. 1938, 52138; clipping, 19 Dec. 1938, 52174; JGG to G.W. Foster, 23 Jan. 1939, 52222; JGG to C.M. Dunn, 20 Mar. 1939, 52284; JGG to P. Walters, 19 June 1939, 523446

41 See Smith, *Prairie Liberalism*, 239.

42 GP, JGG to James Devlin, 4 July 1944, 58209–12

CHAPTER 14 A POLITICIAN AT WAR

1 KP, MG26, J13, vol. 78, 19 Oct. 1935: 788

2 Supra, ch. 6. See also, e.g., GP, 'Canada and the Empire,' 385–93; 'Teaching History to Grade VIII and Higher Pupils,' 415–27; 'Who is the True British Citizen?' 508–9 (all undated but belonging to period 1911–13); JGG to J.A. Clarke, 20 June 1929, 9797–8; JGG to J. Mitrenga, 4 July 1929, 9992; 'Address delivered by Hon. James G. Gardiner to the Rotary District Conference, Regina, Sask., April 26, 1928,' 11379–88.

3 KP, MG26, J1, vol. 267, King to JGG, 10 July 1939; reverse, 15 July 1939, 227061–5

4 Ibid., JGG to King, 4 Aug. 1939, 227080–3

5 GP, 'The Saskatchewan Liberal Association,' 31 Oct. 1939, 56559

6 Most of this paragraph is adapted from G.E. Britnell and V.C. Fowke, *Canadian Agriculture in War and Peace, 1935–1950* (Stanford and London 1962), 119–20.

7 Canada, *Debates*, 1939 (1): 941; 1938: 2032–3

8 Ibid., 1940: 168ff

9 Ibid., 1384–404

10 See King Diary, MG26, J13, vol. 88, 28 June 1940: 659–60; Canada, *Debates*, 1940: 173.

11 GP, G.H. Lash to JGG, 6 May 1941, 43431

12 KP, MG26, J1, vol. 288, JGG to King, 9 July 1940, 243329–31

13 Canada, *Debates*, 1941: 1322

14 Ibid., 1940: 1398–411, 1441–2, 1444–5, 1492, 1566–7, 1571–95

15 See R. MacG. Dawson, *Canada in World Affairs*, II, *Two Years of War 1939–41* (London, Toronto, and New York 1943), 47–8.

16 E.g., Canada, *Debates*, 1941: 1520, 4079; Dawson, *Canada in World Affairs*

17 *Canada Year Book*, 1940; 70–1; Canada, *Debates*, 1941: 1322

18 E.g., ibid., 1941: 1333–5

19 Ibid., 1940: 2308–9

20 KP, MG26, J1, vol. 304, JGG to King, 28 Feb. 1941, 257570–4

21 King Diary, MG26, J13, vol. 88, 27 Nov. 1940: 1026; Lambert Diary, 30 Nov. 1940; King Diary, MG26, J13, vol. 89, 9 Jan. 1941: 21–2

22 M.C. Urquhart and K.A.H. Buckley, eds., *Historical Statistics of Canada* (Cambridge and Toronto 1965), 621–3

23 King Diary, MG26, J13, vol. 89, 20 Jan. 1941: 54

24 KP, MG26, J1, vol. 304, JGG to King, 7 Feb. 1941: 257530–8; same, 28 Feb. 1941; same, 8 May 1941: 257601–4. Gardiner's own files on the Department of National War Services begin in GP, 43414; most of the letters to and from King are repeated therein.

25 The actual proposal is in GP, G.H. Lash to JGG, 6 May 1941: 43427–31.

26 King Diary, MG26, J13, vol. 89, 14 May 1941: 391

27 KP, MG26, J1, vol. 304, JGG to King with attachments, 19 May 1941: 257611–4

28 Lambert Diary, 2 June 1941

29 KP, MG26, J1, vol. 304, JGG to King, 11 June 1941: 257619

30 Canada, *Debates*, 1941: 3780–1

31 King Diary, MG26, J13, vol. 89, 9 Jan. 1941: 22

CHAPTER 15 WAR AND AGRICULTURE

1 GP, Mrs C. Carson to 'Dear Soldier' [Edwin Gardiner], 2 June 1942 (unnumbered personal papers, Box 1a)

2 Canada, *Debates*, 1940: 591, 1582, 1583; 1941: 105, 3426, 3441; 1942: 160; 1943: 4491; 1944: 5138

3 GP, JGG to Edwin Gardiner, 9 Nov. 1941 (unnumbered personal papers, Box 1a)

4 Canada, *Debates*, 1941: 2498; see also, for example, GP, JGG to Don B. McLean, 3 Jan. 1956, 29948–9.

5 GP, Don [D.A. McNiven] to JGG, 30 Dec. 1955, 33425–7; W.R. Motherwell to JGG, 15 Mar. 1943, 52827

6 King Diary, 14 Oct. 1941: 909; see also Douglas Library, Queen's University,

Grant Dexter Papers, Max Freedman to Dexter, 30 Mar. 1947, and GP, 'Speech ... to Rotary Club of Ottawa,' 21 Mar. 1949.

7 GP, JGG to P.M. Anderson, 10 Aug. 1948, 60224–5; JGG to George G. Grant, 9 Aug. 1948, 60213

8 C.F. Wilson, *A Century of Canadian Grain: Government Policy to 1951* (Saskatoon 1978), 527

9 G.E. Britnell and V.C. Fowke, *Canadian Agriculture in War and Peace, 1935–1950* (Stanford 1962), 72

10 Canada, *Debates*, 16 Feb. 1939: 1036. Gardiner's summation of key features of PFAA, ibid., 5 Apr. 1939: 2627–8; periodic recapitulations, 10 June 1941: 3777–8; 25 July 1942: 4757: 3 Mar. 1944: 1137; and 20 July 1944: 5141

11 Ibid., 16 Feb. 1939: 1036

12 GP, JGG to Paul Martin, 4 July 1959, 66781; see also speech to the Canadian Club, Regina, 16 Sept. 1936; Canada, *Debates*, 5 June, 1941: 3586–7 and 20 July 1944: 5140–1; GP, Address to Kiwanis Club of Montreal, 18 May 1944, and 30 Sept. 1954; address to annual meeting of the Lethbridge Board of Trade, 15 Jan. 1947; speech to the Kansas State Board of Agriculture, Topeka, 13 Jan. 1955; address to the closing session of the Eighteenth Federal-Provincial Agricultural Conference, 5 Dec. 1956.

13 Ibid., address to Canadian Federation of Agriculture, 29 Jan. 1942; see also radio address during Gravelbourg provincial by-election, 3 July, 1951.

14 GP, JGG to P.C. Davis, 18 Mar. 1943, 41685–6; King Diary, 30 July 1940: 667, and 20 Mar. 1941: 231; Canada, *Debates*, 9 Mar. 1942: 1143 (Walter Tucker) and 14 June 1943: 3603–4 (John Diefenbaker); Lambert Diary, 18 Feb. 1941

15 GP, John J. Bowlen to JGG, 1 Sept. 1940, 49654–5

16 Ibid., address on agriculture's contribution to the war effort, Ottawa, 10 Nov. 1941

17 Ibid., JGG to T.H. Wood, 30 Jan. 1943, 45576–7

18 Canada *Debates*, 9 Mar. 1942: 1130

19 GP, Les Mutch to JGG, 4 Jan. 1947, 48034

20 Ibid., JGG to T.C. Davis, 3 July 1943, 41598–601

21 Ibid., JGG to Wilfrid H. Heffernan, 30 Oct. 1941, 42790–2. The importance of these developments on the growth of the Co-operative Commonwealth Federation is noted by Seymour Martin Lipset, *Agrarian Socialism: The Co-operative Commonwealth Federation in Saskatchewan* (Garden City 1968), 149–50.

22 GP, Don [D.A. McNiven] to JGG, 17 Oct. 1941, 43713–6; see also ibid., H.R. Fleming to JGG, 10 Oct. 1941, 57244.

23 King Diary, 5–7 March 1941, in Wilson, *Century of Canadian Grain*, 650;

King Diary, 23 Feb. 1942: 175; 18 Dec. 1942: 1106; 21 Feb. 1944: 184; and 8 June 1944: 570; Dexter Papers, Dexter to George [Ferguson], 1 Nov. 1943

24 Britnell and Fowke, *Canadian Agriculture*, 107 and appendix, table IX, 451–3

25 Standing Committee on Agriculture and Colonization, *Minutes of Proceedings and Evidence* (No. 5, 10, 15 June 1943 to No. 15, 8 July, 1943): 101–392; (No. 16, 16, 19 July 1943): iii–iv (Third and Fourth Reports). Except where otherwise noted, the committee hearings constitute the source of the next several paragraphs. The evidence of the following people is found at the pages cited: Gardiner, 101–8; G.S.H. Barton, 109–23 at 110; A.M. Shaw, 125–47 at 126; Nelson Young, 163–72 at 164; J.F. Singleton, 227–53 at 249 and 240.

26 Canada, *Debates*, 8 July 1943: 4500

27 Ibid., 22 May 1944: 3147

28 Ibid., 25 June 1940: 1151

29 King Diary, 9 Jan. 1943: 20; KP, JGG to King, 20 Apr. 1942, 27583–7; GP, JGG to King, 1 Dec. 1942, 43393–4; Canada, *Debates*, 'Wartime Prices and Trade Board: Statement as to Relationships with Departments of Agriculture, Fisheries and Munitions and Supply,' 9 Feb. 1943: 258–60

30 GP, JGG to J.C. Lewis, 17 Dec. 1956, 48132–6; Speech to the sixteenth annual meeting of the Canadian Federation of Agriculture, 23 Jan. 1952

31 *Minutes of Proceedings and Evidence*, 187, 243, 391

32 'What Will We Eat This Year?' *Maclean's*, 1 May 1943: 17, 42–3

33 KP, MG26, J1, vol. 340, 292869, J.W.P. to King, 3 Mar. 1943

34 Dexter Papers, Dexter to [George Ferguson], 13 Sept. 1943

35 GP, JGG to T.C. Davis, 3 July 1943, 41598-01; see also JGG to King, 11 Sept. 1942, 25978–81.

36 Canada, *Debates*, 1944: 673–4 and 1612–3; 1942: 3000

37 GP, JGG to Mrs E.M. Pattulo, 18 Aug. 1949, 24210–3; Dominion Provincial Conference on Reconstruction: Address to Sub-Committee on Agriculture, 9 Aug. 1945, 2–4; address to Ontario Crop Improvement Association, Toronto, 17 Jan. 1951

38 Britnell and Fowke, *Canadian Agriculture* 116

39 Glenbow Tapes, 29 Dec. 1961–5 Jan. 1962, tape 6

40 GP, JGG to Robert Campbell, 10 May 1954, 27888–91

41 Ibid., JGG to Col. E.A. McCusker, 18 June 1940, 43643–5; JGG to J. Mildenberger, 22 July 1940, 43776–7; 'Agriculture and War Service,' n.d. 65043–51 (in file on Trip to United Kingdom, October 1940)

CHAPTER 16 A LESS THAN PERFECT ORGANIZATION

1 GP, JGG to Albert Simmons, 12 Feb. 1946, 65306–7
2 Bruce Hutchison, *The Incredible Canadian* (Toronto 1952), 431
3 GP, JGG to Gilbert H. Yule, 5 June 1947, 59630–3. See also C.M. Dunn to JGG, 23 June 1938, 42558–62.
4 Glenbow Tapes, tape 1
5 GP, JGG to W.W. Dawson, 27 Dec. 1944, 58562–3; JGG to H.M. Salter, 29 Jan. 1944, 52930–1; JGG to V.P. Deshaye, 21 Jan. 1949, 53765–6 and to W.R. Bird, 7 July 1944, 53079–83, Wood to JGG, 3 Jan. 1944, 45652–4
6 Ibid, Ken Mayhew to JGG, 24 June 1943, 57452–3 and Reg. J. Jones to JGG, 30 Aug. 1943, 57564–6
7 Ibid., J.J. Tynman to JGG, 26 Jan. 1945, 58602–3
8 Ibid., W.J. Patterson to JGG, 12 Sept. 1939, 44035; JGG to Thos. Miller, 22 June 1940, 43910
9 Ibid., Tommy Dawkins to Gardner [*sic*], 13 Feb. 1942, 57272–5; see also George W. Hayes, 19 June 1944, 58097–100.
10 Ibid., J.R. Hill to JGG, 20 Jan. 1944, 57800–1; Tommy Dawkins to JGG, 13 Feb. 1942, 57272–5; T.H. Wood to JGG, 20 Jan. 1942, 45427–8; and Wood to JGG, 10 Jan. 1944, 45661
11 Ibid., Bird to JGG, 15 June 1944, 53030–3
12 Ibid., Dunn to JGG, 24 May 1944, 58040–2; T.H. Wood to JGG, 20 Jan. 1944, 45665–7 and 21 Jan. 1944, 45668–71
13 Ibid., JGG to Mart Salter, 17 July 1944, 53119–21
14 Ibid., JGG to H.A. Ross, 15 Feb. 1945, 58698–700
15 Ibid., T.H. Wood to JGG, 28 Dec. 1939, 45106–9; JGG to Wilfrid H. Heffernan, 20 Mar. 1942, 42800–2; Dexter Papers, R.H. Milliken to Dexter, 9 Jan. 1942, file 21
16 GP, JGG to Edwin Gardiner, 22 Feb. 1942 and 9 Nov. 1941, unnumbered personal papers, box 3a and box 1a
17 Ibid., JGG to T.C. Davis, 5 Oct. 1943, 41630–2
18 Canada, *Debates*, 10 Feb. 1944: 334–5, 420–4
19 GP, unnumbered pages in 'Humboldt Election Material, 1943,' file 46498ff
20 Ibid., JGG to D.A. McNiven, 25 Nov. 1942, 57396–7, Wood to JGG, 20 Jan. 1944, 45665–7
21 Ibid., Albert Simmons to Archie [Campbell], 19 July 1941, 45348–54; Wood to JGG, 9 Sept. 1941, 45370–1
22 Ibid., JGG to J.A. Watson, 20 Apr. 1940, 52592–3; same to Ellen Devlin, 20 Sept. 1944, 58407–9

23 Ibid., Wood to JGG, 5 June 1940, 45171; W.J. Patterson to JGG, 25 May 1940, 37595–6

24 Ibid., JGG to Patterson, 1 June 1940, 37597–8; see also JGG to W.C. Barrie, 22 June 1940, 49181–2.

25 Ibid., JGG to Mulock, 22 July 1942, 37622–6

26 King Diary, 11 Feb. 1943: 110; 5 May 1943: 331. For more on the Uhrich story, see GP, Uhrich to JGG, 21 Jan. 1940, 44735–7; JGG to King, memo, 8 Sept. 1941, 43358–60; P.J. Monahan (Archbishop of Regina) to JGG, 24 Jan. 1945, 35275, and reply, 29 Jan. 1945, 35276–9. On the respective roles of Gardiner and King in regard to patronage, see ibid., JGG to Austin E. Dewar, 31 Dec. 1954, 42533–7.

27 GP, JGG to J.D. Munro, 5 May 1941, 52701–2; same to same, 29 May 1941, 52708

28 King Diary, 14 Sept. 1939: 1025

29 GP, Lapointe to King, 8 Dec. 1939, 43544–5; JGG to Lapointe, 9 Dec. 1939, 43547–8

30 Ibid., JGG to Wood, 8 Sept. 1943, 45618–2; same to same, 30 Aug. 1942, 45535

31 Ibid., Wood to JGG, 27 Aug. 1942, 45531–33

32 Ibid., H.S. Athey to Bill Bird, 17 Apr. 1945, 54995; H.S. Athey to Bill Bird, 15 Feb. 1945, 54980; JGG to Bird, 12 Dec. 1944, 55036

33 Ibid., Herbert D. Bishop to JGG, 21 Sept. 1942, 57370–2

34 Ibid., Geo. C. Avery to Donald M. Allan (private secretary, minister of agriculture), 24 Oct. 1940, 37762–3

35 Ibid., Wood to Don Allan, secretary to the minister of agriculture, 4 June 1940, 45162–3

36 Dexter Papers, Dexter to ?, 14 Sept. 1943; GP, JGG to Wood, 6 Sept. 1945, 45616–7

37 GP, JGG to James Matthews, 28 Dec. 1944, 53233–9

38 Ibid., JGG to T.H. Wood, 15 Sept. 1943, 45630–1

39 Dexter Papers, Chester A. Bloom to Victor Sifton, 10 Nov. 1944; KP, JGG to King, 14 Aug. 1943, 292875–6

40 For a more balanced perspective on the crisis, see J.L. Granatstein, *Canada's War: The Politics of the Mackenzie King Government, 1939–1945* (Toronto 1975), ch. 9.

41 GP, JGG to W.H. Heffernan, 3 Aug. 1944, 42887–92

42 Ibid., JGG to F.O. Wright, 3 Sept. 1945, 59093–5

43 King Diary, 16 June 1944: 591

44 GP, JGG to J.W. Estey, 5 July 1944, 58228–9

45 Ibid., Dunn to JGG, 27 July 1944, 58313–6

59 Ibid., Allan G. McLean to JGG, 2 Sept. 1953, 62533–4

CHAPTER 18 DEFEAT AND RETIREMENT

1 John A. Munro and Alex I. Inglis, *Mike: The Memoirs of the Right Honourable Lester B. Pearson*, 3 vols. (Toronto 1975), III, 20–1; GP, JGG to Hon. David A. Croll, 15 June 1957, 66589; JGG to Paul Martin, 12 Dec. 1958, 66775–6; JGG to Howard Winkler, 9 Dec. 1958, 67498
2 GP, 'Report from Parliament Hill,' CKCK (Regina), 9 Nov. 1957
3 Ibid., JGG to W.C. Barrie, 23 Dec. 1933, 17159, and to R.H. Milliken, 6 May 1958, 43813
4 Ibid., Ellen (Mrs V.) Hadley to JGG, 9 Apr. 1956, 25189–92
5 Ibid., JGG to Ross Thatcher, 31 Dec. 1959, 67059; JGG to Fred S. Orpen, 9 July 1960, 67731
6 Ibid., JGG to William A. Robinson, 18 June 1957, 67010
7 Ibid., JGG to Hector L. Watson, 19 May 1958, 67086–7
8 Canada, *Debates*, 18 Feb. 1944: 659–60
9 GP, JGG to F.W. Anderson, 8 Aug. 1959, 64311
10 Ibid., *Western Producer* (newsclipping), 66195
11 Ibid., JGG to Marc Letellier, 9 Mar. 1961, personal files IX, 12a
12 Ibid., Mr and Mrs A. Monchier to JGG, 4 Jan. 1962, 67931
13 Ibid., JGG to Howe, 20 May 1958, 66676–7. See also JGG to Howe, 10 Nov. 1958, 66683; and JGG to Paul Martin, 12 Dec. 1958, 66775–6. Also see Howe to JGG, 19 Apr. 1958, 66674–5, and 24 May 1958, 66678–9.
14 Ibid., JGG to T.C. Davis, 10 Dec. 1958, 42463–4, and JGG to Howard Winkler, 9 Dec. 1958, 67498
15 Ibid., David A. Croll to JGG, 1 Jan. 1958, 66590, and Douglas S. Harkness to JGG, 9 Jan. 1958, 66640

EPILOGUE

1 GP, JGG to Martin, 4 July 1959, 66781
2 Dexter Papers, 30 May 1947
3 GP, JGG to Wilna Moore, 9 Jan. 1940, 43861–6
4 Ibid., JGG to W.H. Heffernan, 3 Aug. 1944, 42887–92; radio address, 'Social Planning, Liberalism and the War,' 21 Apr. 1943, 46536–42
5 Ibid., JGG to Oscar A. Hagen, 20 May 1955, 62926
6 Ibid., Speech delivered to Alberta Liberal Convention, 21 Nov. 1959, 64780–3; JGG to Ross Thatcher, 22 Aug. 1959, 64323, and to J.A. Kernahan, 12 Sept. 1952, 61844–50

7 Ibid., JGG to C.L. Burton, 22 Dec. 1937, 41139–40, and to F.J. Knudsen, 10 Sept. 1938, 52054–8
8 Ibid., JGG to Peter R. Kreutzwieser, 3 Mar. 1954, 62616
9 Ibid., JGG to W.E. Jopp, 2 Apr. 1945, 58796–8
10 Ibid., Address to National Office Management Association on 'The South Saskatchewan River Project,' 15 Sept. 1959, 27410–1
11 Ibid., JGG to Howard Winkler, 9 Dec. 1958, 67498; JGG to Peter Newman, 11 Feb. 1959, 67219
12 See O.L. Symes, 'Agricultural Technology and Changing Life on the Prairies,' Canadian Plains Research Centre, 28 Feb. 1975, typescript. See also V.C. Fowke, 'The Effects of the War on the Prairie Economy,' *Canadian Journal of Economics and Political Science* (August 1945), and GP, G.E. Britnell, 'The Implications of United States Policy for the Canadian Wheat Economy,' presented at meeting of the Royal Society of Canada, Section II, Toronto, 6 June 1955, 29399–425.
13 GP, E.D. Gardiner to Claude Schaller, 24 Jan. 1955, 33465; Albert G. Hughes to JGG, 30 May 1955, 35936. See Phelps-Gardiner correspondence, 18 Mar. 1949, 28180–1, passim, to 20 Dec. 1957, 28306–7.
14 King Diary, 19 Jan. 1946: 61
15 GP, speech to the sixteenth annual meeting of the Canadian Federation of Agriculture, 23 Jan. 1952; JGG to J.C. Lewis, 17 Dec. 1956, 48132–6
16 Ibid., JGG to A.C. Stewart, 19 Oct. 1950, 61094–6; JGG to Karl Jaeger, 15 Mar. 1947, 59570–3; W.A. Boucher to JGG, 30 Dec. 1953, 35392–3; reply, 5 Jan. 1954, 35394; JGG to Rhys Williams, 10 Feb. 1951, 53906–8
17 Ibid., Memorandum to the Prime Minister, the Right Honourable Louis S. St Laurent, 31 July 1951, 24413–6
18 Ibid., J.L. Phelps to JGG, 15 Nov. 1953, 24635–6
19 Ibid, JGG to George Spence, 13 Oct. 1915, 29602–5; JGG to A.H. Parker, 31 Jan. 1954, 28769–72; JGG to H.H. Hannam, 26 Jan. 1961, 67754
20 Ibid., speech to Rotary Club, Ottawa, 21 Mar. 1949
21 Ibid., speech by C.D. Howe to Junior Investment Dealers Association, 28 Oct. 1952, 28626–38
22 Ibid., JGG to T.C. Davis, 4 Jan. 1957, 42445–6; JGG to W. Wallace Lynd, 31 Jan. 1956, 63112–4; H.B. Whiteside to JGG, 10 Apr. 1957, 34238–40
23 Ibid., M.L. Tallant to JGG, 14 May 1954, 31852–3; May Penman to JGG, 15 Dec. 1955, 33383
24 Ibid., JGG to J.J. McCann, 8 Jan. 1955, 32664. See also JGG to R.H. Winters, 28 Nov. 1956, 32639–40, and J.J. McCann to JGG, 20 Dec. 1950, 32642–3; also 32712–60, passim, for radio correspondence in 1938–39.
25 Ibid., cited in J.F. Sweeney to JGG, 30 Sept. 1950, 32632

26 Ibid., JGG to J.J. McCann, 20 Nov. 1953, 32545 with enclosure; J.G. Crepeau to JGG, 16 Nov. 1953, 32542–3

27 Ibid., JGG to Rev. Dan McIvor, 18 June 1957, 66737–8

28 Ibid., notes on speech (handwritten and undated)

29 Ibid., JGG to Ken Mayhew, 9 July 1957, 66815–7

30 Ibid., JGG to J.J. Tyman, 17 Nov. 1954, 64156–8; JGG to Most Rev. M.C. O'Neill, 9 Dec. 1955, 34772–5

31 Ibid., JGG to L.B. Pearson, 16 Jan. 1959, 66896

32 Ibid., JGG to Dr G.E. Dragan, 27 Dec. 1952, 62133–5

33 Ibid., JGG to W.R. Bird, 17 Feb. 1953, 62245–6. For a different view, see King Diary, 10 May 1941: 406, and 11 June 1941: 473.

34 GP, JGG to J.C. Lewis, 17 Dec. 1956, 48132–6, and speech to the sixteenth annual meeting of the Canadian Federation of Agriculture, 23 Jan. 1952

35 Ibid., W. Greer to JGG, 25 June 1951, 61208–11; and St Laurent to JGG, 30 Sept. 1951, 61256

Index

Abbott, Douglas 244, 297

Aberhart, William 3, 161, 190, 206, 221

Agar, Charles 171

Agricultural Supplies Board 236, 260

Agriculture: development prior to 1939 251–4; farm income and wheat prices 61, 139, 255, 257, 258, 259, 263–4, 307; image of 248, 257–9; politics of 203, 209, 241, 248, 294, 295, 307, 330–1, 333; post-war declining importance of 248–9, 265, 266, 297, 299. *See also* Canada–United Kingdom Wheat Agreement, Shaw report

Agriculture, Department of: administration 204–5, 214, 226, 306; and farm organizations 331–3; Gardiner as minister 247, 248, 255–6, 265, 266, 268, 270, 294; policies of 207–8, 233, 250, 253–5, 262–3, 264–5, 274, 306–9; politics of 197–8, 251; and the war 234, 235–7, 257, 260–2, 265–6; and the wheat acreage

reduction program 255–7, 260. *See also* Board of Grain Commissioners, Wartime Prices and Trade Board

Anderson, J.T.M. 54, 102, 103, 194; and immigration and education issues 88, 94, 99, 128; and patronage 76, 85, 127; as premier and leader 44, 83, 121, 143–4, 174. *See also* Co-operative government

Anderson, P.M. 148, 150, 171, 172

Barrymore, John 133

Barton, G.S.H. 261

Bell, George 102, 103, 131, 132

Bennett, R.B. 138, 174, 182–7 *passim*, 188, 193, 198; and Gardiner 207, 208–9

Benson, Nathaniel 4, 131, 294

Bird, Bill 272, 286

Blackmore, J.H. 235

Bland, Salem 149

Board of Grain Commissioners 198, 199, 200, 202, 203, 209, 218

Borden, Sir Robert 94

Bracken, John 33, 67, 68, 69, 173

Endicott, Rev. C. 131
Estevan Riot 168, 187
Estey, J.W. 171, 172
Euler, W.D. 209, 210, 251, 252, 253
Evans, Una MacLean 322

farmers' movements 32, 33, 35–6, 40, 47
Farmers' Union 47, 332
Farm Loan Board 62, 77, 118–19, 120, 147
Fielding, W.S. 35, 49
Forke, Robert 45–6

Gardiner, Florence Ellen (daughter) 123
Gardiner, James C. (father) 5
Gardiner, Mrs. James C. 5, 10, 59
Gardiner, James G: and agricultural pressure groups 11, 16, 37, 40, 44, 75, 132, 233, 256, 332–3; attitude toward women 5, 133; British connection 9, 13, 27, 178, 231–2; dcfcat and last years 319–22, 323; early life and education 4–11, 23; family and war 25, 249–50; performance in House of Commons 207, 208–9, 211; and Lemberg farm 26, 320–1; move to federal politics 55–8, 159, 190, 194–8, 200–1, 213–14; political style 269–70, 285, 297, 298–9; political views 12–15, 29, 130, 214, 269, 302, 318, 325–30, 332, 336–9; and religion 12–13, 29; as teetotaller and prohibitionist 6, 28–9, 34; views on being a

Liberal 34, 39, 73, 74, 132–3, 202, 215, 221, 298
Gardiner, James Wilfred (son) 123, 304
Gardiner, John Edwin (son) 123, 231, 247, 249, 322, 336
Gardiner, Maude (Mrs Hugh Christie) 321, 323
Gardiner, Robert (brother) 25
Gardiner, Robert (grandfather) 5
Gardiner, Rosetta Jane (Etta) 7, 14, 32
Gardiner, Violet (McEwen) 32, 35, 213, 249, 282
Gardiner, Violet Elizabeth (daughter) 123
Gardiner, William (brother) 25
Gardiner, William (uncle) 5, 7
Gardiner machine 8, 21–2, 32–3, 51–2, 75–8, 85, 117, 193, 196, 270–1, 334, 339, 341–4
Gillespie, J.B. 4, 15
Gordon, Donald 257, 261
Grain Growers 16, 37, 40, 42, 44; Saskatchewan Grain Growers' Association 33, 40, 47
Grain Growers' Guide 26
Gray, E.L. 221, 227
Gray, James H. 298
Graydon, Gordon 247
Greenway, Harvey 10
Greenway, Thomas 7

Hall, R.H. 15, 16, 44
Hamilton, Charles M. 59
Hanson, R.B. 247, 248
Harkness, Douglas 323
Haultain, F.W. 20, 31
Hawkins, J.H. 92–3